CAPTAIN COOK
VOYAGER BETWEEN WORLDS

John Webber, Portrait of Captain James Cook RN 1782 (National Portrait Gallery, Canberra, 2000.25)

Captain Cook
Voyager Between Worlds

John Gascoigne

hambledon
continuum

Hambledon Continuum is an imprint of Continuum Books
Continuum UK, The Tower Building, 11 York Road, London SE1 7NX
Continuum US, 80 Maiden Lane, Suite 704, New York, NY 10038

www.continuumbooks.com

First published 2007

British Library Cataloguing-in-Publication Data
A catalogue record for this book is available from the British Library.

ISBN 978 1 84725 002 5

Typeset by Egan Reid Ltd, Auckland, New Zealand
Printed and bound by MPG Books Ltd, Cornwall, Great Britain

Contents

Illustrations

Maps

Abbreviations

Add.   Additional
Adm.   Admiralty
ATL   Alexander Turnbull Library, National Library of New Zealand
AJCP   Australian Joint Copying Project
BL   British Library, London
DL   Dixson Library, State Library of New South Wales, Sydney
ML   Mitchell Library, State Library of New South Wales, Sydney
NLA   National Library of Australia, Canberra
NYCRO   North Yorkshire County Record Office
TNA   The National Archives (formerly the Public Record Office)
UCMAA   University of Cambridge Museum of Archaeology and
          Anthropology

Note: when reproducing quotations contractions and abbreviations in the
original have been spelt out.

For Kate,
once more

Preface

Among the objects that Mrs Cook long treasured after her husband's tragic death in distant Hawai'i was an unfinished waistcoat made from Polynesian *tapa* (bark) cloth.[1] It continued to be revered long after her death in 1835, being kept in the family before its sale to the government of New South Wales in 1887, following its display as part of a 'Collection of Relics of the late Captain Cook, RN, FRS' at the Colonial and Indian Exhibition, London in the previous year. In time it, and other objects from this collection, made their way to that great repository of Australia's historical memory, the Mitchell Library, Sydney, where, like saints' relics of old, it is kept as a tangible link with another world made visible through such physical remnants. Cook stood for the British origins of Australia and any objects connected to him – especially when on Australian soil – served to heighten such associations.

The *tapa* waistcoat captures much about Cook and his journeying. The cloth presumably derives from the second voyage and Mrs Cook was at work on it in the years while Cook was on his fatal third voyage – its unfinished state a reminder that he never returned. The many hours that she lovingly devoted to embroidering it with an intricate multi-coloured floral design were intended to make it fit for Cook to appear at court – underlining the long distance Cook had travelled socially, as well as across the globe, since his origins as a farm boy. Above all, it was an object that brought together two worlds, that of Georgian England, with its waistcoats and fine needlework, and that of the Pacific, to which Cook had devoted much of his adult life and which had brought him the fame that such invitations to court betokened. His contact with the Pacific made manifest in *tapa* cloth had been cut into the forms of English dress, but this attempt to bring together such diverse worlds in what was to be an unfinished garment was never fully realized. Though Cook generally did not attempt to change the Pacific in the image and likeness of England others later did, and their endeavours to cut Pacific cloth on a European pattern often remained incomplete as well.

Through his Pacific explorations, wrote Darwin, reflecting the Eurocentric outlook of Victorian Britain, Cook 'added a hemisphere to the civilized world'.[2] Cook himself was more willing than Darwin to acknowledge that the Pacific world that he encountered had much to teach him, but inevitably he saw the Pacific through British eyes and tried to make sense of it by means of the cultural baggage that he brought with him. It is this interaction between the world from which Cook came and the world he encountered which is the theme of this book. Like insects or plants trapped in resin and then fossilized in amber, the copious records of Cook's voyages capture that rare moment when two different cultures viewed each other across a frontier that was relatively open and uncluttered by the weight of many previous encounters – though, inevitably, we know much more about the vantage point of those on Cook's boats than the peoples who looked back at them from the other side of the shore. Cook's arrival both marked a link with the traditional way of life of the peoples of the Pacific, much of which he recorded, and presaged profound change – for Cook's presence and the maps and other records he brought back to England connected such peoples with global forces that would profoundly transform their way of life.

Cook's voyages did much to clear up the dark corners of Europe's map of the globe and to sweep away such long-standing chimeras as the existence of the great southern land that would supposedly balance the land masses of the northern hemisphere. By doing so, he underlined the extent to which the world was one and helped to plant the seed of a more global perspective on the world and humanity's place in it.[3] News of his death prompted one contemporary to write: 'he has twice put a girdle round the world, and had prepared a third with which he had half encircled it again'.[4] Greater globalization was to be linked to the forces unleashed by the Industrial Revolution – a profound transformation of the economy, and the social order with which it was intertwined, which was in its incipient stages in Cook's England. It was, moreover, a transformation closely associated with the part of England from which Cook came. For Cook was born in the Cleveland area of the North Riding of Yorkshire, the northern border of which was the River Tees, one of the cradles of the Industrial Revolution. On the northern and southern banks of this river the towns of Stockton and Middlesbrough were to be connected with that great icon of industrialization, the Stockton–Darlington railway – the opening of which in 1825 with George Stephenson driving the *Locomotion* heralded a new chapter in human history.

The impact of Cook's voyages had global consequences but understanding the forces that shaped him and his responses to the Pacific means focusing on the local and the regional as well as the global, and utilizing the microscope as well as the telescope. Much of the book is devoted to sketching the Cleveland world from which Cook came as well as the Pacific world to which he voyaged. Chapter 1 'Worlds' is divided into three parts, the first of which seeks to anchor Cook firmly in his Yorkshire setting before venturing in the second part to the world of London and the Atlantic (and especially the eastern coast of Canada where he served in the Seven Years' War and its aftermath) and finally to the Pacific. The other chapters link Cook's own life experience to the cultural encounter between Europeans and the peoples of the Pacific concluding, inevitably, with a chapter on death. In understanding the world from which Cook came I have learnt much from the work of others who have devoted much time to exploring archives which shed light on his local setting, and have benefited particularly from reading works by Rosalin Barker, Barrie Farnill, John Howard, Dan O'Sullivan, Julia Rae, Tom and Cordelia Stamp and Cliff Thornton.[5]

Any exploration of that remarkable moment of first (or, at least, very early) contact between the worlds of Europe and the Pacific is made possible by the cargo that Cook brought back with him and which has been made available to a larger world through much scholarly labour. Any quest to follow in the wake of Cook owes much in the first place to the monumental edition of Cook's journals by J.C. Beaglehole.[6] Beaglehole crowned this achievement with a posthumously-published authoritative life of Cook. More recently, two further major biographies of Cook have appeared by Anne Salmond and Nicholas Thomas which have enriched our understanding of Cook and his Pacific encounters by the perspectives brought to bear by these anthropologist-historians.[7] The remarkable visual record of Cook's voyages, which did much to etch the Pacific into European consciousness, has been comprehensively edited by Rüdiger Joppien and Bernard Smith in four beautiful volumes and has also been the subject of classic studies by the latter.[8] Along with the artistic record of Cook's voyages, probably the greatest of any voyage of exploration, another form of pictorial representation of Cook's voyages has recently been made available in the authoritative three-volumed edition of his charts and coastal profiles edited by Andrew David.[9] Another way in which Cook's voyages established a record of the way of life of the peoples of the Pacific is through the large number of artefacts that were brought back to England from whence they were to be disseminated around much of the world. Tracing these over two thousand objects and their present location has been the life's work of Adrienne Kaeppler and her major work on the subject will provide the foundation for further work on this important but, as yet, by no means fully-plumbed aspect of Cook's encounters.[10] Any student of Cook is also much indebted to invaluable reference works on the subject: notably M.K. Beddie's *Bibliography of Captain James Cook* (now rather dated but nonetheless indispensable), John Robson's enlightening cartographic guide to Cook's voyages, *Captain Cook's World*, as well as his comprehensive *The Captain Cook Encyclopaedia*, together with the great amount of useful material drawn from Cook's day and our own made readily available on the National Library of Australia-sponsored 'South Seas website', the work of Paul Turnbull. Such works have ever been at my (physical or cybernetic) side while writing this book.[11]

My thanks to my institution, the University of New South Wales, for sabbatical support which made possible work in overseas archives. I have benefited from conversations with many people, among them Anne Salmond who offered some useful comments following a seminar based on the present Chapter 3 at the University of Auckland, Tim Beaglehole for insights into his father's great project and Robin Inglis, my guide at Nootka Sound. My thanks, too, to Tony Morris of Hambledon Continuum for the infectious enthusiasm which helped to sustain this long-gestating project and to his colleague, Martin Sheppard, for his careful attention to my text and its possibilities. The maps and the index have greatly enhanced this work – for the former I owe thanks to Ian Faulkner and the latter to Alan Walker. I am particularly indebted to Rosalin Barker, John Robson and Paul Turnbull for their kindness in reading and commenting on this work when in manuscript – though any remaining errors are of course my own.

This work was made possible by the often unsung work of librarians around the world, particularly at the Mitchell and Dixson Libraries of the State Library of New South Wales, Sydney; the Australian National Library, Canberra; the Alexander Turnbull Library of the National Library of New Zealand, Wellington; the British Library, London; the North Yorkshire County Record Office, Northallerton and the local studies section of the Northallerton Library and Information Centre. I also owe thanks to the following museums, custodians of some of the artefacts brought back by Cook and his men, for providing access to material in store: The Australian Museum, Sydney (and especially Yvonne Carrillo-Huffman and Logan Metcalf); the Berne Historisches Museum (and especially Dr Thomas Psota); the Bishop Museum, Honolulu (even though I there had to pay by the hour); Bristol City Museum and Art Gallery (and especially Sue Giles); the Canterbury Museum, Christchurch (and especially Roger Fyfe); the Captain Cook Memorial Museum, Whitby; the Institut für Ethnologie, Göttingen; the Museo Nazionale di Anthropologico e Ethnologia, Florence (and especially Dr Marco Piccardi and Vito Stanco); the Museo Nazionale Preistorico, Ethnografico 'Luigi Pigorini', Rome (and especially Dr Carlo Nobili); the National Maritime Museum, Greenwich; the National Museum of Ireland; the Otago Museum, Dunedin (and especially Scott Reeves); the Pitt Rivers Museum, Oxford (and especially Jeremy Coote); the Royal Albert Memorial Museum, Exeter (and especially Jane Burkinshaw); the South African Museum, Capetown (and especially June Hosford); Te Papa Tongarewa (the Museum of New Zealand, Wellington); the University of Cambridge Museum of Archaeology and Anthropology (and especially Anita Herle and Peter Gathercole) and the Whitby Museum.

The 'Cook book' has been an intermittent presence in my family for many years and I thank them for their patience in accommodating its long presence and for their companionship on some of my voyages in search of Cook (especially in Hawai'i and New Zealand) – even if, like Cook and Furneaux on the second voyage, we became separated at Queen Charlotte Sound.

Worlds

When James Cook was born in 1728 the hold of tradition was strong, with many of the patterns and rhythms of life being determined by the agricultural calendar. By the time he died in 1779 there were the first stirrings of that great transformation which were to reshape England into the first industrial nation – a change that was to be particularly evident in the area near the River Tees where he spent his formative years.

Cook was born a Yorkshire man – a vast county which had anciently been divided into three more manageable portions with its East, West and North Thridings (corrupted to Ridings), the last of which encompassed Cook's boyhood world. But the North Riding had its further subdivisions and the portion that framed Cook's early years was the district known as Cleveland. It took its name from the hills (or cliffs as they were once known) which divided it from the North Yorkshire moors to the south. As one approached the formidable eastern border of Cleveland, the North Sea (or, as it was known in Cook's time, the German Sea), these hills merged into sheer coastal cliffs – a topographical feature which also contributed to the area being known as Cliffland or what eventually was termed Cleveland. To the north Cleveland had a natural boundary in the form of the River Tees and to the west it was bounded by the foothills of the Pennines. All in all it comprised an area of some forty miles long by eighteen broad and largely corresponded to the wapentake of Langbaurgh ('Long Hill') – the traditional Anglo-Saxon unit of local government (based on the royal levy of armed retainers) that persisted in Yorkshire.[1] (Strictly, the area around Whitby fell outside this area since it belonged to the wapentake and liberty of Whitby Strand, but in practice was generally regarded as a part of Cleveland.)

Cleveland was a largely self-contained world. The journey to the county capital of York from the west of Cleveland was a long and arduous one of at least a day over roads that were just beginning to be improved on any scale during Cook's own lifetime. To travel from the coast was even more demanding: an uncertain pack road linked the western border of Cleveland with the main coastal port of Whitby. When Cook visited his family in 1772 at Great Ayton, after his first great Pacific voyage, the road to Whitby was still too rough to subject his pregnant wife to its exigencies.[2] The easiest access from Cleveland to the outside world was by

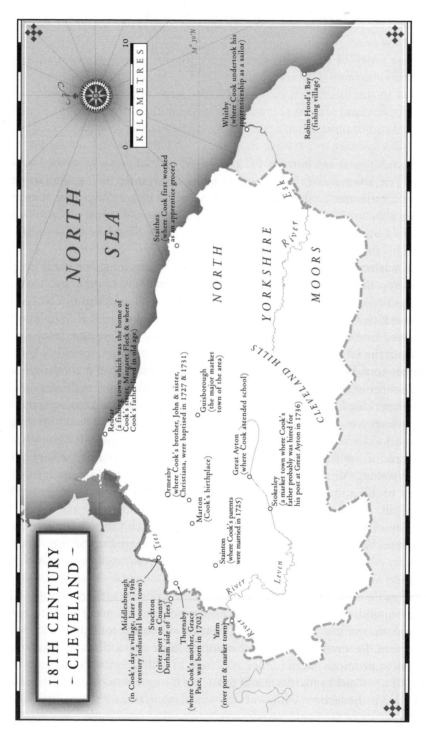

Eighteenth-Century Cleveland

the sea and the sea and the character of seafaring life did much to shape the way of life of the area.

The sea provided a highway which could help foe as well as friend, making Cleveland vulnerable to attack from outside. This weakness the Norsemen had exploited to the full, which accounts for the large number of Scandinavian names in Cleveland and the survival of some Scandinavian words and customs in isolated communities, such as the fishing village of Staithes where Cook spent his early adolescence as a trainee shopkeeper.[3] Whitby, where Cook served his apprenticeship as a sailor, takes the second part of its name from the Norse ending for a town (hence 'white town') and had been the site of the Danish 'Thing' or parliament. When the place names of the area around Whitby were recorded after the Norman Conquest, almost all were of Danish origin.[4] Such traditions, combined with the difficulty of travel, strengthened the self-contained character of much of Cleveland.

If the journey to the county's capital of York was a demanding one, a coach trip to London could consume three days or more.[5] There was, however, increasing contact with the capital by sea in Cook's lifetime through the ever-growing coal trade in which Cook served his nautical apprenticeship. More accessible was Edinburgh, once the capital of the independent kingdom of Scotland but, after 1707, a provincial city within Great Britain. But whatever the formal political divide between England and Scotland there had always been a good deal of coming and going across the border regions which had once formed the ancient Anglo-Saxon kingdom of Northumbria. An instance of such informal migration was the journey south of Cook's father, James, from near Kelso in Roxburghshire in Scotland to Cleveland in the early 1720s. It was a journey probably prompted by the need to obtain work as an agricultural labourer, though perhaps the political unrest within Scotland, which had been highlighted by the Jacobite uprising of 1715, may also have played some part in the decision to leave for England.

The life of an agricultural labourer was determined by season and harvest. Hours were the immemorial ones of 'daylight to dusk in winter, and from 6 to 6 in summer'.[6] The timeless pattern of agricultural life was, however, being slowly changed by an agricultural economy that was beginning to move to larger-scale farming more conditioned by regional or even national markets. As one of the most abundant producers of high-quality wheat in the north of England,[7] Cleveland was well placed to participate in such a widening economy. There, over the course of the seventeenth and eighteenth centuries, agricultural innovations designed to promote greater efficiency were breaking down the traditional pattern of open-field agriculture and replacing it by enclosed individual farms surrounded by hedgerows – innovations which, ironically, are often considered the ancient face of the English landscape.[8]

The North Riding of Yorkshire in relation to England and Scotland

Investment in measures such as better draining, more effective rotation of crops to overcome the necessity of leaving the land fallow and the breeding of more valuable livestock were difficult to combine with the traditional village-based pattern of agriculture. Traditionally, the rotation of crops on large open fields was determined communally and animals were grazed on the surrounding commons – a brake on innovation by individuals. The increasing pace of enclosure – whereby individual ownership of the land was made evident by its being enclosed by a fence or hedge – was to mean increasing profits, increasing concentration of land in the hands of a few, and vastly increased production which broke for ever the primeval fear of dearth and starvation. But these developments also meant fewer self-sufficient small farmers and more waged agricultural labourers dependent for their livelihood on employers. The result was a more fluid and mobile market for agricultural labour which accentuated the peripatetic nature of an agricultural labourer's life.[9] An agricultural labourer was traditionally employed on a yearly basis at the end of which he might be re-engaged, or another chosen, at the annual 'hiring fairs' at the major market towns.[10]

In the early years of his marriage Cook's father moved about a good deal (though within a fairly restricted area near the River Tees). When Cook's parents were married in 1725 it was at Stainton-in-Cleveland, but when their first son, John, was born in 1727 he was baptized at Ormesby. James Cook came next and was baptized at Marton ('Marsh-town') in 1728 and the event was duly recorded in the parish register of the local church with Cook's father being termed a 'day labourer'. By 1731, when Cook's sister Christiana was baptized, the family was back near Ormesby but they had returned to Marton by 1733 where the fourth child, Mary, was baptized.

One now approaches St Cuthbert's, Marton, where Cook and his sister were baptized, along a busy road and it takes an effort of imagination to conjure up that bygone village in what is now an outer suburb of Middlesbrough. In Cook's boyhood Middlesbrough had been a tiny hamlet on the River Tees on the eve of its rapid growth which mirrored the early industrialization of the country as a whole. Coal and iron ore, together with water transport, made nineteenth-century Middlesbrough one of the major sites of the 'workshop of the world' that Britain had become. Its pivotal role in the early stages of industrialization was underlined by the fact that in 1831 it was linked to the Stockton–Darlington railway – six years after this historic railway opened with great ceremony with George Stephenson ushering in the railway age by driving the *Locomotion*.

Linked to the epicentre of early industrialization, Middlesbrough mushroomed. Two Quaker businessmen, Edward and Joseph Pease, were greatly enriched by sponsoring the railway and by foreseeing the commercial possibilities of the then hamlet of Middlesbrough, having purchased the river-front land around it in

1828,[11] when it had a population of a mere twenty souls. To them is attributed the prophecy: 'Yarm was, Stockton is, Middlesbrough will be'. For, along with Stockton on the northern side of the River Tees, Middlesbrough, on the southern, provided a port for the coal that was fuelling the ever-quickening pace of industrialization – the main purpose of the railway being to transport coal (though it did carry some passengers). In 1830, within two years of the coming of the Peases, the first of many coal-laden ships left the new port of Middlesbrough.

Not only was Middlesbrough well situated for the transport of coal, it was also strategically located near another of the vital ingredients of industrialization: iron ore from the Cleveland Hills. Thus in 1851 the town's first blast furnace was opened, and by 1900 Middlesbrough produced one third of the country's total output of iron and steel.[12] Appropriately the Sydney Harbour Bridge (opened in 1932) was built from Middlesbrough steel, as was the Auckland Harbour Bridge (opened 1959) – a distant link between Cook's place of origin and the world he opened up to European scrutiny.

Although Marton has been swallowed by its erstwhile sleepier neighbour of Middlesbrough, Cook's birthplace is still remembered. The site where Cook once lived became part of the grounds of a country house and, in 1858, after it fell into disrepair and was demolished, a granite vase was erected to mark the place of Cook's parents' cottage. The whole area is now known as Stewart Park and includes a well-conceived high-tech museum devoted to Cook's life and voyages. Marton's metamorphosis from village to suburb of a large industrial town captures in miniature the larger transformation of England into an industrial power – a transformation that was gathering momentum in Cook's own lifetime.

By contrast, Great Ayton, where Cook spent most of his boyhood, remained unmarked by industrialization – indeed Airyholme, the estate on which his father worked as hind (overseer) for Thomas Skottowe, the lord of the manor, still functions as a farm on the outskirts of a picturesque village, bisected by the River Leven, with a statue of the young Cook on the village green. The farm lies under the shadow of the great eminence of Roseberry Topping, beyond which lies Easby Moor and a vast stone pillar erected in 1827 to the memory of Cook. The Great Ayton of Cook's day was characteristic of the pre-industrial revolution economy, combining both agricultural diversity (growing wheat, oats, barley and beans) with small-scale local processing of agricultural products. At the end of the eighteenth century it still supported such businesses as a tanning works, a brewery and a comb and horn manufactory, though its alum works had closed down in the 1770s.[13] There was an attempt in 1790 to establish a water-driven flax-spinning mill – the production of linen being one of the major local industries – but it did not prove profitable.[14] As factory-based industrialization gathered pace elsewhere there was less and less of this merging of agriculture

Late Eighteenth-Century Great Ayton, South-East View (Wakefield Art Gallery, Gott3/42)

and manufacturing, and city and country became more and more distinct. In Cook's time, however, Great Ayton's diversification enabled it to support some two hundred families – about twice the population of Marton.[15]

Cook's father probably gained his post with Skottowe at one of the annual Martinmas 'Hirings' held in late October at the gracious, still largely Georgian, town of Stokesley, a few miles miles from Great Ayton and, like it, located on the River Leven.[16] For the Cook family the move from Marton to Great Ayton in 1736 brought with it an end to their itinerant existence and for Cook's father a sense of responsibility and permanency as a trusted employee of one of the prominent local landowners. Such employment still carried with it reciprocal obligations and could not entirely be reduced to a cash contract. Skottowe considered that he owed Cook's father as a loyal employee not only a wage but help in other ways. It was he, for example, who helped young Cook to attend the local school,[17] and it seems clear that it was he who obtained for him his first post as a trainee storekeeper at Staithes.

For a future navigator Great Ayton was in some ways a surprising boyhood home. It was the other side of Cleveland from the sea coast and not connected with the sea by a river – which, together with the fact that Great Ayton had no coal, is one of the reasons it has remained agricultural in character. But the town was part of a regional economy which linked it to surrounding market towns, chiefly Guisborough, Stokesley, Yarm and Stockton – the last two being on the River Tees and thus part of the waterways that led on to the North Sea and the wider world to which the sea was the gateway. Glimpses of the coast could be seen on a clear day from Roseberry Topping (or, as it was known in Cook's day, Ounesbury Topping), 'Cleveland's Matterhorn', which loomed over Great Ayton. As a boy Cook must have climbed its 1,052 feet made of a hard sandstone cap which protected Roseberry Topping from the erosion which has worn away the surrounding shales and clay. The very name was a link with the Norsemen who had both ravaged and settled the area in the late eighth and early ninth centuries and had given Cleveland its name,[18] for the term 'topping' had come from 'toppen', the Norse word for a hill. For sailors approaching the coast it was a clear landmark and an indication of changing weather:

> When Roseberry Topping wears a cap,
> Let Cleveland then beware of a clap![19]

As in most villages, the central focus of Great Ayton was the church. It had been renovated in 1743 to accommodate a gallery with a separate entrance which allowed the local squire, Cook's employer Thomas Skottowe, to enter without having to rub shoulders with his tenants.[20] In a symbolic linkage of squire and parson the Skottowes lived in Ayton Hall alongside the church. By 1761, however, the hall was bought by Commodore William Wilson. Wilson was renowned for his discovery in 1758 of a new route to China through the Pitt Passage between the Moluccas and New Guinea (achievements commemorated in a memorial tablet on the church wall).[21] Though Cook and Wilson only came to know each other as adults, it was appropriate that these two Great Ayton explorers became friends. Cook, for example, stayed with him in 1772.

While the church was intended to draw together the village's living community, its churchyard accommodated the dead. The Cooks had their place in the graveyard where Cook's mother was buried, along with five of her children who were all cut down well before their prime. Cook's lifetime saw a steady increase in the size of the British population, which eventually was to people not only a vastly more populous Britain but also the 'new Europes' of North America, Australasia and parts of Africa. When Cook was born the population of England and Wales was around 5.3 million and by the time he died it was near 7.04 million. In the decades that followed growth was more spectacular: 7.74 million in 1791, 8.7 in 1801, 9.5 in 1811 and 11.2 in 1821.[22] However, the main motor of such increase was not a drop in the death rate but a rise in the birthrate, occasioned by earlier marriage made possible by a more buoyant economy. But death remained a frequent visitor and, as the Cook tombstone and the sorry fate of Cook's own

South-East View of Airy Holme Farm near Great Ayton, Wakefield Art Gallery, Gott Collection, 3/43

six children (none of whom outlived their mother) remind us, the Cooks were well acquainted with early death.

Not all Cook's family succumbed early to the Grim Reaper. His mother is commemorated in the Great Ayton churchyard as 'Grace, wife of James Cook, who died Feb 18th 1765, aged 63 years'. Though Cook's elder brother, John, died at the age of twenty-three leaving James Cook the eldest of the children, his sister, Christiana (who was next in line), lived to the age of sixty four. We know that she married a Mr Cocker, but otherwise she and any progeny have disappeared from history. Cook's other sister, Margaret (who married a man by the name of Fleck, a fisherman in the small Cleveland coastal town of Redcar), lived to the age of sixty-two, and it is from her that any surviving genealogical links with Cook derive. Longest lived of all was Cook's father, who survived until the ripe old age of eighty-four. He died at his daughter's house at the fishing village of Redcar on 1 April 1779 – mercifully before news of Cook's death at the hands of Hawaiians on 14 February 1779 reached England.

Before he moved to his daughter's in 1772, Cook's father had lived in a small cottage in Great Ayton, the site of which he had obtained from his employer, in 1755. The purchase documents reflect the social divide between the two with

Photograph of 'Captain Cook's Cottage' [actually that of his father], Melbourne
(National Archives of Australia, A1200:L546)

their record of a contract between 'Thomas Skottowe, Gentleman' and 'James
Cooke [sic], yeoman'. Like his son, James Cook senior was a resourceful man
and built the cottage himself, having turned more and more to the trade of
mason.[23] He also knew how to make a tidy profit (even allowing for the addition
of the cottage). Having purchased the site for 26 shillings, he eventually sold
it for £82 15 shillings when in old age he moved to his daughter's at Redcar.[24]
This cottage is where his son James visited him on his infrequent visits home.
Prior to a visit in early 1772, for example, he had sought leave of absence from
the Admiralty, 'Having some business to transact down in Yorkshire as well as
to see an Aged father'.[25] The cottage is now a symbol of how far Cook travelled
from Great Ayton, having been re-erected in the Fitzroy Gardens at the centre of
Melbourne in 1934. Reciprocally, a column of stone from the area in Australia
that Cook first sighted near Point Hicks marks the spot of the missing cottage
in distant England.[26]

Like a relic brought from distant lands, the cottage, when erected in the 1930s,
was a tangible reassurance that Australians were connected with the island on

the other side of the world from which European Australia traced its origins. Few concerned themselves with the fact that it was the cottage of Cook's aged father rather than the cottage in which James Cook had grown up – for most in Melbourne it was 'Cook's cottage' and a shrine to the Great Navigator whose exploits had led to the British colonization of Australia. The better to fulfill the goal of 'introduc[ing] some old, reminder of the old world to this young country' a cutting of ivy was also brought from the original site to Melbourne to link organically Great Ayton and the antipodes.[27]

The documents concerning the sale of the cottage by James Cook the elder show that he could sign his name. There was also said to be a family Bible which he could read – a tribute to the Scottish parochial school system which educated a much larger percentage of the labouring population than in England.[28] One of the paths out of Great Ayton was via its school, which could provide sufficient education to open up careers beyond the timeless routine of agricultural life. Cook the younger had learnt his alphabet from 'Dame Walker' at Marton and was fortunate in being able to build on this at the Postgate School at Great Ayton when he moved there at the age of eight. The school had been founded in 1703 by a local landowner, Michael Postgate, and had originally been intended for a mere eight boys. But by the time Cook came to attend it the school had expanded, for we know that in 1743 it was catering to twenty or thirty children.[29] When Cook finished there, probably around the age of twelve, he was able to read and write with facility and had some basic mathematical knowledge, which he later built on to good effect in the merchant and Royal Navy. Evidently Cook's sisters did not receive the same opportunities, for his sister, Margaret, was illiterate.[30] This typified a society in which, among the labouring classes, something like a half of boys and a third of girls received a basic education which generally lasted for only about three to four years.[31]

Like many such schools, Postgate School was the result of local philanthropy rather than government action, as government did not get involved with mass education on any scale in England until 1870. Since the level of such philanthropy varied from place to place some towns could offer a reasonable level of schooling, while others had little more than individuals (usually women) teaching at the most rudimentary level – the sort of dame's school that Cook attended at Marton. There, as the vicar of Marton reported in 1743, 'a widdow Woman teaches a few small children to read in her own house'.[32] The school at Great Ayton offered a curriculum that was to suit Cook's future needs better than the traditional grammar schools characteristic of the larger towns – institutions which, as their name suggests, were largely devoted to the teaching of Latin and in some cases Greek and even Hebrew. Like many such schools, Great Ayton's was closely tied with the established church and the training of youth in the principles of the Church of England was one of its declared goals.

In between school terms, and for a few years after finishing school, Cook worked on the farm. Though Cook left agricultural life as soon as possible it left a lasting mark which helps to account for the great preoccupation on his voyages with spreading the fruits of the agricultural improvement which was transforming Cleveland and Britain more generally during his lifetime.[33] The main instrument Cook could employ in linking British agricultural advances with the Pacific was through the export of farm animals[34] – 'the leaving of some of them', hoped Cook, 'might prove usefull to posterity'.[35] His determination to make his ships floating arks which would make his voyages sources of human betterment gathered pace on the second and third voyages, as his status and ability to impose his own goals increased. His lack of success on the second voyage – when he bemoaned the fact that in New Zealand 'every method I have taken to stock this Country with Sheep and Goats have proved ineffectual' – only made him more determined to bring more animals on the third voyage.[36] Throughout his life Cook was not one to be deflected from his goals: as James King, his lieutenant on the *Resolution* wrote, his 'most distinguishing feature was that unremitting perseverance in the pursuit of his object'.[37]

The result, as Cook wrote to Sandwich, was that on the third voyage 'Nothing is wanting but a few females of our own species to make the *Resolution* a Compleate ark'. Cook justified to Sandwich increasing the number of animals on board since 'my intention for so doing is for the good of posterity'.[38] The outcome was mixed – on the Hawaiian island of Kaua'i, for example, the introduction of new animals led to conflict and bloodshed,[39] but Cook nonetheless felt that his efforts had been worthwhile. Having delivered much of his animal cargo to Tahiti, he reflected on 'the satisfaction I felt in having been so fortunate as to fulfill His Majestys design in sending such usefull Animals', something which 'sufficiently recompenced me for the many anxious hours I had on their account'.[40] Cook's vessels also brought new crops, some of which took root in the Pacific. In 1823, for example, it was reported that wild spinach, celery and carrots were growing in the Bay of Islands area in New Zealand, where wild pigs could also be found – all deriving from Cook's visit.[41]

For all his subsequent enthusiasm for agricultural improvement the young Cook had sufficient ambition to look beyond what the largely agricultural Great Ayton had to offer. Even at this early stage there is some foreshadowing of the man who, in a rare moment of self-disclosure, wrote in January 1774, when he finally turned back from the Antarctic ice: 'I whose ambition leads me not only farther, than any other man has been before me, but as far as I think it possible for man to go, was not sorry at meeting with this interruption'.[42] At the age of sixteen, then, he set off to the fishing village of Staithes to train as a shopkeeper with a Mr William Sanderson – a post he appears to have owed to the good offices of his father's employer, Thomas Skottowe.

The friendship between Skottowe and Sanderson was an instance of the ties that linked the larger world of Cleveland together – at least at the level of the elite. Skottowe was a justice of the peace, one of those workhorses of local government who provided much of the day to day administration in an age when the chief function of central government was simply to fight wars. The post of justice of peace was an honorary one, but it brought public recognition and status and was regarded as a natural part of the life of a major landowner or prominent citizen. At the sessions held at the Cleveland market town of Guisborough, Skottowe would have come to know Sanderson, who served as a constable; the two men indeed were later linked by the marriage of their sons, who married two sisters.[43]

Though Cook soon tired of the life of a shopkeeper and remained only eighteen months, Sanderson still looked favourably upon him, since it was he that helped to find him another post and, indeed, another career: as an apprentice to a shipowner, John Walker, in the nearby town of Whitby. Sanderson's solicitude for the young Cook owed much to Skottowe's goodwill towards the Cook family. Sanderson had a wide range of business interests, ranging from shops to shipping, which no doubt drew him into contact with Whitby shipowners such as the Walker brothers. Victualling ships was, after all, closely aligned to supplying groceries. Sanderson probably combined both.[44]

In some ways, too, Cook was also to draw on his shopkeeping background in the provisioning of the ships for his great Pacific voyages. He arranged the victualling of the *Endeavour* and was both captain and purser of the first *Resolution* voyage. It was a combination of offices which, as the Swedish naturalist Anders Sparrman caustically observed, 'was extremely lucrative for our captain', since he could barter cheap trade goods for local food 'instead of having to use the Government salt provisions to which he was entitled'.[45] Pursers were well known for their 'tricks' and Cook had learnt a few of them. 'As a purser', noted Lieutenant Richard Pickersgill on the same voyage, 'Cook knew how to prolong' the naval day (which finished at midday), 'in order to save the day's allowance, of wine by the Ships Company'.[46] Such practices continued on his last voyage: hence his men's complaint, about being supplied with beer brewed from local sugar cane rather than the Admiralty-provided spirits, which reportedly led the irate Cook to respond that 'He did not chuse to keep turning & working among these Isles without having some Profit'.[47] Cook the captain still retained something of the young trainee grocer.

Staithes was a brief interlude in Cook's life but it was his first lengthy exposure to the sea. Precariously poised at the foot of the cliffs that plunge down to the North Sea, the fishing town had fought a long battle with the sea. A small stream had gradually carved its way down to sea level so that the town lay between two vast cliffs, the one to the north forming a part of the highest sea cliffs in England.

Contemporary Lithograph of Staithes c. 1820. John Jordison after sketch by Thomas Thorpe (Dixson Library, Sydney, Pf 83)

The natural harbour so formed was the heart of the village and its very name, coming from the Norse word for a 'landing place', evokes much of its history. Periodically parts of the town – including eventually the shop in which Cook worked – were reclaimed by the sea, but the town continued to earn its living from the sea until the indiscriminate methods of the large trawler fleets rendered line fishing obsolete in the late nineteenth century.[48] Today its narrow lanes and houses and shops strung out along a steep climb down to the sea are a reminder of how isolated and self-contained the village once was – so much so that it was a natural haven for smugglers. How far Cook was accepted into this closed community we have no way of telling, but it is not unlikely that loneliness was one of the reasons that he moved down the coast to Whitby.

The trip to Whitby was the beginning of Cook's larger voyages beyond Cleveland. Whitby opened the door to the sea and, with it, to the expanding world that British trade and naval power were prising wider and wider over the course of the eighteenth century. Whitby was growing fast, reflecting the increasing demand for coal, particularly in London. Though most of this coal originated up the coast in Newcastle-on-Tyne, Whitby, as the only effective harbour between the River Tees and the River Humber, was an important stopping-place on the way south – as well as an increasingly important source of ships and the men to sail them. Over the course of the eighteenth century the port of Whitby had blossomed, despite the fact that the River Esk, on which it nestles between sea and

Late Eighteenth-Century Whitby, Southeast View of (Wakefield Art Gallery, Gott Collection, 3/38)

land, was too small, too shallow and too rapid in current to allow access to much of the hinterland. 'At the entrance of a little, nameless river', wrote Daniel Defoe in 1724, 'scarce indeed worth a name, stands Whitby, which, however, is an excellent harbour, and where they build very good ships for the coal trade'.[49] Whitby therefore had to survive as a harbour not by servicing its immediate region but by providing a fleet and other maritime skills to meet the needs of national industries, whether coal, whaling or the transportation of soldiers and convicts. Its role as shipbuilding centre also meant that it was active in the importation of timber and other naval supplies, such as hemp and iron, from the Baltic[50] – by the end of the eighteenth century some twenty per cent of the very important Baltic trade was carried in Whitby ships.[51] Thus the town and its surrounding parish could support a rising population which, by 1776, when Cook set out on his third great Pacific voyage, had reached over eleven thousand.[52]

Whitby also served as a port for the alum that had, since the sixteenth century, been Cleveland's most important non-agricultural product. Alum was essential in two major industries that preceded the industrial revolution, being used in the textile industry as an agent for fixing dye to cloth and in tanning to make the leather soft and supple. The erection of works fuelled by coal to extract alum from the alum shales in seventeenth-century Cleveland was an instance of the early beginnings of industrialization on which the industrial revolution of the late eighteenth century could build.[53] The increasing momentum of a capitalist economy was also evident in the way in which some Cleveland farmers combined agriculture with weaving coarse linens and other textiles – much of which would have been used in Whitby for naval supplies.[54]

Within Whitby itself much of the ever-expanding demand for sail cloth was met in the traditional way through 'the domestic system' – spinning and weaving at home with the raw materials provided by a middleman. From 1807, however, such manufacture moved to factories within Whitby – an instance of the increasing separation between home and workplace which industrialization brought in its wake.[55]

Like Staithes, though on a much larger scale, Whitby in Cook's time was something of a world unto itself – particularly if one approached it by land. The steep descent down to Whitby and the valley of the River Esk which runs through the town made it difficult to transport goods by land – quite apart from the inadequacies of the road across the twenty miles of moors. Indeed there had been no road suitable for wheeled traffic until as late as 1759.[56]

The mighty ruined abbey on the headlands added to Whitby's strong sense of local identity. Its origins dated back to time of the Synod of Whitby at which, in 664, the Celtic Church was corralled very reluctantly into the fold of the universal Roman Catholic Church. The ruins of the abbey, originally founded by St Hilda in 657, were a distant reminder of the Viking invasions that had destroyed the abbey in 870. More potently the destruction of the rebuilt abbey was a symbol of the Reformation and the might of Henry VIII, to whom in 1539 the monks reportedly had 'voluntarily and willingly … granted … All our said Monastery'.[57] Further destruction of the abbey ruins by a German cruiser during the First World War was a reminder that the sea could be an avenue for one's enemies as well as a gateway to the world.

The house in which Cook served his apprenticeship still survives in Grape Lane, together with the large attic in which he and up to sixteen other apprentices slept. Appropriately, it is now the Captain Cook Memorial Museum.[58] Its situation underlines how closely Whitby was linked to the sea, since ships could tie up on the river at the bottom of the property. There they could be unloaded, provisioned or, in winter, subjected to the constant maintenance that was a necessity if they were to survive the rigours of the North Sea. One abiding lesson, above all, that Cook would have learned from the Walker household (and from his own parents) was to avoid idleness or vacillation: on the third voyage Midshipman Trevenen thought that 'indefatigability was a leading feature of his Character … Action was life to him & repose a sort of death'.[59]

In Mr Walker's business, as in most pre-industrial concerns, home and work merged together. Apprentices became part of the household of their masters, which meant for Cook being subject not only to the disciplines of a merchant man but also those of Mr Walker's Quaker way of life. Traditionally, apprenticeships lasted seven years, but Cook's apprenticeship was only three (from 1746 to 1749) – perhaps because Cook was relatively old at seventeen when he joined Walker. In any case the demands of the Elizabethan Statute of Artificers (1563), which had codified traditional practice, were being eroded by the quickening pace of the British economy. But, whatever the period of service, an apprentice's life was so closely intertwined with that of his master that there was no such thing as a private life: Walker's apprentices had to undertake 'not to play dice, cards or bowls, not to haunt taverns or playhouses, not to commit fornication, and not to contract matrimony'. In return, Walker promised to instruct his apprentice in 'the trade, mystery, and occupation of a mariner; and for the period of apprenticeship find and provide meat, drink, washing and lodging'.[60] For Cook, as for other Whitby sailing apprentices, on-the-job training would have probably been supplemented by classes run by local teachers, especially in the winter months when there was less shipping activity because of the menacing North Sea storms. In such classes he would have learnt to calculate latitude by the position of the sun, using what few instruments were available, such as the backstaff for measuring the height of the sun above the horizon. Possibly there was also some instruction in the use of the sextant after its invention in the 1730s (or of its predecessor the octant) – though its cost may have limited its use in the Whitby ships in which Cook sailed.[61]

In many cases apprentices (or, in practice, their parents or guardians) had to pay the master a lump sum on signing the indentures, with the amount varying according to the value of the trade – the theory being that the apprentice was in effect purchasing tuition. There is no record of this in Cook's case which indicates either the extent of goodwill between Mr Walker and Cook's patrons or the eagerness to acquire promising young apprentices such as Cook. It was in Walker's service that Cook acquired his grounding as a seaman and much of the personal discipline that made him such an effective leader of men. Along with the three years as apprentice, Cook was to spend another six with the Walkers in between his trips away. The result was that John Walker became a father figure to whom he later sent detailed reports of his travels. The pre-industrial apprenticeship system, tying an apprentice to one master for a long period of time, was one that offered much room for conflict, but the relationship between Cook and Walker shows the system working at its best.

Service with Walker, on the ships the *Freelove* (1747–48), *Three Brothers* (1748–49, 51) and *Friendship* (1751–55), exposed Cook to a much larger world. The North Sea, one of Cleveland's most forbidding boundaries, now became a route to foreign lands. On a few voyages Cook crossed the North Sea reaching Norway and the Baltic, possibly travelling as far as St Petersburg. We know little of these voyages, but it is fair guess that they were linked to the Whitby shipbuilding trade,

Thomas Bowles, *A General View of the City of London, next to the River Thames*
(London, 1794) (British Library, Maps 3518. (14))

since the Baltic produced some of the best shipbuilding timbers and Russia was a
major source of hemp from which ships' ropes were woven. There was also a trip
in the *Three Brothers* to take British troops and horses from the Netherlands to
Dublin and Liverpool in 1748–49, at the end of the War of Austrian Succession,
a journey that linked Cook with the conflicts associated with Britain's growing
status as a European Power – conflicts which were later to form the backdrop to
his naval career.

Such voyages provided valuable ocean-going experience, but Cook's main task
was to sail ships from the Tyne to London to slake the capital's insatiable thirst
for coal. His first such voyage to London was around 1746–47, and thereafter
the area near the Thames was to remain one of the central foci of his itinerant
life. The East End was then a mass of ships and much depended on having
good London agents who could smooth one's path through this nautical mêlée.
Business was often conducted at the alehouses and it was at one of these, the
'Bell', that Cook met his future wife, Elizabeth Cook. Elizabeth was a Londoner
born and bred, having been baptized at St John's, Wapping, in 1741 – she was
thirteen years younger than her husband. When she and Cook married in 1762
the ceremony was at St Margaret's Barking and their children were baptized at St
Paul's, Shadwell and St Dunstan's, Stepney, further grounding Cook in the once
alien world of the metropolis.

Their married life was conducted within easy reach of the Thames and,
more remotely, the larger world of the Atlantic and the Pacific to which it was a

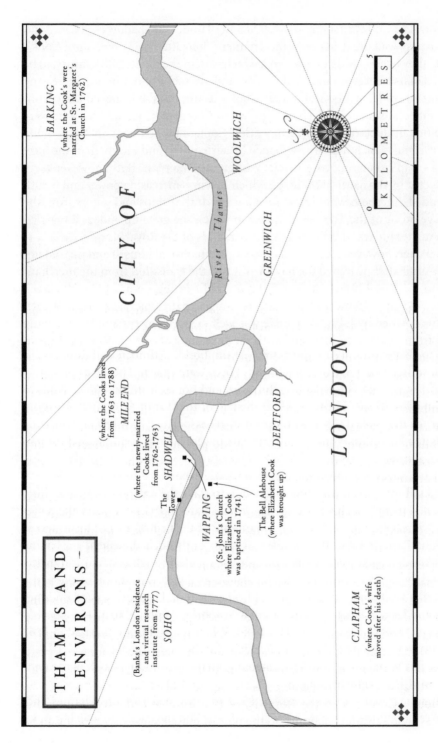

The Thames and Environs

gateway. The Cooks' first home was at Shadwell under the shadow of St Paul's and within easy walking distance of the Thames. Thereafter, from 1763 until Cook's death, they lived in Mile End, an area which was, in the nineteenth century, to be cleared of its houses as London docks expanded to cope with the ever-increasing volume of trade. Symbolically, after Cook's death, Elizabeth moved away from the immediate area of the Thames to live in Clapham. Cook and his wife were therefore products of two different worlds: Cook of the self-contained way of life of Cleveland, which was largely shaped by agriculture, and Elizabeth of the busy world of an expanding commercially orientated London. Both, however, were connected by the nautical trades on which Britain's increasing power and wealth depended. Elizabeth would have seen a great deal of ships and sailors from the vantage point of the Thames alehouse in which she grew up and, as a married woman, her life was dominated by the demands of the Royal Navy.[62]

Marriage, however, had to wait until Cook established himself and this did not occur until after he joined the navy. For it was the transition from the merchant fleet to the Royal Navy that was to be the key turning-point of Cook's career. From 1747 to 1755 most of the sixteen voyages that Cook had made had been on ships owned by John Walker. He was well favoured by his employer, having risen from 'servant' to mate and with the captaincy of one of Walker's ships in prospect.[63] Despite all this, in 1755 Cook decided to leave Walker's employment and join the Royal Navy, commenting laconically that he had determined to 'take his future fortune' that way. Walker later remarked that Cook 'had always an ambition to go into the Navy' – so this change of direction may not have come as a complete surprise to him.[64] We can only speculate on Cook's motives: patriotism, boredom with the coal trade and perhaps life in provincial Whitby or, most likely, a belief that the navy offered more security and a chance of more rapid promotion as well as the spoils of battle.

For, in 1755, on the eve of the Seven Years' War (1756–63), it must have seemed likely that Britain would go to war again. Ever since the Dutch King William had been crowned as king of England in 1689, Britain, which had previously tended to distance itself from continental conflicts, had been involved in a series of struggles against France. For France and Britain were competing not simply for dominance within Europe but also for commercial and strategic advantage in the wider imperial world which European power had prised open. Such increasing assertiveness was made possible by the wealth that flowed from the growing volume of British commerce and the efficiency of its agriculture. In these conflicts Britain's major weapon was the Royal Navy and the prestige and, for a lucky few, the wealth in the form of prize money that thereby accrued, made service with it an attractive calling to an ambitious young sailor like Cook.

Though Cook joined the Royal Navy as a humble ordinary seaman, his abilities soon saw him promoted to the post of master's mate – a promotion he gained while on his first naval ship, HMS *Eagle*, which patrolled the southern waters between England and Ireland in 1755. Before the *Eagle* again set out from Plymouth in 1755, to patrol the western approaches to the English Channel, Cook acquired a new captain and, all importantly, a patron for life, in the person of Hugh Palliser, a future admiral and comptroller of the navy. The close bond between these socially very distant men is apparent in the fact that Cook named his son Hugh after his patron.

If, as is very likely, Cook's decision to join the Royal Navy was prompted in part by the hope of prize money, he could rejoice in 1756 at the small amount that came his way (for prize money was divided by a formula based on rank) with the capture of the French ship, the *Triton*, in 1756. Cook's growing reputation was evident, too, in the fact that he was chosen to sail the prize vessel back to London. In the following year, the *Eagle* went further afield to the Bay of Biscay. Again fortune smiled on her with the capture of a French East Indiaman, the *Duc d'Aquitaine*. Again Cook was given the responsibility of being a member of the crew which sailed the vessel back to England.

The lustre of such achievements could be overlooked without patrons to draw attention to them. At this critical point in Cook's early naval career the earliest of Cook's patrons, his father's employer, Thomas Skottowe, appears to have prompted the MP for Scarborough, William Osbaldeston, to write on Cook's behalf to Palliser, suggesting that Cook be made an officer.[65] This was, however, too much of a leap to be contemplated at such an early stage – particularly as Cook had not achieved the necessary seniority. But after Cook had passed the required examination at Trinity House (the body charged with training pilots) in 1757, he was promoted to the post of master.

Cook's early patrons may have played a part in this promotion or it may simply reflect Cook's abilities. Naval service, even more than army service, required competence – appointments based solely on good connections offered too many opportunities for disaster. But, despite his obvious competence, the humbly-born Cook was slow to pass the all important line that separated officers and men. A master was a residue of the days when fighting ships were largely transports for the army or marines who fought hand to hand combats with enemy crews. The master was there to sail the ship but lacked the authority and status that accrued to an officer who could command it (though they walked the quarterdeck in the company of the officers).

After a voyage on the HMS *Solebay* up the east coast of Scotland to the Shetland Islands in 1757, Cook became master of the HMS *Pembroke*. As such he was part of the naval machine devoted to consolidating British control over North America as Britain and France extended their European conflict to a more global arena – making the Seven Years' War (1756–63) one of the first world wars. On board the HMS *Pembroke*, he sailed in 1758 to Halifax, Nova Scotia, the British

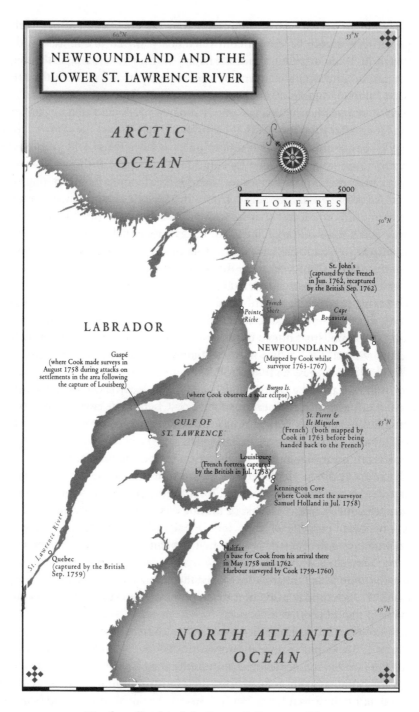

Newfoundland and the Lower St Lawrence River

base in eastern Canada – an area dominated by the French and of considerable economic importance because it controlled entry to that major seaway, the St Lawrence. After undertaking repairs at Halifax the *Pembroke* joined in the siege of the fortress of Louisbourg which controlled entry to the St Lawrence, the French garrison surrendering on 26 July.

British victory also ushered in an important new phase in the shaping of Cook's skills as a cartographer, for it was at Louisbourg that he met the army engineer, Samuel Holland. As part of his examination by Trinity House, and, possibly, too, at Whitby, Cook would have received some basic training in hydrography and the making of sea charts. The encounter with Holland meant, however, that Cook could link such nautical mapping with the increasingly sophisticated techniques being employed by land surveyors – in particular the establishment of a reliable baseline and the use of triangulation and trigonometrical readings from a series of landmarks to establish accurate coordinates. Cook's time in Canada also later led to a meeting with another land surveyor, James Des Barres, at Newfoundland in 1762 which further strengthened Cook's determination to produce accurate sea charts by scientifically-based observation of the shore – bringing together the techniques of both land and sea cartography.[66] Cook's command of such cartographical skills was honed by his work on a series of charts of key Canadian sites, the most notable of which was to be the 'New Chart of the River St Lawrence' compiled by him and Holland in 1759.

Knowledge is power and such charts played a role in the British defeat of the French. Wolfe's landing and surprise attack on Quebec was partly made possible by such detailed mapping of the St Lawrence. Cook assisted further in the attack, as he later told Lieutenant King on board the *Resolution*, since he 'conducted the embarkation to the Heights of Abraham; examined the passage and laid buoys for the security of the large ships in proceeding up the river'.[67] Such service prompted the payment to Cook in 1761 of 'Fifty pounds in consideration of his indefatigable industry in making himself Master of the Pilotage of the River Saint Lawrence'.[68]

Though they surrendered this key stronghold in September 1759, the French were not altogether a spent force. In 1762 they captured St John's, the British base on Newfoundland – an island of considerable importance since it provided access to the rich fishing fields of the Grand Banks. At the time Cook was based in Halifax, and it was from there he sailed on board the *Northumberland* as part of the fleet to recapture St John's. With his reputation as a cartographer now firmly established, he was allocated the task of charting the coast adjacent to St John's before the British recaptured the town in September 1762. Victory gave Cook, now a rising man within the navy, the opportunity to return to England and marry. Early married life was for Elizabeth dominated by almost continuous pregnancies and for Cook by the return across the Atlantic every summer from 1763 to 1767 to chart the coast of Newfoundland in his new role as 'Surveyor of Newfoundland'. Winter would see Cook back in London with his growing family, drawing together the data collected in the form of accurate maps and painstaking sailing instructions. The office brought with it the (rather limited) services of an assistant draughtsman from the Tower of London where the embryonic Ordnance Survey was based – thus further linking Cook with the techniques of land as well as sea surveying.[69] For Cook the charting of coastlines became as essential a record of a voyage as the maintenance of a log – hence his admonition that 'The world will hardly admit of an excuse for a man leaving a coast unexplored [uncharted] he has once discovered'.[70]

Cook's work as surveyor stimulated his interest in astronomy – indeed, he later recounted that it was in Canada, particularly in the winter of 1758, that he 'first read Euclid, and applied himself to the study of mathematics and astronomy'.[71] Such studies bore fruit in his observations of an eclipse of the sun from Newfoundland in 1766. These were published by the Royal Society, together with calculations by John Bevis, the society's foreign secretary, on the exact longitude of Cook's position in Canada and praise for Cook as 'a good mathematician, and very expert in his business'.[72] Astronomical observations to establish precise coordinates was particularly important when it was not possible to make observations from a clearly defined shore station – a situation that was generally to prevail on his Pacific voyages. In many ways, Cook's work in the Atlantic established the cartographic techniques that he was to employ in the Pacific. There was even continuity in some of the men that he employed, as well as the instruments on which their observations were based. In Newfoundland and the Pacific, too, Cook utilized the expertise of local pilots where that was possible and in both he learned to deal with the indigenous populations.[73] In a very tangible form the charts that derived from Cook's Canadian years proclaimed British control over its new territories in North America and offered further opportunity for their economic exploitation – and his Pacific charts later served similar goals. Cook's careful surveys combined nautical data with information on the economic advantages to be derived from coasts and harbours; and his thorough survey of Newfoundland kept the French pinned down to the terms of the treaty, to the detriment of French fishermen and the benefit of the English.[74] Cook's maps were part of the projection of British power across the Atlantic; soon they were to become an agent of British influence in a much less familiar part of the globe, the Pacific.

While the British had been regularly traversing the Atlantic since the sixteenth century, the Pacific was in many respects a *terra incognita* (or at least a *mare incognitum*). The Spanish had largely claimed it for themselves since Vasco de Balboa had become the first recorded European to immerse himself in its waters in 1513, claiming the vast watery expanse for Spain. This high claim was made a little more plausible by the epic voyage of Ferdinand Magellan from 1519 to 1521, the first recorded circumnavigation of the globe and the voyage that gave the Pacific its name.

Spanish penetration of the Pacific was followed up by the voyages of Alvaro de Mendaña of 1567–69 and 1595–97 and that of his pilot, Pedro de Quirós, of 1605–6. These voyages were shaped by the Spanish preoccupation with gold, God and glory adding to the mystique of the Pacific with tales of King Solomon's mines (hence the name the Solomon Islands) and the possible site of a New Jerusalem as part of the Great South Land – Quirós's messianic vision being captured in the bestowal of the name Austrialia del Espíritu Santo (South Land of the Holy Spirit) on what eventually turned out to be a island in the New Hebrides group (now Vanuatu). But, apart from Spanish consolidation of power in the Phillippines, such voyages were not the prelude to further Spanish exploration and exploitation of the Pacific. Spain had enough problems dealing with its economic and dynastic problems at home, as well as digesting its already vast imperial possessions, without taking on new territories.

The Dutch mapped much of Australia (apart from the east coast, which was left to Cook) as a by-product of their voyages from the Netherlands to the East Indies. They did sponsor two major voyages of Pacific exploration in the form of Tasman's expeditions of 1642–43 and 1644. Tasman sailed around parts of Australia and New Zealand, together with Tonga, Fiji and New Guinea, but his reports indicated that there was little profit to be made in further exploration or colonization. The British William Dampier's account of his voyages to western Australia in 1688 and 1699 was even less encouraging and so, generally speaking, the Pacific was largely left untroubled by importunate European voyagers and Spanish claims to the Pacific were left unchallenged.

European nations, however, and particularly the British and the French, came to regard the Pacific with renewed interest after the Seven Years' War came to an end in 1763. The war had resulted in clear British dominance of North America and India and there was a natural rush to seek new worlds for imperial expansion in the Southern Hemisphere. The French had hopes that the Great Southland – about which the influential Charles de Brosses had speculated in his *Histoire des navigations aux terres australes* (1756) – might redress their waning fortunes in the Northern Hemisphere. There is an appropriate symbolism in the fact that Bougainville, the first of the great French Pacific explorers, was an aide-de-camp to General Montcalm, who had been defeated at the battle for Quebec with the aid of Cook's cartography. Another presage of the way in which, for the French, the Pacific was a possible arena for balancing Atlantic losses is the career of La Pérouse. He had been involved in the attack on St John's, Newfoundland, in 1762, which Cook's cartography played a small part in reversing, and later led the ill-fated Pacific expedition of 1785–88 which represented the French response to Cook's Pacific voyages.

For the British, French interest in the Pacific further stimulated their own determination to ensure that any new Americas or other riches should, as far as possible, flow to them. The expedition of John Byron in 1764 was an early, but abortive, indication of an interest in promoting such a British Pacific presence. It was followed, however, by the more successful voyage of Samuel Wallis in 1776–78, which placed Tahiti on the map of the globe and helped to establish its supposed sybaritic delights in the European imagination. Accompanying Wallis's *Dolphin* was Cartaret's *Swallow*, though the two ships (as in Cook's second voyage), parted company, leaving Cartaret with the honour of being the first European to sight Pitcairn Island. He mischarted it, however, enabling the *Bounty* mutineers later to hide there safe from the wrath of the British navy.

Such was the state of British knowledge of the Pacific on the eve of Cook's *Endeavour* voyage – a voyage that led eventually to the British dominating the 'neo-Europes' of Australia and New Zealand, even if it did not lead to the discovery of another America. If such another America had been found, there would probably have been an Antipodean equivalent of the Seven Years' War, as Britain and France fought it out for dominance; but, from a European perspective, the Pacific did not offer prizes worth such a conflict. Indeed, in the nineteenth century Britain was prepared to forfeit its claims – which owed much to Cook's voyages – to Tahiti and New Caledonia to France.

The route that led to Cook's command of the *Endeavour* in 1768 and the first of his three great Pacific voyages is an obscure one. Very likely Palliser had an hand in recommending him for the voyage. The case for Cook's appointment was probably greatly strengthened by his published observations of the solar eclipse of 1766, making him an appropriate commander for a voyage the primary (or at least overt) purpose of which was to view the transit of Venus of 1769 in close (and very rare) succession to that of 1761. The transit of Venus across the face of the sun offered an opportunity to measure precisely the distance from the earth to the sun. The black dot, as Venus appeared in its transit across the sun, offered a fixed point on which to focus. Such calculations could, by fairly straightforward trigonometry, be used to establish accurate figures for that basic astronomical yardstick, the distance from the earth to the sun. The great advantage of having two transits of Venus so close together was that it meant that the first one could act, as it were, as a dress rehearsal for the second.

One of the lessons learnt from the first transit of Venus was that the calculations would be more accurate if there were an observation post in the Southern Hemisphere, as well as the multiple points of observation in the Northern Hemisphere used in 1761. The return of Wallis in 1768, having, in the previous year, been the first European to visit Tahiti, made the island the obvious choice for this major British contribution to astronomy. Continuity between the Wallis voyage and Cook's *Endeavour* was provided by some of the crew, and by a goat which graced the deck of both vessels, providing milk for the crew throughout the two long voyages.

Great Power rivalry between France and Britain was played out in science as well as in more overt forms of conflict. Though the observation of the transit of Venus involved a very considerable degree of international cooperation, it was important for national prestige that the British did not appear to be too much in the shadow of the formidable French scientific establishment which had first drawn attention to the forthcoming double transits of Venus. The British contribution of observations from the Southern Hemisphere offered something distinctive; it also provided a plausible alibi for exploration of the South Seas and investigation of whether or not there was a great South Land – discovery of which had at least the potential to have a similar impact on Europe to Columbus's arrival in the Americas.

The Royal Society, which had been Britain's premier scientific body since its foundation in 1660, had initiated the voyage with the support of its patron, King George III. Its choice for commander was Alexander Dalrymple, the chief exponent of the view that there was a yet undiscovered Great South Land. The Royal Navy, however, drew the line at having one of its ships commanded by a civilian and Cook was the compromise choice. Perhaps one of the reasons that Cook was chosen was that his background was a natural complement to the ship: a Whitby-built collier, the *Earl of Pembroke*, which was rechristened the *Endeavour*. No doubt his reputation as a cartographer also played a major role in his obtaining the post, particularly as surveying was ineluctably linked with astronomy, as calculations of latitude depended on taking readings from the heavens. Moreover, until the method of calculating longitude at sea by the use of chronometer became widespread (a method not used by Cook until his second Pacific voyage), longitude was commonly calculated by the method of lunar differences, which involved using the moon to measure the passage of time: in effect turning the moon into a distant clock. Such calculations required some astronomical skill, since one had to measure the angular distance between the moon and the sun or a particular star.[75]

For Cook the post meant a new form of naval career based on scientific exploration rather than the customary one based on capturing or sinking as many enemy vessels as possible. To some extent his career had been moving in that direction with his mapping work in Newfoundland, but the *Endeavour* voyage brought with it his own command and elevation to the officer class, albeit as a mere lieutenant. The *Endeavour* was to establish the mould for a series of voyages of scientific exploration, among them George Vancouver's exploration of the north-west coast of America in 1791–94, Matthew Flinders' *Investigator* voyage

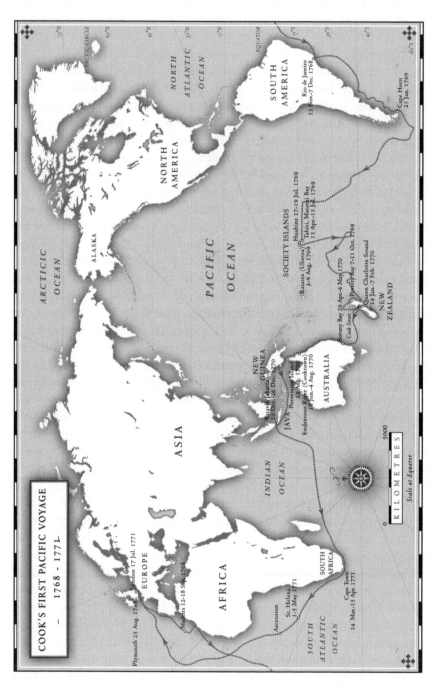

Cook's First Pacific Voyage, 1768–1771

around Australia in 1801–3 and, most momentously of all, Robert Fitzroy's voyage of the *Beagle* in 1831–36, which set the young Darwin on course for his theory of evolution.

The scientific character of the *Endeavour* voyage was strengthened by its being a voyage to promote the study of natural history as well as astronomy. For not only was one of the chief missions of the *Endeavour* to view the transit of Venus, but also it carried with it Joseph Banks who, as the Royal Society described him in its letter to the Admiralty requesting his passage, was 'a gentleman of large fortune, who is well versed in natural history' and who wished to promote 'the advancement of useful knowledge'.[76] Banks was subsequently to be the longest serving of all presidents of the Royal Society and, as president from 1778 to 1820, he did much to steer the British government towards the promotion of such voyages of discovery which he had helped to initiate through his presence on board the *Endeavour* – together with his party consisting of two Swedish naturalists, Daniel Solander and Herman Sporing, two draughtsmen, Sydney Parkinson and Alexander Buchan, along with four servants and two dogs.

How Cook responded to the Banks entourage, which must have been an alien presence in the set routines of naval life, is difficult to discern. The enormous difference in social status between the humbly-born Cook and Banks, with his broad Lincolnshire acres and Eton and Oxford education, must have created a gulf that took some bridging. Though Cook's authority in matters relating to the sailing of the ship would have been apparent, Cook does seem to have deferred to Banks in more academic matters – passages of their journals, which they would have written up together in the great cabin, are very similar and it would appear that Cook followed Banks in some of his descriptions of the Pacific island societies they encountered. Cook found more of his own voice as time went on, however, setting the tone for the second and third Pacific voyages when he would write quite independently of the absent Banks.[77]

Though Banks was due to sail aboard the second voyage of 1772 to 1775, he withdrew in high dudgeon when the expedition was not reorganized to meet the extensive demands of his much enlarged entourage. These 'cross circumstances' (as Cook put in a letter to Banks sent when the *Resolution* called in Cape Town in November 1775) caused some 'coolness betwixt you and I', but it was not a lasting break. Cook was well aware of his 'many obligations' to Banks – including some 'Pickled and dryed Salmon' which Banks contributed to an expedition from which he had withdrawn so acrimoniously.[78] Banks actively promoted Cook's career and did much to recommend him to Banks' fellow London clubman, the earl of Sandwich, the First Lord of the Admiralty – one of the ties between Sandwich and Banks being the close friendship of their respective mistresses. No doubt it was Banks, too, who played a role in securing for Cook the Royal Society's Copley Medal in 1776 as recognition of the importance of his paper on

Fort Venus, Tahiti. Engraving by S. Middiman after Parkinson (from Sydney Parkinson,
A Journal of a Voyage to the South Seas (London, 1773), plate 4, facing p. 16)

'The Method Taken for Preserving the Health of the Crew of His Majesty's Ship
the *Resolution*'.[79] After Cook's death Banks' good offices went as far as assisting
Cook's sister financially (though her case was later weakened when it was revealed
she was inclined to drink more than was considered respectable).[80]

From the point of view of Cook as commander of the *Endeavour*, the most
valuable service that Banks provided was his ability to learn Tahitian and to
study closely the Pacific peoples they encountered. The *Endeavour* arrived at
Matavai Bay, Tahiti, on 13 April 1769 after a voyage around South America.
Today it is difficult to discern a great deal of interest in this landfall in French-
speaking Tahiti. There is a monument marking the site of Point Venus where the
astronomical observatory was established to study the transit of Venus. Erected in
1901 it owes its existence, not to local initiative, but to the British Royal Society
and Royal Geographical Society and has a neglected air. Bligh, who learned his
trade as a seaman on board Cook's third voyage, is better remembered – not
so much for himself as for the mutiny on the *Bounty*. For the mutineers took
Tahitian wives with them to Pitcairn Island and their descendants can still be
found there and on Norfolk Island.

Although there is little at Matavai Bay to mark Cook's arrival, the fact that Cook made this the chief harbour for European vessels visiting Tahiti helped to establish the tribal chieftains of this area, the Pomare clan, as the paramount chiefs of the island of Tahiti as a whole.[81] In a culture where gestures of friendship and respect counted for much, the gifts given to the Pomare clan and the meals and other courtesies shared with them by Cook and subsequent European visitors, added significantly to its standing, and access to European trading goods provided opportunities for valuable patronage.[82] A tangible symbol of British favour was the Union Jack left behind at Matavai Bay by Samuel Wallis. In an amalgam of European and Tahitian symbolism, it was, as the astronomer William Bayly remarked in his journal of Cook's third Pacific voyage, 'worked over with Feathers of various Colours and … put on the King when Crowned or invested with the Royal Authority'.[83] The red and yellow feathers thus added linked this symbol of European power with potent sources of Tahitian status since the feathers indicated a line of descent dating back to the arrival of such feathers from the sacred island of Ra'iatea in the late seventeenth century.[84] Surgeon Anderson thought it 'answer[ed] exactly in signification to a Europaean crown and is amongst these people held to be full as sacred'.[85] The growth of Pomare power was later further consolidated by the arrival at Matavai Bay of members of the London Missionary Society in 1796. They are more enthusiastically commemorated than Cook there today with a monument displaying a diagram charting the way in which they fanned out across the Pacific after they established themselves with much initial travail on Tahiti.

For Cook and his men, Tahiti was to be one of the continuing bright spots amidst the hardships and deprivations that were an inseparable part of shipboard life. The three months spent there to study the transit of Venus gave considerable opportunity to study Tahitian life, which most regarded warmly and often contrasted to the laborious disciplines of chilly Britain. Though Cook bemoaned his sailors' corruption of local morals and the spread of venereal disease this occasioned, he grasped every opportunity to return to Tahiti both on his second and third voyages.

In turn, Tahiti sent its ambassadors to Britain in the form of the priest Tupaia, who travelled with the *Endeavour* before succumbing to dysentery at Batavia (now Jakarta) in the Dutch East Indies (Indonesia). Though he joined the *Endeavour* at Tahiti he was originally from another of the Society Islands, Ra'iatea, the religious centre of the archipelago where he probably received some of his priestly training before moving to Tahiti, probably as a result of an invasion from the nearby island of Bora Bora in around 1760. He was to be of considerable service to Cook as a pilot within his home waters and as an interpreter throughout the Polynesian diaspora, and the accounts by Cook and Banks of Tahitian society owe much to conversations with him. In contrast to the unfortunate Tupaia,

Mai (or Omai), who was taken aboard on the second voyage, reached England and made a considerable stir there, being presented to the king and painted by Joshua Reynolds.[86] Like Tupaia, he had fled from Ra'iatea to Tahiti. By the time he joined Cook's expedition in 1773 he had, however, moved on to Huahine. Others would have come, too, but Cook on his second voyage grew wary of acquiring passengers who might never be returned – indeed, Mai's voyage to Britain was not due to Cook but to his fellow captain, Tobias Furneaux. Tupaia's abilities were rated more highly than those of Mai but both, along with Hitihiti (or Odidday) who completed a circuit of the Pacific before being returned to Tahiti on Cook's second voyage), were regarded with affection by their British shipmates.

After three months' opportunity to soak up the sun, food and other comforts of Tahiti, the *Endeavour* explored some of the outer (Leeward Islands) of the group of islands around Tahiti. This group Cook collectively called the Society Islands, 'as they lay contiguous to one another';[87] perhaps, too, the name was intended to echo that of the Royal Society which had initiated the voyage.[88] He stopped briefly at Huahine and at Ra'iatea in July 1769, his interest in them being sufficiently stimulated to return on later voyages. Then he steered towards New Zealand to fill out the sketchy maps that Tasman had made in 1642. There the Tahitian Tupaia was able to converse with the indigenous people, making it apparent that they were of a common stock. It was the beginning of Cook's continuing education in the vast extent of Polynesian voyaging, which was heightened by the visit to Easter Island on the second voyage and Hawai'i on the third. At Tahiti there had been three months of continuing residence in one place; by contrast, the six month period spent charting New Zealand was peripatetic with occasional landfalls to restock with water and, if possible, fresh food. On 4 November 1769 there was an echo of its mission to Tahiti when the *Endeavour* landed to observe the transit of Mercury at an inlet which Cook predictably named Mercury Bay.

There had been little major conflict in Tahiti – perhaps because Wallis had previously made a display of British naval might by firing on and killing some Tahitians in retaliation for an initial attack when the British vessels arrived. Like Wallis's arrival in Tahiti, however, Cook's arrival in New Zealand began with bloodshed. When on 9 October 1769 he landed at the mouth of the Turanganui River at the site of what is now the town of Gisborne, Cook was soon involved in a clash with local Māoris which resulted in the death of one of them. His attempt to kidnap others from a canoe, to persuade these captives by good treatment that he meant no harm, badly miscarried and more bloodshed ensued, with several Māoris on board the canoe being shot. Today, the monuments around Gisborne attempt to do justice to the perspectives of both sides of that timeworn frontier. The landing site itself, now some distance from the shifting river, is ignominiously positioned in front of an industrial site. More evocative is the relatively unspoiled

Tolaga Bay a little north, where Cook successfully found water and wood while Banks and Solander collected plants and the crew traded with Māoris on amicable terms. The three-mile bushwalk from the road to Cook's Cove within Tolaga Bay is rewarded by superb vistas of the coast and views of a natural curiosity which much intrigued Cook's men, being described by Parkinson as 'a curious Arched Rock, having a River running under it'.[89] There is also a plain monument to mark Cook's stay there from 23 to 29 October 1769.

Sporadic conflict continued on this and Cook's subsequent visits to New Zealand, as the British punished theft or stumbled into intertribal conflicts or violations of taboo. On the second voyage, this resulted in eleven of the crew of Cook's companion vessel, the *Adventure*, under Furneaux being killed and eaten.[90] Yet, though Cook and his men did not regard the New Zealanders with the same warm affection that they showed towards the Tahitians, they had a certain respect for the Māoris and their martial virtues. Like Tahiti, New Zealand was a common thread to the three voyages and Queen Charlotte Sound at the top of the South Island became a virtual base for Cook's Pacific operations. He visited Ship Cove with its sheltered anchorage and supply of water five times in all – as one is reminded by a substantial and blockish monument on the site which overlooks the wide and scenic vista of the mouth of the Sound.

From New Zealand Cook began to make his way home. Though he could have headed back directly via South America, he turned north. This gave him the opportunity to explore the hitherto largely unknown east coast of New Holland (as Australia was then known) and to institute much needed repairs at the Dutch East India Company's dockyards at Batavia. In Australia he made few landfalls and his contact with the Aborigines was minimal. His most extended stays were at Botany Bay (near present-day Sydney) and on the Endeavour River, near what is now Cooktown in Northern Queensland, where he had to beach his vessel after it was very nearly wrecked on the Great Barrier Reef. At Botany Bay – named for the profusion of new plants collected by Banks and Solander – the Aboriginal men from the Gweagal tribe threw spears at the British when they landed, but then retreated, these and other spears being gathered up to add to the *Endeavour*'s large collection of 'artificial curiosities'.[91]

The landing at Botany Bay was a defining moment for two cultures. Today the recently-refurbished Captain Cook Landing Site Museum at Kurnell underlines the traditional (though waning) iconic significance of Cook as the founding father of European Australia. Nearby a stone pillar erected in 1870 duly records the place and date of the landing on 28 April 1770. It is set at the edge of a park, the well-ordered state of which contrasts with the descriptions by Cook and his men of a place that was well-forested – though archaeological excavation of the site records the extent of the Aboriginal presence evident when Cook landed.[92] Overhead is the noise of the planes from the large airport nearby,

The *Endeavour* Beached for Repairs after Hitting the Great Barrier Reef. Engraving by Will Byrne, probably after a lost drawing by Parkinson (from J. Hawkesworth, *An Account of the Voyages* … (3 vols, London, 1773), iii, plate 19, facing p. 557)

which now provides Sydney's major link with the larger world – taking much further the globalization of which Cook's *Endeavour* was a harbinger. The other side of Cook's presence is also remembered around Australia in Aboriginal oral tradition, with the representation and character of Cook being shaped by the varying Aboriginal experience of white settlement of which he is seen as the progenitor.[93] From their differing perspectives, both white and black accord Cook a symbolic importance which in Australia and around the Pacific generally often makes him a controversial figure.

Both at Botany Bay and Cooktown the British were amazed at how little interest the Aborigines had in trading – in conspicuous contrast to the Polynesian peoples. Indeed the Gogo-Yimidir people around Cooktown showed very little interest in the British generally during their seven weeks' enforced sojourn there, though they retaliated when the British caught what they considered their turtles by attempting to burn their camp. The Aborigines' general indifference to the goods that the British had to offer led both Cook and Banks to comment on how content the Australian Aborigines were with their lot. For Cook 'they are far more happier than we Europeans; being wholy unacquainted not only with the superfluous but the necessary Conveniencies so much sought after in Europe'.[94] Nonetheless, Cook showed no great desire to return to Australia, visiting it again only briefly on the third voyage, with a few days' stay at Van Diemen's Land (Tasmania). Nor did such ruminations deflect Cook from his imperial purposes and, at Possession Island off the tip of Cape York (and thus as far to the north of Australia as Cook could go), he paused to take formal possession of the east coast of New Holland (which he named New South Wales) in the name of the British crown.

From there he made his way through Torres Strait (the existence of which he probably knew from Spanish accounts collected by Dalrymple) and thence to Batavia. There the fit and healthy crew of the *Endeavour* died in large numbers: seven at Batavia itself and twenty-four on the way home as a consequence of disease contracted at Batavia or possibly from polluted water from another East Indies island, Princes Island (Pulau Panaitan). It was a tragic dénouement to a voyage that had hitherto suffered a remarkably low mortality rate. Cook had ensured that his men escaped the customary curse of Pacific voyaging: scurvy brought on by lack of fresh food with, as we would put it today, a consequent loss of vitamin C. This he had done by insisting that his crew varied their customary diet of weevil-infected ship's biscuit and salted meat with a range of antiscorbutics: sauerkraut, portable soup (somewhat like stock cubes), essence of wort (a yeast preparation like marmite), and concentrated lemon and lime juice.

Such dietary measures, together with an insistence on cleanliness, had led to a remarkably low loss of life. By the time he got back to England, the overall loss for the voyage was forty-one (thirty-one died as a result of dysentery caught in the East Indies, with another ten dying chiefly of the familiar naval afflictions of alcoholic excess, drowning and tuberculosis).[95] Nonetheless, by the standards of the time, this was not a high figure. On the second voyage the *Resolution* lost a mere two, and on the third it lost eleven (including Cook himself and the four marines killed at Hawai'i). These were figures that underlined the fact that Cook had conquered one of the most formidable obstacles to Pacific travel: the human body's need for fresh food or its equivalent.

Cook returned to much applause, but the applause was still louder for Banks, whose social rank and connections ensured that he received much of the attention of London society. Nonetheless, Cook did achieve some tangible recognition, being presented to the king, who confirmed Cook's promotion from lieutenant to the rank of commander. In the first instance, he was appointed to command HMS *Scorpion* on a cartographical mission to revise the maps of British waters, but, by January 1772, plans were afoot for a second voyage to settle once and for all the question of whether or not there was a Great South Land. It was a quest that Cook himself had proposed, and his enthusiasm for it had probably been heightened by Dalrymple's vocal objections that Cook's *Endeavour* voyage still left the issue in doubt. Important political support for the voyage came from the earl of Sandwich, now first lord of the admiralty, who was in close touch with Joseph Banks – at least until Banks attempted to take over much of the organization of the voyage himself. The fact that Cook's early patron, Hugh Palliser, was comptroller of the navy also helped to smooth Cook's path. On 21 June 1772 Cook set off once again to explore the unknown reaches of the Pacific and, indeed, of the southern latitudes of the globe as a whole.

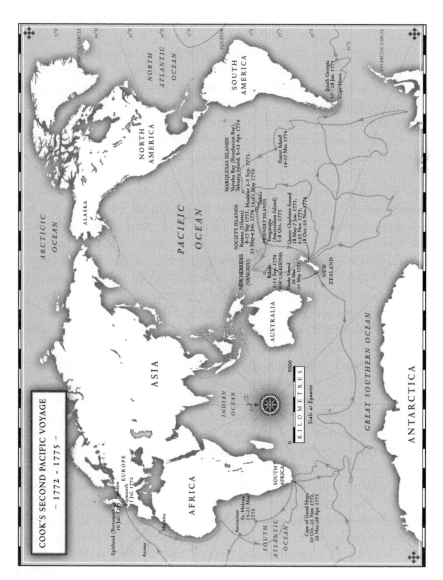

Cook's Second Pacific Voyage, 1772–1775

The second and third voyages were both quests to find something that did not exist – the Great South Land and the North-West Passage from the Pacific to the Atlantic. But there have been few more productive voyages than Cook's great second voyage: not only did it definitively prove the non-existence of an alleged continent – a considerable demystification of the map of the Southern Hemisphere – but, in the process, it opened up much of the southern latitudes to European scrutiny and, during the winter months, further unravelled the map of the Pacific. After his encounter with the Barrier Reef, he was adamant that in future voyages he would have a back-up vessel so his own ship, the *Resolution*, was accompanied by the *Adventure* under the command of Tobias Furneaux. Both were Whitby colliers – ships which had a low draft and were able to come in close to land, as was essential to produce the maps which were to be the most tangible legacy of Cook's voyaging.

After Banks and his party withdrew in pique, the place of resident scientist was taken by the impecunious but vastly learned German Johann Reinhold Forster and his son George. Forster senior, in particular, made few friends and he seems to have had a particular knack for alienating powerful patrons like Sandwich and Banks. Yet we owe much to their presence on board: their accounts of the voyage drew on deep wells of erudition and a fascination with the new worlds that they encountered.[96] The post of artist went to William Hodges, whose background as an landscape artist is evident in some of the vivid, almost cinematic, depictions of the scenery he encountered on the voyage.

The second voyage fundamentally consisted of three sweeps through the southern latitudes as close to the ice cape as was prudent, thereby proving the non-existence of the alleged Great Southern Land in the Indian, Pacific and Atlantic Oceans. These great circuits consumed the summers of 1772–73 (crossing the Antarctic Circle on 17 January 1773), 1773–74 and 1774–75 respectively. In the winter months, when exploration in these icy latitudes was impossible, Cook returned to the South Pacific with two great circles which both predictably took in Tahiti. The geographical pivot of the second voyage was Queen Charlotte Sound at the top of the South Island of New Zealand, which was meant to serve as the point of rendezvous for the two ships, though eventually they became separated. In November 1773 Cook waited in vain there for three weeks but eventually gave up: ironically, Furneaux and the *Adventure* arrived five days later. With no prospect of finding Cook, and demoralized by the death of eleven of his men at the hands of local Māoris, Furneaux decided to return to England.

Furneaux and his men therefore participated in only the first of the two great Pacific sweeps. Since he stopped off at Tasmania on his way north from the southern reaches of the Indian Ocean before rejoining Cook at Queen Charlotte Sound in May 1773, Furneaux was also not with Cook during what appears to have been the most fondly-remembered sojourn in New Zealand, the *Resolution*'s six-week stay at Dusky Sound in 1773 near the south-west tip of the South Island – a visit vividly captured in William Hodges's superb artwork. Cook had sighted the Sound on the first voyage – a gash in the great sea wall that surrounded a thickly-forested sheer coastline dotted with small islands carved off by the fury of the sea – but had not dared venture into its unknown depths. After four months in Antarctic waters he thought it worth the risk and, on 28 March 1773, successfully negotiated his way through the many islands within the Sound (one for every day of the year) to a calm anchorage in the small cove off Astronomer's Point. In contrast to the ravages of the frozen south, Dusky Sound came to seem a little Eden, with a mild climate and plentiful food in the form of fish, birds and seals readily available – a preoccupation that has left a lasting legacy in the form in such names as Luncheon Cove and Supper Cove. There was little contact with Māori people, apart from a family group of a man, a few women and some children, on whom was focused the full ethnological gaze of the Forsters and others of Cook's crew, and the artistic licence of Hodges. Today Dusky Sound – inaccessible by land except to the hardiest of long-distance bushwalkers – remains very much as Cook left it, unencumbered by monuments (a discreet plaque excepted), apart from the stumps of trees on Astronomer's Point, the felling of which was the work of Cook's long-vanished crew. [97]

Such sojourns did much to restore morale to sailors who had had to contend with the icy blasts and the frozen sails and ropes of the southern latitudes. The two great Pacific sweeps also filled in some of the blank spaces on the map of the Pacific. In the first sweep, in the winter of 1773, they headed first to the blandishments of Tahiti, taking in not only Tahiti itself but also other islands within the Society Islands: Huahine (where they picked up their celebrated passenger, Mai) and Ra'iatea (the main centre of Tahitean religious traditions). Thence they sailed by way of some outlying islands of what is now the Cook Islands to the Tonga group, unvisited by Europeans since Tasman passed through in 1643. At the island of Tongatapu the reception was so hospitable that Cook gave the name the Friendly Islands to the whole archipelago.

After the ice cruise of the southern Pacific latitudes of late 1773 and early 1774, Cook had more time for his second Pacific sweep. By March 1774 he reached Easter Island (previously visited by the Dutch explorer Jacob Roggeveen in 1722). The next major port of call was the Marquesas, which had been described by the Spanish Mendaña in 1595 but accorded only a very uncertain place on the map. Then it was time for another visit to Tahiti. From there the *Resolution* sailed via some of the Cook Islands and Niue (or Savage Island as Cook termed it because of the hostile reception he received) back to the Friendly Islands (Tonga). Cook's next destination was, like the Marquesas, determined by the inexact accounts left by the Spanish: in this case that of Quirós. His religious enthusiasm had prompted him to regard Espiritu Santo, one of the islands of Vanuatu, as part of a great southern continent which could offer fertile ground for the spread of Christian civilization. After stopping briefly at Vatoa, an outer island of the Fiji Group (the nearest Cook ever came to Fiji), Cook landed on Malekula, one of the New Hebrides Group (present day Vanuatu), on 22 July.

Having become so used to the farflung character of Polynesian culture, Cook was surprised to find that a different people populated these islands. They became known as the Melanesians and their language was quite different to Polynesian. The fact that there was no common language intensified the suspicion and uncertainty on both sides, and Cook's visits to Melanesian societies were much more tense affairs than those to Polynesian islands. Eventually, after visits to Erromango and Tanna, Cook arrived at Quirós's Tierra del Espiritu Santo, where Cook paid a modest tribute to his distant Spanish counterpart by naming one of the island's headlands Cape Quiros.

Sailing south from the New Hebrides (Vanuatu), Cook encountered New Caledonia on 4 September, where again the population was Melanesian rather than Polynesian. It was then time to head back to base in New Zealand, but on the way Cook encountered another uncharted island, which he called Norfolk Island. It was unpopulated but was later to serve as one of the grimmest of New South Wales's early 'places of secondary punishment' before being ceded by Queen Victoria to the descendants of the *Bounty* mutineers who were outgrowing their home on Pitcairn Island. Thence back to Queen Charlotte Sound, where some of the Māoris passed on rumours about the fate of the eleven members of Furneaux's crew who had been killed.

Cook's chief priority, however, was to leave as soon as possible on his last ice cruise, which would take him to the bottom of South America and, then, via the South Atlantic, back to England. As in the Indian and the Pacific Oceans, Cook could confirm the non-existence of a major land mass apart from Antarctica – the frozen expanse of which was plainly no new America. Otherwise all that the South Atlantic had to offer by way of new discoveries were small uninhabited islands such as South Georgia or the South Sandwich Islands (a tribute to his aristocratic patron). Then it was high time to return home, so he headed for Cape Town, where he found a long letter from Furneaux recounting his misfortunes. On the journey from there to England he stopped at St Helena, where the governor was the son of Thomas Skottowe, his father's employer and Cook's first patron.

Back in London, Cook received greater recognition than he had on his return from the *Endeavour* voyage. He was presented at court and promoted to post-captain (which meant that, in due course and given sufficient longevity, he could eventually work his way up the seniority list to admiral). As something of a celebrity, Cook was duly scrutinized by some of the leading diarists of the age. James Boswell met him at a dinner hosted by Sir John Pringle, the President of the Royal Society, and remarked on his judicious air, regarding Cook as having 'a ballance in his mind for truth as nice as scales for weighing a guinea'.[98] Fanny Burney was not so appreciative of his reserve and caution. Although she thought 'This truly great man appeared to be full of sense and thought', she also regarded him as being 'studiously wrapped up in his own purposes and pursuits; and apparently under a pressure of mental fatigue when called upon to speak'.[99] Perhaps rather bashful about having foregone the opportunity to serve on such a great voyage, Banks took a month to greet Cook, but his hand is evident in such honours as Cook's election to the Royal Society in March 1776. As a reward for his exertions, Cook was offered one of the choicest sinecures the navy had to offer: a captaincy at the Greenwich Hospital, which carried with it a pension, accommodation and, appropriately for a former collier hand, free coals.

Cook the explorer was not easily satisfied with such genteel blandishments. As he wrote to his old friend and employer, John Walker: 'a fews [sic] Months ago the whole Southern hemisphere was hardly big enough for me and now I am to be confined within the limits of Greenwich Hospital, which are far too small for an active mind like mine'.[100] In search of new worlds to discover, Cook willingly acceded to the earl of Sandwich's proposal that he command a voyage in search of the North-West Passage – naturally enough Cook, who had spent so much time unravelling the map of the South Pacific, welcomed the opportunity to explore the unknown regions of the North Pacific. He would also have been very mindful of the twenty thousand pounds reward to be shared amongst the company of the ship which successfully charted the elusive but much sought after passage. The expedition also offered an opportunity to return Mai – whose celebrity value had been waning – to Tahiti or, more exactly, to his adopted home on the island of Huahine. Before setting off Cook had responded to a would-be French Pacific explorer with advice which conveys his own determination to make his mark in the annals of exploration by seizing whatever opportunities that came his way: 'It seems certain to me that the man who does no more than carry out his instructions will never get very far in discovery'.[101]

The two ships chosen were again Whitby colliers: the *Resolution* was pressed into service once more, this time accompanied by the *Discovery* under Charles Clerke, who had served with Cook on his two previous Pacific voyages. The *Resolution* was given an overhaul but the trip was to show that the ravages of the previous voyage had left their mark, just as they had left their mark on Cook. The troubles of the third voyage arose in large measure from a tired ship commanded by a tired man, though perhaps this was compounded by other factors: for other explanations for Cook's behaviour on the third voyage have been advanced, including physical illness and reaction to the massacre of Furneaux's men at Grass Cove on the second voyage, and the contempt that his lack of revenge for this engendered in the Polynesians (including Mai) and some of his men.[102]

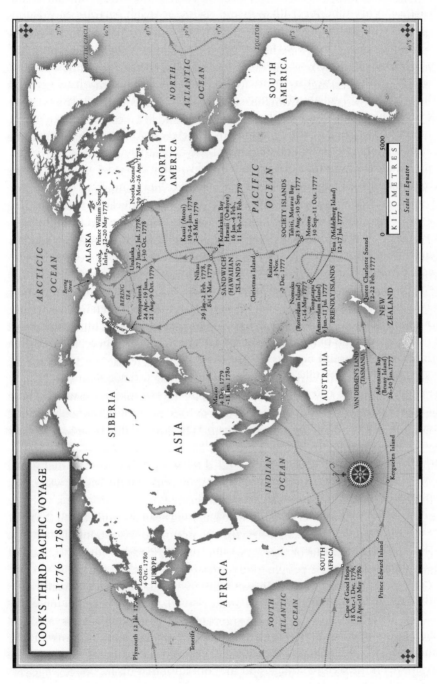

Cook's Third Pacific Voyage, 1776–1780

On the third voyage Cook's anger level varied according to circumstances and the pattern of behaviour was different more in degree than kind from the previous voyages – one certainly cannot talk of a sort of Jekyll to Hyde transformation on the third voyage.[103] Nonetheless, his men plainly thought something had changed – particularly when it came to dealing with the indigenous peoples. Cook became increasingly sensitive to any challenge to his authority, whether it came from his own men or from the native peoples he encountered. The extent to which 'he was so much respected by the islanders and at times worshipped', wrote Heinrich Zimmerman in his account of the third voyage, meant, 'that he became so enraged when they ceased to honour him or when they ridiculed him'.[104]

His most extreme bout of temper came on the island of Mo'orea in the Society Islands over the theft of a goat, when, wrote Lieutenant Williamson, 'we destroyed ten large & several small Canoes, besides houses & etc. loading the launches with the plank to build a house for Omai, we also brought away several hogs'.[105] George Gilbert, a midshipman and son of the *Resolution*'s sailing master on the second voyage, sadly remarked of the affair: 'I can't well account for Captain Cooks proceedings on this occasion as they were so very different from his conduct in like cases in his former voyages'. The truth of Gilbert's remark is borne out by Cook's reflections on the first voyage, when a theft of an iron rake in Tahiti led him to threaten to burn every canoe he could find unless the object was returned. Tellingly, Cook himself added 'not that I ever intend to put this in execution'; and, indeed, on this occasion – in contrast to the third voyage – he returned the canoes unharmed even though the rake was not returned.[106]

Cook's actions at Mo'orea were prompted by the fact that the goat stood for a number of things that were very important to him. First for the ennobling cause of agricultural improvement. As he wrote: 'The loss of this Goat would have been nothing if it had not interfered with my views of Stocking other islands with these Animals'.[107] It was also intended to be a gift and the fact that it had been, as he plausibly suspected, taken by Mahine, ruler of the island, was an act of flagrant defiance. It also was an act that indicated contempt for Cook's ally, Tu (or Otoo), the leading chief of Tahiti who had long been in conflict with the ruler of Mo'orea. Hence Gilbert's half-hearted defence of Cook's actions: 'If anything may be offered in favour of them; t'was his great friendship for Otoo (king of Otaheite) to whom these people were professed enemies'.[108]

On the third voyage Cook ensured that there would be no civilian naturalists on board who could challenge his authority (though he countenanced the presence of David Nelson, a gardener and plant collector, who knew his place and was answerable to Joseph Banks). Other civilians on board were the astronomer William Bayly (and his servant), who was sent out by the Board of Longitude on both the second and third voyages, and the Swiss-born John Webber. Like his predecessor on the second voyage, William Hodges, Webber was by background a landscape artist. He carried on the tradition of Sydney Parkinson on the first voyage and Hodges on the second by bringing back a splendid pictorial record of the voyage. After the charming but rather *prima donnish* Banks and the quarrelsome Forsters, Cook had had enough of civilian scientists on board, so the task of naturalist and anthropologist was allocated to a sharp-eyed naval surgeon, William Anderson. Cook's reaction to this issue indicates that, even before setting off, he was, as the suave Lieutenant King diplomatically put it, 'subject to hastiness and passion'.[109] For, when King raised the matter, Cook responded, 'Curse the scientists, and all science into the bargain'. When retailing this anecdote Johann Reinhold Forster advanced the view that, if he or Solander or Banks had been on board, Cook would not have met his death. No doubt, this greatly exaggerated the naturalists' importance but, possibly, having a scientist who had some standing but was not subject to Cook's full naval authority might have provided some independent advice.[110]

Firmly under Cook's command, the *Resolution* set off from Plymouth on 12 July 1776. Because Clerke had been imprisoned as guarantor for his brother's debt, the *Discovery* came later with orders to rendezvous at Cape Town. Despite this inauspicious start, the two ships succeeded in keeping together throughout the voyage – in contrast to the second voyage. From Cape Town Cook headed for his customary South Pacific base at Queen Charlotte Sound, New Zealand, on the way clearing up some uncertain patches of the map of the south Indian Ocean by definitively locating the Prince Edward Islands and Kerguelen. The latter had been sighted by the French explorer, Yves-Joseph de Kerguelen-Trémarec, but its place on the charts was far from clear. Cook also made a brief return to Australia with a stop at Adventure Bay off the southern coast of Van Diemen's Land – a harbour charted by Furneaux (and named after his ship) in March 1773 on his way to rendezvous with Cook at Queen Charlotte Sound. He was not the first to do so, for Abel Tasman had charted it when he arrived there in November 1642.

Cook did not realize that Adventure Bay was actually part of an island which was in turn off the large island of Van Diemen's Land. Bruny Island was charted by the Frenchman, Bruni D'Entrecasteaux, in 1792 while on his unsuccessful voyage to find the missing La Pérouse. Though he had reproached the hapless Furneaux for not investigating whether Van Diemen's Land was an island, Cook himself did not pursue the matter and the insularity of Van Diemen's Land was subsequently established by Matthew Flinders, together with his fellow Lincolnshire sea companion, George Bass, in 1798. Through a sort of maritime apostolic succession, Flinders was linked with Cook, as Flinders served his apprenticeship under Bligh who himself sailed on Cook's third voyage. Indeed Bligh returned to Adventure Bay with its well-sheltered harbour in 1792 while commanding the *Providence* – on the voyage which successfully completed the transfer of breadfruit from Tahiti to the West Indies, a task that had been previously rudely interrupted by the mutiny on the *Bounty*. The task of charting Adventure Bay Bligh allocated to the young Flinders – an apprenticeship exercise which helped train him for his subsequent life's work: the charting of his circumnavigation of Australia aboard the *Investigator* in 1801–3. Appropriately there now stands near the largely unspoiled Adventure Bay a small museum principally devoted to the memory of Bligh, together with a few plaques near the beachline to remind the few travellers that make their way there of Cook's visit long ago.

From Adventure Bay Cook returned to the familiar site of Queen Charlotte Sound, New Zealand. After some two weeks of resting, repairs and reprovisioning, the ships turned east for a wide and leisurely sweep of the South Pacific, retracing some of the ground covered in the second voyage. After brief stops at some of the Cook Islands, Cook arrived at the Friendly Islands (Tonga group) on 28 April 1777, staying on various islands of that group until 17 June 1777. For the customarily energetic Cook it was a long sojourn. The unhurried nature of his stay at the Friendly Islands was heightened by the fact that, contrary to custom, he declined to investigate reports of the existence of such uncharted and relatively nearby island groups as Fiji and Samoa. From the Friendly Islands the expedition headed for the inevitable visit to Tahiti and then on to Huahine in October to deliver back a very reluctant Mai whose return was greeted with less than rapturous enthusiasm.

This visit was an opportunity to visit Mo'orea and Bora Bora – islands within the Society group that Cook had missed on the first and second voyages. One of the attractions of Bora Bora was that the chief there had custody of the anchor from one of Bougainville's ships – something that Cook purchased in order to provide a ready source of iron for trading. It is possible that the anchor provided some of the iron with which Cook was struck down at Hawai'i – if so it was a distant revenge for the fall of Quebec where Bougainville and Cook had been distant adversaries.

After leaving Tahiti in December 1777, Cook encountered a whole new island group in January 1778 – a group to which he subsequently gave the name the Sandwich Islands (Hawai'i), the most notable of the many eponymous tributes he paid his aristocratic patron. The first of the Hawaiian islands he encountered was O'ahu, followed shortly afterwards by Kaua'i and Ni'ihau. He landed on these latter two islands and found that he could, to some degree, converse with the people in Tahitian – thus underlining yet again that the Polynesians, as well as the British, had traversed vast expanses of the Pacific Ocean.

After this remarkable and unexpected find, it was high time to devote himself to the chief goal of the voyage, the search for the North-West Passage from the Pacific side of the American continent. The north-west coast of America was largely unknown to the European world. Under the patronage of the Russian monarchy the Danish explorer Vitus Bering had shown in 1728 that there was a strait – appropriately named after him – between America and Asia. On a subsequent voyage in 1741 he had charted part of the Gulf of Alaska and some of the Aleutian Islands. On Beringa, one of the Komandor Islands, he died of scurvy. While the Russians worked south, the Spanish – vigilant about protecting their territories in America – had sent exploring parties north from their possessions in California, but had been slow to publish their findings. Overall Cook was entering territory that was only very sketchily mapped on the European picture of the globe.

Cook first sighted the western coast of America on 7 March 1778, giving the first discernible piece of land the name Cape Foulweather (in present-day Oregon). Like a number of the names Cook bestowed (such as Cape Tribulation on the Great Barrier Reef, Queensland, or Doubtful Sound, New Zealand), it is a graphic indication of his state of mind at the time. On 29 March 1778 he finally pulled in for much needed rest and refreshment further north at Nootka Sound which, unbeknown to Cook, was part of an island – later named Vancouver and Quadra Island by Vancouver himself, who had served with Cook on both the second and third voyage. Nootka Sound, like Dusky Sound in New Zealand, is a break in a sheer coastline thickly covered with timber. Indeed timber-getting is still a major industry, but the forest is so impenetrable in some places that the logs have to be extracted by helicopter. Like Dusky Sound, too, Nootka Sound itself is well endowed with islands and it was in a convenient crescent of one such, Bligh Island, that, as the name Resolution Cove suggests, Cook found secure refuge. True to the astronomical preoccupations of all of his voyages (as instanced by Astronomers' Point at Dusky Sound) an observatory was soon erected nearby.

Across the sound was an Indian settlement at what Cook called Friendly Cove (locally known as Yuquot). Though there was no common language, the Nootka people were keen traders and Cook and his men spent a productive month there. Cook's account of their fur trade (particularly sea otter pelts) later led other English vessels there. This caused such anxiety to the Spanish about their hold over the west coast of America that control of Nootka Sound almost became the cause of a war between Britain and Spain in 1790. Thereafter it faded from European gaze and today it is an out of the way former Indian reserve where, symbolically, the defunct Catholic mission church at Yuquot now has a totem pole where the altar used to be.

From Nootka Sound Cook followed the coast north, looking for any inlet that might lead to the much prized North-West Passage and not stopping again until he reached Prince William Sound in the Gulf of Alaska. This originally Cook named Sandwich Sound, but the earl seems to have thought, with some reason, that his name had already been cast about the globe sufficiently, so he rechristened it after Prince William. In any case a nearby headland was named

Cape Hinchinbrook after the Sandwich country seat, and there was also closeby a Montague Strait and Montague Island, Montagu being Sandwich's family name. Such geographical immortality was one of the few currencies in which Cook could repay his patron in a system where the goodwill of a patron could overcome many obstacles.

After a brief stay at English Bay on Unalaska, the most significant of the easterly Aleutian Islands, the ships sailed out into the Bering Sea on 2 July, reaching Bering Strait on 8 August. By 18 August they reached the aptly named Icy Point at the top of Alaska, where the expanse of ice stopped any further progress north. But Cook could have the consolation of knowing that, as far as any European account indicated, he had travelled the furthest north into the Arctic Circle, just as, on the second voyage, he had travelled further south into the Antarctic Circle than any other explorer. After travelling west to the Asian mainland, he made his way down to Bering Strait and then, weary of ice and snow, headed back to Hawai'i – for it was pointless to continue the search for the North-West Passage until the next summer.

By 26 November he reached Maui, sailing around its northern coast before heading for Hawai'i, the largest and, in pre-European times, the most densely populated island, with the greatest number of sacred sites. On 17 January 1779 the ships anchored in the vast mile-wide, roughly semi-circular Kealakekua Bay, the place where Cook was to meet his death. It was a place that was central to the political and religious culture of Hawai'i: Ka'awaloa, the village at the north-western end of the bay (near where Cook met his end) was the seat of royal power, while at the southwestern was the major religious centre with the great *heiau* (temple) of Hikiau – the remains of which are still to be seen. Nearby is a plaque to commemorate the death of William Watman, one of Cook's veteran sailors who died on 1 February 1779, 'and the first recorded Christian service in the Hawaiian Islands'. Though it was to be a fateful visit, the initial welcome from the Hawaiians was warm. Over a thousand canoes greeted the ships before Cook was taken off to meet the leading chiefs and priests.

By the time Cook left for the first time on 4 February enthusiasm for the British presence was waning. It was with the greatest reluctance that he returned a week later after the *Resolution*'s mast was damaged in a gale. This time there was a much more chilly welcome and increasing outbreaks of theft, one of which was to lead to Cook's undoing. When a cutter was taken for its iron fittings, Cook responded by attempting to take King Kalaniopu'u hostage. In the scuffle that broke out as a consequence Cook, four marines and seventeen Hawaiians died. The site of Cook's death on the northern end of the bay has subsided into the sea, but there is a plaque some fifty feet back from the spot.[111] He died on the edge of a small cove which marks the coastal end of a promontory on which once stood the royal village of Ka'awaloa. Some twenty yards away is a large and still well-maintained monument that dates from 1874. It was further embellished in the lavish sesquicentenary celebrations of 1928 to mark Cook's first arrival in 1778. Access to it is limited today, however, since it has been frequently defaced by local activists. The slippery lava shelf that marks a fluctuating shoreline (since it is subject to the vagaries of the tide and seismic uplift and fall) makes clear the problems that Cook and his men faced in effecting a rapid exit from their troubled situation. Looming over the coast is the mighty backdrop of thousand-feet sheer cliffs in the crevices of which were secreted the remains of royalty and which perhaps still contain some of the dust from Cook's bones, which were treated with the royal respect and awe.

The British navy was used to losing commanders and, as protocol demanded, there was a quick shuffle in the upper ranks. Clerke took over the command of the *Resolution* and the expedition as a whole, while Gore (who had also sailed with Cook on the *Endeavour* voyage) assumed command of the *Discovery*. Subsequently, when Clerke succumbed to the tuberculosis he had probably contracted whilst in debtors' prison, Gore duly moved up to command of the *Resolution*, while Lieutenant James King captained the *Discovery*. After as many of Cook's remains as possible had been reclaimed from the Hawaiians, they were dispatched with all ceremony into the depths of Kealakekua Bay on 21 February. The following day, the ships departed from those waters that had brought such tragedy.

As far as possible, the expedition continued to follow the path that Cook would have chosen. The ships continued to explore the Hawaiian archipelago before heading back to search once more for the elusive North-West Passage. This time it was decided to approach the Bering Strait, and the American coast beyond, along the Asian mainland. En route the ships stopped near Petropavlovsk, the main Russian base within Kamchatka, which had been recently colonized by the Russians as part of their incorporation of Siberia. After a five-day dog-sled ride across the peninsula to Bol'sheretsk, King and Gore were welcomed by the governor of Kamchatka, Magnus von Behm, who accompanied them back to Petropavlovsk to greet the ailing Clerke.

As had happened under Cook's command the summer before, the ships' progress north beyond the Bering Strait was arrested by pack ice and, at a point not far from where Cook had turned back, the ships turned south again, following the Asian mainland. They stopped again at Petropavlovsk and entrusted to Governor Behm (who was setting out for St Petersburg) letters and journals for dispatch to England. By this roundabout route, the tragic news of Cook's death reached London in January 1780. Clerke, who had died at sea, was buried at Petropavlovsk on 30 August 1779.

By this time both men and ships were too weary to attempt further exploration. When they set off from Petropavlovsk, on 10 October 1779, the only thought was to get home as soon as possible. They proceeded down along the coast of the Japanese island Honshu (where the local ships, true to the Japanese policy of isolation, ignored them) before anchoring at the Portuguese port of Macao. Thence they sailed through the Sunda Strait between Sumatra and Java and across the Indian Ocean to Cape Town, before setting off across the Atlantic to London, arriving on 7 October 1780 after an absence of four and a half years.

The mourning for Cook had already taken place. The returned ships could offer various relics and many tales, but no body or physical remains, since these had been consigned to the waters of Kealakekua Bay which had become at once Cook's killing place and his shrine. Indeed, part of it is for ever England, since the small patch of land immediately surrounding his monument near where he was killed was ceded by the then kingdom of Hawai'i to Great Britain in 1874. A less overt tribute was the surreptitious withholding of portions of Cook's bones among the Hawaiian chiefs as a means of absorbing some of the spirit and power that had once been Cook's. It was a long way from Cleveland, but in a tangible way Cook had become part of the Pacific, that vast portion of the globe that had dominated the last decade of his life before his death at fifty.

2

The Sea

What connected Cook's different worlds – Cleveland, London and the Atlantic and the Pacific – was the sea.[1] The sea, with its different moods and manifestations, was the central reality around which his life and career turned. For Cook, the sea with all its dangers never lost its fascination and siren-like drew him back to his disastrous third voyage when he was comfortably and safely ensconced in Greenwich Hospital. In the preface to his published account of his second Pacific voyage, he wrote of himself as one 'who has been constantly at sea from his youth' and who 'has passed through all the Stations belonging to a seaman, from an apprentice boy in the coal trade to a Post Captain in the Royal Navy'.[2] The result was that he developed an instinct for the proper functioning of ships. George Forster captured this in his description of Cook walking on deck and being able to 'notice at once in the tangle of ropes and lines … that one or the other of these lines were either hauled too taut or paid out too much, thus preventing the ship from moving faster'.[3]

Indeed he spent more time with the sea – that fickle mistress – than with his wife, who had to bear his long absences and his many children as best she could. Even when back with his family in London, it was the concerns of the sea that continued to dominate his life as he spent his time compiling charts or preparing for the next voyage. For Elizabeth, the sea extracted a grim toll: a husband dead in distant Hawai'i; her son Nathaniel lost in a hurricane off Jamaica nine months after the death of his father; and her eldest son, James (the last remaining of her six children), drowned off the Isle of Wight in 1794.

Cook was raised a farm boy, but even in the areas of Cleveland furthest from the sea its importance and power were evident. The River Tees ran a mere three miles from his birthplace at Marton, where the masts of ships making their way to and fro from the town of Yarm were an everyday sight.[4] Great Ayton was about as far away from the sea as one could get in Cleveland, but there were plenty of ships to be seen on the River Tees on market days at Stockton and Yarm. Seafaring was a natural part of the life of the village: not only did Cook go to sea but so too did one of his class mates, Thomas Bloyd, whom Cook literally ran into when their two colliers collided in the Thames in 1767. Nicholas Skottowe, the son of Cook's father's employer, later commanded a ship which had as its surgeon the son of William Sanderson, Cook's employer at the shop at Staithes.[5]

When he moved to Staithes and Whitby, Cook became part of communities dominated by the sea. In Staithes the struggle with the sea was fought with simpler weapons than at the thriving port of Whitby. There, the Staithes fishermen set out for their harvest of fish in small fishing boats or cobles which, with their high bow to face the surf, distantly resembled the Viking vessels from which they were descended.[6] Cobles came in two main sizes: the larger 'plosher', about forty feet long and meant for herring fishing; and a smaller boat of about thirty feet long and meant for line fishing. The fish were mainly sold fresh (or as fresh as poor transport and poorer storage made possible) at Whitby or other major nearby markets, such as Newcastle, though some was dried and about a quarter of the catch would be preserved in brine in barrels.[7] Fresh fish was something of a luxury – particularly in towns removed from the coast – until the coming of the railways.[8]

Like agriculture, fishing had its seasons and the main one for the people of Staithes or other Cleveland fishing villages, such as the neighbouring Robin Hood's Bay, was the herring season. July marked the time when the large 'ploshers' would set off for Yarmouth, returning at the beginning of November. If all went well the boats could net thirty to sixty 'lasts' – each last comprising ten thousand herrings – in a season.[9] Many of those returning home would then set off on the one hundred miles to the Dogger Bank, the large North Sea sandbank, whence they would return in February with more herrings (and cod).[10] Other tasks belonged to other seasons. The winter, for example, was a time for mending boats and nets.

In a fishing village such as Staithes all were expected to help. Sometimes the fishermen's womenfolk would accompany them, as was common practice on the Scottish fishing vessels that often made their way down the Yorkshire coast. At home women were expected to help haul the boats on shore and to bait the lines.[11] In their spare moments they knitted the jerseys (locally known as 'garnseys') for which each village had a distinctive design.[12] The village of a washed-up drowned sailor could thus frequently be identified by the garnsey. Boys were introduced to the life that most would follow by tasks such as mending lobster pots. As the fishermen grew older they fished closer to shore, searching for lobsters or crabs.[13]

The sea and its moods shaped everyone's life. The North Sea could be cruel and shipwrecks and drowning were the constant backdrop to a fishing village's way of life. Even in Whitby, with its bigger craft, something like a third of captains perished at sea.[14] A tombstone at St Stephen's Church in nearby Robin Hood's Bay captures the poignancy of loss which many had to endure:

> By storms at sea two sons I lost
> Which sore distresses me,
> Because I could not have their bones,
> To anchor here with me.[15]

Faced by constant danger, sailors became superstitious in their attempt to use any means to ward off the perils of the deep. Encountering a woman or a pig on the way to the slipway could prompt some fishermen to turn back.

Ten miles down the coast from Staithes, the flourishing port of Whitby offered a much greater range of nautical activity. Whitby largely left fishing to smaller sub- (or 'creek') ports like Staithes – in 1817 there were only about nine full-time Whitby fishermen.[16] With its generally larger vessels, Whitby had bigger fish to fry: the staple trade of Whitby ships in Cook's day was the carrying of coal, but Whitby ship owners were very ready to diversify. One lucrative market that was later to link Whitby with Cook's exploration of the east coast of Australia was the transportation of convicts.[17]

Along with its colliers, Whitby was famous for its whalers. The Whitby Greenland whaling trade began around the mid eighteenth century and grew fast.[18] By 1776 Whitby had fifteen whaling vessels with crews of about forty to fifty. While the herring fishers sought their catches in autumn, whalers were busy in summer, often being absent from Whitby from April to September. Departing whalers were farewelled by their womenfolk throwing old shoes and wearing their shifts inside out to bring fair weather. The perils of the deep fostered other superstitions, such as avoiding departing on a Friday, the day of Christ's death.[19] The whaling industry was a very immediate presence in the town as the Try Works which rendered blubber into oil emitted their stench into the atmosphere. Some sense of its pungent odour was captured by Banks when he sought for a way of describing the smell of the rancid oil used by the Māoris to daub their hair. This he likened to a 'Greenland dock when they are trying Whale Blubber'.[20] Giant jawbones of whales were a common sight in Whitby and even today there is a large monument made of whale bones on the West Cliff, adjacent to a statue of Cook framing the view of the ruined abbey on the other headland. In Cook's time, and for some decades afterwards, whaling brought considerable wealth to the town. Between 1767 and 1816 Whitby ships brought back 2,761 whales, but the industry thereafter became less and less profitable and ceased in Whitby from 1837.[21]

Like Cook, William Scoresby, Whitby's most famous whaler, started life as an agricultural labourer. Another link with Cook was a connection with Joseph Banks, with whom Scoresby corresponded extensively on Greenland whaling. Much of Scoresby's success lay in his skill in navigating through ice-encumbered seas and reaching the whaling fields before his competitors. In 1806 his ability to sail in such treacherous waters led to his coming nearer to the North Pole than anyone previously.[22] Such interest in Arctic exploration led Banks to enlist Scoresby in various experiments for measuring sea temperature.[23]

Whaling and the ever-increasing volume of the coal trade meant an expansion in the size of Whitby's fleet. This had grown steadily over the course of the

Painting by Thomas Luny c. 1790 of the *Bark, Earl of Pembroke*, later *Endeavour*, leaving
Whitby Harbour in 1768 (Australian National Library pic-an2280897)

eighteenth century, from 130 in 1734 to over 195 in 1755; a figure that rose
sharply to 251 by 1776. Thereafter the number of ships levelled out, but in 1828
Whitby was still a significant port, with the number of ships registered there
being the eighth largest in Britain.[24]

Along with sailors went shipbuilding – another area where Whitby was
becoming increasingly prominent in Cook's time. All the vessels used on
Cook's great voyages of Pacific exploration were Whitby-built. Perhaps Cook's
achievements, along with the demands of the American war, may have done
something to spread Whitby's renown as a centre for shipbuilding; in 1779,
the year of Cook's death, a Whitby historian could write proudly that 'Whitby
has long been noted for building good ships ... but never was in so much
fame on that account as at present'.[25] The *Endeavour*, the *Resolution* and the
Adventure were all built at Whitby at Thomas Fishburn's shipyard, while the
Discovery was built nearby at George and Nathaniel Langborne's.[26] Along with
colliers, Fishburn – who, in partnership with Thomas Brodrick was the largest
of Whitby shipbuilders[27] – built the reinforced vessels needed for whaling,
among them Scoresby's famed vessel, named after Cook's *Resolution* and built
in 1803. Shipbuilders, in turn, required other maritime trades, such as rope
and sail making. In 1779, for example, Whitby had four canvas factories, giving
employment to seven or eight hundred spinners.[28] Since it was necessary to find
the capital for such ships and their ventures, and to insure them against loss,
Whitby had its own insurance brokers together with largely informal methods
of raising finance until the foundation of a bank in 1785.

In an age of poor roads, sea transport was the lifeblood of Britain's commerce.

Indeed, the fact that nowhere in England is very far from the sea or a connecting river is often put forward as one of the reasons for the 'take off' of the Industrial Revolution. The trade in coals (or 'sea coals' as contemporaries referred to them) was the largest branch of the ever-growing coastal shipping trade and Whitby rose with it. London demanded ever more coal: over the course of the eighteenth century the volume consumed by the capital more than doubled, reaching 2.5 million tons by 1790.[29] For Cook the trip from Whitby up to the Tyne and then down to London was an introduction to the disciplines of shipboard life that he was to come to know so well. The need for a constant watch meant broken sleep as the crew was divided into two watches, each with five hours on and five hours off. The food was 'hard tack' (ship's biscuit) or preserved meat well pickled in brine – with perhaps an immersion in the sea to wash off some of the preservative. Luxuries, such as tea or sugar, could be restricted by rank, or the cost sometimes deducted from the pay.[30] Part of Cook's success as a captain was that he had an iron digestion – something for which the Whitby coal trade was an excellent preparation. James King, one of Cook's lieutenants on the third voyage, thought 'his stomach bore, without difficulty the coarsest and most ungrateful food'.[31]

Characteristically, a Whitby ship would take about two days to sail up to the mouth of the Tyne to be loaded with coal. There it spent about a week while the coal was brought down from the mines by a horse-drawn railway and then poured, as a observer noted in 1802, 'by covered wooden channels called staiths … into boats, or keels as they are here denominated'.[32] These small boats or keels in turn conveyed the coal to the waiting colliers into which the coal was laboriously shoveled.[33] The colliers then set off for London – about a week's journey, but the time varied according to weather.

This trip demanded careful navigation to deal with the uncertain behaviour of the North Sea and the shifting sands that were a feature of the coast. It was a route on which Cook learned not to be afraid of coastal navigation, which was far more hazardous and far less amenable to the use of instruments than deep-sea navigation where the prospect of a sudden collision with the land was much more remote.[34] Sailors had charts and coastal profiles which provided an outline of particular landmarks and ports, but there was still a good deal of traditional lore. Navigation relied on very simple instruments: lead-line, a compass and a backstaff to determine latitude. Sand, shells and pebbles from the seafloor were brought on board by a line, the end of which was primed with tallow and used to give some idea of depth and location – a practice Cook observed on his Pacific voyages. North Sea sailors claimed that they could tell west from east by the fragility of the pebbles – if they could be broken with one's teeth then one was west.[35] Whitby sailors reminded themselves of the landmarks as they sailed north with a rhyme:

> When Flamborough we pass by,
> Filey Brigg we mayn't come nigh,
> Scarborough Castle lies out to sea,
> Whitby three points northerly.[36]

Fixing one's position at sea meant keeping a constant track of the ship's speed. The methods of doing so were simple and time-honoured. A line was run out and weighted at the end with what was called a 'log' but may have been a variety of weights. The time taken by the line to reach a certain length as measured by a glass with sand usually designed to run through in half a minute was a guide to the speed, which was measured by the number of knots set at a fixed distance apart on the line – usually every fifty feet.[37] Such are the remote origins both of the term 'a ship's log' and of the measurement of nautical speed in knots.

Taking coals to London meant bringing ships up the Thames to the very heart of the city. Today the area of London that Cook best knew has lost its docklands, as ships are dealt with at a much greater remove and the East End's office blocks and urban renewal mask its historical character. Probably the biggest problem that Cook's captain would have had to deal with was congestion, as more and more ships vied for attention in the pool of London, where the collier was likely to spend around a week depending on traffic.[38] Part of the success of John Walker as a shipowner derived from the fact that he had good contacts in the London maritime world as a consequence of his Quaker connections. Ensuring that the port was ready to receive the vessel was all important in avoiding long and costly delays. This could mean sending a man overland before the ship arrived in London.

Unloading the ships meant calling in a team of coal-heavers: that hapless race of drudges often to be found in London riots. The hold was emptied by shovelling the coal onto a series of wooden platforms that raised it up to the deck. There the coal was deposited into large vats – the number of which was recorded to pay the tax due to both the city and the king.[39] The vats in turn were tipped into waiting lighters, for there were simply too many ships and too little wharf space to unload directly onto land.[40] With its heavy cargo unloaded, the ships needed ballast to keep an even keel. This meant the services of another group of London's proletariat: the ballast heavers, who used long poles with a bag attached to raise gravel from the bottom of the Thames. To get work coal-heavers and ballast-heavers were dependent on middlemen, or 'undertakers', usually drawn from the tavern keepers along the Thames. Indeed, it was probably through these connections that Cook met his wife. A coal-heaver's or ballast-heaver's life depended very much on the good will of the undertaker: they decided who would work, the cost of renting out equipment and they often clawed back even more of any wages to pay for the large quantities of beer that such back-breaking work required.[41]

Once the coal had been so arduously unloaded it was time to return to Whitby and start the cycle again. The round trip took up to about four weeks so that during a year it was possible to make something like ten journeys.[42] The winter months of December and January were given over to repairs, during which Cook would have come to know well the structure of the boats he was later to sail around the world. Being a collier captain was a dirty and demanding life. This may have been one of the reasons why, in 1755, Cook decided to join the Royal Navy. Service in the navy brought great prestige, as much of Britain's national pride was invested in its navy – the main instrument in securing and maintaining the Great Power status which it established steadily throughout the eighteenth century. The navy was the biggest operation in the land and indeed the biggest organization in Europe,[43] soaking up something like sixty per cent of the national budget for the armed forces in an age when over three-quarters of national expenditure was devoted to the armed forces.[44] No other major state devoted so much of its treasure to the navy.[45]

Since the time of Queen Anne there had no longer been one supreme admiral but rather an admiralty board, with the first lord of the admiralty (an office held by Cook's patron, Lord Sandwich, from 1748–55 and 1771–82) generally sitting in cabinet. The admiralty board oversaw an array of bureaucracies on the performance of which the navy depended. The navy board built, purchased and maintained ships; the victualling board provided the food and drink to sustain the seamen; the ordnance board provided the guns on which victory depended, and the board of sick and hurt had to deal with the after-effects of the guns of the other side or, more likely, the ravages of shipboard life – for far more sailors died of disease than wounds.

Manoeuvring his way around these tributaries of the navy and cultivating the patrons to make such navigation possible became more and more important as Cook advanced up the naval ladder. In 1755, however, Cook was a mere common seaman receiving rather than giving orders. For such lowly beings there was no sharp line between the merchant and the royal navy – indeed there was no real notion of joining the navy (as there was for officers); rather a sailor signed on for service on a specific ship.[46] Hands were generally taken on for particular voyages and paid off at the end (as happened with most of Cook's men at the end of his Pacific voyages).

Britain's growing naval might over the course of the eighteenth century – the period when songs such as 'Rule Britannia' gained currency – was built on the rapid growth of its merchant fleet, under the stimulus of ever-increasing trade at home and abroad. Naval success depended on having an ample quantity of that valuable commodity, trained seamen, and, like Cook, most seamen learnt their trade in civilian life. The ability to climb up masts in heaving seas could only be acquired when young, so skilled seamen had to be trained as apprentices.

When the navy was short of hands and sent out press gangs, it chiefly sought the 'topmen' who were essential to attend to the rigging and sails; those landsmen caught within the press gang's net were, like inferior fish, used grudgingly or discarded.[47] The chief hunting ground of the press gangs were therefore dockside pubs where trained sailors congregated. The risk of falling prey to a press gang was particularly strong in a port such as Whitby: hence the presence there of houses full of hidey holes for sailors and the occurrence of a major riot in 1793 when sailors rose up against their naval captors.[48] Trained sailors were not even safe at sea: in 1756 the short-handed *Eagle*, Cook's first naval ship, stopped a merchant vessel heading from Barbados to London on the high seas and impressed four men.[49]

Just as the line between the merchant and royal navies was often blurred in regards to its men, so, too, it could be about the ships in which they sailed. The vessels in which Cook sailed on his great Pacific voyages were all Whitby colliers. The navy described them as 'cat-built vessels' or 'cats' (though the term was not used in Yorkshire). An authoritative contemporary marine dictionary described such 'cats' as being 'distinguished by a narrow stern, projecting quarters, a deep waist, & by having no ornamental figure on the prow. These vessels are generally built remarkably strong, & carry from five to six hundred tons'.[50] They were, then, built for their carrying capacity rather than their speed and thus attracted some disdain for the way they lumbered along. When commenting on the return of the *Endeavour* in 1771, one newspaper remarked that 'tho' well contrived for stowage', it was 'a very dull sailing vessel'.[51] Cats were also built for sailing close to the shore and for extricating themselves when grounded. They therefore suited Cook's purposes in closely following and mapping the coast. As Lord Sandwich wrote in defence of the vessels, when Banks attempted to secure another type of vessel for the second Pacific voyage, they were 'of a construction that will admit of their going on shore with less danger than ships of war'. He also pointed out that they 'would work with fewer hands, which in an expedition of this nature is no considerable advantage'.[52]

Joining the Royal Navy or being press-ganged into it brought with it a real risk of death or dismemberment; but there were also compensations. The navy offered better developed medical services and the chance of some sort of pension. Naval life also brought the chance of prize money, greater certainty of being paid regularly and a consistent quality of food – it might have been basic but, by the standards of the poor, it was plentiful and offered such luxuries as meat four days a week.[53] The larger naval ships meant that there were more hands to share around the duties and, with luck, shorter watches. Cook generally replaced the customary draconian practice of one watch on and one off (giving no more than four hours' connected sleep) with three watches, allowing the luxury of up to eight hours' straight sleep.[54] This was made possible, as George Forster observed, by the fact that Cook was allocated more than the customary number of officers. Thus the men could be organized into three rather than two watches.[55] When the weather became very rough, however, Cook would sometimes revert to the system of 'watch and watch', with half the men on duty at any one time.

Sailors were very much creatures of habit, demonstrating, as George Forster put it, 'a trait of obstinacy where any innovations are concerned'.[56] Nowhere was this truer than in the matter of food – as Cook wrote with some feeling: 'To interduce any New article of food among Seamen, let it be ever so much for their good, requires both the example and Authority of the Commander'[57]. Though Cook was a popular commander, his dietary innovations brought considerable resistance. The attempt to introduce sauerkraut to ward off scurvy required both the stick in the form of floggings and the carrot of seeing this novel food being treated as a luxury at the officers' table. On the third voyage, Cook, in this as in other ways, lost something of his touch, incurring great displeasure by insisting that his men eat the flesh of walruses. Cook could eat anything but his men gagged on this rancid offering. Alongside Cook's remark in his published account of the voyage that 'there were few on board who did not prefer them to our salt meat', Midshipman Trevenen vented his distaste: 'Captain Cook here speaks entirely from his own taste which was, surely, the coarsest that ever mortal was endowed with'.[58]

By Cook's time, sailors had, however, accepted one innovation in an area close to their hearts: the issue of rum that was regarded as a sailor's natural entitlement. In the 1740s Lord Vernon issued spirits which were one part rum and three parts water in the hope that his men were more likely to be fit for work. It came to be known as 'grog' because Vernon wore an overcoat made of grogram and hence was nicknamed 'Old Grog'. Cook used the same recipe, to which could be added lemon or lime juice to help ward off scurvy. The standard ration was a pint for dinner and another for supper.[59]

Discipline in the navy could be very severe, as Cook witnessed early in his career when a sailor on board HMS Eagle, on which Cook was serving in 1756, was given 200 lashes for desertion.[60] In the course of active service in Canada he witnessed still more draconian punishments for desertion: one sailor was hanged at the yardarm and another two subject to what generally amounted to a barbarous death sentence: flogging around the fleet with eighty to hundred lashes alongside each ship.[61] Cook himself was not a great flogger – in his whole naval career he never gave more than two dozen lashes at a time, no doubt realizing that on the long voyages across the Pacific it was important not to undermine morale with excessive punishment.

On the Endeavour Cook punished a mere twenty-one men (six twice) and even less on the first Resolution voyage with a figure of twenty (one man, the journalist John Marra, was disciplined four times, another two thrice and six twice). The tired and cranky Cook of the third voyage did go considerably higher: on the second *Resolution* trip forty-four men were punished (one four times, five three times and eleven twice).[62] But even this figure – forty-four men out of a total complement of 112, nearly one in four – is close to the average for Pacific voyages in the period from 1767 to 1795 when something like one in five seamen were flogged.[63] Flogging had the advantage from the captain's point of view of being highly public, being over quickly and of ensuring that the men were available for work again reasonably soon. Not surprisingly, then, the vast majority of punishments that Cook inflicted took the form of floggings: of the 127 disciplinary cases all but nine involved flogging though in five cases flogging was combined with being confined. Cook confined four other men but it was a punishment that deprived him of the use of the men thus punished. The other form of punishment (used on five occasions) was to deprive men of their rank or their privileges by sending warrant officers or junior offices before the mast or denying them access to the quarterdeck.

The two offences which most commonly warranted flogging were 'neglect of duty' and theft with disobedience, drunkenness and insolence, absence without leave and desertion following in their wake.[64] Desertion was the offence that Cook took most seriously: the prospect of having to sail a short-handed ship back around the world must have been a worrying one. He would go to almost any length – delaying his departure or using threats to ensure that Pacific islanders assisted in the recapture of deserters – to make an example of deserters. Nonetheless, he, like most captains, did lose men: four from the *Endeavour*, two from the *Resolution* on the second voyage and three on the third voyage.[65]

Cook came in for criticism on the second voyage for breaking the line between officers and men by flogging a drunken and troublesome midshipman. As an officer in training, this was a gross indignity, particularly as it was accompanied by the symbolic, but very real, undermining of his position as an officer and a gentleman by denying him the quarterdeck – the area reserved for the officers. Its association with rank probably grew out of its practical advantage of being at the back at the ship and therefore being less likely to be showered by sea spray as the ship moved forward. Even Cook seems to have thought he had gone too far when he '*Flogged* him like a common sailor and then turned him before the Mast', for the offending midshipman was soon back on the quarterdeck where Cook 'paid every attention to him afterwards'.[66]

Cook seems to have been aware on occasions that his temper had got the better of him – as happened in this instance with the hapless midshipman. On the second voyage, his exasperation with the learned but extremely prickly German naturalist, Johann Reinhold Forster, led to a confrontation from which (according at least to Forster) Cook had later to extricate himself with the good offices of his second-in-command. For, wrote Forster, 'Captain *Furneaux* brought me word Captain Cook was sorry for having acted with such violence against me'. There followed a meeting in the great cabin (from which Cook had ejected him) 'where after several Discourses, we both yielded without giving any thing up of honour, & then shook hands'.[67] Like the midshipman's return to the quarter-deck, Forster's return to the great cabin (where the officers and those, like the travelling scientists, deemed to be of officer rank, gathered) was a reminder of the importance of different spaces of the ship as markers of status.

What held these fragile vessels together as functioning entities was an elaborate system of conventions that enabled a body of men to work together in often appalling and stressful conditions. Seamen would put up with all manner of barbarities if they considered them justified by tradition or sanctioned by a sort of 'moral economy'. If these conventions broke down, the sense of shared identity and acceptable standards of fairness could be undermined with disastrous results – as Bligh discovered on the *Bounty*. Cook was a successful captain as he had a strong sense of what was, by the rough and ready standards of shipboard life, acceptable behaviour – even to the point, as we have seen, of acknowledging when he was in the wrong. Very importantly, he also gained the respect of the men by his sheer competence – nothing could be more unnerving then sailing on board a ship where the captain did not appear to know what he was doing. But to retain that respect a captain had to be seen to be in command. This meant being a rather distant figure. Isaac Smith, Cook's wife's cousin who sailed with him on his first two voyages and later reached the status of admiral, remarked of Cook that, though 'I never thought him severe', 'he was both loved and properly feared by the ship's company'.[68]

It is significant that Smith did not serve on the third voyage, when the tired Cook was sometimes living on the prestige that had accrued from the earlier voyages, for his men's patience was tried by his rages and obstinacy. On this voyage Midshipman Trevenen caught the lash of his temper and was subjected to one of Cook's *heivas* – 'the name of the dances of the Southern Islanders, which bore so great a resemblance to the violent motions and stampings on the Deck of Captain Cooke in the paroxysms of passion'. Trevenen, however, also experienced some rare moments when, off the ship, Cook would 'relax from his almost constant severity of disposition, & condescend now and then, to converse familiarly with us'. Once on board, Cook 'became again the despot'.[69]

By the third voyage, however, Cook had attained a stature that his increasingly volatile temper could only partially undermine. The high regard in which his men held him is evident in the passionate grief that followed his death. It is evident also in the often brutal revenge that his men took on the Hawaiians before proper order was restored by Clerke, who took over from Cook as commander. Such events remind us of how fragile any code of civility was on board a ship far from home, manned by men who were expected to endure all manner of hardships and to be ready for brutal combat in war. Without discipline it was very easy for such ships to become anarchic – a point forcefully made by George Forster in his remarks on the crew of Cook's second voyage: 'Though they are members of a civilized society, they may in some measure be looked upon as a body of uncivilized men, rough, passionate, revengeful, but likewise brave, sincere, and true to each other'.[70]

Occasionally, some hints surface of the tensions between members of the crew that must often have reached boiling point on Cook's long voyages – voyages which would have exacerbated all the usual problems caused by overcrowding and poor conditions. On the *Endeavour* voyage, two such incidents stand out. On 25 March 1769 a young marine by the name of William Greenslade threw himself overboard in the face of strong peer disapproval of his taking, without permission, part of a piece of seal skin which he used for making a tobacco pouch. What blew this trivial incident up to such tragic proportions was the attitude of his fellow marines, who, as Banks wrote, 'drove the young fellow almost mad by representing his crime in the blackest coulours as a breach of trust of the worst consequence'.[71] More mysterious was an incident that took place over a year later, on 22 May 1770, over a fortnight after the *Endeavour* left Botany Bay: while Cook's clerk, Dick Orton, was dead drunk in his hammock, someone cut off his clothes and, subsequently and much more menacingly, part of both his ears. Suspicion fell on the American midshipman James Magra, who, as Cook wrote with a revealing comment on shipboard life, 'had once or twice before this in their drunken frolicks cut of his Cloaths and had been heard to say (as I was told) that if it was not for the Law he would Murder him'.[72] Though he could not firmly establish his guilt, Cook suspended Magra from duty and barred him from the quarterdeck for a time.

Cook took considerable personal umbrage at these unsavory events, regarding them as 'the greatest insult that could be offered to my authority in this Ship'. If there was a complaint against an individual, it was for him to administer discipline: as he insisted, 'I have always been ready to hear and redress every complaint that have been made against any Person in the Ship'.[73] He was so incensed that, when the ship reached Batavia, he offered a reward to anyone who would reveal the culprit. As a consequence another midshipman, Patrick Saunders, deserted and was never seen again. It was a saga pointing to the depths of animosity that could fester in a vessel where some ninety-five men were crammed together in a ship ninety-seven feet long on her lower deck and about twenty-eight feet wide – only a small part of which could be devoted to living quarters.[74]

The Lilliputian polity that made a ship function was kept together by ritual, routine and custom – practices which mirrored those of the larger society of late eighteenth-century Britain. For both late eighteenth-century naval vessels and British society more generally the dominant motif was a hierarchical ordering, tempered by some elements of meritocracy and an increasing demand for efficiency. The ships themselves were products of a society on the verge of industrialization – a fundamental change that would in time undermine much of the traditional hierarchical ordering of society. Such changes, however, lay in the future: the navy that Cook knew was one where birth and station counted for a great deal and where ships could only be constructed with the power made possible by human or animal exertion. The materials from which Cook's ships were largely constructed were the traditional ones of wood, hemp and cloth.

Cook's ships did, however, include some metal, a material which clearly differentiated European and Pacific vessels. For the Pacific islanders metal was the European commodity which had the most obvious application within their own society – hence it was one of the main items of trade. Very rapidly the Tahitians replaced traditional materials with metal: even while he was on the island on the first voyage Cook noted the way in which spike nails were taking the place of bone in chisels used for ship building.[75] Without metal the wood of the *Endeavour* would have been eaten away by teredo worm, which inhabits tropical waters and spectacularly chewed its way through solid oak anchor stocks at Tahiti. Hence the *Endeavour*'s hull was 'sheathed and filled'[76] – given an extra wooden skin which was then covered by wrought-iron nails with broad heads closely placed together so that the rust would cover the remaining surface.[77] Iron also formed a part of the ship's rudder fittings and fastenings. Where possible, however, the actual fabric of the ship was kept together with wooden dowels to prevent rust contaminating the wood.[78]

Important though it was, the use of metal was still in keeping with a pre-industrial age in which metal was laboriously and expensively produced in small-scale workshops not yet transformed in scale and efficiency by the techniques of industrialization. Metal was too expensive to be used extensively and iron was used wherever possible rather than still more expensive metals such as copper. Copper had begun to be used by the navy from the 1760s for protecting the bottom of vessels from barnacles, but using copper and iron together caused problems with electrolysis that were not properly solved until the nineteenth century. 'Therefore', wrote Cook, in the preface to his account of the second voyage, 'till a remedy is found to prevent the effect of copper upon the iron work, it would not be adviseable to use it on a voyage of this kind'.[79] Using it on Cook's Pacific vessels would not have been practical, as it would not have been possible to conduct running repairs on the copper so far from home. By the third voyage Cook was willing, however, to participate in a naval experiment to see if tin plates on some areas that had not been filled with nails could act as a substitute for copper sheathing.[80]

When Cook's ships entered the world of the peoples of the South Pacific the gulf between the two cultures was not nearly as vast as it was to be a century later, when ships made entirely of metal and powered by steam were able to expand and enforce European empires. In their different ways both the British and the peoples of the Pacific had to battle the sea and its moods with timber vessels powered by sail or human muscle. Both cultures, too, were profoundly shaped by strong conceptions of hierarchy – though this was truer of some Pacific peoples than others, being very much the case among the Polynesians but barely so among Australian Aborigines.

There were parallels, too, in the practical skills of seamanship employed by the British and the peoples of the Pacific, particularly when it came to navigation along the coast, where instruments were of less use than in blue water sailing. Cook's training as a seaman on the Whitby coal run, with its constant exposure to the vagaries of the coast, had depended to a large extent on craft skills that the Polynesian sailors, who traversed much of the Pacific, would have recognized: training in the location of prominent landmarks and shore outlines often reinforced by chants handed down by word of mouth; close observation of markers of the changing pattern of tides, such as sandbanks or pebbles; and discernment of incipient weather changes. Like the British, Polynesian navigators used estimates of the speed of their boat as a rough and ready way of working out their position through a form of dead reckoning. The stars also offered some directional guidance: a Polynesian navigator could locate and name up to two hundred stars and recognize the star formation associated with particular islands.[81] It was a skill that Cook's sailors regarded with respect: 'it is astonishing', wrote John Marra in his account of the second voyage, 'with what exactness their navigators can describe the motions and changes of those luminaries'.[82] The Polynesians had also developed a form of mental compass based on the position of the stars or the winds. The British and Polynesian sailor even shared some common superstitions, such as fear of contact with women before sailing, and both had their rituals to attempt to ward off the perils of the sea.[83] Cook's men commented, too, on the similarities in the basic equipment used for fishing in both societies: the Māori fishing lines made from flax were, wrote the astronomer William Bayly, 'twisted the very same as ours are & they knot their nets using the same knot as we do'.[84]

Needless to say there were also profound differences between the two cultures. Discipline and cohesion aboard a Polynesian vessel was generally the outcome of kinship ties, whereas on European ships more impersonal codes had to be devised and enforced. Hence the astonishment of the Marquesans when Cook struck one of his men and their exclamation that 'He beats his brother!'[85] While the British could rely to some extent on their instruments, Polynesian navigators, lacking such aids, needed to become even closer students of possible clues as to the presence of islands or reefs. They would closely scrutinize the movement and behaviour of birds or clouds – at dawn or dusk, for example, it was important to watch the direction of birds which nested on land but fed at sea. Clouds might indicate the presence of an island with a high peak, and even their colour might be an indication of the reflection of an atoll lagoon. Deep sea phosphorescence could provide another indication of the direction of land. The need to discern the presence of coral reefs was an inseparable part of Pacific voyaging and the Polynesian voyagers became expert at detecting their presence through subtle changes in the colour of the sea or the behaviour of waves; it was sometimes even possible to smell a reef.[86] Underlying Polynesian navigational techniques was a system of beliefs quite foreign to the European voyagers in which aid could be sought from ancestors and chants could invoke the aid of ancestral gods.[87]

The need to draw on spiritual as well as practical lore meant that a navigator was also often a priest, as in the case of Tupaia who accompanied Cook on the *Endeavour* voyage from Tahiti to Batavia, where he died. Just as Cook used local pilots in Newfoundland so, too, he sought local expertise in the Pacific. The extent to which he relied on Tupaia underlines the points of intersection between the maritime cultures of Britain and parts of the Pacific. As Banks wrote of Tupaia, 'what makes him more than any thing else desireable is his experience in the navigation of these people and knowledge of the Islands in these seas'.[88] Along with Tupaia the muster-book for the voyage includes mention of two other Tahitians as 'Guides for the interior Parts of the Island & Pilots for the Coast'.[89]

The coming of Cook's ships, then, meant one maritime people encountering another. The nature of Cook's voyages were such that, when he landed in the Pacific, he rarely strayed far from the coast, so the peoples he encountered led lives which were themselves closely intertwined with the sea. From the perspective of the peoples of the Pacific, the men Cook's ships disgorged were wayfarers from the sea and their view of them was necessarily shaped by their view of what the sea was likely to bring. For the Māoris, for example, the sea was a favoured route of enemies (much like the Vikings centuries ago in Cleveland) and they often adopted a belligerent attitude towards strangers. The beaches and coastal areas on which Cook landed were, then, places where two different cultures either rapidly reached some level of understanding and accommodation or they could become places of conflict where, at least, the sea offered a means of escape.

In places such as the Society or Friendly Islands, where the British remained for an extended period, there was an opportunity for the sailors from afar to admire the boats and seamanship of the local seafarers. It was soon realized that the Tahitians had a range of boats for different purposes, ranging from single dugout canoes of about six feet (which could be sailed or paddled) and small outrigger canoes from ten to twenty feet long up to double-canoes which could carry up to sixty passengers and their provisions, being up to ninety

Huahine Harbour. Engraving by W. Byrne after Webber (from J. Cook and J. King, *Voyage to the Pacific Ocean* ... (3 vols, London, 1784), ii, p. 91, plate 31)

feet long – vessels which could be used for the great Polynesian voyages of discovery.[90]

As someone familiar with the shipyards at Whitby and elsewhere, Cook naturally took a close interest in the construction of these craft. The building of the large double-canoes intended primarily for war he described in terms similar to those that would have been used in a British shipyard: 'the sides are of plank of nearly the same thickness and are built nearly perpendicular rounding in a little towards the gunwhale'. When he came to the way in which the parts of the boat were put together, however, the process was so unfamiliar that he reached for a distinctly unnautical metaphor: 'the peices in which they are built are well fited and fastened or sewed together with strong platting something in the same manner as old China wooden bowls etc. are mended'. The carving on the prow and stern Cook described approvingly as 'very little inferior [to the] work of the like kind done by common ship carvers in England', adding that:

> When one considers the tools these people have to work with one cannot help but admire their workmanship, these are Adzes and small hatchets made of a hard stone, Chisels or gouges made of human bones ... with these ordinary tools that a European workman would expect to break the first stroke I have seen them work surprisingly fast.[91]

Soon afterwards Cook visited another of the Society Islands, Ulietea (Ra'iatea), which was renowned as a centre of boat building. Here he was particularly taken by the boat houses and the care taken of canoes – a contrast with Tahiti where boats did not appear to be as valued (perhaps because that large and fertile island was not as dependent on seafaring as the outlying islands). 'This people are very

A View of the Island of Ulietea [Ra'iatea], with a Double Canoe and a Boathouse. Engraving by E. Rooker after Parkinson. (from J. Hawkesworth, *An Account of the Voyages* ... (3 vols, London, 1773), ii, plate 3, facing p. 258)

ingenious in building their Proes or Canoes', he wrote, 'and seem to take as much care of them, having large shades or houses to put them in built for the purpose and in these houses they likewise build and repair them and in this they shew a great deal of ingenuity, far more than one could expect'.[92]

Cook and his men were equally admiring of the craft of the Friendly Islands. Indeed, William Wales, the astronomer on the second voyage, considered the Tongan canoes the best in the Pacific: 'No Canoes that we have seen in these seas can bear the least Comparison with these in point of neatness & workmanship'.[93] The seamanship of the other Polynesian peoples encountered on Cook's voyages was regarded a little less enthusiastically. On the first voyage, Banks praised the Māoris for their abilities in paddling canoes – 'never did men I beleive keep better time with the strokes, driving on the boat with immense velocity' – but thought them wanting as sailors: 'in sailing they are not so expert, we very seldom saw them make use of Sails and indeed never unless when they were to go right before the wind'.[94]

The Māoris took the art of elaborately carving ornaments on both the prow and stern to an even higher plane than the Tahitians.[95] Banks' servant, James Roberts, thought that their canoes 'have Excessive Neat Carved work on their head and stern in the form of Spirales in a very Elegant manner so as to out pass any thing I ever saw before'.[96] Although the Māoris developed the art of carving in particularly elaborate forms, there were parallels with Polynesian carving elsewhere – a common characteristic that, like the basic unity of the Polynesian language, emphasized the cultural similarities of the widely dispersed Polynesian peoples.

Boats of the Friendly Isles. Engraving by W. Watts after Hodges (from J. Cook, *A Voyage towards the South Pole and Round the World* ... (2 vols, London, 1777), ii, plate 42, facing p. 18)

This shared identity of the farflung Polynesian peoples was also reinforced by the similarities in their design of boats. When the voyagers first encountered Hawai'i on the third voyage, Midshipman Gilbert described their small single canoes as being 'nearly like those at the Friendly Islands with out riggers to them, in the same manner', adding that 'both in their form and workmanship [they] are the neatest we have ever seen'.[97] His shipmate, Lieutenant King, was less complimentary about the larger canoes there, writing that 'there are no Canoes equal, or to be compared to theirs [the Tahitians] in size or Grandeur'.[98] One skill that the Hawaiians had that was completely outside the British range of experience was surfboard riding, described by Midshipman Gilbert. They 'have a method of swimming upon a piece of wood nearly in the form of a blade of an Oar ... These pieces of wood are so nicely ballanced that the most expert of our people at swimming, could not keep upon them half a minute with out rolling off'.[99] But this aspect of Polynesian seagoing culture had already been encountered in Tahiti on Cook's *Endeavour* voyage. While there, Banks remarked on the way in which 'their cheif amusement was carried on by the stern of an old canoe, with this before them they swam out as far as the outermost breach, then one or two would get into it and opposing the blunt end to the breaking wave were hurried in with incredible swiftness'.[100]

Polynesian seamanship set a standard by which the British judged other Pacific cultures – usually to their disadvantage. For Banks the outrigger canoes of the

A Māori War Canoe. Engraving by R.B. Godfrey after Parkinson (from Sydney Parkinson, *A Journal of a Voyage to the South Seas* (London, 1773), plate 18, facing p. 93)

Australian Aborigines of what is now Cooktown in northern Queensland had some similarities with Polynesian craft but were 'far inferior'. He did, however, remark on their adaptability, being capable of being paddled in deep water and propelled by poles in shallow.[101] Cook was even more dismissive: 'Their Canoes are as mean as can be conceived, especially to the southward'. He did concede, however, that 'they do very well for the purpose they apply them to, better then if they were larger', since they were well suited for foraging on mud banks for shell fish and the like.[102] William Wales regarded the canoes of the Melanesian New Caledonians as heavy and slow, but he did note that they were capable of being both sailed and rowed with large oars in a manner that he likened to 'sculling' in Britain – a novelty in the Pacific where canoes were normally paddled.[103]

On the third voyage the British encountered the maritime cultures of the peoples of the Pacific north west of the American continent, where the standard of boat building impressed them as perhaps being even superior to that of the Polynesians. The surgeon David Samwell regarded the canoes of the Nootka

Australian Aborigines in Bark Canoes [by Tupaia] (British Library, Add. MS 15508,
f.10(a) (no. 10))

on the western side of what is now Vancouver Island as being 'much the best
Canoes we have seen this Voyage'. In particular, he remarked that the canoes were
so 'well constructed' with such a 'good breadth' that, unlike Polynesian boats,
'they require no outrigger'. In contrast to the Polynesians, too, the Nootka 'know
nothing of the use of sails'. Samwell, who, like all the voyagers, naturally groped
for an analogy from his own world, likened the larger Nootka canoes (which
varied from ten to forty feet) to a 'Thames Wherry' (a light shallow rowing-boat
used for carrying passengers). The Nootka's use of a decorative white line along
the gunwhale he thought was 'much like the greenland Fishing boats', while
Cook likened the Nootka vessels to 'a Norway yawl'.[104] On the first voyage, Cook
showed a similar penchant for analogy by describing the Māori canoes as being
'much like a New England Whale boat'.[105]

Like the peoples of the South Pacific, the Nootka used wood for constructing
their canoes – a material with which the British were very familiar. When he
moved further north to Prince William Sound (South Alaska), Samwell was
particularly impressed with the use of very different materials for boat building
– in the form of the animal skins used by the indigenous peoples of the near
Arctic Pacific waters around Alaska. He described their canoes, in which timber

Kayaks of Unalaska. Engraving by W. Angus after Webber (from J. Cook and J. King,
Voyage to the Pacific Ocean ... (3 vols, London, 1784), ii, p. 371, plate 50)

was largely replaced by animal skins (stretched over a wooden frame), as 'being
very light and buoyant they will carry great Weights and they hardly make any
Water, being much superior in both these respects to wooden Canoes, which
generally admit so much water as to keep one person almost constantly bailing'.
These canoes came in two main sizes: one capable of carrying one or two; and the
larger version which could accommodate up to thirty or forty people. This latter
variety Samwell again described as being 'something in the shape of a London
Wherry' – another instance of the natural instinct to render the unfamiliar
intelligible by analogy with the familiar.[106] His shipmate Midshipman Gilbert
used the comparison of a British cutter, which also had a timber frame, the
difference being that the Prince William Sound canoes were 'covered with whale
skins instead of plank'.[107]

While there were enough points of similarity between British craft and
those of the peoples of the Pacific for Cook and his men to admire the skill of
the Pacific boatbuilders, there was no ready bridge across the cultural divide
when it came to different ways of understanding mapping. Mapping was the
basic thread that ran through Cook's entire career: from his early instruction in
navigational techniques at Whitby; to the maps of the St Lawrence that made a

contribution to the British victory over the French in Canada; and, finally, and most momentously, to the great maps of the Pacific that rendered much of the globe familiar and accessible to Europeans.

But Cook's maps were the highly abstract maps of a Europe whose elite increasingly thought in scientific terms shaped by mathematics.[108] The all-encompassing grid of latitude and longitude both stripped away much of the physical appearance of the world and focused attention on essentials. The maps of Cook were ones well removed from the pictorial forms out of which maps had grown: even the winsome decorations of mermaids and seabeasts which still festooned some maps before the eighteenth century were absent from Cook's chaste and cerebral charts.[109]

There was a partial exception to this: the coastal profiles which Cook and his men amassed in quantity on their voyages.[110] These pictorial outlines of ports and coastal stretches had long been a part of seaman's lore, since they enabled a captain or pilot to identify the chief landmarks of a port as the ship made its way through the often tricky and treacherous heads. For close work such as this, they were often of greater use than larger-scale charts. It was easier, too, in new waters such as the Pacific to draw a profile than to compile an accurate chart of a confined waterway when time and the possibility of accurate observation were often limited. Once again the continued use of these pictorial aids rather than grid-based maps underlines the difference between coastal and blue water navigation. The former required more in the way of the craft skills that Cook had learned on the Whitby run, while the latter was more amenable to the scientific techniques to which Cook was more fully exposed in the Royal Navy.

The faint concession to pictorial forms embodied in Cook's coastal profiles does not nullify the fact that for Cook the world was fundamentally only intelligible through the discipline of accurate grid measurements of latitude and longitude.[111] Thanks to major advances in the eighteenth century, it was possible to arrive at such measurements with increasing precision. A series of devices for measuring latitude had culminated in the sextant. This allowed for highly accurate astronomical readings, which were improved further by the publication of ever more comprehensive astronomical tables. Such tables also went a long way towards solving the age-old problem of measuring longitude through the method of lunar differences, by which the moon's movement is measured against the fixed backdrop of the stars.[112] It was the method that Cook used to good effect on the first voyage and which he continued to use on the second voyage. George Forster even regarded it as superior to that based on a chronometer (perhaps out of patriotic pride in the fact that the astronomical tables on which the method of lunar difference were based had been compiled by the German Tobias Meyer). Chronometers, thought Forster, were less reliable since they 'frequently change their rates of going'.[113]

Despite Forster's comments, the second voyage did establish the superiority of measuring the difference in time between local time and Greenwich time – the calculation on which establishing longitude was based – by means of a chronometer rather than the lunar differences.[114] On his two ships Cook took with him a replica of the famous Harrison chronometer made by Larcum Kendall, together with three chronometers of a different design by Arnold. The second voyage, among its many other accomplishments, included establishing categorically the greater accuracy of longitude deduced by a Harrison chronometer. Furthermore, a chronometer could be used in circumstances such as a cloudy day or turbulent seas which could render impossible the observations necessary for the method of lunar differences. For the method of lunar differences was limited by the fact that it was often only possible to make the necessary observations on fifteen days in any lunar month.[115] A chronometer was also much simpler to use, though its cost meant that experienced sailors went on using the astronomical method for some time.

Cook's view of the world, with its insistent focus on the grid of latitude and longitude, could not be readily combined with indigenous forms of mapping. The 'stick charts' of the Marshall Islanders used to map islands and the swell patterns that surrounded them would have meant little to Cook, any more than his men could altogether understand the way in which the Tahitian Hitihiti, who was on board for some of the second voyage, used twigs to represent new lands.[116] Nor did Cook seem to be able to make much use of the map of seventy-four islands surrounding Tahiti compiled by Tupaia while on board the *Endeavour*[117] – interested though he was in any light that Tupaia could shed on Polynesian society. The pictorial form of Tupaia's chart and the placing of islands according to sailing times from Tahiti meant that there was no ready way of translating it into what Cook meant by a map with co-ordinates and a scale. These problems were compounded by the fact that the British misunderstood the Tahitian notions of north and south.[118] It was to take much more extended contact between the maritime cultures of Europe and Polynesia for both to understand each other's maps and to appreciate the form of knowledge and the skills they embodied.

Cook admired the way that Tupaia assisted him in finding his way about the Society Islands but, fundamentally, he had little confidence in Polynesian navigation and did not pursue this subject with him. The mental map of the islands on which Tupaia drew in compiling his chart (possibly in collaboration with some of the *Endeavour*'s crew) Cook attributed to scraps of information derived from 'natives of those islands, driven accidentally upon their coasts ... We may thus account for that extensive knowledge attributed ... to Tupaia in such matters'. This made explicable Tupaia being able to direct the *Endeavour* to the island of Rurutu 'without ever having been there himself, as he pretended, which on many accounts is very improbable'.[119]

Cook's lack of confidence in Polynesian navigation – which reflects his fundamental scepticism about their mapping – accounts, too, for his inability to understand how the great Polynesian voyages of exploration could have been conducted. The remarkable spread of Polynesian culture greatly exercised Cook's considerable curiosity. When he encountered the Hawaiians he asked: 'How shall we account for this Nation spreading itself so far over this Vast Ocean? We find them from New Zealand to the South, to these islands to the North and from Easter Island to the Hebrides'.[120] Cook had found it difficult to grasp how they could have achieved this in the absence of navigational methods as he understood them.

In his admiring description of the large canoes on Ra'iatea in the Society Islands, Cook vaguely remarked that with such craft they could sail 'for several hundred Leagues, the Sun serving them for a compass by day and the Moon and Stars by night'.[121] But the question remained how the Polynesians had succeeded in encompassing the vast distances that made it possible to colonize much of the Pacific within the 'Polynesian triangle' of Hawai'i, Easter Island and New Zealand. Possibly, he thought, it was the result of accident. Such was the conclusion he drew from the encounter with a group of Tahitians on Atiu, one of the Cook Islands, who had been blown off course: 'This circumstance', he wrote, 'very well accounts for the manner the inhabited islands in this Sea have been at first peopled'.[122] Modern investigation, using computer simulations of wind and tide, has established conclusively, however, that the wide geographical diffusion of the Polynesians cannot be explained by chance. Moreover, the large canoes quite deliberately took with them sufficient men and women and plants and animals to establish new colonies.[123] But, for Cook, the methods of accomplishing such heroic voyages were too remote from his conception of navigation to be comprehensible.

Reconstructing the nature of Polynesian navigation and seafaring at the time of Cook's voyages is limited by one very real practical difficulty: that the canoes were too bulky to bring back to Europe, even if the owners had been willing to sell them. (On his third voyage Cook was offered a Tahitian canoe but understandably decided that there was already more than enough clutter on board.)[124] Cook's men did bring back some lesser items of Pacific maritime culture such as finely carved bailers and paddles from New Zealand and the Marquesas.[125] Such artefacts represented the same collecting mentality evident in the large-scale acquisition of natural history specimens – the attempt to bring back as much of the Pacific as possible in order to study it closely back in Europe. Out of such study came both greater knowledge and the possibility of greater control of the Pacific for European ends. While plants, animals and minerals could be conveniently and neatly filed away, using the systems of Linnaeus and his followers, 'artificial curiosities' (as ethnographic specimens were known) did not lend themselves to such ready ordering. As a consequence, they often languished in the back rooms of museums or in the homes of the wealthy collectors who were the main immediate purchasers of the specimens brought back by Cook's crews.

From such collections it is possible to reconstruct many aspects of first contact Pacific life, particularly when such specimens are used in conjunction with the

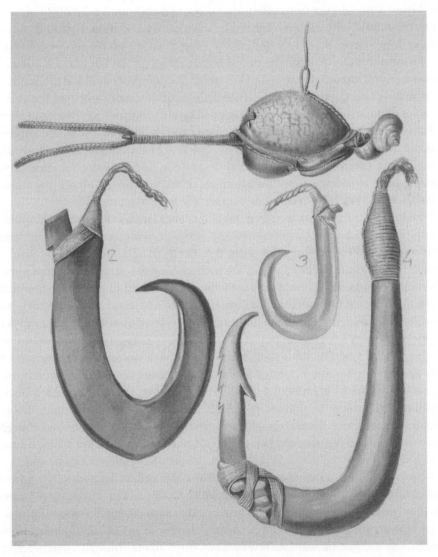

Fishing Hooks from Tahiti and New Zealand by John F. Miller (British Library, Add. MS 15508, f.25 (no. 27))

written and pictorial records. One thing that it was easy for Cook and his crew to bring home was a quantity of fish-hooks or lures, so we have a fairly detailed knowledge of first-contact fishing practices – an important aspect of these Pacific societies which were (like Cook's Britain) very dependent on fish. What stands out is the ingenuity of different societies in using the available materials to construct a range of artefacts for capturing the full gamut of marine life from small fish to seals and even whales. Banks remarked of the Tahitians, for example, that 'In every expedient for taking fish they are vastly ingenious'.[126] The Hawaiian fish hooks were particularly praised by the voyagers: Midshipman Trevenen reported that his crewmen who used them 'found them superior to all of European construction'.[127] Octopuses were caught in the Friendly Islands and elsewhere in Polynesia by using lures to which the octopuses attached themselves. These were cunningly made to resemble fish, using pieces of cowrie shell to make a head and coconut fibre strings to make a tail.[128] Tongan line fishermen were also equipped with sinkers such as the one brought back by the Forsters made of calcite and camouflaged with cowrie shells.[129] Fish stocks were preserved by social restraints such as the Hawaiian *kapu* (equivalent of the Tahitian *tapu*) on catching particular fish at certain times of the year or the Māori practice of confining the catching of shark or dogfish to a few days a year.[130]

Polynesian nets were woven from vegetable fibre (such as flax in New Zealand) with floats and sinkers.[131] Māori nets could be vast, with seines 1,000 yards long demanding 500 people to draw them effectively.[132] Such nets, thought Banks, must be 'the joint work of a whole town'.[133] Fishing was largely a male preserve though women might hunt for shell-fish.[134] In some cases the hooks were unbaited, being dragged along at a speed that would emulate a small fish, the hook being hidden by a feather or attached to a shiny shell which, under water, appeared to be a fish as it was pulled along rapidly.[135] Larger fish meant, of course, bigger hooks, which in both New Zealand and Tahiti were sometimes produced by deliberately training saplings so that as they grew they would produce the required curves.[136] (Similarly, English keels often incorporated curved timbers deliberately grown for that purpose.) Sharks called for especially large hooks such as the one that Banks brought back from Tahiti and gave to his old college, Christ Church: it was made of two pieces of wood (one ground to a point) bound with sennit.[137]

The Polynesians also used fishing spears, but not as systematically as the Melanesians of Tanna (Vanuatu) who, wrote Cook, lacked 'any sort of fishing tackle' but were 'expert' at spearing fish.[138] Australian Aborigines also frequently used fishing spears (which could be up to fifteen feet long) which Cook described as having '2, 3, or 4 prongs each very ingeniously made'; they also had 'wooden Harpoons for striking Turtle'.[139] In addition, Aborigines fished with hook and line though this (in contrast to spear fishing) was a female preserve.[140] Australian

Aborigines and the Polynesians also caught fish using fish traps, as did the peoples of the coast of north-west America.[141]

The peoples of the American Pacific north west, who were very dependent on hunting large maritime mammals, made harpoons from the bones of their prey rendered sharper still by using resin to cement on a large, sharp mussel shell.[142] Their harpoons (which would have been of particular interest to Cook with his familiarity with the Whitby whalers) took the form either of lances or missiles propelled by spear throwers. The Nootka people had a form of hinged harpoon to which was attached skin bladders which slowed down the whale and enabled them to follow the progress of the stricken animal: the whole process was explained to Captain Clerke by means of a drawing on the Nootka's clothing.[143] A further refinement of the Aleutians was to use slate tips which had been poisoned. Hauling a whale to shore was beyond their boats so they had to rely on the sea washing up the dead whale. Like British fishermen, the Nootka people of the west coast of Vancouver Island made the most of the time of the year when fish were abundant to dry fish (and particularly salmon) for leaner months.[144] Cook also admired an original device that they used for catching small fish in shoals: a twenty-foot long instrument like an oar with bone teeth on which the fish were caught.[145]

As well as food, fish could produce other materials (as whales did in Europe, the flexible baleen being used for making corsets and the like). Throughout Polynesia and Micronesia the sharp bones from the backbone of the stingray were used to point spears, arrows or daggers and the skin of the stingray (or shark) was used to make rasps to serve as an abrasive for woodworking,[146] Hawaiians used sharp shark teeth to make knives and even weapon-like rings.[147] Whale bone was put to many uses especially by the peoples of the American Pacific north west: the Nootka people, for example, commonly used it to make clubs – though so, too, did the Māoris.[148] The Tierra del Fuegans turned whalebone into harpoons with which to hunt sea lions,[149] and seal skin was used for a number of purposes including making coats and quivers for their arrows.[150]

The sea also provided the peoples of the Pacific with forms of jewellery such as the Tierra del Fuegan necklaces made of small iridescent shells threaded together with plaited, fibrous strings or the Easter Island neck or chest ornament (brought back by Forster the elder) made of turtle or porpoise bone with a cord of twisted human hair.[151] Mrs Cook passed on to her sister a beautiful Tongan ornament made from carved bone (probably of marine origin) decorated with small shells and fragments of turtle shells.[152] Even instruments for making music came form the ocean, including a Māori trumpet made of a triton shell with a carved wooden mouthpiece, the sound of which could be varied with a modulator made of flax.[153] Other Polynesian peoples also had similar trumpets.[154]

Like the British, the peoples of the Pacific had to rely heavily on the sea for food, transport and raw materials. For all the attractions of staying safe on dry land, both cultures had learned in their different ways to engage with the sea and to lessen if not eliminate its dangers. In dealing with the sea and its often savage moods both had to turn the available material derived from plants and animals into craft or implements which could make the sea more manageable. In the preindustrial Britain of Cook ships were chiefly the products of the vegetable kingdom in the form of wood or plant-derived cloth. The mineral kingdom was represented in the form of some metal – an advantage not enjoyed by the Pacific islanders – but its use was limited.

What chiefly made it possible for Cook's ships to traverse the huge distances across the Pacific was the complexity of social organization that had produced these large ships in the first place and which allowed the degree of division of labour and specialization with which to man and navigate them. This in turn reflected the size and relative wealth of the British state, which could extract sufficient surplus from its population to fund such large-scale enterprises as the naval dockyards. Pacific societies, too, had their social differentiation – particularly in the skilled occupations associated with the sea such as shipbuilding, fishing and navigation – but these island or coastal peoples lived in polities which were too small to erect the social ordering necessary to build vessels which could circumnavigate the world.

Cook's voyages also depended on a scientifically-inclined culture that could provide the expertise to make precise navigation possible. Though still a preindustrial society, Cook's England had achieved a high level of skill in manufacturing the sort of precision instruments which were his stock in trade: sextants, telescopes, compasses and chronometers. Both in their precise workmanship and scientific accuracy, such instruments were very much the harbingers of the machine age. The great Polynesian navigators had traversed the Pacific using techniques that took aspects of scientific method such as close observation and trial and error to a remarkable level of sophistication. These craft skills could not, however, readily be systematized and reproduced. There was a high degree of craft skill imparted by oral tradition in European voyaging (and Cook had been exposed to it as an Whitby apprentice), but, particularly in the Royal Navy, this was beginning to be supplanted by navigation more overtly reliant on instruments.

Though such differences existed between the maritime cultures of the British and the peoples of the Pacific, they were much less pronounced in Cook's time than they were to become in the nineteenth century. As the pace of industrialization gathered momentum, European ships became less and less dependent on timber and cloth and more on tougher metals less likely to break under the strain of the sea's demands. The development of the steam engine meant less reliance on the fickle winds to which both Cook and the Polynesians had to bow. The coal that Cook had once carried to London found a new use as the fuel for replacing the human exertion that had once been the only available motive force to move anchors or ropes. Cook's ships, which so changed the lives of the peoples of the Pacific, were to be both one of the last emissaries of preindustrial Europe and heralds of a new era of European industrially-based dominance over much of the globe.

3

Trade

The demands of trade increasingly drove eighteenth-century Britons down to the sea in ships. 'There was never from the earliest ages', wrote Dr Johnson, 'a time in which trade so much engaged the attention of mankind, or commercial gain was sought with such general emulation'.[1] The quickening pace of commerce was closely linked with more effective use of Britain's natural advantage as an island, securing ready access to the sea and, with it, an efficient means of transporting goods both at home and abroad. In the eighteenth century it was considered that sea transport was about one twentieth the cost of carriage by land.[2] Much of the eighteenth century's very substantial investment in transport infrastructure was designed to make sea and water transport more effective: harbours were 'improved' (a favourite eighteenth-century word), rivers providing access to the sea were made navigable and, eventually, a system of man-made waterways, canals, extended Britain's watery arteries of trade further inland.

Land transport was also considerably improved, thanks to the spread of turnpikes. These required payment of a toll in return for the capital outlay needed to improve the roads. Much of Britain was more effectively knitted together and trade flourished accordingly: in 1760 the single stage coach that left Edinburgh for London took fifteen days to arrive; by 1783 there were fifteen coaches a week and the journey took four days.[3] By 1770 (the date when Cook first encountered Australia) there were more than 15,000 miles of turnpike road in England.[4]

But there were corners of the land, such as Cleveland, still largely dependent on sea transport. Cleveland's remoteness from the major trunk routes meant there was little incentive to invest large sums in roads, though by 1765 Whitby was linked to York by turnpike which opened up an economy previously linked more to sea than land.[5] In many parts of the country the local roads had declined markedly since Roman times: the wording of a 1752 Yorkshire Turnpike Act is testimony to their often sorry state, since the existing road was described as being 'so very ruinous and bad, especially in the winter season, that travellers cannot pass without great danger'.[6] Cleveland did have a tradition of local initiative in maintaining its parish roads with the JPs enforcing the communal obligation to devote a few days a year their upkeep,[7] but to judge from a popular rhyme, Cleveland roads left much to be desired, especially in wet weather:

> Cleveland in the clay
> Bring two shoes and carry one away.[8]

The need for turnpike roads in Cleveland was, however, lessened by access to water transport. As Adam Smith wrote in his seminal *Wealth of Nations* (1776), 'by means of water-carriage a more extensive market is opened to every sort of industry than what land-carriage alone can afford' – a comment that applied with particular force to Cleveland.

Road transport remained tiring and time-consuming. The roads themselves often continued to deteriorate until the late eighteenth and early nineteenth centuries when the innovations of engineers, like John McAdam, to ensure proper drainage were widely adopted (hence 'macadamized' roads and, ultimately, 'tarmac'). Eighteenth-century roads were not equal to the burden of the carriage of heavy goods as Smith went on to emphasize: 'Six or eight men ... by the help of water-carriage, can carry and bring back in the same time the same quantity of goods between London and Edinburgh, as fifty broad-wheeled waggons, attended by a hundred men, and drawn by four hundred horses'.[9]

Nowhere was this more evident than in the carriage of what contemporaries called 'sea-coals' – the trade in which Cook learnt his seagoing skills. Coals and water went together, whether it was salt water or man-made freshwater canals. The duke of Bridgewater perceptively remarked that 'A navigation must have coals at the heels of it'.[10] He could speak with authority: the ten-mile canal he commissioned to link coal mines on his estate with Manchester ushered in the canal age when it was opened in 1761. Thanks to improved water transport, coals became cheaper and more widely used. Shipments from the north east of England climbed from around 1.2 million tons in 1750 to 2.25 million tons in 1800 – an increase that outshot the growth in population underlining the ever-increasing demand for coals.[11]

The greatly expanding volume of coals shipped around the country was an index of the growth of trade generally. After the political upheavals of the seventeenth century, eighteenth-century Britain was politically more stable (apart from sporadic Jacobite uprisings) and, after the Act of Union of 1707 between England and Scotland, formed the largest free trade area in Europe. Increasingly Britain's population was drawn into a money economy: the near-subsistence peasant farmers who still loomed large in continental Europe were, in Britain, being changed into a paid work force as land holdings became bigger and more capital intensive. Cook's father, an agricultural labourer who subsequently became an overseer, with a wage that made him a customer rather than a subsistence farmer, typified the lot of many. Commerce was also driven by the increasingly multi-layered nature of British society with its many gradations, few of which lay completely outside the reach of the market.[12] As one contemporary put it in 1757 (with an oblique comparison with continental society), in England there was a 'gradual and easy transition from rank to rank'.[13] The possibility of social advancement of the kind achieved by Cook himself was reflected in a vigorous market for the goods that proclaimed improved status, from better clothes to the keyboard instrument in the parlour.

Domestic trade was the main engine of the 'commercial revolution.' This, in turn, provided the economic momentum that was eventually to energize Britain down the path to the Industrial Revolution.[14] As the century wore on, however, overseas trade became increasingly important. British naval power secured for Britain an ever greater role in international commerce. Over the course of the century British imports and exports swelled more than fivefold.[15] It was still an age when war and trade were closely aligned: the nineteenth-century assumption that free trade would bring peace and disarmament rested on British success in largely eliminating the power of its rivals to thwart its own trade.[16] One of the themes that runs throughout Cook's work as a naval officer and explorer is the imperative of securing British trading interests at the expense of its chief rival, France. Cook's superiors had long grasped the nexus between national power and trade: naval supremacy brought more trade and more trade brought greater naval might. One eighteenth-century writer had pithily summed matters up in 1747 with his remark that Britain's 'rising greatness' was 'all owing to trade'.[17]

From the point of view of government one great advantage of foreign trade was that it could be readily taxed as it came into the kingdom. A natural reaction to the growth of foreign trade was, inevitably, the growth of smuggling. The scale of smuggling is borne out by an estimate by the East India Company in 1784 that only about one third of the tea sold in Britain had been legally imported. The only viable government response was in the same year to drop the import duty on tea from 119 to 12.5 per cent and thus to drive the smugglers out of business.[18]

Smuggling was a trade well known to the fishermen of the Cleveland coast and Cook must have heard much of it in a place like Staithes. In 1776 Cook was drawn into the affairs of his own brother-in-law, James Fleck, a fisherman at the small fishing town of Redcar who had fallen foul of the customs officials. The prosecution refused to give the time and place of the alleged offence which, wrote Cook to a lawyer in Guisborough, meant that his brother-in-law was placed in the position of having to deny having ever been engaged in smuggling. This, as Cook candidly admitted, 'I suppose is not the Case'.[19] Cook knew the fishermen of Cleveland too well to pretend that they never resorted to supplementing their hard-won income by smuggling.

Cook, therefore, was shaped by a society increasingly preoccupied with trade, whether licit or illicit. After all, he began his working life as a trainee with Mr William Sanderson, the grocer and haberdasher of Staithes with whom he spent eighteen months. The very fact that such a shop existed in a small fishing village is an indication of the growing sophistication of the retailing network linking the most remote areas with the metropolis and beyond. Traditionally, outlying areas had supplemented those goods that could not be produced locally with those bought from itinerant pedlars and chapmen or at seasonal fairs.[20] Fairs met the needs of a society that had been largely self-sufficient, needing only occasional contact with the market. Elsewhere in eighteenth-century Europe their role continued: in Russia there were fairs in spring to sell the handicrafts made during winter and in autumn to sell the harvest.[21] But in ever more market-orientated Britain such fairs were beginning to be replaced by the sort of shops maintained by Mr Sanderson.

Twenty miles down the coast from Whitby lay Scarborough, once the site of one of the greatest fairs in the nation, the origins of which went back to a royal charter of 1235. The fair is etched in historical memory by the ballad (or at least its nineteenth-century rendition):

> Are you going to Scarborough Fair?
> Parsley, sage, rosemary and thyme.

But Scarborough Fair closed in 1788. After this, the town more and more concentrated its energies on building up the resort trade that had begun with the discovery of a spa, with supposedly health-sustaining properties, in 1620. By the eighteenth century Scarborough's future as a seaside resort was well established and it pioneered the use of bathing machines to shield maidenly modesty from naked male bathers. The growth of such luxuries as seaside holidays was a telling indication of the increasing wealth of at least some sections of the eighteenth-century population.

While Scarborough had been the site of the largest provincial fair of northern England, Stourbridge (just outside Cambridge) had been that of southern England – forming the original of the 'Vanity Fair' referred to in the *Pilgrim's Progress* by John Bunyan, who came from nearby Bedford. It, too, was falling on hard times in the eighteenth century – though it lasted longer than its rival at Scarborough, not being formally closed until 1855. Some of the smaller fairs survived better, especially where they acquired a reputation for some speciality. The Cleveland town of Yarm was known for its cheese fair held in October. Eighteenth-century Yarm, however, was in decline, as larger boats could not make their way up the Tees to Yarm and had to anchor nearer the sea at Stockton and, eventually, Middlesbrough – the need for such bigger boats carrying more goods being another indication of the growing volume of trade.[22]

Occasional fairs also lost their trade to weekly markets which were facilitated by improvements in transport.[23] These markets were particularly important for fresh food: at the Saturday market at Whitby, for example, one could find farmers' wives and daughters standing in rows offering their produce for sale.[24]

Such markets, in turn, served shopkeepers by attracting customers to town. Great Ayton lost its market probably because of its proximity to the market town of Stokesley (some two miles away), an example of the way in which improved transport led to the growth of some towns and the decline of others.[25]

Improved transport meant more shops. Shops also responded to the demands of the market, becoming more accessible and orientated to the needs of the customer. Over the course of the eighteenth century shops began their evolution from cellars cluttered with higgledy-piggledy piles of goods, or warehouses with an open window or counter, to the bow-windowed, glass-plated specialist shops already to be found in major towns by the end of the century.[26] When Cook began work as a grocer he entered a thriving trade, the number of grocers' shops expanding considerably to cater to the rising demand for a greater variety of foodstuffs. Grocers came to specialize in dry goods, selling such petty luxuries as tea, sugar, coffee, currents and spices – imported goods that reflected the growing significance of eighteenth-century British trade.[27] Adam Smith famously observed that Britain was increasingly coming to be a 'nation of shopkeepers', though, as he sagely added, its foreign policy, with its emphasis on trade, was not so much the direct outcome of mercantile interests as of 'a nation whose government is influenced by shopkeepers'.[28] Britain's aristocratic governing class had learnt the value of trade as a means of building up strategic as well as economic power.

So vibrant was British trade that it increasingly outgrew the available supply of currency, particularly in the period after the end of the Seven Years' War in 1763. Cook's travelling companion, Joseph Banks, was later to play an important part in modernizing the antiquated practices and equipment of the Mint. In particular, he encouraged the role of the great industrialist, Matthew Boulton, in the use of innovative steam technology to bring about the great recoinage of copper coin from 1797 to 1799.[29] Until the coinage of the realm caught up with the volume of the trade, however, other forms of currency had to be devised – the value of which rested on the metal itself rather than the fiat of the state. In sea-faring communities the range of coins that fetched up from near and far was particularly diverse. A shopkeeper at Staithes would have seen a wide range of coins pass through his till: among them tokens struck in Whitby, the half-pennies minted at Robin's Hood Bay in the reign of King Charles and the copper trade tokens minted in bulk by the industrialist John Wilkinson of Birmingham, with the assistance of Matthew Boulton.[30] There is a (perhaps apocryphal) story that Cook's parting with Mr Sanderson and his shop was prompted by the accusation that Cook had stolen a shilling when all that he had done was swap an old shilling for a shiny one issued by the South Sea Company;[31] an anecdote that underlines the range of coins pressed into service to keep the wheels of eighteenth-century Britain's commerce turning.

Paper currency became ever more widespread, though there were periodic panics as customers demanded precious metal in return for paper. This increasing reliance on promissory notes, bills of exchange and the like was an indication of the relative stability and growing sophistication of the economy. As with coins, there were regional variations as local banks issued their own notes.[32] Such local initiatives were needed, since up until 1793 the Bank of England did not issue notes smaller than the then major sum of ten pounds. Nevertheless, the Bank of England guaranteed the ever-expanding edifice of paper money – an edifice that rested on the right to exchange paper money for gold.[33] This was one of the many instances of the increasingly close ties between London and the provinces since the growth of country banks led to an increasing use of paper money and less dependence on gold coins.[34] Along with bank notes went the persistence of some forms of non-monetary payment: thus the wages of many of the working population were still partly paid in kind.[35] Servants, for example, received cast-off clothes. Naval dockyard workers were entitled to an allotment of fire wood – a proposal in 1756 to substitute this for an increase in money wages led to a riot at Chatham.[36] When Cook sailed to the Pacific he was certainly used to a money economy, but the idea of a range of currencies and even some form of barter came naturally to him as he engaged in forms of trade based on a wide range of mediums of exchange from iron nails to red feathers.

Where Cook's world had diverged widely from the world that he and his men encountered in the Pacific was in the extent to which trade in Britain had become divorced from the ritual and ceremonial life of the society. Like most societies, Britain had traditionally linked trade with other values. When established in the middle ages, fairs were often linked to religious festivals. The original charter of Scarborough Fair specified that the town was permitted to hold an annual fair from the Feast of the Assumption of the Blessed Virgin Mary until the Feast of St Michael next following, that is that the fair should last forty-five days from 15 August. The ritual character of the fair was further heightened by the welcome accorded to outsiders to the town (together with an admonition to trade fairly) which was issued by town officers riding on decorated horses led by a band. Jugglers, morris dances, sports and probably puppet shows all formed part of the festivities.[37]

By the eighteenth century many of these ceremonial flourishes had been lost, although some residual elements remained. Fairs were often still linked with a religious feast, though this probably had little true religious significance, since such festivals had often lost their ritual importance at the Reformation. More important was their seasonal character. Fairs were generally held in late spring and early summer (Easter and Whitsuntide) and in early autumn.[38] Cook's father probably gained his post at Great Ayton at the Martinmas hirings held at Stokesley in October. The contract was generally sealed in ritual fashion with the payment of the 'godspenny'.[39] Many fairs continued to mix business and pleasure, so that at the October cheese fair at Yarm one could find acrobats, jugglers and musicians.[40] On the whole, however, the serious business of making money was becoming distinct from public entertainment. One of the reasons that London's Bartholomew Fair (held in September at Smithfield on the feast of St Bartholomew) survived, unlike that of Scarborough, was that it lost much of its commercial importance and became largely an amusement fair, complete with puppets, freak shows and waxworks.[41] When Cook's men saw the Tahitian *arioi* entertainers they thought them like the 'drolls at St. Bartholomew's Fair'.[42] Even it eventually was closed down in 1854, the victim of increasing suspicion of the effect on public order of such unruliness in the heart of the capital.[43]

Eighteenth-century Britain had become the first thorough-going capitalist society, where getting and spending had become largely ends in themselves. Marx was later in 1848 to decry in the *Communist Manifesto* the extent to which the bourgeoisie (led by Britain)

> has pitilessly torn asunder the motley feudal ties that bound man to his 'natural superiors', and has left remaining no other nexus between man and man than naked self-interest, than callous 'cash payment'. It has drowned the most heavenly ecstasies of religious fervor, of chivalrous enthusiasm, of philistine sentimentalism, in the icy waters of egotistical calculation.[44]

As even Marx's remarks indicate, the increasing transparency of social relations, highlighted by monetary payment, brought gains as well as losses as traditional obligations were transmuted into overt financial transactions. When, however, he came to trade with the Pacific islanders Cook found a world that in some ways he could not fully understand. It was one in which trade could not simply be reduced to the exchange of goods and where hierarchical loyalties shaped the conduct of everything, including economic life. Many of his men, too, were to discover that one commodity they particularly valued, the sexual services of Pacific women, involved expectations that could not simply be met by monetary payment or its equivalent.

While the whole fabric of British life was increasingly shaped by trade, the Pacific societies encountered by Cook were largely self-sufficient, generally relying on local agriculture and fishing. Some Pacific societies did have trading relations with others but this was generally only for a very limited supply of a valuable commodity such as the Tongan–Fiji trade in the sacred red feathers or trade in metal by the peoples of the Pacific Northwest. When goods were exchanged within a society it often reflected not so much the needs of everyday life but, rather, the outward and manifest expression of a social bond, whether between members of the same society linked by hierarchical ties or between different societies expressing their willingness to live at peace.[45] The arrival of strangers in the form of the European explorers was deeply unsettling to such traditions. The Europeans brought with them goods, such as iron, which had an immediate use and value and which challenged the reliance on a subsistence economy. Eventually, prolonged contact with the Europeans led to a breakdown in the traditional way of life as the peoples of the Pacific were drawn into a ever more complex network of trade and, with it, reliance on imported goods. But first contact with Europeans also led to confusion and conflict on both sides as different conceptions of what was involved in the exchange of goods became evident.

Deeply embedded in many Pacific societies was the notion that contact between two different peoples should be cemented by the exchange of gifts. This could be a source of embarrassment and confusion to British reared on the workings of a market economy. When the *Endeavour* left Tahiti, for example, the local people attempted to give Cook four hogs, but these were declined since 'they would take no thing for them'.[46] He had the same response on the third voyage when the people of the Hawaiian island of Kaua'i again offered him some pigs: 'he refused', wrote Bayly, 'to receive them as presents, but paid the people for them'.[47] To Pacific islanders Cook and his men often appeared ungenerous when it came to giving such presents, and their preoccupation with payment seemed both foreign and lacking in munificence.[48] For the Pacific islanders largesse and munificence in gift-giving was both an indication of status and the tribute that status demanded[49] – values difficult to combine with British understandings of exchange based on the values of the market. Interestingly, Lieutenant King reported that the Tahitians considered that the less commercialized Spanish were thought less calculating since they 'made them many presents without expecting anything in return'.[50]

A common response to the British lack of familiarity with a gift-exchange culture was for the islanders to help themselves to the goods the big ships brought – something which did much to sour cross-cultural relations.[51] On occasions, what the Europeans interpreted as theft when goods were handed over and none returned may have been to Pacific islanders the acceptance of a gift or, at least, a ritual exchange that required some delay between the giving of goods. In some instances such confusion was evident even to the British. When Cook landed in Kaua'i in the Hawaiian islands the local people obviously considered that they were entitled to gifts and, accordingly, started to load a number of objects from the *Resolution* into their canoes. When they were stopped, wrote Midshipman George Gilbert, they 'seemed greatly surprized … for they could not believe that we were in earnest but imagined that we could allow them to take what they chose'.[52] In this case, however, good relations were preserved once the Kauaians grasped that these strangers did things differently.

Whether the instances of Māoris taking goods without reciprocating was the outcome of similar confusion about the line between gift-giving and trade is more doubtful.[53] Such a situation led to tragedy when the *Endeavour* called into Mercury Bay, New Zealand. There Lieutenant Gore impulsively shot a man who attempted to make off with a roll of cloth without surrendering the dogskin cloak that had (at least in Gore's estimation) been the agreed price. Very likely the Māori had staged an act of defiance against strangers he regarded as potential enemies – hence the fact that he and his companions 'shook their Paddles at the People in the Ship'.[54] Cook and Banks were dismayed at Gore's over reaction; Banks, however, thought that some response of a less deadly kind was necessary, lest they were subjected 'to the derision and consequently to the attacks of these people'.[55] The local Māoris appear to have decided that the death should not be

Englishman bartering with a Māori, 1769 probably at Tolaga Bay [by Tupaia] (British Library, Add. MS 15508, f.11(a) (no. 12))

avenged since their companion had committed an action that invited retaliation and simply buried him 'in the cloth which he had paid for with his life'.[56] Whatever the motives, it was an exchange that illustrated the dangerous course that trade across cultures could take.

To the Māoris, notions of reciprocity – what they termed *utu* – went beyond the exchange of goods to encompass a balance in the dealings between peoples which could extend to due retribution for insults that challenged the *mana*, the well-springs of power and prestige on which the status of an individual or a group was based.[58] In the case of the Māori killed by Gore, they evidently decided that it did not require the vengeance which *utu* normally demanded since the balance had been originally upset by the Māori himself. One way in which *utu* could be expressed was through the giving of gifts, but its multi-faceted character did not readily lend itself to the mundane black and white dealings of the market. In New Zealand the voyagers might have stumbled into trouble by appearing to favour one group over another in their trading, which in Māori eyes was a form of gift exchange with strong political overtones – this may even have been one of the causes of the Grass Cove massacre of Furneaux's men on the second voyage.[59]

There was also the issue of what, for both societies, required payment. The explorers thought many of the things they needed most, such as fresh water, firewood and fresh fish, should be free, since, as they saw it, they did not belong to anyone. But some Pacific societies took a different view. This again helps to explain why the islanders thought they were entitled to take European goods by way of exchange. Even some of Cook's men were aware of the conflict their often rather cavalier ways could cause. In his account of Cook's second voyage, John Marra urged his readers not to be too critical of the South Islanders' propensity to theft, writing:

> Is it not very natural, when a people see a company of strangers come among them, and without ceremony cut down their trees, gather their fruits, seize their animals, and, in short, take whatever they want, that such a people should use as little ceremony with the stranger, as the strangers do with them?[60]

While the Polynesian people may have sought compensation for the loss of their local produce by taking European goods, this was of little relevance to the Australian Aborigines who had no interest in such goods. When they objected to the capture by Cook's men of some local turtles, their response was to use fire as a weapon. Though little damage was done, many of the supplies of the *Endeavour*, then beached after its grounding on the Great Barrier Reef, might have been incinerated.[61]

By contrast, the Nootka people, whom Cook encountered on his third voyage on the western side of what is now Vancouver Island, were very ready to put a price in terms of European goods on all forms of local produce. These were a people used to trade: 'They had much Iron & Copper among them', wrote the astronomer, William Bayly, '& seemed not suprized in the least at the sight of the Ships'.[62] Cook's company was, however, surprised to find among them a couple of silver table spoons, the result of an exchange with earlier Spanish visitors.[63] A further indication of their exposure to a market which ultimately stretched back to Europe was the fact that many of them had 'a small crooked Knife, made of a very white sort of Iron' which they considered so valuable they would not sell.[64]

Such familiarity with the market brought with it a much greater readiness to demand compensation for the use of local supplies. 'No people', wrote Lieutenant King, 'had higher Ideas of exclusive property', adding that they made Cook pay for grass (which was used to feed the livestock on board), 'although useless to themselves'. Cook drew the line at paying for wood and water which, in his scheme of things, belonged to no one. When payment was not forthcoming, however, the Nootka people pointed out to the British that they had received a gift. For, added King, they 'made a merit … of giving it to us, & often told us that they had done it out of Friendship'.[65]

The Nootka's long experience of trade with other groups along the Pacific north-west coast meant that they generally drove much harder bargains than the Polynesians. On the other hand, there was much less of what the British considered theft, perhaps because both sides better understood the terms of exchange (though the Nootka had learnt a few sales tricks such as making a sailor believe a bird's head artefact had a whistle when it was simply one of the Nootka themselves making the sound).[66] The Nootka did, however, distinguish between trade goods, which were not fair game for pilfering, and other goods which were – perhaps viewing the latter as in the same category as salvage goods that drifted ashore to which they had a traditional right.[67]

Though accustomed to trade, the Nootka retained some ritual elements in their trading – ritual which appears to have been intended to underline the authority of the chief and the exclusive right of the Nootka rather than other groups to deal with the British. When the day's trading began, with the approach of several canoes to the British ships, a leader would rise, spear (or sometimes rattle) in hand, and face covered with a mask. The market would not begin until this exalted personage had made a speech. Sometimes, too, the Nootka would sing together before trading.[68]

For the Nootka, as for the British, establishing firm rights to trade meant conflict with other groups seeking to do exactly the same. Just as the British had fought many times with the French and the Spanish to establish their trading empire, so, too, the Nootka had a history of conflict with other neighbouring groups engaged in trade – conflict that was greatly exacerbated by the coming of Europeans trading valuable and much sought after goods.[69] Cook and his men were aware of these tensions, even though they did not lead to overt local warfare at the time. 'It appeared', wrote Bayly, 'that the first party who came to us [the Yuquot people] claimed the part of the Sound ... & could not be prevailed on to suffer their tribe to share any of the trade'.[70] Subsequently, the life of the peoples of the Nootka region was reshaped by the imperatives of the market, with the population becoming more mobile in the quest to obtain as many animal furs as possible to engage in trade. This increasingly peripatetic and competitive way of life brought with it sporadic warfare between different groups.[71]

Among the New Zealand Māoris the need to obtain trade goods exacerbated already existing endemic and internecine warfare. Even Cook's landings prompted Māori raiding parties to capture objects such as artefacts, particularly those made from the precious greenstone (nephrite) which was obtained from the west coast of the South Island. After a battle in Admiralty Bay in which many were killed, Johann Reinhold Forster ruefully reflected in his journal of the second voyage that 'I am afraid we are the innocent cause of this war'. He saw it as being the outcome of Māori determination 'to possess themselves of these things which are so much coveted by the Europeans'.[72] Such conflicts help to explain why the Māoris parted with such valuable objects as greenstone *patus* (hand clubs): the ones they traded with the British may have lost much of their potency and *mana* since they had been taken from conquered adversaries.[73]

As the British well knew from their own experience at home and abroad, the darker underside of trade was the ability to enforce bargains. Without sanctions attempts at trade could degenerate into chaos. The English legal system was largely focused on the importance of contracts and the sanctity of property – breaches attracted heavy penalties at home; abroad, the armed forces were vigilant in defence of British trading interests. Not surprisingly, when the peoples of the Pacific encountered the British with their valuable goods, there was sometimes an element of testing to see whether such goods could be simply be taken by conquest. What Europeans saw as exchange of property may have been for many of the Pacific chiefs a more important transaction: locating these strangers in a hierarchy of relative power and status. This may also explain why sometimes goods which seemingly had no value to the indigenous people were taken. They were possibly seen as a way of acquiring something of the spirit or *mana* of these strangers and potential adversaries.[74] The astronomical quadrant that was so essential to the *Endeavour* voyage may have been stolen since it was considered to have some important ritual function, while the clothes of key figures, such as Cook and Banks, may have been thought to contain some of their power.[75]

For societies such as the Māoris, used to war and to regarding strangers as enemies, it was natural to probe the defences of new arrivals. This could take the form of outright attack or of taking valuable goods. Such a dynamic seems to have been at work in the incident when Gore shot a Māori for, as Gore saw it, not honouring a bargain. Probably with this incident in mind, Banks alluded to the way in which attempts to institute trade with some Māoris could take on the forms of war. Sometimes, 'before peace was concluded', they would 'entice us to trust something of ours into their hands, [and] refuse to return it with all the coolness in the world, seeming to look upon it as the plunder of an enemy'.[76] Yet Cook regarded the Māoris as 'far less addicted to thieving than the other Islanders', adding that they 'are I believe strictly honest among them-selves'.[77] He seems to have found the occasional attempt at outright appropriation more acceptable than a whole series of surreptitious thefts.

The longer Cook was in the Pacific, the more sensitive he became to the challenges to his authority implied by theft. By the third voyage he had become ever more draconian in his responses to what he saw as such defiance. For Cook, therefore, quite trivial thefts became battlegrounds against those he saw as treating him with contempt. This accounts for the way in which in Tahiti and Tonga on the third voyage he was prepared to go any length, short of death, to punish thieves: hence such extreme measures as cutting off ears or cutting one man's arms and another's shoulder with crosses right through to the bone so that they would be permanently marked.

Cook became more and more aware that the chiefs were often behind such thefts – which accounts for the scale of destruction he inflicted on Mo'orea, in the Society Islands, during the third voyage, over the theft of a goat. Here much more than a goat was at stake, for Cook was demonstrating his power against what he perceived as the attempt by a local chief to defy him. His frustration and anger were compounded by the fact that Cook and other European captains in Pacific waters were very dependent on the local chiefs for the conduct of trade and for much else. If the chiefs chose to deter thefts from the ships, relations could be harmonious; if they did not or, more menacingly still, actively encouraged them, severe conflict was often the result. Cook's death on Hawai'i appears to have been partly the outcome of a change of attitude on the part of the chiefs. When Cook and his men had first arrived they had been treated with great munificence and been given many gifts of food. The chiefs had also, as Surgeon Samwell put it, been 'of great use to us in preventing the Indians from thieving' – there, as elsewhere, 'there is hardly any thing can be stole, be it ever so secretly done, but they are able to recover if they choose it'.[78] After Cook's unwelcome return, however, the chiefs' attitude changed markedly and some, at least, appear to have encouraged the taking of metal goods,[79] perhaps regarding them as their due after their earlier lavish hospitality.

While Pacific societies had their own concept of theft, it had much less force when dealing with outsiders – particularly outsiders as exotic as Cook and his men. Johann Reinhold Forster thought that for the Tahitians 'theft is only forbidden in regard

to their brethren' and that no such prohibition applied to foreigners.[80] The
gravity with which theft was regarded also depended on the extent to which
effective sanctions could be enforced.[81] Here, again, the attitude of the chiefs was
all important. As in European peasant societies,[82] the successful trickster or thief
was often admired as someone who had shown resourcefulness, skill and courage
in the struggle for survival.[83] In his journal of Cook's third voyage, John Rickman
remarked on the way in which in Tahiti thieving was commonly regarded not
'so much a vice in the light we are apt to consider it, as a craft synonymous to
cunning'.[84]

The unsuccessful thief, however, was often considered to have deserved
whatever punishment came his way: 'if one were caught in the fact', wrote Forster,
'& severely beaten by our people, they thought it but just & none pitied or assisted
the Thief'.[85] After the British flogged a Māori who had attempted to steal one
of the half-minute glasses, the would-be thief was again flogged by an old man
(who was possibly his father).[86] Such an object would have been valueless to the
Māori, though it was essential for the navigation of the ship, since it established
the basis for measuring the number of knots which were played out on the rope
attached to the ship's log. Once again the glass may have been seen as having
some ritual or talismanic function and hence have carried with it access to some
of the strangers' power.

Theft not only meant the loss of goods; it could also lead to the corruption
of the market as the Europeans lost the advantage of forms of valuable currency
such as pieces of metal.[87] Hence the dismay when it was discovered that some
of the Hawaiians were prising out some of the sheathing nails out of the ship's
bottom, thereby reducing the Europeans' capacity to trade.[88]

If good relations were to be retained and the necessary supplies obtained,
some thefts had to be overlooked. As Cook wrote when visiting Ra'iatea in the
Society Islands on the second voyage: 'it will be better to put up with the loss, for
one no sooner attempts to force a restitution then the whole country is alarmed
and a total stop put to all manner of supplies'.[89] One solution was to spend as
little time as possible on shore to lessen the number of thefts: this Cook did at
the Marquesas, writing that he there 'put up' with many such misdemeanors
since 'our stay was likely to be but short among them'.[90] Cook might, however,
have had mutiny on his hands if had attempted to pass by all such Pacific islands
so rapidly, quite apart from the fact that some tasks, such as the observation of
Venus, required a lengthy stay. Where Europeans stayed for longer periods the
severity of the sanctions against theft became more and more pronounced. After
all, they themselves came from a society where thefts above a petty amount were
frequently punished with death – a punishment that, as Samwell noted when the
third voyage visited Unalaska, was meted out by the Russians resident there to
any native caught stealing.[91]

Though there was a continual litany of complaints about theft in the journals, the incentives for both sides to engage in trade were too strong for resentment about stolen goods to stand in their way. For the Europeans trade was vital to the success of their Pacific missions, as they needed fresh supplies during their long absences abroad. Without them they were reliant on their dwindling supply of salted provisions and weevil-infested ships' biscuits. On the other hand, for many Pacific societies, the Europeans had objects that were of inestimable value, above all metal, the value of which to some societies had already been evident from the occasional piece that had come their way, probably attached to driftwood. In the Cook Islands, thought Midshipman John Martin, it was 'evident these people never had seen an European before, yet they appeared to know the use of Iron'.[92] The Pacific islanders quickly learnt that trade was the most reliable means of acquiring such goods – particularly as European firearms generally ruled out seizing them. Trade of some kind was therefore an integral part of Cook's voyages. Inevitably, in some places it proceeded more smoothly than others: on his third voyage Cook wrote of Tonga (where relations later soured) that 'No Nation in the world understand Traffick or Barter ... better than these people' – even to the point where 'if either party repented of the bargen the goods were re-exchanged with mutual consent on both sides'.[93] One of the objects that the Tongans sought most avidly was what Cook called 'Togies, that is a Iron tool made in emmitation of one of theirs' – underlining the extent to which the Tongans, like most societies, were most interested in goods which were already familiar to them.[94] Such harmonious trading probably reflected the good will of the local chiefs and perhaps, also, indigenous experience of trade since there was some trading between Tonga and Fiji and even occasional contact with Samoa.[95] But even in Tahiti, where there were constant complaints about the amount of thieving, trade continued at a brisk pace.

The most conspicuous exceptions to this willingness of Pacific societies to engage in trade were the Australian Aborigines. In the period of first contact, they set little store by what the Europeans had to offer – such goods having little relevance to their hunter-gatherer way of life. While the *Endeavour* was under repair near what is now Cooktown, North Queensland, Banks encountered 'the greatest part of the clothes which had been given to the Indians [the Aborigines] left all in a heap together, doubtless as lumber not worth carriage'. If, he added, they had looked further 'we should have found our other trinkets, for they seemed to set no value upon any thing we had'.[96] The Aborigines' indifference to European goods prompted the admiration of Benjamin Franklin, who, when he heard of it from Banks and Solander, recorded in his diary in 1771: 'Behold a Nation of Philosophers! [S]uch as him whom we celebrate for saying as he went thro' a Fair, "*How many things there are in the World that I don't want!*"'[97]

The encounter with Aboriginal society was part of the long education of Europeans in what the peoples of the Pacific considered valuable. The assumption that a lot of beads and trinkets would be sufficient was to be soon disproved. Over and over again they discovered the value of metal objects so, on the second and third voyages, they set out equipped with more of these. But they were also to discover the value of objects which could be obtained in the Pacific itself as they sailed from one part of that vast sea to the next. On the first voyage it was discovered that the Māoris of Tolaga Bay 'Valued more than any thing we could give them' the tapa bark cloth that had been purchased in quantity in Tahiti.[98] On the second voyage George Forster noted how the Tahitians urged Cook and his men 'to give them curiosities from Tonga-Tabboo, Waihoo, and Waitahoo, instead of English goods', in exchange while on Tanna (Vanuatu). 'They set no value', he remarked, 'on our iron-ware but preferred Taheitee cloth, small pieces of green nephritic stone from New Zealand, mother of pearl shells, and, above all, pieces of tortoise-shell'.[99]

Given the wide disparity of objects being exchanged, it is not surprising that both sides sometimes seem to have felt that they were getting the better side of the bargain. While in New Zealand on the third voyage, Thomas Edgar, master of Cook's sister ship, the *Discovery*, remarked on the 'great Contempt' with which the Māoris treated Cook's men. This he attributed in part to 'their getting from us so many valuable things for which they regarded us as Dupes to their Superior Cunning'.[100]

The objects which did most to highlight the wide gulf between cultures and their greatly varying sense of value were the red parrot feathers traded in Polynesia on the second and third voyages. Cook and his men discovered by accident the vast value that the Tahitians and others accorded these objects. As George Forster realized, these had a particular ritual significance in Tahiti: 'These red feathers, with which they ornament the dress of their warriors, and which perhaps are made use of on some other solemn occasions, are valued at an incredible rate in this island'.[101] The colour red, it has been suggested, had particular cultic significance since the gods entered the world through miscarriages and were thus covered in blood.[102] Though in Tahiti there were no birds with red plumage, such feathers formed an integral part of religious and political life, being used in prayer rituals and, in the form of feather girdles, as a mark of political status[103] – for the greater the quantity of red feathers the greater the presence of the divine.

These feathers were obtained by Cook and his men at Tonga on the second voyage with little sense of their value, or so we are told. There, as Elliott wrote, 'We got a great many of them as curiosities ... We bought them because we thought them handsome and curious'.[104] This is a little strange since the Tongans put a reasonably high price on them – though not to the same extent as the Tahitians. The Tongans obtained them from the Fijians and, so Cook learned on the third voyage, would even fight to get them if trade was not available.[105] Perhaps their purchase owed something to the Tahitian Hitihiti alerting Cook to their worth in Tahiti.[106] If Cook and his men had not fully appreciated this, they were to do so when they arrived at the Marquesas. The flourishing trade there (which included exchanging local artefacts for those obtained on other islands) was undermined when the red feathers were produced. Anxious to secure fresh supplies, Cook was angry at the gaucherie of one of his men who 'ruined our Market' by exchanging a pig for 'a very large quantity of Red feathers ... which these people much value'. The result, inevitably, was that the customary currency of metal objects was quite devalued since 'Red feathers was what they wanted'.[107]

At Tahiti the response to the arrival of large quantities of these red feathers was even more spectacular. As Cook wrote, they are 'as valuable here as Jewels are in Europe'. He added, with an aside that helps to explain the frequent suspicion that accompanied such cross-cultural trading, that 'many of our people attempted to deceive them [the Tahitians] by dying other feathers, but I never heard that any one succeeded'. Cook was aware that the value accorded to these feathers was linked to their being 'used as Symbols of the Eatua's or Divinities in all their religious ceremonies'. With an eye to the future, he strongly recommended that future expeditions to Tahiti should come with 'Red feathers, the finest and smallest that are to be got'.[108]

Cook followed his own precept: when he and his men returned to Tonga on the third voyage they purchased large quantities of red feathers: 'Our people giving any price for them', as Thomas Edgar wrote, 'on a supposition that they would turn to good account at Otaheite'.[109] Inevitably, market forces started to take effect: the Tongans, wrote Surgeon Samwell, 'in a short time perceiving our eagerness after them raised the Price of them' to the point where 'it was hardly worth our while to purchase them'.[110] They were to discover, too, on arrival at Tahiti that the flooding of this small market inevitably led to inflation: 'but as every one in the Ships had some', wrote Cook, 'they fell in their value above five hundred per cent before night' – though he added 'but even than the ballance of trade was much in our favour and they never lessened in their value afterwards'.[111]

The inflationary effects of valuable objects such as the red feathers suddenly arriving in quantity in a small market was an instance of a wider problem: the extent to which the purchasing power of trading objects could be subverted. To deal with such problems, Cook generally sought to control as much as possible the terms of trade. Not for him the open market of the sort advocated by his contemporary, Adam Smith. Cook leaned more towards mercantilism, ensuring that the rate of exchange would be controlled through centralized control. The experience of the subversion of the market at the Marquesas, where he lost 'a plentifull supply of refreshments' by the introduction of the red feathers, confirmed him in such views. From it he drew the moral that this 'will ever be

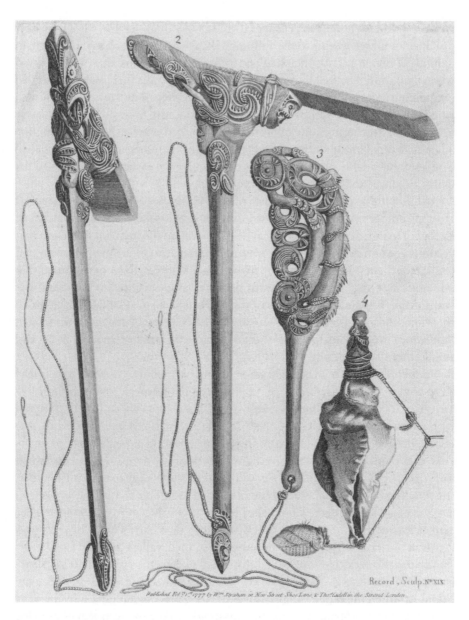

Specimens of New Zealand Workmanship. 1, and 2. Different Views of an Adze. – 3.
A Saw – 4. A Shell. Engraving by Record (from J. Cook, *A Voyage towards the South Pole
and Round the World* … (2 vols, London, 1777), i, plate 19, facing p. 245)

the case so long as every one is allowed to make exchanges for what he pleaseth and in what manner he pleases'.[112]

From Cook's point of view such an approach was particularly necessary, since there were conflicting economic interests within his crew which complicated the conduct of trade. The officers wanted supplies for their ship, especially fruit and vegetables and fresh fish and meat (which usually meant pigs). The men (and not a few of the officers) were interested, above all, in purchasing sex and to that end would sell objects necessary for the effective running of the vessels, such as nails used to hold up hammocks or other objects.[113] The theft at Tahiti by some of the *Endeavour*'s men of 'a large part of our stock of Nails' was a serious threat to the trade in basic supplies for, as Banks wrote, 'these nails if circulated by the people among the Indians will much lessen the value of Iron, our staple commodity'.[114]

Another commodity which the men were interested in acquiring was native artefacts, or what the eighteenth century called 'artificial curiosities', which could be exchanged at profit either in the Pacific or when they returned home. The journals frequently indicate how the trade in curiosities could subvert what the officers regarded as the primary purpose of exchange: the obtaining of fresh supplies. While in New Zealand Johann Reinhold Forster wrote of how 'the Ship's-Crew are mad after Curiosities; & buy them preferably to fresh Fish'.[115] Hence the introduction of regulations such as those laid down by Cook at Tonga on the third voyage: 'No curiosities are to be purchased or traded for, till the Ships have obtained a sufficient supply of refreshments, and until leave is given for that purpose'.[116]

Faced by such threats to what he considered the most basic purpose of trade – obtaining fresh supplies – Cook attempted to institute further regulatory controls. The regulations for trade at Tonga also included a further provision that 'Exchanges on board or alongside the ship shall be under the inspection of the Commanding Officer, who is to appoint proper persons to barter with the natives for such Provisions and refreshments as they may bring off'.[117] Similar provisions were enforced when the ships encountered the island of Maui in the Hawaiian archipelago, where again 'proper Persons were appointed to purchase Provisions'. This was accompanied, as Samwell noted, by Cook forbidding 'every person from buying Curiosities of the Indians, which would prevent them in a great measure from bringing off Provisions to the Ships'.[118] Such controls only had limited effect and were widely evaded. As Adam Smith could have told Cook, the market could not be controlled as closely as Cook wished. Over successive voyages both sides of the market got to know each other better and the terms of trade changed as a consequence. On the first voyage metal objects had enormous scarcity value in the Pacific, but this became less true by the third. Inadvertently, too, the Europeans increasingly devalued their own mediums of exchange by bringing more and more of what the peoples of the Pacific wanted.

On the second voyage, Cook drew up a list for provisioning future expeditions to Tahiti. This, along with red feathers, extended to 'Axes and Hatchets, Spike Nails, Files, Knives, Looking Glasses, Beads & etc. Sheets and Shirts are much sought after, especially by the Ladies as many of our gentlemen found by experience'.[119] Many such objects had indeed been brought on the first and second voyage, but the store of them was expanded substantially for the third. The result, inevitably, was that their trading value diminished. Edgar complained at Queen Charlotte Sound in 1777 that 'our folks were all so eager after Curiosities and withall so much better provided than in any voyage that our traffic with the Indians was quite spoilt'.[120] Lieutenant James Burney thought that the increase in the volume of trading goods meant 'that Traffick was greatly altered in favour of the Indians, a Nail the last Voyage purchasing more than an Axe or Hatchet now'.[121]

The Hawaiians, since they were encountered on the third voyage, unlike the Tahitians or Māoris, had not had the experience of the previous voyages to act as a guide to relative value when trading. They seem, however, to have had a strong sense of what was a fair exchange and would not budge if this was not honoured. Cook remarked on the way in which 'they bring off things in great plenty, particularly pigs, yet they keep up their price and rather than despose of them for less than they demand will take them a shore again'.[122] The Hawaiians soon adapted the metal gained by trade to their own needs: even while Cook's men were there they were turning it into fish hooks and adzes[123] – and, as Cook and his marines were to be all too forcefully made aware, they soon utilized metal weapons.

As always, Cook was concerned to ensure that the men's trading did not interfere with the flow of fresh provisions: he therefore restricted trade to a few officials appointed by himself and his fellow commander, Clerke. '[K]nowing from experience', wrote Cook, that the needs of the ship could not be properly served 'if a free trade was allowed, that is every man allowed to trade for what he pleased and as he pleased'.[124] Perhaps because of the Hawaiians' own sense of what constituted a fair trade, such precautions proved less necessary than in most other places. Eventually, wrote Samwell, 'Trade was made free for every one to day as it was evident that it would not hinder the Indians from supplying the Ships with Provisions'.[125]

Trade was therefore one of the threads that bound Cook's voyages together. It brought together the Europeans and the peoples of the Pacific but also highlighted the differences between their cultures. Although it led to multiple misunderstandings, the strong impulse to exchange goods was largely undimmed.

Trade brought new objects, notably metal, which were to transform such fundamental practices as agriculture and war, eventually drawing the peoples of the Pacific into a web of exchange that made them part of a global market. As elsewhere, the market became a generator for energizing change both for good and ill: trade made available new goods and metal tools lessened toil, but trade in sexual services brought to the Pacific the scourge of venereal disease and new weapons sharpened and intensified old conflicts.

Cook and his men came from a society where trade had become ubiquitous and had begun to weaken the old foundations of society based on religion and hierarchy. When they sailed into the Pacific they encountered societies where the values of the market had had little impact. By bringing in new goods, and by creating new needs, the Europeans began the process of undermining some of the traditional sanctions which had been gradually eroded within Europe itself. But the peoples of the Pacific also used the market for their own ends. Chiefs sought to use European goods to strengthen their own power and some, such as Kamehameha, the first king of a unified Hawai'i, found it possible greatly to expand their power over rival chiefs by the use of western military technology. Iron tools also led to the transformation rather than destruction of some traditional crafts, so that Māori carving, for example, reached new heights with the coming of metal. On Tonga, metal traded on the second Cook voyage had already resulted in new styles of carving by the third.[126]

For Cook, the former trainee shopkeeper, to trade was one of the most natural of human activities. During his voyages, he was slowly educated into the ways in which in the Pacific the seemingly straightforward operations of the market were still intermeshed with other values. The consequences were in some ways to be destructive as Cook became both more aware and more sensitive to the extent to which trade and its mirror image, theft, were shaped by the hierarchical demands of many of the societies he visited. Cook was to learn, too, what would sell best in the Pacific, which meant expanding his repertoire of European goods and recognizing the importance of cross-Pacific trade in objects such as artefacts and red feathers.

Trade formed an integral part of Pacific voyages, since the long absences from home that they demanded meant that obtaining fresh supplies was essential. When the British, the world's leading trading nation, began to explore the Pacific in the late eighteenth century, they naturally assumed that they could buy their way around this new part of the globe as they had elsewhere. In many ways the British were successful, but trade proved a powerful solvent which was to reshape the lives of the peoples of the Pacific into new forms. The encounter between the vigorous market society that was propelling Britain into the Industrial Revolution and the largely subsistence economies of the Pacific was to prove an asymmetrical one. Trade with the Pacific had little effect on Britain but was to

create a new Pacific. The encounter between the peoples of the Pacific and Cook
and his men was to prove an object lesson in the power of the market both to
build and destroy.

4

War

War and trade were close cousins. Britain's increasing commercial wealth made it possible to support a large military and an even larger naval establishment and hence to secure its victory by outspending its rivals.[1] Contemporaries were well aware that the Ciceronian dictum that 'the sinews of War are infinite money' had become even more true in their own times – as one British pamphleteer wrote in 1788: 'Modern wars especially between England and France have been in great measure competition of expence'.[2] Not only did commercial success ease the path to victory but, reciprocally, victory enhanced the scale of commerce. Only when Britain was secure in its commercial domination of the world in the nineteenth century could it forget that its markets had had to be fought for and defended.[3] The nineteenth century might have embraced Adam Smith's roseate view of an ever-expanding economy based on free trade which could benefit all. The eighteenth century, however, was still under the long shadow of mercantilism which viewed the economy as a cake of fixed size with a bigger slice for Britain meaning a smaller one for France or some other rival.

Waging war successfully meant creating effective state structures to mobilize the nation's population and wealth. As one historian has pithily put it: 'War made the state, and the state made war'.[4] Government spending was in effect a war budget with some 75–85 per cent of state expenditure being soaked up by the army or the still more expensive navy (in wartime a sailor cost more than twice a soldier because of the cost of building and maintaining ships).[5] The British taxpayer, however, more willingly parted with funds for a navy than an army, the latter being seen as a potentially dangerous instrument of the state which might be used to create the sort of absolutist monarchy so common on the Continent. Nonetheless, Britain's increasing involvement in European conflicts meant that the eighteenth-century army inexorably continued to grow in size: before the Seven Years' War it was 35, 000 but afterwards it was 45,000.[6] The army, however, continued to be regarded as in some sense unEnglish, the creation of the Dutch King William III and the German Hanoverians in contrast to the navy with its misty descent from King Alfred.[7]

As an island kingdom England had the advantage of having a centuries-old unified kingdom, but even within England there had been border zones that had only slowly and reluctantly been brought under the full sway of the English crown. Cook's county of Yorkshire and the North generally had a long history of being a frontier region, and the major chapters of English history had all left their bloody mark. In the battles between the Anglo-Saxon kingdoms and against the Viking invaders out of which emerged the infant state of England, Whitby had been at the eye of the storm. The foundation of St Hilda's Abbey at Whitby was linked with the great victory at Winwidfield (Leeds) in 655 of the Christian kingdom of Northumbria over the pagan Mercians and the fulfillment of the Northumbrian king's oath to offer his infant daughter in consecrated service to the Christian lord of battles.[8] The end of Anglo-Saxon kingdom and the North's failure to comply readily with the Norman Conquest led to the terrible 'Harrowing of the North' which long remained etched in the north's ambivalent attitude to its southern masters. So, too, did the recollection of the brutal suppression of the Pilgrimage of Grace of 1536–37, following Henry VIII's break with Rome and the suppression of the monasteries which formed such an important part of the northern landscape. In the English Civil War Yorkshire tended to side with the crown and much of it again had to be subjugated, with the parliamentary victories at Marston Moor in 1644 (the largest battle of the war) and the capture of Scarborough Castle in 1645.

But such northern backsliding did little to imperil the unity of the English realm. More threatening was the challenge from England's northern neighbour, the kingdom of Scotland. Caught between the expanding energies of England and the spirited resistance of Scotland, Yorkshire and Whitby, in particular, was subject to regular raids from across the border. In 1328, for example, Edward III ordered the Archbishop of York 'to survey the benefices pertaining to Whiteby abbey that have been destroyed by the Scots'.[9] Nor did the Act of Union between England and Scotland in 1707 bring such conflicts to an end. Northern England was the frontline for the Jacobite uprisings of 1715 and 1745, as one of the tombstones in Whitby parish church poignantly reminds us:

> To the memory of Peregrin Lasells of His Majesty's Forces, who served his country from the year 1706. In the reign of Queen Anne, he served in Spain and performed the duty of a brave and gallant officer. In the rebellion of the year 1715, he served in Scotland and in that of 1745, after a fruitless exertion of his spirit and ability, of the disgraceful rout, Prestonpans, he remained forsaken on the field.[10]

Yet, when Cook joined the navy in 1755 on the eve of the Seven Years' War (1756–63), Great Britain was once again a functioning state. Its victory in that war and eventual dominance over France with the defeat of Napoleon in 1815 largely derived from its ability to draw effectively on the resources, both human and commercial, of the British Isles as a whole. Cook's own ships were themselves microcosms of a state that had become Great Britain rather than simply England. On the *Resolution*, for example, the crew consisted of sixty-one English, eight

Scottish, seven Irish and five Welsh (together with five Americans and one German), while on board the *Discovery* were fifty English, three Scottish and one from Guernsey (along with two Americans and two Germans).[11] War, then, brought together and imparted a national identity to these far-flung residents of the British Isles and even strengthened the use of English – especially for those from the Celtic lands whose first language may have been Welsh or Scottish or Irish Gaelic. Though the English on board were very much in the majority, war service helped to bring different regions together and make those (like Cook) who came from outside the metropolitan centres an integral part of that most national of institutions, the Royal Navy.[12]

Tellingly, Cook's first duties in the Seven Years' War were to assist in undermining French commerce by blockading ports such as Brest as well as protecting British shipping from the French. Cook had an early taste of command when he escorted the prize vessels, the *Triton* and the *Duc d'Aquitaine* (a French Indiaman), back to England in 1756 and 1757. The French, of course, regularly did likewise and Whitby, for example, had had a long history of having been blockaded by the French.[13] The quest for commercial advantage widened the war from its European theatre to an increasingly world-wide one as the rival European powers sought to weaken their enemies' imperial reach and to deny to them the resources and captive markets which colonies could provide. An instance of this was that, after three years' harassing the French coast and its shipping, Cook was moved in 1758 to North America and the battle for Canada.

As master of the *Pembroke*, Cook took an active part in the bombardment of Quebec, recording in his logbook on 5 August 1759 that 'At 1 am the bombarding set on fire the lower town which burnt with great violence and consumed a great part of the lower town'. On 13 September Cook reported the victory which led to British dominance over all of North America: 'At 10 the English Army commanded by General Wolfe, attacked the French under the command of General Montcalm on the field of Abraham behind Quebec, and totally defeated them!'[14] The surrender of the town soon followed, as Cook noted on 18 September: 'at 4 pm the Town Capitulated and the English Troops Marched in and took Possession'.[15] Back in Cook's boyhood village of Great Ayton, the news was received with such enthusiasm that not only were the bell-ringers paid one pound 'for ringing an account of Good News' but a further sixpence had to be spent 'for mending Bellropes' which had been pulled with unaccustomed vigour.[16]

In both peace and war Cook's main contribution was to be chiefly his cartography which both aided the movement of troops in the British victories and, after victory, helped establish clearly the boundaries of Britain's domains within North America (and the limitations to France's remaining fishing rights off Newfoundland). His subsequent great feats in the Pacific carried on this cartographic expansion of Britain's sway and his exploration was never totally

Siege and Taking of Quebec, 1759. Anonymous engraving (National Archives of Canada, C-77769)

divorced from the great power rivalry which had been so nakedly on display in Canada. The French, ever watchful of the wiles of the 'perfidious Albion', made sure that Cook's discoveries (and those of his predecessors such as Wallis) were soon followed by their own expeditions to the Pacific – though, in the event, the South Pacific, unlike North America, did not have spoils that were worth a war.

Though Cook's Pacific ships were converted colliers, chosen for their capaciousness and suitability for exploration, they were nonetheless warships and were armed as such. The *Endeavour* carried twelve swivel guns or blunderbusses which could be mounted on posts in the boats, together with ten four-pounder carriage guns which could either fire an iron ball weighing four pounds or a large number of musket balls.[17] The carriages on which these guns were fixed enabled them to be run out and back through a port on the side of the ship, and it was possible to raise or lower the barrel. As was true of all naval ships after the outbreak of the Seven Years' War, Cook's ships carried a force of marines – floating soldiers – under the captain's direct control (rather than as before the Seven Years' War under army command). On the first voyage there were twelve, on the second thirty-three and on the third thirty-two.[18] Their task was to protect the ship and its shore parties from external foes, but they were also there to deal with internal threats in the form of mutiny. Apart from lending a hand when brute force was needed to pull on ropes or a wayward anchor, their duties were quite distinct from those of the sailors and they had separate quarters – an indication of their role as a buffer between crew and officers.[19]

The ship's marines (and, in emergencies, the sailors) were equipped with muskets very similar to the smooth-bore flintlock muskets issued to land forces, except that they had a shorter barrel. (The smooth bore made muskets less accurate than the grooves or rifling inside the barrel of the weapons which came to be known as rifles). Like land troops, the marines were constantly drilled so that they could rapidly load and fire. Ideally, they should be able to achieve this every twenty to thirty seconds, no mean feat when one considers that this involved taking a sewn-up cartridge, biting off the end and pouring the powder both into a small priming pan and the rest into the muzzle followed by a ball, then using the empty cartridge as wadding as the charge was packed down using a ramrod. On a good day an experienced musketman might be able to hit a target about over two hundred feet away but had little chance of accuracy beyond this.[20]

Nor could Cook and his men ever forget the possibility that they might be obliged to defend themselves against a European enemy. In any European port in any part of the world Cook was likely to meet with suspicion and a considerable degree of scepticism about the alleged scientific goals of his voyage, whether from the Portuguese authorities when he called into Rio de Janiero in 1768 on the first voyage or the Russians when the third voyage arrived at Kamchatka.[21] In 1780, when the third voyage reached Macao on its way back to England after the death of Cook, news finally reached it that Britain was again at war and, as a consequence, wrote William Griffin, ship's corporal on the *Resolution*, we 'Put the Ship in the best state of defence we could'.[22]

Becalmed between the religious zeal of the seventeenth century and the murderous ideologies of the twentieth century, warfare in the eighteenth century was chiefly a matter for paid professionals (such as Cook) rather than the population as a whole. Both on land and sea battles were largely fought at terrifyingly close proximity with the rival sides blasting away at each other. This was largely dictated by the fact that the weapons then available were not accurate at long range, so that warfare meant firing in close formation at a nearby enemy. Since these weapons were single shot, the need to reload led to infantry warfare being based around ranks of men, so that while one rank was reloading the other could fire. Even at close range these weapons were not very accurate – something like one musket ball in four hundred hit an enemy – which again dictated large formations as each side tried to make up in numbers what it lacked in precision.[23]

Compelling large numbers of men to move around in such set formations – often while under fire – meant turning them into virtual automata through rigorous drill and draconian discipline. Frederick the Great of Prussia, the exponent, *par excellence*, of this style of warfare, set out to ensure 'that order, discipline and astonishing precision which made these troops like the work of a watch, the wheels of which by artful gearing produce an exact and regular movement'.[24] Naval warfare was also highly formalized – again with the opposing parties drawn up in opposing lines (hence battle ships were known as 'ships of the line'). Keeping a number of ships in formation again meant complying with very set routines. War had settled into a fixed pattern familiar to the professionals on both sides, leaving little room for strategic brilliance. Victory generally went to those with more men or more ships (which meant more money). The British naval victories in the Revolutionary and Napoleonic wars, which finally ensured that Britain ruled the waves, largely derived from the fact that it had more capital ships than anyone else: of the approximately 440 European ships-of-the-line in 1789 Britain had 153, over one-third.[25] By this time the size of armies and navies had stabilized, since the European states had reached the limits of their resources.[26] Indeed France had overshot hers and the ensuing bankruptcy helped to trigger off the French Revolution.

As the 'sport of kings', rather than a conflict between whole nations, pre-revolutionary warfare had become like a chess game where the moves were well known and in which, as a consequence, stalemate was a likely outcome.[27] The main goal was to preserve one's ships or troops to fight another day, so battles often were inconclusive.[28] Victory, however, could be won through superior numbers or through the ability to bring superior firepower against the enemy: the British navy, for example, owed much of its success to having more and better equipped ships and well-trained guncrews who could fire more broadsides than their opponents – a crack crew could blast off three in five minutes.[29]

In many cases the civilians could get on with their daily lives while the armed forces played out their familiar rituals: Laurence Sterne, author of *Tristram Shandy* (1760–67) (a novel which drew on Yorkshire characters), was surprised, for example, to find that his country was at war with France while he was there at the outbreak of the Seven Years' War, nor did it prevent him remaining for another year. Rulers actively discouraged civilians from getting involved with warfare, a pursuit that belonged to the professionals: Frederick the Great went so far as to imprison some civilians who engaged with retreating French soldiers.[30] The military forces were a sub-culture of their own cut off from the larger society by their uniforms and arcane rituals,[31] though they also acted as the state's arm of enforcement, especially in Britain, which lacked a police force. Coastal villages like Staithes, where the population often combined fishing with smuggling, became very familiar with the army's intrusion in the running battle to maintain customs dues.[32] The divide between the military and the civilian spheres was also lessened by the growth of the militia, the formation of which was prompted by the Jacobite uprising of 1745 and the threat of invasion during the Seven Years' War.[33] But Britons, with their longheld suspicion of the military, did not rush to become part-time soldiers. In Yorkshire the Militia Act of 1757 was followed by riots which led to the trial of one hundred and the execution of two individuals.[34]

Though the eighteenth century was a much safer century in which to be a civilian than the seventeenth or the twentieth, civilians could become casualties, especially when it was considered necessary to undercut the commercial foundations of war. Not only were ports blockaded and merchant ships captured but the livelihood of the civilian population could be devastated if this was seen as a way of denying supplies to the enemy. Before fighting enemies abroad in Canada, General Wolfe had fought the king's enemies at home in the form of the Scottish Highlanders who gave aid and comfort to the Jacobites. He returned to this unheroic work of devastating farms, impounding livestock and subjugating and even killing those who resisted in Canada in late 1758 with a force which included Cook's ship, the *Pembroke*. Though the great French fortress of Louisbourg near the mouth of the St Lawrence had been captured earlier that year with winter coming on it was decided to leave the next and major step of the campaign – the siege of Quebec – until the following year. Meanwhile Quebec was to be weakened by denying it, as far as possible, its food supply, which meant destroying the French settlements on the Bay of Gaspé and other sites around the Gulf of St Lawrence. Quebec lost much of its fish and other supplies and the French fishermen lost their livelihood and, in some cases, their lives.[35]

When he moved from the European wars, fought out on both sides of the Atlantic to the Pacific, Cook moved to a world where the distinction between civilians and the armed forces had little meaning. In the tribal societies of the Pacific every able-bodied man was potentially a warrior, and the society as a whole was, for good or ill, caught up in the consequences of victory or defeat. The lack of any clear dividing line between soldier and civilian also meant that, important though it was, the conduct of war was one among the range of occupations that the population might pursue. The idea of a full-time military, the only business of which was to fight, seemed both strange and rather menacing in Pacific eyes. Hence the warning of the great Māori warrior chief Hongi Hika at his death in 1828 to be beware of

> a people who wear red garments, but who do no work, who neither buy or sell, and who always have arms in their hands, then be aware that these are a people called soldiers, a dangerous people, whose only occupation is war. When you see them, make war against them.

From a Pacific vantage point things were further complicated by the division between army and navy, with their different tasks and uniforms and rituals, leading to an early Māori belief that the soldiers and sailors belonged to different tribal groups.[36]

The lack of any divide between the military and civilian spheres in Pacific societies meant that there were few of the checks and conventions that, at least in theory, were meant to protect non-combatants in Europe. Defeat of one tribal group by another could mean potentially the annihilation of a whole group or, at least, the defeated party being taken into slavery and a very uncertain future. The scale of victory was often determined by the rank of those killed, since the elimination of the elite destroyed the identity of the rival group and left their resources free to be distributed to the conquerors. After Cook's death the Hawaiians seemed to think, as one of Cook's men noted, that 'their Conquest over us was compleat and that we would be able to make no resistance without our Leader'.[37] Bligh, however, did detect a sense that, though the British had been defeated with Cook's death, that the Hawaiians 'feared that when another Chief of equal power to Captain Cook (for [they] thought none present) should be send from Brittania ... that they would all be killed by [the] Number of Men he [would] bring with him'.[38]

European weapons were of course much more suited to mass slaughter than those of the peoples of the Pacific – which helps to explain why various conventions had grown up in Europe (however imperfectly observed) about limiting the spread of carnage to the civilian population. The peoples of the Pacific used the available materials, wood, stone and bone, to create a range of weapons which, in very general terms, can be classed as projectile (especially spears and arrows), thrusting (spears again) and striking (clubs or the Māori hand held *patu*). *Patus* – the word derived from the word 'to strike' – were commonly made of wood, whalebone or basalt, but the most valuable and treasured form of the Māori *patu* was the *patu-pounamu* made of the rare greenstone which could only be obtained on the west coast of the South Island.[39] Curiously the Nootka people of Vancouver Island also used short wooden and bone handheld clubs 'exactly resembling the Pattipatows at New Zealand' – as Midshipman Edward Riou put it.[40] *Patus* and other such stone weapons were often given an edge though patient and time-consuming grinding with sand and water,[41] but lack of metal meant that there were not many edged weapons as Europeans understood them. However, the Tahitians used a sharp rasp made from the serrated backbone of a stingray,[42] and both Tahitians and Hawaiians used knives made from sharpened wood inset with shark teeth.

Strangely enough Polynesian societies made little use of bows and arrows – Māoris did not possess them at all while the Tahitians used them for sport rather than war; so, too, did the Hawaiians who as, the astronomer, William Bayly put it, looked on them as 'fit for amusement only'.[43] The Tongans used bows and arrows for hunting, though in the early nineteenth century they were to adopt a much more effective and deadly variety probably derived from Fiji[44] – for, as Captain Clerke put it: 'The Natives of Fidgi are the only people in this

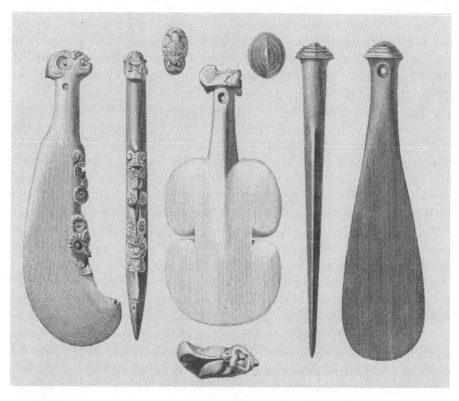

Māori Patus: Side, Edge and End Views. Engraving by Record after J.F. Miller (from J. Hawkesworth, *An Account of the Voyages ...* (3 vols, London, 1773), iii, plate 14, facing p. 466)

part of the World, who use Bows & Arrows in Battle'.[45] But they were employed to deadly effect by the Tierra del Fuegians, who tipped their arrows with flint or volcanic glass,[46] and the Vanuatans, who added further potency to their arrows by coating them with poison.[47] Midshipman Gilbert considered the bows used by the Nootka People as 'the best I ever saw and are rendered very strong and elastick by having a number of Whole Sinews along the grove at the back of them'. The arrow heads were sharpened with hardened wood, bone or flint and, interestingly, 'some few with copper roughly beat out'.[48] Elsewhere, along the Pacific north west and across the Bering Sea in Siberia, bows and arrows were used to deadly effect: 'At the use of the Bow & Arrow', wrote Surgeon Samwell of the Chukchi people of Siberia, 'they seemed very expert'.[49] Another projectile weapon was the sling which was widely used throughout the Pacific.[50]

Throughout the Pacific north west there was evidence of some use of metal for weapons, an indication of trading, probably with Europeans. At Prince William

Sound in Alaska, surgeon David Samwell noted that 'The Spears which they used in war were long & pointed with Iron of which they seemed to have much among them of European Manufacture'.[51] Iron also made possible edged weapons of the kind that Bayly saw there consisting of 'a piece of Iron like a sword blade fixed in the end of a long stick'.[52]

The Australian Aborigines did not use bows and arrows but they had developed unique forms of projectile weapons, such as the boomerang, and an array of spears and objects such as *woomeras* to assist in throwing them further and more accurately. The Unalaskans also used a different type of spear thrower.[53] Throughout the Pacific there was little in the way of protection: Aborigines used shields and the Alaskans had a curious form of wooden armour which, as Samwell wrote, was 'made of thin pieces of wood tyed together with strings ... & will effectually answer the Purpose of defending their Bodies from the point of an Arrow'.[54] The Polynesians did not make much use of armour, though the Tahitians did employ a form of protection made out of wound sennit cords.[55] Māori warriors, however, generally distained such devices and went into battle in little more than a kind of kilt (though chiefs would be marked out by their dogskin coats, the *pauku*, which could be used as a very flimsy shield.)[56]

As island and coastal societies, the peoples of the Pacific often used the sea as well as the land to fight each other – put in European terms they often had navies as well as armies. As in Europe before the development of better artillery, Polynesian naval combat used similar weapons and tactics to land warfare, except that the forces had to engage at sea. The main task of the seagoing vessels was to act as transport to bring the two sides together. In some parts of the Pacific, however, vessels were specifically designed to facilitate combat at sea: towards the front of the large twin-hulled Tahitian naval vessels, for example, was a raised stage which served as a fighting platform. '[T]he use of these platforms', wrote Cook, 'as we were told are for the club men to stand and fight upon in time of battle'. For apart from blasts of stone – the nearest equivalent to artillery[57] – naval warfare was similar to that on land and was played out close to shore often inside the coral reefs where the seas would generally be calm.[58] As Cook put it: 'their method of fighting is to grapple one a nother and fight it out with Clubs, spears & stones'.[59]

In Tahiti this linking of the ships appears to have been ritualized, with conventions protecting those whose task it was to tie the boats so that the real fighting could begin. The artist Sydney Parkinson described, in his journal of the first voyage, how 'they generally throw a string to one another to fasten the canoes together; and the men who are employed in doing this are never struck at'.[60] In his account of Tahitian naval combat, observed during the third voyage, Alexander Home, a master's mate on the *Discovery*, makes the same point even more forcefully, underlining the extent to which war in the Pacific, as in Europe,

Māori Warrior in a Dogskin Coat and Armed with a *Tewhatewha* (Wooden staff with chopping-blade and pointed end). Engraving by T. Chambers after Parkinson (from Sydney Parkinson, *A Journal of a Voyage to the South Seas* (London, 1773), plate 15, facing p. 88)

The Tahitian Fleet assembled at Oparee. Engraved by Woolett after the painting by Hodges (From J. Cook, *A Voyage towards the South Pole and Round the World* ... (2 vols, London, 1777), i, plate 61, facing p. 341)

had its rules and conventions which outlawed totally indiscriminate killing: 'They rush their Vessels Alongside of one Another and they will hand the ropes to one another from the different Vessels and assist one another in the work of Lashing or Casting off ... with out the Least Ill will'. Moreover, when warriors up on the fighting stage who were engaged in 'annoying' the enemy (as Home euphemistically put it) were killed or disabled, they were replaced by others below but, until that happened, these reserves 'are only Spectators ... and as much care is taken by the Men that are fighting as possible that none of their weapons Should do any hurt to those who are Not Engaged'.[61] Ironically, defeat could be more dangerous than the battle itself, since once taken prisoner there was a real possibility of being sacrificed or enslaved.

Though the weapons of the peoples of the Pacific killed fewer than those of the Europeans, Pacific war was, then, a high stake venture, but there were strong forces at work to make war an endemic part of life. War was the ultimate test of a chieftain's power and the command of both material and spiritual forces which in Polynesian societies was known as *mana*. Success in war gave chiefs the resources with which to reward and retain the support of ambitious clients.[62] It was also an opportunity for rivals to demonstrate their *mana* and hence their right to higher social position.[63] For in societies with very strong hierarchical orders, as in Polynesia, war provided some mobility for the less well entrenched. War meant a reconfiguration of the social landscape which would enable those with rank but no position to move into the elite.[64]

Something of the same could be said of Europe, too, where younger sons of the elite – who often only had rather marginal prospects – looked to war as a means of elevating their status and wealth. Again, there was plenty of European precedent for the use of booty to reward retainers, though, particularly by the eighteenth century, this had become constrained by some concept of international law which had arisen in reaction to the horrors of the age of the religious wars. Europe, however, still certainly believed that in many cases it was a case of 'to the victors the spoils' – something deeply entrenched in the navy with its pursuit of prize money. Such booty could also lead to the fortunate few joining the elite: hence Sir Walter Elliott in Jane Austen's *Persuasion* – the gentleman 'who, for his own amusement, never took up any book but the Baronetage' – lamented that the navy was 'the means of bringing persons of obscure birth into undue distinction, and raising men to honours which their fathers and grandfathers never dreamed of'.[65]

Victory among the Polynesians would be followed by a distribution of the lands and goods of the defeated, allowing the victor's supporters to raise their status. Generally speaking this would mean the decimation of the defeated elite – a message underlined by the twenty decapitated heads of defeated Maui chiefs which adorned the wooden fence around an Hawaiian temple (a fence which Cook's party acquired for firewood just before his death).[66] The European parallel to such a public display of a foe's total subjection was a practice such as displaying the heads of executed traitors on London bridge. But defeated Polynesian aristocrats were not always treated thus. Alexander Home was pleasantly surprised to find that on Tahitian island of Ra'iatea the deposed king 'was permitted to live on a piece of ground Not exceeding half an Acre', adding, with an implied criticism of his own society, 'that the cruel follies of civilized Nations is not Need full here'. However, the war in which this ruler had been deposed which had 'happened about the time that the Endeavour arrived' meant, as Home put it in European terms, that 'the Conqueror Divide[d] the Estates of the Vanquished Amongst his Officers' and that his general was 'Now the Viceroy'.[67]

Pacific societies with a less pronounced hierarchy – such as those of the Australian Aborigines – struck Cook and his men as being much less warlike than those of Polynesia. As Cook wrote of the Aborigines in his *Endeavour* journal, 'I do not look upon them to be a warlike People, on the Contrary I think them a timorous and inoffensive race, no ways inclinable to cruelty'.[68] The encounter with the Tasmanian Aborigines on the third voyage prompted similar comment from William Bayly: 'They appeared to be a harmless inoffensive people having no weapons of war of any kind, & seemed not in the least to suspect or fear us, which in my opinion is a strong indication of their living Amicable & happy with each other'.[69] In what came to be known as Micronesia, too, warfare seemed to

Two Australian Aboriginal Warriors. Engraving by T. Chambers after Parkinson (from
Sydney Parkinson, *A Journal of a Voyage to the South Seas* (London, 1773), plate 27,
facing p. 134)

be much more constrained than in much of Polynesia. Johann Reinhold Forster remarked that on the island of Uhlee (one of the Carolines) that 'their wars are by no means bloody and cruel; the death of two or three men commonly decides the victory'.[70]

Within Polynesia, warfare seemed much less a feature of the Friendly Islands than elsewhere – an indication of the stability of the Tongan monarchy. On the third voyage Cook wrote of Tonga that 'The art of War is not unknown to these people though perhaps they practise it as little as any nation upon earth; for except their occasional disputes with Fidge [Fiji] ... they seem to have no Enimies round them'.[71] Tonga had, however, a safety valve for its restless young aristocrats, since they frequently went off to Fiji to learn the arts of war from the Fijian warriors who, as William Bayly put it, were 'certainly masters in the field'.[72] Such apprentice warriors brought back with them expertise which influenced the design of the formidable Tongan clubs which, as Midshipman George Gilbert wrote, 'are made of a hard kind of wood and about 4 feet in length which they manage very dexterously'.[73] Though relatively peaceful in Cook's time, soon afterwards Tonga was to be racked by war – perhaps in part because of the unsettling impact of the Europeans.[74]

It is, however, an indication of the strongly militarist nature of European society that being less warlike did not always lead to respect. After the Aborigines of Botany Bay from the Gweagal clan had retreated, following their initial confrontation with Cook's landing party, Joseph Banks pursued his botanizing 'now quite void of fear as our neighbours have turned out such rank cowards'.[75] Conversely, the more martial Māoris were praised for their courage: Furneaux, for example, considered them 'a bold, fearless race of beings, insensible of danger'.[76] Cook did, however, recognize the toll that virtually continuous warfare exacted on Māori society, remarking on the first voyage that even the 'manner when they laid down to sleep as plainly shewed that it was necessary for them to be always upon their guard'.[77] More emphatically, in his second voyage journal, Lieutenant Pickersgill wrote in fractured prose that 'They are very miserable on account of their Intestine wars, every sound or bay being at varience with their Neighbours'.[78]

The Māoris with their constant warfare were a source of particular fascination to the fighting men on board Cook's ships. Māori warfare with its frequent reliance on surprise attack and stealth (pitched battles were reserved for the few occasions when both sides were confident of victory) differed from European conceptions of proper battle etiquette, as Cook and his men frequently complained in their journals.[79] Anders Sparrman, a naturalist on the second voyage, recognized, however, a common humanity between Europeans and Māoris. He philosophically observed that 'in New Zealand its wild conditions I thought I recognised many of the methods of war and murder of our Gothic

Viking forefathers'. He added – with an aside that indicates the increasing influence of evolutionary ideas in the realm of the infant science of anthropology – that 'we ourselves are descended from forefathers of olden times who were no less barbarous'.[80]

One aspect of Māori warfare that had some parallels with the Europeans' experience was the extensive use of fortresses or *pas* – something which Cook and his men did not encounter elsewhere in the Pacific. Indeed, eighteenth-century European warfare had become ever more reliant on fortresses as bases to preserve both troops and supplies, and ever more elaborate curtain walls and earthworks had been developed to provide a ring of protection around them[81] – not unlike the way in which Māori fortresses, usually located on a hill, were surrounded by terraces to prevent a surprise attack.[82] As Joseph Banks discerned, the need for these fortresses was linked to 'the state of war in which they live, constantly in danger of being surprized, when least upon their guard'. The result was that they lived together and 'fortif[ied] those towns; which they do by a broad ditch and a palisade within it of no despicable construction'.[83] More accurately, James Matra in his *Endeavour* journal distinguished between the villages and 'the castle', 'which serves them for a place of retreat, and a magazine for securing their dried fish, fern root, and other provisions'.[84] For, as with European fortresses, one of the main functions of Māori *pas* was to preserve large reserves of food. The lack of cereal crops which did not spoil, however, limited the length of time Māoris could withstand a siege.[85]

Cook and his men could understand enough of the workings of society to appreciate the importance in Māori culture of what the Europeans regarded as revenge. As the botanist Anders Sparrman put it: 'At the slightest annoyance (and that often quite unjustified) they would threaten revenge'.[86] In Māori eyes a more appropriate term would have been '*utu*' – the very broad term which described a whole understanding of the workings of society based on the concept of balance and even harmony. *Utu* meant keeping an even score, whether it be in relation to gifts and favours or insults and attacks. Friendly gestures had to be reciprocated, but so too did acts which were regarded as hostile.[87] An unrevenged slight upset such harmony and was a source of ongoing shame that it was the duty of the group as a whole to rectify, even if they had to wait for some generations to achieve it. Until this was done the group as a whole was weakened not only in its reputation but in its sustaining spiritual force, its *mana*.[88] When (and if) victory finally came, revenge might be sweetened by post-mortem desecrations such as cannibalism. Swallowing the eyes of the slain enemy had particular significance, since this was a means of incorporating his spirit, as the eyes were the seat of a person's spiritual force.[89] Using his bones for mundane purposes such as fish hooks further served to destroy any remaining *mana* harboured by the enemy and to hamper the malign intervention of the enemy gods.[90] Until

Māori Pa or Fort built on a Natural Arch at Mercury Bay. Engraving after J. Barralet (from J. Hawkesworth, *An Account of the Voyages* … (3 vols, London, 1773), ii, plate 18, facing p. 340)

accounts, both physical and spiritual, had thus been squared up things were out of joint. Those who failed to live by the law of *utu* were less than men, mere slaves lacking in *mana*.[91] Hence the Māoris' low opinion of Cook and his men when, on their return to Queen Charlotte Sound on the third voyage, they did not exact vengeance for the killing and eating of eleven of Captain Furneaux's men at Grass Cove in November 1772. As Thomas Edgar put it: 'It seemed evident to me that some of the Zealanders held us in great Contempt – one Reason I believe was our not revenging the affair of Grass Cove – so contrary to the principles by which they would have been actuated in the like case'.[92]

Though the desire for revenge (which was linked to kinship obligations) was the most important cause for war throughout Polynesia,[93] Cook and his men remarked on the extent to which other Polynesian societies (notably the Tahitians) seemed less preoccupied with the need to exact vengeance. Despite the bloodshed exacted when Europeans first encountered Tahiti, with the arrival of the *Dolphin* in 1767, Sparrman commented on the good relations between

Tahitians and Europeans which he attributed to the former's 'complete lack of any desire for revenge, which is one of the most laudable characteristics of the Otaheitians'.[94] After the third voyage, John Rickman wrote glowingly (if rather simplistically) of the Tahitians that 'They seem to be the only people upon earth who, in principle and practice, are true Christians … They may be truly said to love their enemies, though they never heard the precept that enjoins it'.[95]

The idea of slighted honour, so strong among the Māoris, was something that European military and naval officers could well understand. Coming from a society, the values of which had shaped by a hierarchy whose origins went back to a warrior class, officers were much preoccupied with questions of status and nice codes of honour. Hence the prevalence of duelling – a practice that was so much a part of military and naval life that the army turned a blind eye to its regular occurrence. After all, what else could be expected of ambitious young men much preoccupied with glory – if necessary at the price of their own life – who regularly used firearms? Technically, duelling was a breach of the articles of war, but the practice was not actively stamped out until the 1840s. As one pamphleteer mordantly put it in 1795: 'such is the unaccountable prevalence of custom, that the disobeyer of these orders is generally applauded, while the obeyer of them is obliged to quit the army with disgrace!'[96] While the official journals on Cook's voyages tended to keep quiet about duels, there were a few on his voyages: on the *Endeavour* voyage a long simmering dispute between two officers was to be settled by a duel when they reached Tahiti in 1769 but, as Midshipman James Matra put it in his anonymous journal, 'after a few discharges they were arrested and reconducted on board, by a party sent for that purpose, before any mischief had happened'.[97]

On the third voyage things went further when Molesworth Phillips, the lieutenant of marines, and John Williamson, the third lieutenant of the *Resolution*, fought a duel in 1777 – again at Tahiti. But like most duels it was inconclusive, leaving honour satisfied and two live protagonists (which was one of the reasons the practice was obliquely tolerated). For, as William Griffin wrote, 'after one or two rounds neither being wounded, the seconds interfered & ended the affair'. Griffin did not disguise his disappointment at seeing Williamson back on board: 'Many person would have rejoiced if Mr. Williamson our third Lieutenant had fell, as he was a very bad man & a great Tyrant'.[98] Williamson's unpopularity continued to rise, particularly since he was in command of the launch which did little to prevent Cook's death though nearby – which possibly led to another duel with Phillips. But Williamson lived to fight another day and continued to rise in the navy until after the battle of Camperdown in 1797, when his career came to a rapid halt after being tried for cowardice (though he escaped with convictions on the lesser charges of misreading a signal and dereliction of duty), dying a year later.[99]

Duelling was one of the few occasions when members of the armed forces could fight as individuals, for European warfare had become ever larger and to that extent more impersonal. When late eighteenth-century Europeans encountered the world of the Pacific, they therefore focused particularly on the way in which war there still left room for single combat. The most obvious historical parallels for a society where the elite were raised on the classics were those drawn from the Homeric epics. Johann Reinhold Forster thought that the Tahitians' ships were of the same kind as those 'that went to fight the famous city of *Troy*; & perhaps the nature of their wars seems to have been very much the same'.[100] Cook and his men also admired the strong bonds between warriors which meant that they would risk death to rescue a fallen comrade – hence the remark of one of Cook's men that 'one would think the age of old Homer had been revived for it as much the point of Honour here to carry of their dead as ever it was in antient Greece'.[101]

Invoking the classical world was one way that Europeans attempted to make comprehensible the new world of the Pacific. They also had resort to a less distant past to describe the weapons of the peoples of the Pacific in terms that would have meaning for a European audience. The replacement of a separate class of pikemen by musketeers with bayonets in the late seventeenth century meant that there were weapons which had by Cook's time become obsolete but were still remembered. Moreover, these were sometimes retained for ceremonial purposes and symbolically underlined a soldier's rank.[102] Hence Cook singled out the commanders of a Māori war canoe as being 'better clothed' and as carrying 'a halbard or battle axe ... that distinguished them from the others'.[103] Bayly referred to the Māori fighting staffs or *taiaha* as being like 'a Spantoon that the officers (*in Marching Regiments*) have'.[104] Predictably, the Māoris' long spears were referred to as pikes.[105]

While the Europeans sought to translate such weapons into terms familiar to them, so, too, the peoples of the Pacific were faced by the task of rapidly assessing the nature of these strangers (and their weapons) who had so unexpectedly sailed into their world. In their terms there were aspects of these strangers' behaviour that seemed contradictory. The fact that they did not have women with them was in itself an indication that they might be a war party. As in Europe, war (or, at least, frontline combat) was a male domain: while women might be involved in Pacific wars in emergency, the Māori proverb, 'Fighting with men and childbirth with women' summed up the prevailing attitude – and the suspicion that therefore attached to groups consisting solely of men.[106] On the other hand, the Europeans did not particularly look like warriors as the Pacific understood them. They did not make war cries, lacked tattoos or other such markings and, particularly in Polynesian eyes, did not seem all that large and formidable. All this, as Lieutenant King wrote of the Hawaiians, was 'a circumstance which puzzled them exceedingly, our having no women with us; together with our quiet conduct, and unwarlike appearance'.[107] Nor did the Hawaiians think highly of the physique of the Europeans asking, as Surgeon Samwell reported, 'who are the Tata Toa or fighting Men among us, they suppose none are such but those who are tall & stout, the same as they are among them'. Cook passed muster as a Toa, since he could show some wounds (which derived from a gunpowder explosion in Canada), but King's lack of any prompted the Hawaiian to display his own battle scars and hence his status as a fighting man.[108] But such ambiguities about the nature of the Europeans did not detract from the fact that people coming from the sea – and especially those without women – were likely to be invaders. Cook himself was well aware of this, ruefully remarking after the attempted landing at Erromango (Vanuatu) on the second voyage led to bloodshed: 'in what light can they at first look upon us but as invaders of their Country; time and some acquaintance with us can only convince them of their mistake'.[109]

Strangely enough, Europeans and the peoples of the Pacific seemed to understand each other better in the rituals of peace than those of war. Both sides acknowledged a white cloth as a symbol of a request for surrender or, at least, a ceasefire. It was a symbol which the Māoris employed on Cook's return to Queen Charlotte Sound in 1777 at a time when Māori–European relations were overshadowed by the massacre at Grass Cove of a boat crew from the *Adventure* on the second voyage. As William Bayly put it: 'They seemed to hesitate some time & halted at a distance' – understandably under the circumstances – 'waving a white Cloth as a signal of peace'.[110] A white cloth was again produced when Cook's ships first arrived at the main island of Hawai'i in December 1778. 'The Natives were shy in their first approaches,' wrote Lieutenant King, '& we saw in many parts upon the Shore, pieces of white Cloth flying, as we supposed mean[t] for emblems of Peace.'[111] In the very different circumstances which prevailed after the death of Cook, the Hawaiians again sought peace by holding up white clothes though, added the German sailor Heinrich Zimmerman they 'mocked at us'. Soon afterwards, he continued, they reinforced their sincerity by 'approach[ing] us with green branches in their hands' – another symbol for peace which Cook and his men encountered throughout the Pacific.[112] In Vanuatu, where Cook landed carrying a green bough, the then Lieutenant Charles Clerke observed that 'the Green Bow is an Emblem of Peace among all the Indians I ever saw'.[113] George Forster agreed, writing that 'almost all nations on our globe have tacitly agreed upon the white colour, or upon green branches, as tokens of a peaceable disposition', adding, in a characteristically philosophical aside, that 'Perhaps this general agreement had its origin anterior to the universal disposition of the human species'.[114]

From the Pacific perspective, determining the fighting prowess of these strangers from abroad meant a good deal of initial testing. Europeans were confident that gunpowder brought with it a natural dominance. Cook thought that 'The best method to preserve good understanding with such people is first to shew them the use of fire arms and to convince them of the Superiority they give you over them'. But the potency of firearms was not always quite so evident to the peoples the voyagers encountered. The strange European weapons that were wielded from afar were so outside the experience of many groups that they did not at first necessarily take them too seriously – Banks, for example, wrote that the Māoris would not 'be convinced by the noise of our fire arms alone that they were superior to their' weapons, while Cook thought that 'Musquetry they never regarded unless they felt the effect but great guns they did because they threw stones further than they could comprehend'.[115] The first reaction of an Aboriginal warrior at Botany Bay to being fired on (with small shot) was to use a shield.[116] Samwell attributed the attack on Cook in 1779 to the fact that the Hawaiians did not realize the power of firearms:

> they thought their Matts would defend them from a ball as well as a stone, & in the heat & fury of Action they were not immediately convinced of the contrary. Holding their Matts before them they advanced up to the very muzzles of our pieces.[117]

Part of the reason that Cook had relatively good relations with the Tahitians may well have been linked to the earlier bombardment by the *Dolphin* in 1767, since the Tahitians had become well aware of the force of European firearms. Anders Sparrman went further, arguing that the fact that Captain Wallis only fired in self-defence further strengthened respect for 'the strangers [who] did not employ their authority and strength to destroy the natives, but only ... to punish insurrection'.[118] Indigenous peoples less familiar with European weapons were more likely to attack the generally vastly outnumbered members of Cook's expeditions. Cook had always to be on his guard and was at pains to demonstrate the effectiveness of his fighting force. In what proved a prophetic description of his own death in Hawai'i he remarked at Tahiti on the second voyage that the indigenous peoples 'are very sencible of the superiority they have over us in numbers and no one knows what an enraged multitude might do'.[119] At Nootka Sound Midshipman Riou reported that it appeared likely that the Nootka might have attacked, 'knowing their superiority in Numbers but seeing as we armed so quickly and appearing always prepared for them it is supposed they Changed their Mind'.[120] On the second voyage, Cook's determination not to allow any display of European weakness went so far as his forbidding further boxing matches between the English and the Tahitians after one such was won by the Tahitians for, as John Elliott reported, he considered it to 'be highly impolitic to let them suppose that they were *equal to us* in anything'.[121]

On the other hand, once European weapons became more familiar so, too, did their limitations – particularly the fact that guns required reloading. The

Māoris around Queen Charlotte Sound, who saw quite a lot of Cook and his men, were well aware of this as Lieutenant Burney emphasized in his report on the Grass Cove massacre of 1773: 'they were sensible a Gun was not infallible, that they sometimes mist & that when discharged they must be loaded again, which time they knew how to take advantage of'.[122] Nor did Cook always take full account of the limitations of his weapons. Most spectacularly this was the case at the time of his own death on Hawai'i when, in the flurry of the moment, he ordered a full volley from the marines to make the maximum impact on the threatening crowd. By discharging all muskets, the result was that they, as Samwell put it, 'left themselves without a Reserve'.[123] The master's mate, Alexander Home, gave the blame for this squarely to Cook who overruled Lieutenant Phillips of the marines, who had previously been adopting the standard tactic of letting one group fire while the other reloaded. Once the full volley was fired, however, 'just as Phillips had predicted, before the marines had time to reload, they were overwhelmed by the natives, and the captain and the two marines murdered'.[124] In characteristically robust language William Bligh, whose stormy career included service as the *Resolution*'s master on the third voyage, took the marines to task for not then proceeding with a bayonet charge, the standard tactic of infantry at close range (and particularly when they could no longer fire) – by doing so, Bligh forcefully contended, 'they might have drove all before them'.[125]

Notwithstanding the limitations of European firearms, those peoples with whom Cook and his men had extended contact could well appreciate their power and, more particularly, appreciate how useful they would be if directed against their own enemies. Part of the reason that Mai accompanied Furneaux back to England on the second voyage was his hope that he could enlist European support and European weapons against his old enemies, the Bora Bora men, who had attacked his native island of Ra'iatea. On the third voyage, Cook's increasing familiarity with the tribal leaders around Matavai Bay, Tahiti, led to a plea from them to help in their battle with the neighbouring island of Mo'orea by sending over one of his ships. Cook, as William Bayly reports it, 'told them that he would not take any part in their quarrel for he was friends with all the Islands'.[126] Such a stance was, however, interpreted by some on Tahiti as a breach of friendship especially by the high-ranking To'ofa (whom Cook's men termed the admiral). He 'fell into a passion' and then, as Surgeon William Anderson reported, exclaimed that 'Is it possible ... that you who pretend to be our friends should be unwilling to assist us against our enemies?'[127] The plea from the Tongans for Cook and his men to destroy the war canoes of the Fijians was equally fruitless.[128]

While the peoples of the Pacific could recognize the enormous power that European weapons brought with them, the military capabilities of Cook's day did not bring with them the overwhelming European global dominance that was to emerge in the nineteenth century. The tactics employed by eighteenth-century Europeans were often more suited to fighting other Europeans than indigenous peoples. European battles both on land and sea relied on elaborate formations on an ever increasing scale. This could make European forces very unwieldy when dealing with the much less structured and less predictable tactics of non-Europeans, who did not obligingly stand in straight lines to be shot at like well-trained European troops. It has been suggested that the development of light troops – who fought in a much looser formation and had to use a degree of initiative in contrast to the machine-like discipline of most troops in their serried ranks – was prompted by the encounter with American Indians.[129] Until Europe developed rapid-fire guns it was tied to a form of mass warfare that was not readily exported.

The style of war that Cook knew was that of a preindustrial society soon to be revolutionized by the impact of the Industrial Revolution. It was a revolution which brought in its wake mass production of devices – such as breech-loading guns (later capable of firing multiple rounds without reloading) and steam-powered ships which meant that naval warfare was less at the mercy of the elements – that made mechanized killing possible on a unprecedented scale. Improved communications such as the telegraph meant it was possible to establish effective systems of supply and command. Such changes were to dwarf the importance of the so-called military revolutions of early modern period which had been linked to such developments as more effective muskets, the invention of the bayonet and the increasing size of armies.[130] As in other ways, Cook lived on the eve of a period of change in warfare which, for good and ill, brought more and more of the globe under European dominance.

5

Politics

The goal of war was to increase power; so, too, in other forms was the exercise of politics. Clausewitz's dictum that war is the continuation of politics by other means underlines the extent to which both activities shared common aspirations. War brought with it booty which enabled a leader to attach his clients more securely to his reign. It also brought what the Europeans considered glory and the Polynesians an increase of *mana*, the divine force from which all power, material and spiritual, flowed.

The means of war in turn reflected the nature of the polity. The strongly hierarchical regimes of both Europe and Polynesia organized their forces in ways which underlined aristocratic power, with the conduct of battle directed by the few, though the fighting was done by the many. Military command in Cook's Britain was closely allied with aristocratic status or the ownership of land. After the Rudd family purchased the manor of Marton-in-Cleveland, Cook's birthplace, in 1786, Bartholomew Rudd's appointment as major in the Cleveland Corps of the Volunteer Infantry in 1803 naturally followed.[1] There were still residues of the notion that an officer's men were his personal following which meant that the officers of old regime Europe expected a greater degree of independence than their more professionalized successors.[2]

In Polynesia, too, status was linked with leadership in war, with war being the ultimate test of the right to rule. In less hierarchical societies, such as the Aborigines, there was less of a divide between the individual warriors and the tribal elders. The bigger the polity the larger the array of troops – a further incentive to employ war or power politics to expand national boundaries, the better to command more men and more treasure to support them. In the Pacific what generally linked such individual polities together, and gave them a common identity and cohesion, were the ties of blood which were renewed and widened by marriage alliance. Such bounds of kinship were of such importance that on Hawai'i it was assumed that Lieutenant King gained his position from being Cook's son – hence the request that King remain behind in order to forge a link between the newcomers and the Hawaiians.[3]

Membership of the same society meant sharing common ancestors, even though the status of the aristocrats was often linked to their descent from the gods. In Tahiti George Forster thought that the commoners' affection for their chiefs sprung from the fact that 'they consider themselves as one family, and respect their eldest-born in the person of the chiefs'. In the Marquesas, he remarked that the aristocratic principle seemed less entrenched and that there the inhabitants 'probably look on themselves as one family, of which the elder born is the chief or king'.[4] Such bonds helped to weld together even those Pacific societies in which social stratification and the creation of an aristocracy had become particularly pronounced. In Hawai'i, the most aristocratic of Pacific societies, there remained a residual sense of all sharing some ties of kinship.[5] In less hierarchical societies outside Polynesia the importance of the family and extended kin as the primary principle of social organization loomed even larger. Johann Reinhold Forster thought that on the Melanesian island of Tanna (Vanuatu) that 'Their government seems to be patriarchal. Each Family having the oldest man at their head, but he is not obeyed or respected like a Sovereign'.[6] Among the Nootka people on Vancouver Island, concluded Midshipman Gilbert, there did not seem to be 'any Cheifs amongst them; as we find at the Tropical Islands; but [they] live in Families quite independent of one another'.[7]

Though ties of kin were important in Europe, they were, by Cook's time, in competition with other forms of social organization. Monarchy and aristocracy were based on the ties of blood and descent, and throughout the society as a whole claims based on kinship, which went well beyond the immediate family, were accorded much greater respect than today. Nonetheless, by the eighteenth century there were signs that the British elite had become less inclined to acknowledge claims of distant cousins and even less inclined to accept that the claims of kith and kin should be primary in the disposal of offices.[8] By this period other ways of conceiving of the transmission of power than the biological one had also taken root. The great theorist of the liberal state, John Locke, had spent the first of his enormously influential *Two Treatises on Government* (1690) debunking the ideas of Sir John Filmer who, in his *Patriarchia: or the Natural Power of Kings Asserted* (1680), had linked both blood and religion by arguing that a king's power derived from his ultimate descent from Adam. Faced by the prospect of overthrowing the unpopular Catholic monarch, James II, Locke had argued that government, including monarchy, should be based primarily not on the principle of descent but rather on that of a contract between the governed and the governed – hence it was legitimate in extreme circumstances to dismiss a monarch who did not live by the terms of this contract. Cook's Britain was to be ruled by the German house of Hanover, which stood as a living (and often divisive) embodiment of this principle, since their claims to the throne were plainly not securely based on right of descent: fifty-eight Catholic Stuarts had been passed over to ensure that the solidly Protestant Hanoverians, with only a very remote royal genealogical claim, were rulers of Britain.[9]

The weakening of the biological basis of rule in Britain brought with it increasing emphasis on more abstract and impersonal principles of government, such as Locke's contractual theorizing or an emphasis on various forms of rights. It also reinforced the importance of institutions, such as the law and parliament, which had both the sanction of tradition and that of providing a check on any attempt at royal despotism. The rule of law was conceived of both as an Englishman's birthright, since the law had been passed on from previous generations, and as an embodiment of the principle that the exercise of power by any individual (including the king) should be kept in check. Cook and his men were therefore particularly struck by the extent to which in the Pacific there appeared to them to be no clear line between chiefly power and the law. On the second voyage the astronomer William Wales expressed scepticism about the proposition that the Tahitians were 'governed by a body of Laws' as in Britain; rather, he thought, matters rested with the chiefs and, when it came to crimes, 'their punishment lies in the breast of the Chief'.[10] The Tongans, thought Surgeon Samwell, might 'have certain Laws by which the conduct & Actions on one chief towards another are regulated, but that the common People are intirely at their Disposal'.[11] Captain Charles Clerke thought similarly, speculating that in Tonga, Tahiti and Hawai'i 'most probably the Aree's [aristocracy] have some determined mode of adjusting matters among themselves; but I believe the immediate pleasure of the principal People is the Law of the inferior subjects in general'.[12] More sweeping still was the gunner's mate, John Marra, who concluded that in Tahiti 'Laws they had none, but such as naturally arose from the idea of superiority and Submission'.[13]

In Britain, parliament, as the body which made law, was invested with increasing prestige throughout the eighteenth century. Parliament provided a means of the monarch consulting the country as whole. The institutionalization and formalization of such consultation was partly a consequence of the size of the country. Such an institution was less necessary in the much smaller Pacific societies, where kinship ties provided more informal mechanisms for a dialogue between rulers and ruled. Though increasingly linked with abstract theorizing about the rule of law and the maintenance of abstract rights, the English parliament had been shaped by the accidents of history and its often arcane composition reflected little system. Cook's county of Yorkshire, the largest in the country with twenty thousand voters, had two representatives – the same as every other county irrespective of size.[14] Under the radicalizing impulse of the War of American Independence, Yorkshire became increasingly vocal about its under-representation, though there was no fundamental change until the Great Reform Bill of 1832.

Along with the two members elected by the county ('the knights of the shire'), there were two representatives (known as 'burgesses') of fourteen Yorkshire towns or boroughs – why one town was so privileged rather than another reflecting historical accident rather than any obvious principle.[15] Medieval Whitby had been represented – after a fashion – in the House of Lords by its abbots, but that tenuous claim to consultation was lost with the Reformation. A little to the south, the town of Scarborough did return two members of parliament but the small number of those entitled to vote (less than fifty) helped to ensure that the seat generally remained firmly under the control of prominent interests. Since secret voting was not introduced until the Ballot Act of 1872, seats such as Scarborough with a small number of voters were readily overawed by such interests and hence were known as pocket or, more derisively, rotten boroughs.

But by no means all seats meekly complied with their social superiors' bidding. A little further south again the Yorkshire seat of Kingston-upon-Hull (Hull) was known for its independence, partly because it was much larger with 1,200 voters and therefore much more difficult to dominate. Elections were therefore more likely to be contested. The result could be very expensive as candidates sought to woo the voters – as the accounts of Sir Charles Turner, MP, who stood in the radical interest in 1796 testify. For, while electioneering at Hull, Sir Charles had to pay for entertainment, ribbons, flags, music and bellringers, as well as compensation for damage done by the mob. To encourage possible voters he had also to meet their travelling costs, including the bills for innkeepers and liquor. Evidently not all these were paid, since after the election he was sued by an innkeeper for the cost of entertainment, liquor and victuals (food).[16] A seat such as the ancient City of London, where Cook was based for most of his adult life, had an even greater number of voters (some seven thousand) and was proportionally even more independent and it was there that reforming impulses such as the movement led by the radical John Wilkes took root. Though there was the requirement that a voter be linked to one of the City Guilds if Cook had chosen to vote (and there is no evidence that he ever did) he would have had little difficulty fulfilling that requirement, the effect of which was to allow the vote to all men above the labouring classes.[17]

Just as there was no evident logic to which town could elect MPs so, too, there was no uniformity about the criteria which established who was allowed to vote. Scarborough had a particularly restrictive franchise, since voting went with membership of the corporation (the local government). At Hull, by contrast, all freemen were allowed to vote. Such freemen boroughs were the most common variety of electorate and were fairly open (if one were male), since one could become a freeman by birth, apprenticeship or marriage. Another variant was the 'scot and lot' borough of which the small Yorkshire town of Aldborough was an example. In such electorates the franchise was based on the payment of local taxes (especially the poor rate) which approximated to modern rates. At Aldborough this only yielded fifty voters and so this seat was rarely troubled by elections. The seat of Westminster, however, was also based on scot and lot and it was the largest electorate in the country with around twelve thousand voters being known for its radicalism.

Boroughbridge, a near neighbour of Aldborough, represented another variant, where the right to vote went with particular properties (known as 'burgages'); again this resulted in a small and very tractable electorate (with sixty four voters). Both these seats were firmly in the pocket of that great eighteenth-century borough manager, the duke of Newcastle, who referred to them as 'my own two boroughs' – an appropriate description since he owned most of the houses in both places, including the Boroughbridge burgages which carried with them the right to vote. None of Yorkshire's fourteen boroughs included a representative of the eleven householder or 'potwalloper' boroughs, the most open of all, since every male householder not receiving poor relief was allowed to vote. Such relatively democratic seats were also known for their venality, as the often politically uninterested voters cheerfully sold off their vote to the highest bidder.[18] In the country as a whole something like fifteen per cent of adult males had the vote.[19] Women of course were not permitted a role in elections until 1918.

Contemporaries had, however, become adept at making this apparent muddle work to represent their interests. For the parliamentary system (if one can use an inappropriate word) made no pretence to be democratic or to represent every individual. Rather, if it had a directing principle, it was that each of the major interest groups in society should be represented, so that law-making and major debates about national policy should be informed by the key sectors on which the society and its economy were based, whether the landed and city interests, or the professions and the armed forces. Since MPs were not paid until 1911, leisured gentlemen with landed estates were disproportionably represented in parliament – hence some two-thirds of MPs between 1660 and 1832 were drawn from about 484 families.[20]

As someone whose career was so closely linked to that key instrument of state policy, the navy, Cook's career on occasions intermeshed with the parliamentary process and the interests it embodied. His early steps in the navy were probably assisted by the intervention of William Osbaldeston, the member for Scarborough, who wrote to his captain, Hugh Palliser, to advance the case for Cook's more rapid promotion. An independent landed gentleman, Osbaldeston held a secure hold on the seat (being MP 1736–47, 1754–5 and 1766) and, following his death in 1765, it passed without fuss to his brother, Fontayne. Unlike his brother, Fontayne had to face the indignity of an election, for in 1768 there were three candidates for the two seats. This was the outcome of the successful campaign by the aristocratic Lord Granby to use his position as master-general of the Ordnance (the government office in charge of military equipment, barracks and fortifications, and all the lucrative contracts that went with them) to ensure the election of his illegimate son – a campaign accompanied by much drinking with the mayor and corporation and alleged bribery. With the support of the administration of the day Lord Granby's son was duly returned, but so too was Osbaldeston, beating his former local parliamentary colleague by a mere two votes before he died in 1770. Both Osbaldestons seem to have been devoid of ambition for high office and neither appear to have spoken in the house. The family was, however, regarded by the duke of Newcastle and the marquis of Rockingham, Yorkshire's most politically influential peer, as being good and faithful servants of the administration of the day.[21]

When William Osbaldeston intervened on Cook's behalf he appears to have been acting at the behest of Cook's first patron, Thomas Skottowe, the squire of Great Ayton and his father's employer with probably, too, some involvement by John Walker, the shipowner of Whitby, Cook's own erstwhile employer.[22] Thus, although Great Ayton and Whitby were not formally represented in parliament, leading citizens such as Skottowe and Walker could still take the view that parliament could respond to their interests through such informal ties with the parliamentarians in nearby towns. They also would have had the more doubtful consolation of being among the twenty thousand Yorkshire voters holding sufficient property to be entitled to vote for the two county representatives. Osbaldeston's early intervention on Cook's behalf was a telling example of the way in which the seeming chaos of the unreformed constitution could be made to work by those who knew how to find their way through its mazes. Like many rotten boroughs, Scarborough also served wider purposes by providing a safe seat for the administration of the day in an age when there was little party discipline. In particular, it helped to provide a voice in parliament for the navy and the interests of Cook's chief patron, the earl of Sandwich.

Prominent among Sandwich's clients was another of Cook's early patrons, Sir Hugh Palliser, MP for Scarborough from 1774 to 1779, a fellow Yorkshireman (though from the West Riding). Palliser was the person whose career intersected most with that of Cook. It was to him as commander of the *Eagle* that the letter from Osbaldeston about his subordinate, James Cook, was addressed in the midst of the Seven Years' War which may have assisted in Cook's elevation to the post of master in 1757. Thereafter Palliser continued to act as Cook's guiding star. In 1759 Palliser was serving in Canada under Admiral Saunders who was overseeing the siege of Quebec and it was possibly he who recommended Cook to the admiral as someone well qualified to undertake the critically important task of measuring the depths of the river St Lawrence at the point where the French army had pitched its camp.[23] Impressed by his work Admiral Saunders appointed Cook Surveyor of Newfoundland in 1763; and a year later Palliser became Governor of Newfoundland and, while there until 1768, he helped to bring Cook's talents to notice as 'a gentleman I have been long acquainted with'.[24]

Captain Hugh Palliser. Portrait engraved by E. Orme (after D. Orme) (in *European Magazine* (April 1796), facing p. 219)

By 1770 Palliser was Comptroller of the Navy, a post he held until 1775. He thus took an active part in the planning of Cook's second voyage (and, very likely, he also played a background role in promoting the first and third). His regard for Cook was proclaimed by his national appeal in 1785 for a monument to him. When this did not eventuate, he erected a shrine to Cook on his own estate at Vache Park at Chalfont St Giles, Buckinghamshire. The fact that the son of an impecunious army officer could die owning such an estate was an indication of the money to be made out of both war and politics, and the extent to which both could promote some degree of social mobility.

Palliser's work with the navy brought him within the orbit of Lord Sandwich's reforming energies, and it was Sandwich's influence which almost certainly played a part in Palliser's election as MP for Scarborough in 1774. As a port, Scarborough was inclined to vote with the government of the day and especially with the first lord of the admiralty, since the administration controlled many aspects of maritime affairs, including the bestowal of offices in the customs service.[25] Palliser was elected unopposed in 1774, being returned along with Lord Granby's son-in-law, who duly took up the seat when Granby's illegitimate son died in 1772 – like the Osbaldestons the Granbys believed in keeping politics in the family. Palliser used his seat to promote vigorously a parliamentary campaign in support of Sandwich's naval reforms.[26] Elevation to a position as one of the lord commissioners of the admiralty in 1775 under Sandwich followed, but this post brought with it the necessity to resign his seat and stand again – a requirement which was one of the few victories of the reforming party, being intended to ensure that MPs who held office would be answerable to their electorate as well as the administration to whom they owed their position. Though duly re-elected, he vacated the seat in 1779 since his recent involvement in the prosecution of the popular Admiral Keppel had made him very unpopular (indeed his sister's house at York had been attacked) – an indication that even a seat as pliable as Scarborough, retained a certain degree of independence. Palliser, however, continued to sit in parliament and to represent both Sandwich and the naval interest more generally as the member for Huntingdon – a seat well and truly in the pocket of the earl of Sandwich, whose Hinchingbrooke estate was nearby.[27]

Though Palliser moved on, the seat of Scarborough remained within the Sandwich connection, since he passed it on to another Sandwich client, Charles Phipp in 1780 – thanks in part to the influence that Palliser exerted on his behalf. The election went unopposed, but it appears to have prompted a petition to parliament for reform of Scarborough's electoral processes.[28] This was a move which reflected the more general calls for reform unleashed by Britain's poor showing in the War of American Independence, the movement for reform being particularly strong in relatively unrepresented Yorkshire, leading to the formation of the Yorkshire Association in 1779, the year before the Scarborough petition.

Charles Phipps, whose election had prompted this petition, was the brother of Lord Mulgrave whose seat, Mulgrave Castle, overlooked the sea about three miles from Whitby. The Mulgrave family naturally saw themselves as entitled to considerable influence in nearby Scarborough and, though Phipps lost his seat to an Osbaldeston in 1780, the Mulgraves continued to play an important role in Scarborough politics for the next fifty years.[29]

Constantine Phipps (from 1775 Lord Mulgrave) was another figure whose career touched that of Cook's at a number of important points. In the first place he was a close confidant of Joseph Banks. Banks and Phipps were Eton school friends and in 1766 travelled together to Newfoundland, missing overlapping with Cook at St John's by a few days. On his return that year Phipps was elected as MP for Lincoln City, with the active support of that prominent Lincolnshire landowner, Joseph Banks. As Banks' steward assured him: 'Your Interest was of vast service to Mr. Phipps, and without it he must inevitably have lost his Election'.[30] Banks helped to steer his old Eton friend more closely into the orbit of Sandwich. By 1775 he could report of Phipps to the first lord of the admiralty that 'I am sure he is well inclined to Government & particularly loud in his applauses of the present measures pursued in American affairs'.[31] Phipps' political reward followed: like Palliser, he became one of the lords of the admiralty, serving until 1782. In 1777 he was also elected to Sandwich's pocket seat of Huntingdon which he held until 1784 when he obligingly passed it on (no doubt at Sandwich's request) to the beleaguered Palliser, moving on himself to the seat of Newark-upon-Trent.

As someone close to both Banks and Sandwich, Constantine Phipps formed part of the backdrop of Cook's life. In 1775 Phipps, along with Banks, the botanist Daniel Solander and others, nominated Cook for membership of the Royal Society.[32] More significantly, Phipps' voyage in 1773 in the *Racehorse*, to seek a new route to India through the Arctic regions, formed part of the background to the Royal Society's agitation for a new expedition in search of the North-West Passage which led to Cook's third voyage. A more distant link with Cook was Phipps' hosting of a house party in July 1775 at Mulgrave Castle for Banks and his protégé, Mai, who came back with Furneaux from Cook's second voyage. Along with a repast prepared by Mai in Polynesian fashion with an earth oven, the visitors to Mulgrave Castle were also entertained by a visit to Cook's father, then aged eighty.[33]

As well as being a client of these clients of Sandwich, Cook's career depended very heavily on Sandwich himself, who, as Cook's first biographer wrote, was 'the great patron of our navigator and the principal power in his mighty under-takings'.[34] As first lord of the admiralty at the beginning of both Cook's second and third voyages Sandwich watched over the arrangements for both. Though a close friend of Banks, Sandwich was too solicitous for the wellbeing of the

John Montagu, Earl of Sandwich, Viscount Hinchingbrooke. 1774. Engraved by
Valentine Green after the painting by Johann Zoffany (Australian National Library,
pic – an 9900680)

navy to allow him virtually to take over the second voyage to suit the needs of his large scientific party: 'you suppose the ships', he admonished Banks, 'to have been wholly fitted out for your use, which I own I by no means apprehend to be the case'.[35] When Banks subsequently left in high dudgeon, it was Sandwich that obtained the prime minister's approval for appointing that prickly polymath Johann Reinhold Forster and his son George as naturalists on the voyage.[36] The return of the voyage brought more trouble with naturalists, as Sandwich incurred the wrath of the Forsters for not being permitted to publish the official account of the voyage, one of Sandwich's motives for doing so being to protect Cook's rights to this highly lucrative publication.[37] Sandwich's admiration for Cook's achievements on the second voyage was underlined by his overseeing his promotion to post-captain and appointment to a sinecure at the naval hospital at Greenwich. It was an appointment that prompted public criticism of Sandwich's well-developed skills as a political patron. For Cook's receipt of this lucrative post prompted comment on the way in which 'some men in power leap over all rules and institutions; and dispose of places according to the pulse of interest, and the complexion of the times'.[38]

Cook accepted command of the third voyage largely at Sandwich's instigation, and Sandwich's name and influence loomed large on that voyage as the choice of name for the Sandwich Islands indicates. Before he was out of Plymouth Sound in July 1776, Cook wrote to Sandwich to acknowledge 'the Very liberal allowance made to Mrs Cook during my absence'. Cook was also mindful in turn of looking after his own clients, asking his lordship for a position as a nurse at Greenwich Hospital for a widow of the late cook from the *Adventure*, his sister ship on the second voyage.[39] Arrival at the Cape of Good Hope in October prompted another letter to Sandwich, assuring him of the good health of Mai and of Cook's strong sense of the favours bestowed by Sandwich.[40] It was Sandwich who broke the news of Cook's death to Banks in January 1780, after word reached him via Siberia, and it fell to Sandwich (in consultation with Banks) to protect Cook's posthumous interests in the sale of the published account of his third voyage[41] – hence Mrs Cook's letter of 1783 thanking him for the 'kind assistance of your interest in securing to me and my family the profits of the publication of my dear husband's last and unfortunate voyage'.[42]

Cook's achievements were such that, as Mrs Cook was relieved to find, his patrons could still be invoked after his death. Along with Sandwich, his close friend Banks was another person on whom to call when the Cooks ran into trouble. Thus it was to him that Benjamin Rudd, a JP of the North Riding, applied in 1801 to seek help for Cook's sister, Margaret Fleck. It was a cameo example of the way in which the patronage chain could work, linking the lowest to the highest. In order to have some hope of access to the upper ranks of the establishment, Mrs Fleck, the wife of a penniless and aged fisherman, needed the help of a member of the political class in the form of Rudd, the owner of the manor of Marton-in-Cleveland. The common link between Mrs Fleck, Rudd and Banks was of course James Cook – indeed Rudd informed Banks that, since he owned the site of the cottage where Cook was born, 'I mean shortly to erect a small Pillar to record the fact, & the honour which this place claims'. Thanks to Rudd's advocacy, Banks forwarded on the then substantial sum of ten pounds to supplement the annuity of twenty pounds granted to the Flecks by Mrs Cook. But the main purpose in applying to Banks was for him to use his considerable connections to gain for Mrs Fleck's son (and Cook's nephew) either 'the place of Revenue officer stationed upon the Coast to prevent smuggling' or 'some office in the Navy'.[43] In a system based on patronage, that was how government posts were obtained, the steps in the patronage ladder emphasizing the hierarchical nature of society more generally.

But in the navy, particularly, patronage had also to be accompanied by demonstrable ability, a truly incompetent officer was too conspicuous even for a well-placed patron to save him.[44] One scandalous exception to this was the continued rise of the notorious John Williamson, who incurred opprobrium for not showing more initiative in coming to Cook's rescue when he was killed in Hawai'i. Despite this, he was promoted to post-captain in 1782 and, most surprisingly of all, was given command of a third-rate ship in 1796, before losing command the following year in disgrace after the Battle of Camperdown. According to his old adversary, Cook's lieutenant of marines, Molesworth Phillips, Williamson owed this command to his vigorous support of the radical politician, Charles James Fox. This in turn attracted the notice of another of Fox's enthusiastic supporters, the duchess of Devonshire who, happily for Williamson, was the sister of Lord Spencer, first lord of the Admiralty from 1794 to 1801. Spencer, so Phillips's story goes, attempted to resist but the 'Duchess in a flood of tears … exclaimed brother you do not love me' and Williamson obtained his ship.[45] It is an anecdote that underlines both the importance of choosing one's political allegiance carefully in the navy and the fact the women (or, at least, duchesses) could play some part in the politics, even though they were excluded from the electoral process.

Taking all these instances of patronage together in an ascending scale, from the widow of the *Adventure*'s cook and the Flecks up to Cook himself, and thence into the ranks of the leisured classes with Sandwich's clients, Palliser and Phipps, serves to underline the way in which British old regime society was held together by chains of connection and dependency which ultimately centred on the small inner circle of aristocratic families (182 in 1780).[46] This social dominance was matched by their control of the political process, both through their direct representation in the House of Lords and their indirect representation through clients and younger sons in the House of Commons. When Cook sailed into the Pacific, then, he departed from a society where the aristocracy set much of the tone and shaped the dominant values. After Cook's death one of the most obvious marks of public acclaim was George III granting his family a coat of arms – something that proclaimed that his achievements warranted a quasi-aristocratic status.[47]

The workings of this aristocratic system of patronage and deference help to explain why Cook and his men sought to understand the workings of Pacific societies largely through the lens of hierarchical ordering, which they were accustomed to think of as part of the natural order of things. Comparisons with aristocracy and monarchy loomed large in their Pacific journals, as did resort to analogies with feudalism, as Pacific societies were compared with earlier stages of Britain's aristocratic order. References to feudalism were a way of connecting the Pacific with Britain's past, though they also carried with them a clear implication that the Pacific was at a earlier stage of historical development than Britain – a point underlined by Joseph Banks' remark about Tahiti that 'the Subordination which takes place among them very much resembles the early state of the feudal laws by which our Ancestors were so long Governed'.[48]

For Cook, Tahitian government was 'of the feudal kind', though he saw that as giving it 'sufficient Stability', for it was 'by no means badly constituted'. To his mind an indication of the successful workings of the Tahitian body politic was the fact that the chiefs 'are more beloved by the bulk of the people than feared', which led him to conclude 'that the government is mild and equitable'.[49] With a broad brush, George Forster described Tahitian society as being 'distinguished into the classes of aree, manahoùna, and towtow, which bear some distant relation to those of the feudal systems of Europe'.[50] Cook adopted a similar tripartite division of Tahitian society, with 'first the *Eares* or Chiefs, second the *Manahoona's* or middling sort and lastly the *Toutou's* which comprehends all the lower class'.[51] The 'towtows' were, in Alexander Home's view, best compared with the lowest rank of feudal society, the villeins – a comparison that extended to the fact that both words have 'got a scandalous Idea'. Extending the feudal analogy further, he described the arrees or aristocrats as having vassals who were obliged to serve them on pain on losing their lands.[52]

Both Cook and Surgeon Anderson reached for comparisons with feudalism when describing the Friendly Islands. In Cook's view, 'a subordination is established among them that resembles the feudal system', while Anderson pursued the analogy further, arguing that, though 'all acknowledge the Sovereignty of the Prince', there were local rulers who, like England's barons of old, 'are in some respects wholly independent unless in the single circumstance of paying the homage due to the Lord of all'.[53] Needless to say, this too easy mapping of the ancient social system of England onto the Pacific produced considerable distortions – among them the too rigid a distinction in the description of Tahitian society between the general class of commoners or *manahune* (or *manahouna*) and the *teuteu* (or *towtows*), who were not like the lowly feudal 'villeins' but rather were hereditary retainers of the aristocratic *arii* (or *arees*).[54]

Along with the feudal past Cook and his men groped for analogies with Europe's present in order to attempt to make comprehensible the unfamiliar world of Pacific polities. The government of Tahiti reminded Midshipman Gilbert of the disunited state of Germany, where many petty princedoms went their own way despite a nominal allegiance to an emperor – the analogy extending to the fact that the Tahitian 'king' had 'no great degree of Authority having but little power of his own without the joint consent and assistance of the Chiefs'.[55] Lieutenant Burney drew a comparison between Tahiti and Poland, focusing on the great gulf between the aristocracy and the commoners, perhaps with an implied comparison with the much more finely graded social hierarchy of Britain. 'The Government here', he wrote of Tahiti, 'in one respect resembles that of the Poles – there are but 2 classes of people, the Arees or Independent Men & the Towtows or Servants – nor are the peasants of Poland more subject or dependent on their Nobility than the Towtows on their respective Arees or Masters'.[56] But Cook's men were also capable of using the Tahitian comparison to draw attention to some of the absurdities of their own country. Alluding to the king of England's ancient claim to be the rightful king of France – a claim going back to the Hundred Years' War and repeated, for example, in the long list of titles appended to the king's name in the preface to the King James Bible – the astronomer William Wales remarked of the nebulous claims of the Tahitian *aree*, Tu, to dominance of the whole island of Tahiti that he made this assertion 'as we do over France'.[57]

Used to centralized states, the British found it difficult to fathom the complexities of polities where more than one ruler held sway. Cook's instinctive question, 'Who is in charge?', did not always have a ready answer. Most confusing of all were the Friendly Islands, where the Englishmen's assumptions that status and power naturally went together were called into question.[58] Burney frankly admitted that 'Their Government and degrees of subordination were too difficult and intricate for us to unriddle'.[59] Having established whom he thought was king, Cook was surprised to find that he was in fact outranked by another. For in Tonga there were three main levels of authority: the sacred Tu'i Tonga of divine origin, who in turn passed on some of his religiously-derived power to a secular authority who then delegated power to the third level of ruler whose title derived from the support of his kin.[60] The fact that this last type of ruler owed his authority to another and was not fully hereditary, prompted Captain Clerke to muse that maybe the government of the Friendly Islands was not really 'Monarchical' since 'the King is elected by the voice and at the pleasure of his subjects'.[61] Moreover, in contrast to Britain, where status was transmitted down the male line, Tongan society had a matrilineal character so that women could outrank men in status if not actual authority. Indeed, the highest ranking woman was so beyond any Tongan in status that she had to marry out and take a Fijian as her consort – a practice that had its analogy in the way in which England's reigning queens either did not marry (as in the case of Elizabeth I) or married foreigners as in the case of Mary Tudor or Queen Anne.[62] Bemused, Cook noted that the late Tongan king 'had a sister of equal rank and elder than himself; she had by a Fidgee man a son and two Daughters, these three as also the Mother rank above Fattafee the King'.[63] Complex though it was, the Friendly Islands system of government meant that, uniquely within pre-contact Polynesia, the one dynasty could establish a fair measure of control and relative peace over a far-flung archipelago.[64]

The European voyagers tended to assume that territorial states were so much the natural order of things that Pacific societies would in due course arrive at such a form of government. When in New Zealand on the first voyage, Cook at first thought that the North Island Māoris were united under one chief but then concluded that 'they were very much divided into parties which make war one with another'. On the second voyage, Cook reflected that this lack of 'any settled form of government' would gradually change, bringing with it greater unity and, he thought, greater civilization. For, in Cook's mind, a larger state brought with it the possibility of greater civility, hence his speculation that, as the New Zealanders became more unified, the practice of cannibalism might die away for, as they became more conscious of belonging to a common polity, there would be a greater sense of 'treating other men as they themselves would wish to be treated'.[65]

Though their politics might differ so much, the European strangers and the Polynesians did share a common preoccupation with status and its forms. It is remarkable, for example, how readily Mai adapted to many of the social niceties in England when he visited there from 1774 to 1776, an adaptation that had much to do with his deeply ingrained Polynesian sense of rank and, with it, the need for the rituals of deference. In both Britain and Polynesia rank was expressed in outward and visible forms, and both sides groped to translate the other's code. When at Tahiti on the second voyage, Cook and his fellow captain, Tobias Furneaux, were invited on shore by the 'king', but on condition that they 'put on their best cloaths ... otherwise he would not see them'. This acknowledgement of both their own rank and that of the Tahitian ruler duly made, the visit proceeded with a ritual display of gifts.[66] Absence of clothes could also be important as in the attempt by one Tongan chief to apply the local practice of demanding that all that were admitted to his presence 'must be naked to the Waist' – including Captain Clerke and his fellow officers. They demurred, saying that they would do no more than they would do for their own king, which was to remove their hats.[67]

The importance of dress was again evident on arrival at Kaua'i on the third voyage – the first European landing on Hawai'i. When the local ruler came to visit the *Discovery*, he would at first only deal with the astronomer William Bayly since the latter was wearing a red jacket (the colour red being associated with divinity and hence chiefly power). When it was explained that it was not he, but Clerke, who was captain of the ship then the gift and ritual embrace was transferred to him. Bayly emphasized the high status of Hawaiian chiefs by writing of this ruler, that the Hawaiian 'people would not suffer any other person to come near him so great was their care & attention to him'.[68] Polynesian aristocrats also expected to mix with those of their own rank, as Cook's men found on Tahiti, where, as Alexander Home reported, the *aree* girls would not allow themselves to be touched by a European man until they had established that 'they think he is of the same rank with themselves'.[69]

Used to an aristocratic culture of conspicuous display, the European voyagers naturally looked for the markings of status. In Tahiti, Bayly noted, the 'king' 'by way of distinction is tattooed or marked all over his body'. The difference in rank was also underlined the fact that 'the King or Aree Always sits on a Stool, & his subjects on Mats round him'.[70] On Tonga, Cook realized by the third voyage that the 'large pieces of Cloth and fine Matting are only worn by the superior people, the inferior sort put up with small pieces'.[71] Lieutenant Burney also could perceive the ritual importance of clothing in the Friendly Islands, where 'Superiority of Birth, is held here in great estimation' and 'the greatest distinction in Dress, is the Hahoo or Cloth worn by people of Rank, being very neatly plaited'.[72] The voyagers brought back, too, examples of the minutely-carved fly whisks which were a symbol of Tahitian chiefly power, the very use of which had its elaborate conventions. The symbolic significance of a fly whisk could be heightened by the elaborate nature of its handle or by making it from another valuable object to increase its power.[73] The use of these objects, like so many aspects of Tongan society, from language to the chiefly monopoly on the kava ceremony, was intended to underscore status.[74]

On Hawai'i status was manifestly displayed in the spectacular feathered helmets and cloaks worn by the highest ranking chiefs. 'The Cloaks', wrote Surgeon Samwell, 'are made of fine Netting with red and yellow feathers curiously worked upon them ... A more rich or elegant Dress than this, perhaps the Arts of Europe have not yet been able to supply'. Mindful of codes of rank, Samwell pointed out, too, that colours betokened status so that 'Inferior Chiefs have Cloaks made of Cock's [dark] Tail feathers'.[75] Tellingly, the same type of red feathers were used both for these cloaks and the images of the Hawaiian gods, an indication of the godlike status with which the Hawaiian aristocracy was

Poulaho, King of the Friendly Islands, drinking Kava. Engraved by W. Sharp after John Webber (from J. Cook and J. King, *Voyage to the Pacific Ocean* ... (3 vols, London, 1784), i, plate 20)

invested.[76] Not surprisingly the Hawaiians, as Lieutenant King found, 'set a great value & were unwilling to part with them' – which makes the gifts made to Cook and Clerke of such objects an indication of the high status with which they were regarded by the Hawaiians.[77] Clerke was presented with a cloak when the ships first encountered the Hawaiian islands at Kaua'i, in January and February 1778, and with another at Maui when the ships returned in November of that year. In January 1779, on the big island of Hawai'i, Clerke was presented with another and King Kalanipou'u himself gave Cook one off his own back, along with a feather helmet and five or six additional cloaks – 'all very beautiful, & to them of the greatest Value' – were laid at Cook's feet.[78] After European contact the red colouring of the coats with its religious associations gave way to the even more valuable yellow feathers, emphasizing the growing concentration of political power – above all that accruing to Kamehameha, the only person to acquire a fabulously valuable all-yellow coat.[79] When the naturalist Andrew Bloxam visited Hawai'i on board HMS *Blonde* in 1825, he estimated that the price of five of the yellow feathers was about one shilling which, it was calculated, would mean such a cloak would cost the equivalent of two hundred thousand pounds and the work involved would take fifty years.[80] That such objects were the ultimate symbol of chiefly authority underlined the extent of chiefly power in Hawai'i for in no other part of Polynesia could so much labour be extracted from the commoners.[81]

Trading in such objects emphasized to Cook and his men that the extent of hierarchical deference could vary significantly even within the overall bounds of Polynesian culture. After the more relaxed usages in Tahiti, Cook and his men were struck by the degree of subservience expected in the Friendly Islands centred around Tonga. There, as George Forster put it, the islanders 'seem to behave with great submission to their men of rank, directly contrary to what we had observed at the Society Isles'.[82] Lieutenant Burney was particularly struck by what he called, using the language of the English elite, how on the Friendly Islands 'people of distinction' were obliged to acknowledge their 'patrons' with a ritual that dramatically underlined their subordination being required to bow the head so low 'that his hair touches the others foot, which he afterwards taps gently with his 2 or 3 times and then rises'.[83]

The extent of subordination was even more marked on Hawai'i. Midshipman Gilbert thought that, though the two societies had a similar form of government, on Hawai'i 'the people are kept under more Subjection than any we have seen'.[84] The first encounter with the Hawaiian islands – the landing on Kaua'i – led to astonishment at the adulation accorded to the high chief. Captain Clerke wrote that 'I never in my Life saw a Person paid such abject Homage to'. Rather gauchely, Clerke responded to his arrival by taking him by the hand and clapping him on the shoulder, but 'they gently took away my hand, and begged I would not touch him'.[85] But Cook, too, was regarded with considerable awe and when he landed there 'the Crowd, fell prostrate on their faces'.[86] Such courtesies were also extended to both Cook and Clerke when they were later on the big island of Hawai'i, an indication that there, too, the two captains were regarded as high-ranking chiefs. Clerke, however, was plainly embarrassed by it 'and by application to the Arees [chiefs] I got this troublesome ceremony taken off'.[87]

Not that the strongly aristocratic character of Polynesian society in general, and that of the Friendly Islands and Hawai'i in particular, was necessarily altogether repugnant to at least some of these voyagers from an aristocratic Europe. Cook rather admired the obedience and discipline that the rulers of the Friendly Islands could command, commenting that 'There is a decorum observed in the presence of their great men and particularly the Kings, that is truly admirable'.[88] Interestingly enough, the American marine corporal John Ledyard responded to Hawai'i by invoking a classic defence of aristocracy as ensuring that 'those in power are in no danger of corruption'. He thought, too, that 'their government possessed that energy which is ever the result of economical jurisprudence'.[89] Rather, the concern of the British voyagers was directed more at autocracy than aristocratic oligarchy – hardly surprisingly so since eighteenth-century Britons prided themselves on their largely aristocratic constitution as a bulwark against what they perceived as continental absolutism. Surgeon Samwell's criticism of the Friendly Islands was not that it was aristocratic but that the powers of a few chiefs were too great, being unhampered by law or other restraints. In his view the islands thus served to point the moral of 'how unfit a human being is to posses an u[n]limited Power over his fellow Creatures'.[90] Cook was more cautious and ambivalent about the politics of the Friendly Islands, acknowledging that there was evidence both for and against the character of government being despotic, but on balance there was 'more against than for a dispotic Government'.[91] Lieutenant King was still more enthusiastic, writing of the Friendly Islands that 'We see many things worthy of imitation; few of blame; would to God they could say the same of us'.[92]

The young George Forster – later a supporter of the early phase of the French Revolution – took a more critical stance, arguing that the Friendly Islands were an instance of the way in which despotism and the corruptions of luxury were linked. The extent of 'obedience and submission' strongly indicated that 'their government, though perhaps not perfectly despotic, is yet far from being democratical; and this kind of political constitution seems likely to facilitate the introduction of luxury'. By contrast, unlike Cook, George Forster admired the politically more fragmented state of New Zealand, where he speculated some of the leaders were possibly elected on the basis of military prowess, the Māoris having concluded 'that hereditary government has a natural tendency towards despotism'.[93] If Forster had been able to spend more time on Easter Island, it might have provided interesting material for reflection on the erosion of the power of the aristocracy as a privileged class, for there status as a warrior had largely undermined the political and religious dominance of the traditional *ariki*.[94] He did, however, comment that, though the island had a monarchy, any tendency towards luxury and hence corruption was checked by the island's barrenness.[95] On the basis of a report by Lieutenant Pickersgill, Cook concluded – for he was severely ill when the *Resolution* visited Easter Island on the second voyage – 'that the Island is under the government of one Man whom they stile Arreeke, that is King or Chief'.[96]

Though they came to appreciate the extent of variation in the patterns of aristocratic power, Cook and his men frequently remarked on the limited opportunities that appeared to exist in the Pacific for individuals to advance beyond the station into which they had been born. It was a natural preoccupation for one such as Cook, who had made the difficult ascent from farmboy to captain. Many others on his ships, too, cherished the ambition that the navy, in which talent was both required and, at least on occasions, rewarded, might provide an avenue for social advancement. Hence they dwelt on the fact that, as Alexander Home put it in his description of Tahiti: 'These people Lays much Stress upon Birth ... they seem Quite blind to Merit in a mean man'. To Home the social divide was underlined by the fact that 'A Towtow [commoner] could not marry the daughter of an Eri [aristocrat]'. The gulf he saw as being made more unbridgeable by the fact that, in contrast to Europe, there were not the middling orders 'that gets their Sustinance Either by Merchantdize Navigation or Mechanically'.[97] On the other hand, as George Forster observed, this meant that at least in Tahiti all commoners were on much the same footing and that there was not 'that disparity between the highest and meanest man, which subsists in England between a reputable tradesman and a labourer'.[98]

This picture of a firmly entrenched elite did not take sufficient account of the way in which Polynesian hierarchies could be reshaped, especially by war. There were also cases of those whose talents as priest or politician, as well as warrior, could raise them beyond their station of birth. Like all aristocratic orders, those of Polynesia had a built-in dynamic, as theory had to be made to conform to an ever-changing social reality.[99] The case of Mai, whose trip to Britain had lifted him out of the normal social categories, provided some insight into the way in which the Polynesian as well as the British aristocracy could widen its ranks when it saw advantages in so doing. Alexander Home records that Tu, the high-ranking chief of Tahiti, had (with Cook's encouragement) offered Mai the hand of his youngest sister in marriage. Tu's motives were clear: as Home put it 'Omiah was rich [in European goods] and Ottou was mercenary & greedy'. Mai refused, however, since he did not want to stay on Tahiti and could marry a well-born bride on his own island. According to the astronomer Bayly, Mai's refusal to remain on Tahiti as an *aree* was also prompted by the chief's declining to send away all Mai's enemies from the island of Bora Bora.[100] Needless to say, Mai's refusal caused considerable offence and meant that he had no future on the island of Tahiti. In language that underlined the natural analogy between European and Polynesian concepts of hierarchy, Home wrote that 'His refusing the Sister of Ottou was as Impolitic as for a plowman with us to Refuse the Sister of a Duke or a private gentleman one of the Ladies of the Royal Family'.[101] Interestingly, Mai had previously also been offered aristocratic status in the Friendly Islands, though, as Lieutenant Burney wrote, 'had he been suffered to have accepted that Station, his continuance in it, after the departure of the Ships, would have been very precarious'.[102] It was an astute remark that underlines the extent to which attempts to draw Mai into the Polynesian elite were linked to his association with Cook – once Cook sailed away, Omai's new found status would probably dwindle (as it appears to have done when finally Cook left him on Huahine).

Cook and his fellow voyagers encountered the Pacific at a time when Europe itself was greatly preoccupied with the problems of government. Britain had long basked in the glory of its constitution and the greater liberty it permitted when compared to the absolutism of France and other continental states – obligingly, such self-congratulation had been echoed by such major figures of the French Enlightenment as Voltaire and Montesquieu. Such complacency had, however, begun to be questioned. The accession in 1760 of George III – the first English-born Hanoverian monarch – and his attempt to free himself from the 'dirty arts' of the politicians, who, in his view, had rendered his forebears 'kings in chains', helped prompt moves for greater controls on the powers of the king and his ministers. These acted as a catalyst for the movement led by John Wilkes with which Cook, like all Londoners, would have been very familiar. For in 1768, a few months before the *Endeavour* sailed, Wilkes was tumultuously elected as a member for the county of Middlesex (though Cook was in the South Seas when, in the following year, Wilkes was expelled from the House of Commons and then vainly re-elected three times not being allowed to take up this seat until 1774). Among the most vigorous supporters of Wilkes were the Thames coal-heavers with whom Cook had so much to do in his early days on Whitby colliers. The coal-heavers' demands for better conditions led to their attempting to stop unloading coal and an ensuing clash in 1768 with the sailors, who continued to do so – there were a few fatalities, among them one of the crew of Cook's old ship, the *Freelove*.[103]

London was the focus of the Wilkite movement, which led to the formation of the Society of the Supporters of the Bill of Rights in 1769, the first of a series of important reform organizations. Cook's county of Yorkshire was to be the major centre for the next phase of the reform movement. This was initiated by the formation of the Yorkshire Association in 1779, dedicated to increasing the county's parliamentary representation and the first of a number of such county-based reform organizations. The main stimulus for the revival of the reform movement was the disastrous war with America which broke out in 1775, the year Cook returned from his second voyage. Further in the future lay the great seismic shock of the French Revolution, though some of the irritants that led to it – such as an hostility to entrenched aristocratic privilege and a degree of anticlericalism – could be found in the journal of the young George Forster, a future leader of the revolutionary government in the German prince-bishopric of Mainz.

Faced by such uncertainties the Pacific provided a distant mirror for Cook and his men to consider their own society and its mode of government. Most, including Cook himself, were too politically conservative or indifferent to turn to the Pacific to provide ammunition to use against their own society – a practice much more likely to be adopted by the rather more alienated French and, to a lesser degree, by Germans such as the Forsters. The encounter with the new world of the Pacific did, however, lead them to ruminate on some familiar themes which formed part of the staple of British political debate: the evils of despotism, the need for checks on centralized power, the corrupting effects of luxury and the importance of the rule of law. Few questioned a system where the aristocracy enjoyed as much power as in Britain, nor was there much hostility to the hierarchical character of Polynesian society, except when the voyagers considered that commoners were treated in an arbitrary manner.

Though the demands of ever larger and more complex European states were placing increasing restraints on the extent to which political life could be governed by kinship obligations, the principle of society being organized around the ties of blood was still familiar enough not to strike the Europeans as overly strange. There was some comment, however, about the extent to which they considered that in much of Polynesia birth rather than merit determined one's lifelong social position – comments which reflected the aspirations of these Britishers hoping to advance their position in their own society. Their brief encounters with the Pacific societies meant that the voyagers tended to view them in static terms. Lengthier acquaintance over a longer period might have done more to indicate that, like all aristocracies, those of the Pacific survived by regularly recruiting new members.

On the whole, the voyagers approached these new societies with a reasonably open mind and with little compulsion to remold them into their own image and likeness. A more intrusive phase of European expansion was, however, soon to arrive. Cook's ships provided the maps and cultural and scientific cargo for a much more thorough-going European penetration of the Pacific. With it came the export of that distinctive European institution, the state, which was transported to the Pacific by various means. In the first place there was the full-blown construction of replicas of the British state from the ground up, as in areas such as Australia or New Zealand, where large European populations arrived with the makings of the state in their physical or mental baggage. There was also the absorption of Pacific islands into the larger state structures of European power, such as in the French Pacific dependencies of New Caledonia or Wallis and Futuna. Another path to statehood was the aggregation of a number of islands into a single state by a indigenous leader, using Western armaments and organization, as happened in Tahiti and Hawai'i, though these island kingdoms were to be absorbed into the states of France and the United States (an outcome which, uniquely, the kingdom of Tonga avoided).

However unintentionally, Cook and his ships were the vanguard of a global movement which was to leave no corner of the earth unconnected with another. The framework in which this global reach was to be realized was through a collection of supposedly independent and sovereign states,[104] a system that Europe itself had evolved as the great medieval international entities of pope and emperor lost their power in the aftermath of the Reformation. But globalization also brought with it the need for such states to become increasingly interdependent, and so in our own time the sovereign state has lost much of its lustre – hence the increasing tendency of states to band together in large-scale trading blocks such as the European Community, which has begun to take on the character of superstate with its own bureaucracy and, possibly, armed forces. A loyal servant of the British crown, Cook encountered the Pacific with the aim of advancing British interests over those of his country's traditional adversaries, notably France and Spain. Though his voyages helped to spread such rivalries over more of the earth's surface, they also served to emphasize the unity and interconnectedness of the globe – a reality that worked gradually to erode the pretensions of individual states to an autonomy which Cook's maps of the globe made less and less plausible.

6

Religion

The practice of politics and that of religion sprang from a common impulse. Both dealt with the forces and powers that controlled human life and gave it structure and meaning. In most times and places the basis of political power was closely intertwined with the religious beliefs that gave a particular community its identity and which shaped its culture. The kings of Britain were sealed with the sacred oils at their coronation which betokened 'the divinity that doth hedge about a king'; the emperors of the Chinese middle kingdom appealed to the 'mandate of heaven' to justify their rule. Polynesian chiefs, in contrast, appealed to the transmission of *mana* – the vital force that moved all things from the sun and the stars to human actions, through a genealogical line that ultimately connected a society's leaders with the gods.

In Cook's Britain, however, this deeply-rooted assumption that political power was ultimately of divine origin had begun to falter. Religion and genealogy were the two deepest and most instinctive bases of political power, but in eighteenth-century Britain both had lost some of their force. God still played a major role in political discourse – after all 'God Save the King' was composed in 1744 – but increasingly there were other ways of understanding the origin of political power which did not rely quite so directly on the divine. The divine right of kings could be countered by the view that kings were parties to a contract which required them to provide good government and observance of the laws – such was the thrust of the Lockean justification for the overthrow of the Catholic James II in 1688 and the rebellion by the American colonists against George III in 1776.

In the post-Reformation world God and politics became harder to keep in harmony, as religion itself began to change. The great schism in Christendom meant that religion – long regarded as the cement that bound society together (the word deriving form the Latin '*res*' = 'thing' and '*ligo*' = 'to bind') – had lost much of its force as a source of social, cultural and political unity. Instead of a culturally binding common set of rituals and beliefs, there gradually emerged diverse denominations with diverse beliefs and practices. True, those churches that split with Rome generally attempted to retain the same all-encompassing role for religion which had been characteristic of the middle ages. When he broke with Rome, Henry VIII used this as an occasion to proclaim the extent of royal power and the degree to which the king was linked to the divine: 'this Realm of England is an Empire ... governed by one supreme Head and King ... unto to whom a Body politick ... divided in Terms, and by Names of Spirituality and Temporality, been bounden and owen to bear, next to God, a natural and humble Obedience'.[1] With the abandonment of the principle of a single united Christendom, however, and the increasing appeal to the private interpretation of Scriptures, the attempt to maintain a single established church which would embrace the nation as a whole slowly began to erode.

Cook himself was brought up in a world where the outward forms of an established church still had considerable meaning. The school he attended at Great Ayton, for example, came under the supervision of the archbishop of York and was obliged to provide religious instruction 'in the Principles of ye Christian religion according to ye doctrines of ye Church of England'; the schoolmaster was also required to ensure that his young charges were 'duly brought to church'.[2] How much impact this early instruction had on the young Cook is difficult to gauge. As the law required, he was married in an Anglican church and baptized his children therein, but otherwise there is nothing to connect the adult Cook with the Church of England. Cook's lack of any real affiliation with the Church of England, like that of so many others, was undermining the assumption on which all established churches were based: that they commanded the religious allegiance of the nation.

In any case, the theory that all royal subjects should belong to the royal church existed in uneasy combination with the reality that many of the king's loyal subjects gave their religious loyalties to churches other than the Church of England. In the first place there still remained a sprinkling of adherents of the 'old (Catholic) religion' who had never accepted the changes of the Reformation. Quite a number of these could be found in the more remote villages of Yorkshire (particularly inland), where the hand of the state-church had never fully reached out to extirpate traditional practice, and the shore near the Whitby district offered many sheltered coastal sites for Catholic missionaries to land.[3] The continuing Catholicism of some Yorkshire gentry families also provided such old believers some protection.

Along with these residues of pre-Reformation belief there were also more recent denominations who had taken such Reformation principles as judgement by Scripture alone and the priesthood of all believers in directions that led to a breach with the established church. Presbyterians and Congregationalists rejected the power of bishops and the forms of church government and liturgical practice associated with them. More radically, Baptists overturned the principle of an established church by rejecting infant baptism, and with it the notion that one was born into a church, in favour of adult baptism and the implied element of religious choice that the ritual underlined.

Most radical of all were the Quakers, the nonconformist denomination with whom Cook had most to do. The origins of the Society of the Friends (to give the Quakers their full and rightful name) lay in the high religious and political enthusiasm of the Civil War period, when events such as the execution of the archbishop of Canterbury in 1645 and the king in 1649 prompted speculation about the end of the world and the coming of the kingdom of Christ. In the face of such upheavals, the Quakers sought divine judgement not in the passing forms of institutions but through the guidance of the inner spirit – hence their rejection of religious rituals and any form of priesthood. More radically still, the Quakers moved beyond the Protestant belief in the primacy of Scripture: while Bible-reading was still important to them as a source of inspiration, it was the inner light, the response of the individual to the Spirit, which came before all.[4]

With the restoration of the monarchy and the established church in 1660 the Quakers had to come to terms with the indefinite postponement of the millennium and the persistence of a kingdom that was manifestly of this world. Gradually, the sect lost some of its radicalism, but in important symbolic ways it maintained its separation from the fallen world around it. Quakers wore antiquated clothes, the simplicity of which implied a rejection of the vanity of others. Quakers married among themselves, or at least they were meant to, as there was a steady stream of Quakers who were lost to the faith since they were expelled after marrying out. And Quaker belief brought with it confrontation with the established order in church and state. True to scriptural injunctions about avoiding oaths and not taking the Lord's name in vain, Quakers refused to take oaths which were an integral part of the system of law. Quakers were pacifists and thus refused to pay taxes for the support of the armed forces. Over time various compromises were arrived at which permitted Quakers to play an active part in British society (and to do remarkably well in business). It remained the case, however, that to be a true Quaker meant to belong to a community within a community, a separate world with its practices and traditions which were a constant reminder to the world at large that Quakers were different – thereby providing a standing challenge to the theory that all belonged to the established church.

For Cook, Quakers would have formed part of his mental universe since childhood. At Great Ayton there was a Quaker buried as early as 1699 and by 1743 there were four Quaker families – no great number, but out of a population of one hundred and forty families, they, along with three Presbyterian families, were a standing reminder of the limits of the established church's hold over the population as a whole. The Great Ayton Quakers also had their own meeting house, in which they conducted regular services though, true to their principles, these were held by travelling laymen rather than by clergy.[5] No doubt it complied with the familiar Quaker pattern of having no pulpit or equivalent, to emphasize the authority of the preacher but rather simply a long bench at the front on which the elders sat in full view of the congregation.[6]

By 1793 their numbers had risen to sixty-two[7] and in the previous decade there were enough Great Ayton Quakers to support regular meetings of their womenfolk, who formed part of the larger Quaker female networks stretching to York and thence to London (an indication of the important role that women played in Quaker life). Their communications give a sense of the character of Quaker life and its preoccupation with the next world, with admonitions to avoid 'the momentary trifling Gratifications of this very uncertain State of Being' and the disapproval of such frivolous activities as 'all vain Sports … frequenting of Fairs, and reading unprofitable Books'. The extent of both separation from and opposition to the established church is underlined by the injunction to stand firm against 'tyths of all sorts and Steeplehouse [church] taxes', together with the strong sense of their historical destiny as virtually a chosen people who had left the blandishments of ritual religion behind, for 'it pleased divine Wisdom … [to] gather us as a People' and to bring 'our worthy Predecessors out of the many dead Forms of Worship'. One of the women Quakers in nearby Guisborough betrayed this heritage by being 'married by a priest' and it was thus concluded that 'we cannot have Unity, with Her'.

Though so strongly opposed to the religious establishment, the Quakers were loyal subjects of the king and indeed more punctilious about observing the law than most, particularly when it came to paying excise dues – hence the proceedings require scrutiny of whether Friends are 'just in their dealings and punctual in fulfilling their engagements and do they stand clear in our Testimony against defrauding the King of his Duties'.[8] Such injunctions help to explain why the Quakers acquired a reputation for probity in business which made them both well respected and frequently very successful in this world.

When Cook moved to Staithes he would have encountered Quakers again, their origins going back to the visit of the Quakers' founder, George Fox, to that village as early as 1651.[9] Subsequently, Fox visited Whitby and there his converts gathered and 'silently waited for the motions of the spirit, and being seized with certain tremors or shakings, they gained from thence the appellation of Quakers'.[10] By the time Cook arrived in Whitby in 1746 the number of Quakers was probably not far short of the three hundred which we know they had reached by 1778.[11] As a member of John Walker's Quaker household for nine years – three as an apprentice and six of more intermittent lodging between trips – Cook in effect received a partial Quaker upbringing.

Residues of this probably help to explain why, when Cook wrote to Walker, he was inclined to use religious language. When, after the *Endeavour* voyage, he told Walker of the Tahitians he invoked the language of Genesis and the Fall since 'These people may be said to be exempted from the curse of our fore fathers, scarce can it be said that they earn thier bread with the sweat of thier brows'. The Australian Aborigines also lived in an Edenic state since, like Adam and Eve, they did not know that they were naked: 'it is said of our first Parents that after they had eat of the forbidden fruit they saw themselves naked and were ashamed; these people are Naked and are not ashamed'.[12] Events, in Cook's rendition of his adventures to Walker, were the outcome of the will of Providence, the inscrutable wishes of which led to the delays and deaths that occurred when the *Endeavour* was under repair in Batavia but which nonetheless, as Cook told Walker when setting off from Cape Town on his second voyage, 'has been very kind to me on many occasions, and I trust in the continuation of the divine protection'.[13]

Otherwise Cook was very sparing indeed in his invocation of Providence, which is not necessarily an indication of disbelief for it is hard to believe that Cook would have used language which he regarded as false simply to please Walker. At whatever level of active belief, Providence did continue to form part of Cook's mental furniture so that on the third voyage, having very nearly come to grief off the coast of Unalaska in June 1778, he wrote that 'and yet Providence had conducted us through between these rocks where I should not have ventured in a clear day'.[14]

How far Cook was won over to the faith of the Society of the Friends we will never know fully, but it is possible that he retained such Quaker characteristics as a liking for simplicity and an aversion to ritual forms of religion. The claim by the German Heinrich Zimmerman, a sailor on the third voyage – that Cook 'never spoke of religion, would tolerate no priest on his ship, seldom observed the Sabbath, but otherwise was a just man in all his dealings'[15] – could reflect a Quaker background both in an aversion to 'priestcraft' and in an emphasis on ethical behaviour.

In any case there was a good deal of anticlericalism in eighteenth-century society which did not necessarily equate with unbelief. Cook's travelling companion on the *Endeavour* and subsequent patron, Joseph Banks, was known for his hostility to the privileges of the clergy but nonetheless is reliably attested to have professed privately that 'he firmly believed that there was a God'.[16] Cook seems to have shared with Cook an Enlightenment-tinctured skepticism about some of the doctrines of Christianity. In his brief 1789 life of Cook the Götttingen polymath, Georg Lichtenberg, remarked on Cook's lack of religious orthodoxy – no doubt on the basis of information from his close friend George Forster who had travelled with Cook on his second voyage. Lichtenberg attributed such infidelity to Cook's meagre education and the reading of too many modish books. He also remarked on Cook's lack of superstition – an unusual trait in sailors who would grasp at any straw to ward off the perils of the deep.[17]

While it is quite possible that Cook admired the Quakers and shared some of their liking for simplicity in all areas of life, including religion, his decision to enter the Royal Navy dramatically indicated that he had no aspiration fully to enter the distinct community that eighteenth-century Quakers were.[18] Pacifism was central to being a Quaker and even using guns to protect one's ships was cause for expulsion. This was an issue that Cook would have known well, for it rumbled on among the Whitby Quakers throughout the eighteenth century: in 1706 Quakers doing so were urged 'in love and tenderness' to desist, but by 1783 John Walker was among the thirteen Whitby Quaker shipowners disowned by their fellow religionaries for possessing vessels equipped with cannon.[19]

Though Cook may not have been a card-carrying Quaker, his association with Walker and the close-knit world of the Whitby Quakers helped to provide him with a social network which was to have important consequences – and which very likely included his choice of wife. One of the reasons that Quakers did so well in business was that their co-religionaries provided a nation-wide set of potential business partners whom they could trust. When Walker sent coal off to London he naturally did business with Quaker London coalfactors.[20] Among these was one James Sheppard with whom Elizabeth Batts, the future Mrs Cook, lived after the death of her father in 1742. It was probably through this connection that Cook met his future bride.[21] The young couple, however, married in the Anglican church of St Margaret's, Barking – an outward and visible sign that they were not members of the Quakers.

Cook was connected to Quakers not only by the coal trade but also by the scientific possibilities of his voyages. Quakers, with their belief that the Creator could be better known through the study of the Creation, were particularly active in the study of natural history. Quaker naturalists like the prominent London physician, John Fothergill, were thus very interested in the plans for the *Endeavour* voyage and eagerly sought information from their fellow naturalists, Solander and Banks, whose chief botanical draughtsman, Sydney Parkinson, was a Quaker. Before Cook set off from Plymouth he, Banks and Solander were entertained by the appropriately named William Cookworthy, a local Quaker businessman with strong scientific interests. Solander remembered the occasion fondly, asking word to be passed on to Fothergill that they had met his friend, Cookworthy, and found him 'as worthy a man as can be, full of knowledge and very communicative'.[22]

The Quakers and other such nonconforming sects were a standing contradiction to the theory that, as Edmund Burke, put it: 'the Church and the State' were 'one and the same thing, being different integral parts of the same whole'.[23] Faced by such a challenge, one option for the established order in church and state was to attempt to impose conformity through persecution. There was some movement in this direction in the period of reaction that followed the restoration of church and king in 1660. The Quaker founder, George Fox, for example, was imprisoned in Scarborough Castle from 1665 to 1666.[24] In the Restoration period suspicion continued to linger that nonconformist sects such as the Quakers might seek to overthrow the restored order – thus the collector of customs at the small Yorkshire port of Bridlington wrote to the Secretary of State in 1675 that 'The Quakers and Nonconformists meet constantly in great numbers, and it is feared their meeting tends more to faction and rebellion than real zeal of religion, godliness and obedience'. The result of such suspicions was that at least twenty-four Bridlington Quakers were fined for attending meetings from December 1682 to February 1683, and, since they refused to pay the fines, their goods were 'destrained by the parish constable'.[25] Much more draconian were the punishments that could be, and occasionally were, visited on the Catholics and especially on their priests. Whipped up by fear of French Catholic power, and the Catholic sympathies of the ruling Stuarts, the fraudulent claims that there was a Popish Plot led to the eighty-two-year-old priest, Nicholas Postgate, being hanged, drawn and quartered at York as a traitor in 1678 after having ministered to the Catholics in the Whitby area for some forty years.[26]

The Glorious Revolution of 1688 and the fall of James II brought in its wake the Toleration Act of 1689 which allowed nonconforming Protestant religions to practise their diverse faiths, though non-Anglicans were excluded from full political rights. Catholics continued to remain in a legal limbo with a fair degree of *de facto* toleration but an uneasy awareness that this had no firm legal footing and persecution might break out if the climate changed again. One instance of this was, that after the failure of the Jacobite uprising of 1745 led by the Catholic Stuart claimant, Bonny Prince Charlie, there were anti-Catholic riots in Stokesley and the Catholic mass house there was destroyed. The magistrate who tried the case was Thomas Skottowe, Cook's father's employer in nearby Great Ayton, who, as a four-square Protestant, showed very little sympathy for the Catholic victims. He 'laughingly' dismissed the charges against the rioters and told the Catholics to pay for the damages themselves.[27]

While Catholics remained outside the political nation, Protestant nonconformists often found ways of getting around laws intended to bolster an Anglican monopoly of political power. But, on occasions, dissenters were reminded of their second-class status. In 1705 the Quakers of Scarborough were not allowed to become freemen (and hence to have the vote) unless they took the customary oath, which Quakers were not permitted to do, while Quaker pacifism led to prosecution of eight Scarborough Friends in 1797 for not paying the militia rate. In 1732 one Scarborough Quaker displayed his contempt for religious festivals by keeping his shop open at Christmas and, in consequence, was prosecuted.[28] Fears that the established church would be weakened, and with it the larger constituted order, also prompted petty persecution of the newly emerging domination of Methodism which became a church within the established church (even though there was not a formal break until 1795). The very fact that the denomination's founder, John Wesley, preached in the open air rather than in church was an affront to Anglican sensibilities. When he did so at Whitby the parish church responded by vainly attempting to silence him by loudly ringing its bells.[29] The bar on dissenters becoming full members of the political nation was not removed until 1828 – hence prominent nonconformists tended to concentrate on business like the shipowning Quakers of Whitby (among them Cook's master, John Walker) or the banking Quakers of Darlington, who, led by Joseph Pease, in 1828 began the development of Middlesbrough

Long before the repeal of the acts limiting the political rights of Protestant Nonconformists in 1828 and the Catholic Emancipation of 1829 – acts which finally acknowledged that, whatever the theory might be, full membership of the state did not depend on being a member of the state church and state. The attempt to impose religious uniformity had been abandoned and the need to accept religious pluralism meant accepting, too, that religion had increasingly retreated from the public, political sphere into that of the private conscience.[30] There was the awkward fact, too, that after the Act of Union of 1707 Britain had two established churches, those of England and Scotland, with different liturgies and theologies. Though the eighteenth century retained the theory of an established church, Britain had became a patchwork of different denominations with their different beliefs and rituals – all of which made resting political power on religious belief increasingly difficult. Gradually, from the Reformation onwards, England moved away from a religious culture held together by common rituals to a much more individualized society where religion remained extremely important but more as a source of private belief.[31]

Yet, wherever one looked, there were reminders of the fact that England had been a society which had been once shaped by a religious culture. There were in the first place the continuing and still important vestiges of the belief that all belonged to the established church. These still had some force in that central institution of the state, the Royal Navy. The first of the articles of war stipulated that naval ships were obliged to hold 'publick Worship of Almighty God, according to the Liturgy of the Church of England established by Law'.[32] Though Cook makes little mention of it, he does appear to have observed this requirement, but it is probably significant that he had others take the services – on the *Endeavour*, for example, Surgeon Monkhouse did so.[33] In doing so he was ignoring the admonition of Lord Morton, the President of the Royal Society, for the 'Captain himself … [to] read prayers, especially on sundays to the Crew', to remind them of 'their continual dependence upon their *Maker*'.[34] The second of the articles of war also dealt with religion and the obligation of all officers to stamp out blasphemous language along with 'drunkenness, uncleanness, or other scandalous action in derogation of God's honour'. The wording reflects something of the ancient belief that the realm as a whole, or in this case the microcosm of a ship, would suffer for the sins of the few if they were not checked. Cook, who was given to rages, does not, however, seem to have been too punctilious himself on the avoidance of 'profane oaths, cursings [and] execrations'.[35]

There was, too, the hold of tradition which meant that the medieval religiously-based calendar still served as a way of organizing time (including, as we have seen, the time of fairs) – hence such folk wisdom as:

> Cut your Thistles before St John
> You will have two instead of one.[36]

In the agricultural year the medieval festivals such as Plough Monday still persisted, despite the Reformers' attempts to stamp them out.[37] Saints' days such as Ladyday (a Marian feast), Michaelmas and Candlemas, not to mention the great feasts of Christmas and Easter, continued to mark the passage of the seasons. In Cook's time Plough Monday, the first Monday after Epiphany, the twelfth day of Christmas, was still marked in Great Ayton by an ancient custom where young men took the place of oxen in drawing the plough, being accompanied by sword dancers and musicians. Thus the village marked the end of Christmas festivities and the return to toil. Great Ayton's parish church was dedicated to All Saints (or Hallows) and something survived of the old customs intended to mark Hallowen (All Hallows' Eve), when the evil spirits subdued by the saints had once been thought to be at large.[38] The continuing importance of the feast days as ways of marking the calendar is reflected in Cook's habit of naming some parts of the globe after the religious feast of the day he encountered them: hence Christmas Harbour (Kerguelen Island, South Indian Ocean), Christmas Island (Pacific Ocean) and Christmas Sound (South America), along with Whitsunday Cape (South Alaska), Whitsunday Islands (Queensland) and Whitsunday Island (Vanuatu) – Whitsunday being a traditional English name for Pentecost.

Most tangibly, the forms of medieval religion had left their mark in Britain's churches, most of which were of medieval origin. True, there had been renovations to turn these buildings, which had been designed for the ritual of the mass, into spaces which better reflected a Protestant religion of the Word. When Cook was baptized at St Cuthbert's Church at Marton-in-Cleveland in 1728, it, like so many eighteenth-century churches, had been whitewashed – emphasizing the simplicity of the Protestant religion and its distance from the medieval past thus hidden from view.[39] At Great Ayton the parish church had long lost such fifteenth-century splendours as a brightly-painted rood screen surmounted by a multi-coloured representation of the crucified Christ with the Virgin and St John on either side which naturally drew the eye towards the altar. By Cook's time such popish pomps had been replaced with a church where the focus was on the great three-decker pulpit (with its clerk's desk, reading desk and preaching platform complete with sounding board).[40]

While the parish churches still formed part of the fabric of everyday life in Cook's time, the 'bare, ruined choirs' of the monasteries for which Yorkshire was famous formed a more compelling reminder of the lost world of medieval religion. There was, above all, the ruined Benedictine monastery of St Hilda's, which overshadowed Whitby and acted as a beacon for its sailors (which is probably why its stones had not been carried away as at so many other monastic sites).[41] Cook would almost certainly have seen the ruins of the once wealthy Augustinian Priory at Guisborough, and would have at least have known of other great sites in Yorkshire such as the Cistercian monasteries at Rievaulx, Byland and Fountains, or the ruins of Mount Grace Priory near Osmotherley, one of the nine Carthusian houses in England. All of these were relics of the great monastic presence in Yorkshire, a county which once had some seventy monasteries, since its relatively unpopulated spaces had attracted the foundation of monasteries – foundations which began the long-flourishing wool trade which was later to make parts of Yorkshire early centres of the Industrial Revolution.[42] The fact, however, that these great buildings were in ruins was a forceful reminder that the Reformation had defied the claims of such monasteries to be a link between the natural and the supernatural. In other ways, too, the Reformation had forcefully attacked many of the sources of the divine protection which had been basic to medieval society. Sacred objects to which pilgrims had flocked, such as the Glastonbury thorn with its reputed connections with Christ though Joseph of Arimathea or the great images of the Virgin at Walsingham, were destroyed without apparent divine retaliation.[43]

To use terms that Cook came to know in his voyages through Polynesia, medieval religious *tapus* which existed to protect the *mana*, the spiritual forces which animated all things and which could both help and harm, had been successfully defied. Thus one strongly Protestant reformer showed his contempt for the *tapus* of the medieval church by using two former holy water stoups as kitchen utensils, while other altar stones ended up as paving stones.[44] One of the reasons for the success of the Reformation was the perception that such desecrations showed that the medieval church had lost its spiritual power and that other forms of protection had to be sought. This stripping of the medieval altars was to have its Pacific parallel in the way in which ancient *tapus* on practices such as men and women eating together were broken on board Cook's ships and those of other explorers. Faced by the fact that the strangers had flouted these and other *tapus*, without apparent divine punishment, the framework of rituals around which society had been structured gradually crumbled. Like the destruction of the medieval monasteries or the pilgrimage shrines, there were also watershed moments such as the celebrated banquet held by Kamehameha II of Hawai'i when he succeeded his father in 1819, in which the old order was spectacularly broken by violating the *tapu* against his eating with his female

Southwest View of the Ruins of the Whitby Abbey (Frontispiece, J. Atkinson, *Memorials of Old Whitby* (London, 1894) State Library of New South Wales, N914.2748/1)

relatives – an event followed by the systematic destruction of the images of the ancient gods.

In both Pacific and medieval religion divine power had been manifest in material objects and in ritual practices, but in Protestant England any such hint of idolatry was generally frowned upon. To the dismay of the more Puritan-inclined, the established church maintained some residues of medieval sacramental rituals, though these fell to a low ebb in the eighteenth century. At Great Ayton, for example, it was recorded in the visitation of 1743 that 'The Sacrement [Holy Communion] is administered five times every year'.[45] Faced by the manifold misfortunes of life, and particularly agricultural life, the English populace appears to have found this austere separation of the natural and supernatural overly demanding and continued to seek for ways of finding protection against malign spiritual forces. Some Yorkshire farmhouses had carved witchposts near the fireplace to keep away such unwanted intruders.[46] When the son of Alexander Home, a master's mate on Cook's third voyage, recorded some of his own and his father's memories, he remarked in passing: 'The time is not long gone by when almost every country village had its witch and warlock'.[47]

In Cook's part of Yorkshire such traditions lingered. Even in the late nineteenth century, older residents of Great Ayton feared witchcraft and remembered the case of one villager who sought to revenge himself on a jilted lover by using the services of a local witch, who employed mould from the grave of a suicide to work her dark mischief. But, along with such black witches, there were also white witches or wisemen or women ('cunning folk') who could ward off spells that afflicted stock – Great Ayton was fortunate in having once had one nearby at Stokesley whose powers derived from his being the seventh son of a seventh daughter. Though this was not quite as good as the seventh son of a seventh son, the belief in the magical quality of seven and particularly of the seventh child gave him particular standing.[48] Posthumous children (particularly if male) also had out of the ordinary powers, particularly over Yorkshire black witches.[49] There were also objects which could be used to ward off harm, such as the whips made of the rowan tree (on sale at the Stokesley Fair) which were particularly useful when crossing bridges, since evil spirits could not cross running water and so haunted crossing-places.[50] One could find similar practices at Staithes where the fear of misfortune was further compounded by the perils of the sea. In 1885 *The Times* recorded that if a Staithes fishing boat or coble had continual bad luck the wives of the crew would gather together at midnight in deep silence and then proceed to kill a pigeon, extract its heart and fill it with pins before burning it. This ritual would in turn attract the witch who had made the fishermen's life so difficult and that person could then be bought off with an appropriate present. Staithes folk were also wary of eggs, which they thought could be used by evil persons – a belief that no doubt was connected with the link between eggs and reproduction.[51]

Cook was probably referring to some such continuing folk belief that the natural world and especially animals could offer some tangible link with the supernatural when he remarked, at the Tahitian island of Ra'itatea, that there birds such as herons and woodpeckers were 'Sacred to them as Robin Red-breasts, Swallows, & etc & etc are to many old women in England'. For Cook, a man of the Enlightenment, however, such beliefs were 'superstitions'.[52] Though the journals of Cook and his men have little to say on the subject there were, however, ample parallels between such folk beliefs and Pacific preoccupation with both the malevolent and benevolent uses of witchcraft, and other ways of harnessing supernatural forces at the level of everyday life.[53]

When Cook and his men entered the Pacific they came from a society in which religion had long been a source of controversy and diversity, and hence they viewed other peoples' religions with considerable fascination and curiosity. These voyagers were, however, products of a society where the role of religion was changing, in ways that had few historical parallels, and this meant that they looked at the religions of the Pacific from a vantage point that could lead to skewed vision. Religion largely meant to them a set of beliefs which were assented to by an individual in the light of the instruction they had received, usually from the Bible or other books, and reinforced by attendance at services held at set times and places. In a manner foreign to most societies, they viewed religion as plural, with the one society containing, however uneasily, a range of different religions. The Protestant culture from which they came also strengthened a strong belief that there was a vast gulf between this world and the next and between the terrestrial and the supernatural. All of which made it difficult for them to grasp the extent to which Pacific religions were concerned with outcomes in this world which they hoped to control through rituals and material objects which could be impregnated with the divine.

Used to buildings which held religious services at set times, the voyagers tended to underestimate the pervasive character of Pacific religion and the extent to which it permeated the culture as a whole, rather than being a matter of individual belief. Though the fear of the gods and their possible retribution was the cement which held society together, Māori culture had few closely prescribed rituals or beliefs or a priesthood marked off from the rest of society by distinctive clothing or dwelling-places.[54] Misled by the absence of what he understood as the hallmarks of religion – churches and priests – Cook was prompted to write on the *Endeavour* voyage that, 'With respect to Religion', the New Zealand Māoris 'trouble themselves very little about it'. He echoed this on the second voyage by describing them as being 'void of all religious principles'.[55] Banks was rather more qualified, remarking that 'We saw few signs of religion among these people; they have no publick places of Worship among them', but concluded, apparently on the basis of Tupaia's enquiries, that they had similar beliefs about the creation of the world and of humankind to the Tahitians.[56]

Early in his Tahitian sojourn Joseph Banks was similarly mislead by the lack of interest of the Tahitians in the religious service held by the men of the *Endeavour*, remarking that 'they did not when the service was over ask any question nor would they attend at all to any explanation we attempted to give them'. Indeed, added Banks, 'We have not yet seen the least traces of religion among these people, maybe they are intirely without it'.[57] Cook thought that the ruinous state of many of the *morais* was an indication that Tahitians had once taken their religion more seriously, adding, with a wry comment that reflected on his own society, 'that Religious customs [are] like most other nations, by these people less observed'.[58] A longer stay in Tahiti led James Matra, another of the *Endeavour*'s crew, to a more qualified appraisal, for he concluded that, although 'They have however no religious establishment, or mode of divine worship', they acknowledged their belief in a Creator who was 'too far elevated above his creatures to be affected by their actions'.[59] When he finally reached Hawai'i, Cook and his men were on religiously more familiar ground, for there religious practices seemed more overt and more analogous to the forms with which the Europeans were familiar.

An Hawaiian *Heiau* (Temple). Engraving by W. Walker after W. Ellis (from W. Ellis, *An Authentic Narrative of a Voyage ...* (2 vols, London, 1782), i, p. 181)

As Lieutenant King wrote: 'They have more outward show of Religion than any people we have seen, which is best witnessed by the number of ceremonies we have mentioned'.[60]

Closer acquaintance with Pacific societies generally led to a greater appreciation of the pervasiveness of religious beliefs. Naturally enough, these voyagers from another cultural universe looked at Pacific religion through the Christian lens with which they were familiar. This led them, for example, to focus excessively on the otherworldly elements in Pacific religions and to look for analogies to the Christian scheme of heaven and hell, when Pacific societies were largely preoccupied with the this-worldly consequences of religious practice and generally regarded reward or punishment as being meted out in the here and now.[61] Alexander Home, for example, was operating within such a Christian framework when he concluded that the Tahitians believed that 'that they themselves become Immortal by Death and that the Deity distributes rewards and punishments without respect to their Rank here', though adding that 'Their Notions of Enjoyments of the Future State are all Sensual'.[62]

The European strangers began, however, to appreciate that they were in a strange new world where people viewed both this and the next world differently. Some of the voyagers were rather more doubtful about any analogy between Tahitian beliefs and that of the Christian dogma of divine judgement. James Matra discerned some 'notion of a future life in another island, to which they expect to be translated after death'. Such a state did not, however, bring with it the consequences, good or bad, of one's actions on earth, for 'it does not seem as if they considered it as a state of retribution for the actions of this life'. Indeed, what stood out for Matra was the extent to which the Tahitians extrapolated the condition of this world into the next, for 'they believe that each individual will there enjoy the same condition in which he has lived here, whether it be that of a prince, a master, or a servant'.[63] On the second voyage, the astronomer William Wales also discerned that the Tahitian next world was similarly constituted to this and that 'they believe their servants, or inferior People, do not go to the same place or abode after death which their Principles do'.[64] The astronomer William Bayly, on the third voyage, drew a similar conclusion at Tonga, where he concluded that the afterlife was reserved for the '*Egees* or *Gentlemen*' while the commoners after death 'rot & return to earth & there is an end of them'.[65]

In religion, as in other areas, the voyagers gradually came to appreciate the difference between their own world and that which they encountered in the Pacific – though the questions they asked were naturally shaped by European concerns. Following the Judeo-Christian preoccupations with 'graven images', they at first tended to assume that the people of the Pacific worshipped idols but the more perceptive of the journalists became more doubtful as they came to know these new cultures better. Surgeon Samwell thought that the Hawaiians 'seem to be great Idolaters from the number of Images we saw among them', adding, however, that 'Though they look upon these Idols as their Gods they pay no great reverence to them'.[66] On the previous voyage, the ethnologically more acute Johann Reinhold Forster had drawn more profound conclusions from similar observations. For he concluded that they were not 'idolatrous, for they never shew any kind of respect to the wooden figures'.[67] Forster's adversary, the astronomer William Wales agreed with him on this point at least, conceding 'that those who have asserted that they are Idolaters are mistaken', and that the images that occasioned this error were those of the deceased and were 'considered by them in the same light as we do the statue of a deceased friend, or the figures on his Monument'.[68] Though Banks had at first been doubtful that religion formed a part of Tahitian society, over the course of his three months' stay he gradually came to look at Tahiti in its own terms, appreciating, for example, that, though the Tahitian *morais* or burying-places often displayed carved representations of human forms, 'these however are in no degrees the objects of adoration, every prayer and sacrafise being here offered to the Invisible deities'.[69]

Slowly the European observers were stumbling towards some understanding of the extent to which the religions of the Pacific used material objects as ways of expressing the force of unseen religious forces – what in the Polynesian world was known as *mana*, which made 'visible what is invisible'.[70] The Hawaiians might, as Surgeon Samwell remarked, treat the images of their gods in a rather casual manner and even sell them,[71] but this did not prevent them from seeing such images as a way of pointing towards the forces that sustained their society – hence feathered images of gods were taken into battle. On the other hand, if such objects did not bring success or prosperity, they could be discarded and replaced as no longer having the potency that came with *mana*.[72] Such a strong belief in the power of material objects to embody spiritual forces vital to human society could also be found outside Polynesia. The Nootka people of Vancouver Island, for example, treasured crystals considered to be endowed with supernatural qualities which promoted good fortune.[73] The vitalism that was so basic a feature of Polynesian religion was also characteristic of other Pacific cultures[74] and, indeed, in other societies around the world – including some aspects of medieval Christian religion.

A vivid sense of the potency of the spiritual in the everyday did not come easily to eighteenth-century Protestant Englishmen, reared in the religious traditions of a gulf between the natural and the supernatural. Europe's elite, too, was increasingly influenced by that radical distinction between matter and spirit that had received its philosophical statement in Descartes and which provided the intellectual underpinning of the Scientific Revolution. Newton and other major thinkers of this period even had difficulty accepting the central Christian doctrine of the Incarnation, with its assumption that the divine could be embodied in the terrestrial. Reared on such a bifurcation between matter and spirit, European observers found the idea of *mana*, with its connotations of a world impregnated by spirit, difficult to fathom. In some ways they found it easier to comprehend, at least to some degree, the obverse of the idea of *mana*, that of *tapu* – the most obvious manifestation of which was a set of prohibitions. So struck were the Europeans by the social force of *tapu* that the term entered the English language as 'taboo'.

Ultimately, all such power, whether in the form of *mana* or *tapu*, was of divine origin. 'At the back of *tapu* and *mana*', wrote the great New Zealand ethnologist, Elsdon Best, 'the gods of the Maori stand'.[75] While *mana* was, as it were, live electricity which animated all things, making them both active and also possibly dangerous,[76] *tapu* was potential electricity stored in particular objects or persons making them sacred but also, again, a possible source of danger. The width of the force-field surrounding a particular *tapued* individual depended on rank and position.[77] The force of a *tapu* could be discharged by objects which were *noa*, profane or, in some sense, spiritually neutral. This applied particularly in relation to those two central elements of human life, food and sex. Contact with women and with cooked food lessened the force of the *tapu* but also meant a loss of spiritual energy.[78] European observers, however, were intrigued that the workings of the *tapu* system and its control over the powerful forces that could bring both prosperity and destruction meant that in much of Polynesia those who slept together could not eat together (since men and women took their meals apart).[79] Defying a *tapu* and yet surviving could be considered a sign of power and, with it, *mana*[80] – which is perhaps why breaches of *tapu* by the European visitors were often overlooked, even when Joseph Banks rushed in where angels feared to tread by unwrapping a divine image on one of the major shrines on the Tahitian island of Ra'iatea.[81] Perhaps, too, there was the sense that the visitors' *mana* might protect those local people who broke *tapus* on board the great European vessels. Women, for example, broke *tapu* when they ate with men and ate foods reserved for men. Thomas Edgar, master of the *Discovery*, commented on how Tahitian women were prevailed upon on board to eat such forbidden foods as 'Pork the best fish & Turtle'.[82]

Europeans found it easiest at first to grasp the negative connections of a *tapu*, the way in which certain practices were forbidden or contact with sacred personages circumscribed. But that acute observer Lieutenant King was perceptive enough to see that in Tonga there was more to the notion of *tapu* than 'simply something not to be touchd or something forbidden'. Rather, he wrote, 'this Custom of tapuing is very general & attended with a mysteriousness that made us conclude we do not understand the full import of it'.[83] The voyagers were particularly curious about the way in which the practice of *tapu* impinged on the relations between the sexes. The libidinous Surgeon Samwell was preoccupied with the way in which Hawaiian *tapus* could restrict access to the local women: the fact that the shore party was located in an area that was *tapued* on account of its proximity to a sacred site meant, as it put it, 'The Gentlemen who sleep on shore are mortified at this as no Women will on any Account come to them'. The attempt to bribe the local priest to lift the *tapu* was fruitless, and the women themselves were afraid of being killed if they defied it, for 'none but the King himself can take the Taboo or Consecration off the Ground'.[84] It was an object lesson for Cook and his men in the strength of *tapus*, particularly those connected with the proximity of the sacred.

As in the Samwell case, the journalists generally focused on the extent to which women played a subordinate role in the religions of the Pacific. This would not have been surprising to them, since generally women played a subordinate role in European religion – with the exception of the Quakers who even permitted women a role in the ministry.[85] There may, too, have been some cultural memory of the role of women as heads of religious houses in the middle ages – women, for example, had played a large part in the foundation of the Whitby monastery which had had houses for both men and women, with common worship at the one great abbey church before such Irish-derived practices were stamped out by Rome.[86]

Some of the voyagers, however, thought that there were also some female spaces in the religion of the Pacific. Banks wrote that in Tahiti, though women were not allowed to enter the main burying places or *morais*, 'The women however have *Morais* of their own where they worship and sacrifice to their Goddesses'.[87] That well-informed observer of Tahitian society, the *Bounty* mutineer James Morrison, was, however, later to be quite categorical in denying such claims: 'Their Weomen bear no part in their relegious rites, and neither them nor their Male servants ever partake of these Ceremonies; they have no place of worship for themselves'.[88] Johann Reinhold Forster did, however, think that Tahitian women played some role at funerals, writing that 'Men perform the Funeral rites at the Death of women, & women again at the decease of a Man'.[89] Remarkably Lieutenant Burney found on the small Hawaiian island of Ni'ihau 'many priests and, what we have not seen at any of these Islands, priestesses, who all act as if they were inspired by some supernatural power'.[90] This was probably an exaggeration, since there does not appear to have been a role for priestesses in Polynesian religion and there was but one major Polynesian female divinity, the moon goddess.[91] Nonetheless, the comments of Burney, together with those of Banks and Forster, do underline the fact that Polynesian women on occasions did play a ceremonial and ritual role.

Fascination with the cultures of the Pacific led some of the voyagers to become more participants than simple observers. By the third voyage Cook's thirst for more information on the religious practices of the societies that he encountered led him literally to shed his European dress and with it some of his European presuppositions. In order to venture into one of the great Tongan temples, Cook agreed to remove his hat and to let his hair hang loose rather than being tied up in a queue as usual. He did, however, draw the line at stripping down to a loin-cloth as his companion Mai did.[92] In order, however, to study the Tongan *Inasiu* ceremony – a central ritual which proclaimed the dedication of the islands and their produce to the god Hikulea as represented by the religious head of state[93] – Cook went further and joined in the 'procession of the Chiefes, with his hair hanging loose & his body naked down to ye waist', to the disgust of Lieutenant Williamson who thought that 'he rather let himself down'. Like many of the journalists, Williamson was inclined to focus on the political aspects of religious practices recording the Tongan king's description of the festival as being held 'prior to his Son being permitted to eat with him'[94] – an accurate enough description of the way in which the festival served to mark a royal coming of age at a time when representatives from throughout the sea-strewn kingdom were brought together.[95] It was yet another illustration of the close integration of the political and the religious in the societies of the Pacific.

Cook did not stay on for another Tongan ritual which, Williamson tells us, was due to be held in a month's time, complete with a human sacrifice, but he was an eager observer of a similar event in Tahiti soon afterwards. Perhaps to assuage his own conscience for this cultural voyeurism, Cook afterwards turned

The Natche, A Ceremony in Honour of the King's Son, in Tongataboo. Engraving by
J. Hall and S. Middiman after Webber (from J. Cook and J. King, *Voyage to the Pacific
Ocean* ... (3 vols, London, 1784), i, plate 22)

from detached observer to critic, telling the chief that God would not be pleased
with such an offering and that it would not bring victory against his enemies as
he hoped.[96] When he came to Hawai'i, however, Cook willingly cooperated with
the rituals which were prescribed for him by the priests, even though he had no
knowledge of their meaning – leading Christian critics later to argue that he had
brought on his own death by acceding to such idolatrous practices. Cook stood
by, too, when the funeral of William Watman, a seaman who had died soon after
arrival on the big island of Hawai'i, was effectively conducted with two sets of
rituals, the traditional Christian burial service and those of the Hawaiian priests,
which bore a close resemblance to those for a human sacrifice.[97]

   Though Cook's men overwhelmingly came from a Protestant culture, their
understanding of Pacific religions was largely shaped around the concept of a
priesthood. The idea of a priest performing ritual functions was familiar enough
to them from their knowledge of Catholic Europe and of classical culture; and,
after all, British clergy, even in the nonconformist churches (Quakers excepted),
conducted the rituals of birth, death and marriage together with the central
Christian ritual of holy communion. Protestant clergy, however, were principally
preachers and custodians of the religion of the Word, a cultural difference that
is reflected in Alexander Home's comments on the extent to which the Tahitian
religion was dominated by the clergy, for 'The priests are the Books of the
Ottihitis'.[98] The journalists remarked, too, on the way in which the priesthood
and the aristocracy were intertwined (something which was very familiar from

'A Human Sacrifice, in a Morai, in Otaheite'. Engraved by W. Woollett after Webber (from J. Cook and J. King, *Voyage to the Pacific Ocean ...* (3 vols, London, 1784), ii, plate 25)

Europe). George Forster, for example, wrote of the Society Islands that 'The priests of these islands continue in office during their life, and their dignity is hereditary. The high-priest of every island is always an aree, who has the highest rank after the king'.[99] It was a judgement of Tahitian society echoed subsequently on the third voyage by Corporal Ledyard, who commented that 'the priests are chiefs by rank though they do not immediately intermeddle in the civil department'.[100]

As Ledyard's remark suggests, the journalists generally did not see any marked separation between what in European terms was considered church and state, even though some separation of sacred and secular rule did exist, for example, in Tonga.[101] The major exception was Hawai'i, where the size and power of the priesthood made the voyagers speculate that there were tensions between the clergy and the chiefs – tensions which coloured the Hawaiians' response to the strangers. Faced by clear divisions among the Hawaiians in their attitude to the voyagers after Cook's death, Captain Clerke considered the clue to such fluctuation lay in the fact that 'Here are clearly party matters subsisting between the Laity and the Clergy'.[102] Midshipman Harvey was of like mind, writing that 'from the beginning of this unfortunate quarrel that two separate interests have been among the Natives, the Priests was our friends'. As he remarked, the distinction between priestly and chiefly interests even had a geographical demarcation, since the priests 'lived the opposite side of the Bay', in contrast to the chiefs whose base was on the inner shore near the great temple or *heiau*.[103]

A Heiva or Priest from Ulietea [Ra'iatea] (from T. Chambers after S. Parkinson, *A
Journal of a Voyage to the South Seas* (London, 1773), plate 11, facing p. 71)

Though in Hawai'i the voyagers had good cause to regard the local priests with favour, the journals from Cook's voyagers frequently reflect a good deal of anticlericalism flowing from both Protestantism and the rationalizing spirit of the eighteenth-century Enlightenment. Both forces were clearly at work in the German Protestant pastor, Johann Reinhold Forster and still more in that of his son George whose critical attitude to church and state culminated in his embrace of the early French Revolution. When he discussed the practice of human sacrifice in Tahiti, Johann Reinhold Forster discoursed on the 'caprice of the High Priest' and the 'abominable scenes of priest-craft'. On the whole, however, he took a more favourable view of Polynesian religion, writing with perhaps an implied critique of some European religious practice, that, though it had 'the stamp of all the inventions and works of mankind in its imperfection and error', it was 'less cruel, and not so much clogged with superstition as many others, which were or still are in use among nations who are reputed to be more civilized and more improved'.[104] George Forster echoed the same sentiments in a higher key, denouncing Tahitian 'priestcraft' but praising Tahitian religion for its similarity with the pure and simple religion which all humankind shared but which had in Tahiti as elsewhere been debased 'by the excessive cunning of a few individuals'.[105] On Tonga, George Forster thought that the priests adopted the common practice of using a different language for religion so that it became 'veiled in mysteries, especially where there are priests to take advantage of the credulity of mankind'.[106] His fellow second-voyage shipmate, the gunner's mate John Marra, made the implied critique of Catholicism explicit in his description of the way in which the Tahitian priests used 'a language which the vulgar do not understand', likening it to 'the Popish custom of praying in an unknown tongue'.[107]

Predictably, the Quaker-influenced Cook took a rather dim view of ritual religion. On the first voyage he commented favourably, for example, that Tahitian offerings to the dead seemed to involve no 'Priest craft'. Indeed, he wrote rather dismissively of religion generally, expressing uncertainty about Tahitian beliefs and ceremonies since 'the Misteries of most Religions are very dark and not easily understud even by those who profess them'.[108] The Tahitian priests, he thought, 'seem to be in no great repute', and he thought well of the fact that they could not 'live wholly by their profession' since this showed that 'these people are no bigots to their regelion'.[109] Banks' anticlericalism was even more overt: when he came to writing of his discussion with the Ra'iatean priest, Tupaia, it confirmed the view that 'Religion has been in ages, is still in all Countreys Cloak'd in mysteries unexplicable to human understanding'. He added, with some cultural detachment, that a British clergyman would have just as much difficulty in 'reconcil[ing] the apparent inconsistencies of our own religion to the faith of an infidel'. While Christian clergymen had obtained a monopoly on conducting the ceremony of marriage by using 'the fear of punishment from above', Tahitian clergy, Banks commented, 'have secured to themselves the profit of two operations', tattowing and circumcizing, 'without being driven to the necessity of so severe a penalty'.[110] When on the third voyage Alexander Home came to describe the Tahitian clergy, he did so in the same spirit as Banks, writing that 'like the Clergy in Most Countrys they advantage themselves by the Credulity of the people'.[111] So did another of Cook's crew on this voyage, George Gilbert, who attributed the Tahitian practice of human sacrifice to 'the power of their priests; and their ignorance and superstition'.[112] Like Banks, Gilbert saw Tahitian and European religion as having much in common: 'Their religion though it is attended with some superstitious practices; yet, the principles of it, are as natural, and agreeable to reason, as what is taught in most of the churches in Europe'.[113]

The frequent invocation of 'priestcraft', with its implied or explicit comparison with the behaviour of the European clergy, was an instance of a wider phenomenon: the way in which the voyagers sought for analogies to relate the new forms of religious culture they encountered to forms with which they were familiar. Here they could draw on a considerable range of religious forms. There was some reference to English Protestantism but very little – an indication that they saw few parallels. Where they did make such allusions it was chiefly to describe what they considered was some sort of religious office or post: thus Cook referred to the Tongan chief who 'seemed to be the head of the Church and was distinguished by us by the name of Canterbury', while at Hawai'i Samwell tried to make comprehensible the religious hierarchy by writing in familiarly Anglican terms of a subordinate priest and his superior that 'This Curate lives in the same House with the rector'.[114]

When it came to ritual, the religious practices of the Pacific were more likely to be compared with Catholicism. Anders Sparrman described a frightened chief 'who in his distress murmured prayers over a little bunch of red feathers like a monk with his rosary'. He continued in a more ecumenical manner to liken the Tahitian practice of swearing on a bunch of red feathers to the way 'we adopt when we swear on the Bible'.[115] Surprisingly, given the strength of anti-Catholicism, the American John Ledyard thought that more ritually-focused religions such as Catholicism or Orthodoxy were more appropriate to the needs of the peoples of the Pacific. After observing an Orthodox service at Kamchatka, Siberia, he commented favourably on the way in which the indigenous people 'went through the multitude of ceremonies attendant on that sort of worship', adding, rather patronizingly, that 'I think it a religion the best calculated in the world to gain proselytes when the people are either unwilling or unable to speculate, or when they cannot be made acquainted with the history and principles of Christianity without a formal education'.[116]

Given that the two great authority systems of European culture were

Christianity and the classics, it is surprising that there was not more reference to the classical world as a point of comparison with Pacific religions, especially when exploring such themes as polytheism. Such an analogy was later used by the *Bounty* mutineer James Morrison in his lengthy description of Tahitian society, where he wrote of the Tahitian account of the stars that it 'may be said to Correspond with the Greek fables'.[117] Though the artists of Cook's voyages frequently drew on classical imagery, and the journalists invoked comparisons between Pacific society and other areas of the classical heritage such as warfare, the religious parallel did not loom large. Johann Reinhold Forster made a fleeting reference to the ancient Greek Orphic myths when describing the cosmogonies of the Tahitians, though he combined this with mention of the ancient religions of the Chaldeans and Egyptians. His fellow naturalist (and indeed his employee), the Swedish Anders Sparrman, also turned to pre-classical societies of the Mediterranean and Middle East when attempting to understand the religions of the Pacific. When Sparrman observed the people of Malekula (Vanuatu) pouring water 'on their heads with their hands' 'as a sign of friendship and peace', it prompted him to speculate that perhaps they 'worship the watery element, as the Persians worshipped its opposite, fire'. Perhaps, too, continued Sparrman, their practice could be likened to the way in which water among the ancient Egyptians and Jews was considered 'as an emblem of cleansing, purity, and truth for body and soul or morals' – beliefs which provided the probable source of the Christian rite of baptism.[118]

For John Marra the most obvious comparisons with the priests of Tahiti were the Druids of ancient Britain. But he also invoked other more contemporary parallels drawn from travellers' accounts of India and the East, likening the use of a specialized Tahitian religious language not only to the 'Popish custom of praying in an unknown tongue' but also to 'the Brahmins in the East' and 'the followers of the great Zaroaster'.[119] Lieutenant King drew on similar travellers' accounts when he sought to describe the position of the individual he considered the chief priest of Hawai'i as 'resembl[ing] pretty much the Delai Lama of the Tartars, and the ecclesiastical emperor of Japan'.[120]

Such were some of the cultural lenses through which the European voyagers attempted to view the character of the religions of the Pacific. What of the reverse – how did the peoples of the Pacific attempt to understand the coming of these strangers? The mental universe of the precontact Pacific was one where the secular and the sacred were much more integrated than in Europe, with its long institutional history of conflict over the borders of church and state and its long intellectual history over the demarcation between matter and spirit. The intrusion of these alien beings meant, then, for the peoples of the Pacific the need to make them explicable, often in terms which Europeans would have considered religious or supernatural.

For the Māoris of the Poverty Bay area of New Zealand, where Cook first landed, the *Endeavour* seemed to be a great bird and the boat that rowed off from it a small bird. When this disgorged 'a number of parti-coloured beings ... apparently in human shape ... the bird was regarded as a houseful of divinities'.[121] Another tradition from the same area records the determination of a local warrior to see whether or not these strangers were indeed supernatural beings by rushing to attack them. After he was shot dead Cook laid a cloak over him. This was carefully preserved by the local people as containing something of the *mana* of these powerful beings.[122] The possible divinity of these strangers did not, of course, preclude them from being enemies whose supernatural character made them still more menacing – after all, in the Māori world (as in the Viking) enemies frequently arrived by sea. One initial reaction was that they were 'demons' and, later, when Cook reached the Mercury Bay area, they were regarded as 'goblins' – a description repeated in traditions from other points of encounter.[123]

As in the case of the Māoris likening the *Endeavour* to a bird, the Nootka people of Vancouver Island also drew on familiar categories from the natural world to make comprehensible the arrival of the *Resolution*, describing the ship as 'a fish come alive into people' and the men on board as fish in human form.[124] Possibly, too, in the strongly totemic world of North-west America such fish, on whom the whole way of life depended, had larger cosmological significance.[125] Other first contact accounts from the Nootka people (which may well have blended Cook's arrival with that of other European ships) liken his ship to an island or a giant seagull or the moon propelled by a sea serpent.[126] The common theme was the need to render the unfamiliar manageable by linking it with familiar objects.

When, on the third voyage, Cook's ships encountered the peoples of the island of Atiu (Cook Islands) – a part of the world that Europeans had not hitherto reached – they were regarded as possibly being gods or, at least, partly gods – not a vast leap in Polynesian culture in which the boundaries between the human and divine were much more porous than in Europe.[127] Hence great chiefs embodied the divine (as had Roman emperors of old and Japanese emperors since time immemorial). It was natural for the chiefs to respond to this strange visitation by attempting to incorporate these beings into a familiar religious cosmogony, especially given their white skins (which were associated with divinity) and remarkable weapons and clothing. They therefore asked (as an oral tradition recorded by a missionary in the late nineteenth century has it): 'Are you a son of the Great Root or Cause, whose children are half divine, half human?'[128] In the strongly hierarchical, chief- and priest-dominated society of Hawai'i, the tendency to treat the strangers as emanations of the divine was particularly strong. When they first arrived in Hawai'i on the island of Kaua'i in January 1778, reported Lieutenant King, the local people 'were very fearful of giving offence' and 'seemed to regard us as Superior beings' some being 'extravagant in their joy

in seeing us'.[129] Famously, of course, the return to Hawai'i at the end of the year
and early the next year brought with it the identification of Cook himself with
the god Lono and, possibly, a set of misunderstandings that contributed to his
death – a theme that will be pursued in the last chapter.

Familiarity between Europeans and the peoples of the Pacific bred, if not
contempt, then a less-exalted view of Europeans and an increasing recognition of
common humanity – not least as a consequence of the very evident humanness
of the Europeans' liking for Pacific women. In Tahiti we hear very little of
any tendency to deify the Europeans, no doubt because the visits of Wallis,
Bougainville and the Spanish, along with Cook himself, had done much to
demystify the Europeans and their strange ships, clothes and weapons. A sense
of common humanity extended to a mutual exchange of information about
religious beliefs. The Protestant pastor, Johann Reinhold Forster, had a lengthy
theological discussion with his cultural equivalent, a Tahitian priest.[130] But even
Tahitian–European interchange left ample room for cross-cultural confusion:
when he returned to England on board Furneaux's *Adventure*, Mai was made to
come to the Anglican service and reportedly 'was much afraid thinking they were
going to sacrifice him'.[131] The peoples of the Pacific Northwest also had some
familiarity with Europeans, whether the Spanish or the Russians, and this, too,
may have reduced the cultural shock of the arrival of Cook. Hawai'i, however,
bore the full brunt of the arrival of the totally unfamiliar and this, together with
the strength of its priestly class and elaborate religious observances, appears to
have meant that the advent of Cook was perceived in strongly religious terms.
For a time this brought considerable advantages to the ships' crews, in the way
of copious supplies of food and sex, but the highly charged nature of such a
religiously-based understanding probably contributed to Cook's Hawaiian
downfall.

In religion, as in much else, the tall ships of the Europeans were precursors of
vast changes in the Pacific. The Europeans' ignorance or defiance of *tabus*, which
had been long integral to the workings of many societies, weakened the force of
a system of religious sanctions and, with them, the framework of a whole way
of life. The need to account for the Europeans' power, and particularly that of
their weapons, raised profound questions for the peoples of the Pacific about the
potency of their own gods. When Christian missionaries arrived, they often found
societies receptive to a new way of understanding the workings of the divine and
its relations with humankind. Some Pacific islanders, too, had begun to wonder
if the God of the Europeans had more *mana* than their own deities and whether,
then, they should accept those that spoke in the name of the Christian God as
their priests. Where a new religious dispensation was erected, however, it was
frequently built on traditional foundations: one set of rituals was transmogrified

into another and one set of *tabus* also gave way to another. The strict observance of the Sabbath, for example, often took deep root in newly-converted Pacific societies, as the idea of a *tabued* day meshed so well with older practices.

For the Europeans, contact with the Pacific did not bring about such fundamental religious changes, but it did help to accelerate changes in mentality that were already in train. The Pacific provided a vast human laboratory which demonstrated the extent of cultural and, particularly, religious diversity, thus further calling into question the view that there could be one religion which could apply to all peoples. The painful acceptance of the need to tolerate religious diversity – a process that had been going on since the Reformation – was given further momentum by the encounter with the Pacific and other non-European peoples. So, too, was the recognition that much that was good and true could be found outside the Christian world. Johann Reinhold Forster thought, for example, that the Tahitians 'exercise[d] all the Social virtues to one another, which are usual among the civilized nations. Charity, the main spring of all morality & virtue, is no where more exercised than among these people'.[132] All of which raised profound questions about the importance of a uniquely Christian revelation and the extent to which true morality and even salvation could be found outside the Christian dispensation. These were not new questions, but the encounter with the Pacific and the widely-read travel accounts that followed gave them a renewed force. Cook's voyages depicted in bright and vivid colours the sheer diversity of human behaviour and its response to the divine and in doing so carried further the long process of accepting the need for a religiously pluralist order. England and Europe more generally emerged from its encounter with the Pacific somewhat less religiously and culturally parochial, and with renewed doubts about the possibility of achieving a religious unity which could serve as the bedrock for society as a whole. The voyage into the Pacific was a further voyage away from the ideal of a single Christendom which had once shaped Western Europe in its formative phase.

7

Sex

Birth, and copulation, and death
That's all the facts when you come to brass tacks.[1]

T.S. Eliot's succinct summation of human existence captures the essential realities and the common humanity on which all cultures are based – including those of the Europeans and the peoples of the Pacific when they encountered each other during Cook's voyages. But such a common humanity was enveloped in cultural forms which rendered the basic biological imperatives diverse, multifarious and frequently difficult for foreigners to fathom. Cook's men thought that casual sexual gratification was straightforward enough and would, in the Pacific, follow the same forms with which they were all too familiar at home: female compliance in return for payment in money or kind. But, in the Pacific, they encountered societies where sex brought with it membership of a foreign society, bringing with it foreign obligations. Homosexuality in Britain was illegal and furtive and yet in Hawai'i the voyagers encountered a society where it was openly practised by the society's elite. Marriage for the British was the bedrock of society, and yet in the Pacific its forms often seemed difficult to discern clearly and it was by no means expected to be a commitment to follow the Book of Common Prayer's injunction to honour 'until death us do part'. Cook was even surprised to find that female nakedness could exist in some parts of the globe, such as Australia, for he had assumed there were 'parts which I allways before now thought nature would have taught a woman to conceal'.[2] Confronted by such diversity on Cook's second voyage, George Forster mused about the variety of human cultures and the way in which 'Their opinions in respect to the sex in particular, have been infinitely various in all ages and countries'. Polynesian sexual practices prompted him to contrast the value that different societies placed on virginity, claiming that 'In some parts of India, no man of consequence will condescend to marry a virgin; [while] in Europe she who has lost that character is universally rejected'.[3]

Religion formed an important part of the cultural fabric which clothed the biological facts of human society in distinctive shapes. In medieval England and in much of Catholic Europe consecrated virginity was an important form of religious life. The origins of the great ruined abbey of Whitby were, for example, linked to the promise made by the Northumbrian King Oswy to God, in return for his victory over the forces of paganism, to give his infant daughter 'to be consecrated to Him in perpetual virginity'.[4] With the Reformation there was a strong rejection of such forms of religious life. Hence convents attracted the sort of prurience Johann Reinhold Forster displayed when the *Resolution* called in at the Portuguese Azores on its return journey. He noted in his unpublished journal of the nuns there that 'If the Stories told us are true, they are even very libidinous, & not being able to satisfy their desires with Men, they endeavour to do it effectually one way or other'. With Protestant fervour he concluded that 'These are the miserable effects of bigotry & false notions of sanctity in religious matters'.[5]

In the Protestant world the weight of religious attention fell almost entirely on the institution of marriage, which was so closely intertwined with religion that the Church of England did not abandon its official monopoly over marriages (Jews and Quakers only excepted) until 1836. It was this close connection between religion and marriage which prompted the young and anticlerical Joseph Banks to remark about the contrast between the very fluid nature of Tahitan marriage customs and that of his own society, where 'our preists have excelled theirs in persuading us that the Sexes can not come lawfully together without having bought their benediction'.[6]

Though Cook's Quaker employer, John Walker, might name one of his ships, *Freelove*, as a metaphor for divine grace, overt sexual imagery was rarely employed in British religion. A rare exception was the way in which nakedness could be linked to the Edenic state of Adam and Eve before the fall, so that Midshipman John Watts could write of his encounter with the Tasmanian Aborigines at Adventure Bay that 'these People, from their affable, friendly, innocent, & good-natured Behaviour ... go naked, because they know no Sin'.[7] Things were very different, however, in the Pacific, where the creative forces linked to sex were closely and explicitly tied to the power of the gods. In the Hawaiian temples the fundamental dualism of the sexes was literally part of the fabric of the building, with the rafters deriving their name from the female genitals and the post into which they fitted from the male.[8] This understanding of the workings of the cosmos in sexual terms flowed through to the most everyday objects, so that a Marquesan food pounder was carved to a phallic design.[9]

The European voyagers encountering this strange new world of the Pacific had, perforce, to view it through the very different categories of their own world, where sex was certainly not absent (how could it be?) but was subject to different levels of control as a potentially destructive force. For in their world both church and state threw its weight behind the institution of the family and hence closely linked sex with marriage. In some ways British society was a federation of diverse families, with the father the head of these social units and the king the father of the nation. Since marriage was so important, sexual practices which would

Elizabeth Cook: aged 81, by William Henderson (Mitchell Library GPO 2-08180)

weaken the family were condemned: adultery above all, but also premarital sex and forms of sex such as homosexuality or masturbation which did not lead to fruitful increase of the nation's population. This called for a very high degree of social discipline, since the marriage age in English society was relatively high by the standards of most societies: in the first half of the eighteenth century it was 27.5 for men and 26.2 for women, while in the second half of the century it dropped slightly, due to greater prosperity, being 26.4 for men and 24.9 for women.[10] This in turn reflected the emphasis in British society on the need for the newly-married couple to have accumulated the resources to be in a position to establish a separate household. James Cook, for example, waited until he was firmly established in the navy before he married at the late age of thirty-four. His bride, Elizabeth Batts, was, however, younger than usual at twenty-one, perhaps because Cook was sufficiently well off to dispense with the contribution that a bride would often bring to a marriage.

Such sexual restraint was enforced by religion and the Judeo-Christian prohibitions of all forms of sexual release outside marriage. In the seventeenth century such religious sanctions had had considerable force, as instanced by the low level of illegitimate births (1.5 per cent in the 1670s) but it was an indication of the increasing secularization of society that in the eighteenth century the illegitimacy rate was increasing considerably (3 per cent by the middle of the century and 6 per cent by 1810).[11] The more secular character of society was evident, too, in the weakening power of the church courts, one of the major functions of which was to deal with sexual misdemeanors. There were certainly plenty of these and always had been – to take one example, in Elizabethan Essex there was a one in four chance of being accused of a richly diverse range of sexual offences, ranging from fornication, adultery and bigamy to buggery, incest and bestiality.[12] Human nature had changed little in eighteenth-century Yorkshire, with the records of the East Riding archdeacon's visitations between 1759 and 1773 uncovering a plentiful (though less lurid) haul of sexual offences: 152 cases of fornication, fifteen of the rather intriguing category of 'anticipated fornication' (probably sexual congress by betrothed but not married couples), six for adultery and two for incest.[13]

It is doubtful that many of these erring souls were obliged to enact the full rigour of the public confession before the entire congregation, 'being bare-headed, barefoot and base-legged' being wrapped in a white sheet with a white wand in hand – for private penance appears to have become much more common.[14] Some form of penalty, however, was, at least on occasions, exacted to judge by the entry for the archbishop's visitation of Staithes in 1743: 'Fornication. AB and CD (Staithes); he did penance, she excommunicated and denied'.[15] On the other hand, in one Yorkshire village in 1743, the parson and churchwardens refrained from prosecuting the sexually delinquent because of fear of reprisal from the villages.[16] The picture was not, then, a uniform one though the historical consensus is that the church courts lost much of their power over sexual offences around the mid-eighteenth century. By 1787 the penalty for pre-nuptial conception – increasingly a dead letter – was abolished.[17]

The church courts, as an arm of the established church, theoretically had the power of the state behind them, but what mattered most was the attitude of the community. Thus the moral force exerted on erring members of nonconformist denominations could often be more effective – especially as it was accompanied by the fear of being excluded from a religious community which was often the bedrock of an individual's social existence. The close-knit Quaker community, which took a very strong line on sexual offences, could thus often better discipline its members than the Church of England. The Guisborough Quakers in 1737 admonished by name a young women for 'giving ear to the allurements of the Enemy of mankind and the carnal Insinuation of her own mind' by committing fornication and becoming pregnant 'for which Lascivious action … we doe deny any Unity or Religious fellowship with her … until she shall manifest a godly sorrow for such offences'.[18] Between 1765 and 1808 the Quakers of York also disowned the handful of sexual offenders that came before them: two unmarried mothers, an unmarried father, a father and daughter who shared the same bed, and the anticipating of marriage by 'criminal intercourse'.[19]

Ultimately, such religious sanctions largely drew what force they possessed from public opinion. The main concern of the community was often the very pragmatic one that it would be left to bear the costs of any illegitimate offspring. Courting couples were often in effect policed by their peers, for in a village society there was no such thing as a 'private life'. In a small-scale society marriage was something that involved the community as a whole. Traditionally in the fishing village of Staithes, for example, a wedding would be marked by a volley of gunfire and a race, the winner of which was allowed to remove the bride's garter.[20] After marriage there was strong pressure to conform to the established norms, so that even in nineteenth-century Yorkshire one could still find the traditional practice of 'rough music' where husband and wife were publicly shamed for adultery or the failure of the husband to maintain control over his wife. The front of their house would be ritually swept to a noisy accompaniment of a crude drum and the chanting of satirical verses.[21]

Such social discipline was, however, beginning to weaken in the eighteenth century as society became more mobile and as the time-honoured rhythms of agriculture were disrupted by the scale of economic change. Community standards were not, however, altogether congruent with the morality of the churches. There was a good deal of tolerance for courting practices which could have a sexual element so long as the end result was marriage if a pregnancy occurred. Many eighteenth-century brides went to the altar pregnant (about 15 per cent at the beginning of the century, rising to 40 per cent by the end)[22] – among them Cook's mother whose first child, John, was baptized three months after the marriage in October 1727. (Cook's own first child was born a respectable ten months after the marriage.)[23] In Yorkshire and elsewhere folk practice often sanctioned 'proving' girls before marriage so that if a pregnancy did not result it was assumed that the marriage was not meant to be.[24]

Official theory and folk practice could also be at variance when it came to establishing that a couple was married. Folk practice placed a great deal of emphasis on betrothal and would often permit sexual relations thereafter, even before the church wedding.[25] To some extent marriage practice was made more uniform and regularized by the Hardwicke Marriage Act of 1753 (though only for England, leaving open the possibility for eloping couples to flee to Gretna Green just across the Scottish border). Under its terms the loose practice of the past, when a public exchange of vows was enough to constitute a marriage, was tightened up and only a marriage sanctioned by the state and the state church had legal force.[26] When Cook married in 1762 he complied with the letter of the new law. He did, however, exercise the option to accelerate the wedding by obtaining a licence from the bishop of London rather than observing the more usual reading of the banns over three weeks. Obtaining a licence (and paying the fee that went with it) was something of a sign of gentility especially as it meant one was not obliged to announce one's marriage plans to a gossipy world. Sea-farers also often favoured it since they did not always have the time to wait for the bans. Cook's marriage bond reflected the wording of the Hardwicke Act in testifying that neither party had 'any Impediment by reason of any precontract Consanquinity Affinity or any other Cause whatsoever'. It also complied with the act in stipulating that both parties were over twenty-one and hence did not require the formal assent of the parents.[27]

When it came to his own daughters, Cook, like many parents, sought to rein-force one of the central elements of the act – to ensure that underage daughters were not carried off by fortune hunters – by framing his will in a manner which, he hoped, would reduce the possibility of his daughters entering into an unsuitable marriage. Though Cook's only daughter, Elizabeth (born 1767), had died in 1771, his will covered the possibility of any further female issue by stipulating that, while the sons could not enter into their inheritance until twenty one, his daughters could do so on marriage, even if below twenty-one but only if 'such marriage be had with the consent of my said Wife but not otherwise'.[28] While the respectable Cooks complied with the legal definitions of marriage, and sought to ensure that their offspring did likewise, lower down in society less formal understandings of marriage continued despite the Hardwicke Act. Though legal marriage became stricter, plebeian common-law marriages continued, particularly among sailors, Cook's own trade.[29]

The need to define marriage more closely rather than to rely on the traditional standards of the local community reflected the growth in size and impersonality of much of English life, especially in the towns. In the bigger towns, and above all in London, the sanctions of eaves-dropping neighbours had little force and it was there that one found the greatest divergence from the official sexual morality. Towns, and particularly port towns, were serviced by large numbers of prostitutes – London, it was said, had some ten thousand ranging from the street-walker to the employees of expensive brothels.[30] Among the latter was the establishment of Mrs Hayes of Pall Mall where, at one point, the entertainment was based on accounts of the sexual encounters between Cook's men with the Tahitians. Mrs Hayes herself took the role of Queen Oberea before an audience drawn 'chiefly of the first Nobility', while her female employees presented their clients 'with a Nail at least twelve inches in length, in imitation of the presents received by the Ladies of *Otaheite*'.[31]

The size and anonymity of London meant, too, that it could shelter illicit practices, such as homosexuality – hence the rise of the 'molly houses' as centres of a homosexual subculture which had its own distinctive clothing, networks and cant speech.[32] Eighteenth-century London had some twenty of these at any one time and these were subject to periodic raids, though few of the clients of such establishments were prosecuted.[33] Nonetheless, homosexuality remained theoretically a capital offence and there were occasional prosecutions, which increased in vigour in the late eighteenth century.[34] There was also much public disapproval – a visiting German remarked that 'In no country are such infamous pleasures spoken of with greater detestation'.[35] Over the course of the eighteenth century, too, the stereotype of the homosexual as a distinct type began to gain ground – hence the rise of such terms for homosexuals as 'mollies' and 'mariannes'.[36] Hitherto homosexuality tended to be regarded more as just another form of sexual licence and was often associated with a degenerate court culture – hence a seventeenth-century libertine might be depicted as having a prostitute on one arm and a catamite on the other.[37]

Homosexuality was particularly an issue in the armed forces and, above all, the navy, where men were cooped up together for long period without female company. There were, however, considerable constraints on homosexual practice on board ship: it was very difficult to hide and British tars were as hostile to homosexuality as the bulk of the population. Not surprisingly, then, there does not seem to have been a great deal of it, to judge by the number of formal charges.[38] The scanty medical evidence (albeit drawn from the nineteenth century merchant navy) also suggests that it was not widespread, for if it had been there should have been a much greater incidence of venereal diseases in boys and young men than there was.[39] Inevitably, however, it did happen and the navy regarded it very sternly for Article XXIX of the 1749 Articles of War stated unequivocally: 'If any Person in the Fleet shall commit the unnatural and detestable Sin of Buggery or Sodomy with Man or Beast, he shall be punished with Death by the Sentence of a Court-martial'.[40] On occasion such a draconian punishment was enforced, generally, it would seem, in a period of crisis such as after the momentous mutiny at Nore and Spithead in 1797 or at the peak of war, suggesting a link between fear of treason and hostility to homosexuality.[41] Around nineteen men were executed for the offence between 1767 and 1795 and in the last stages of the Napoleonic War, from 1810 to 1816, there were three to four executions a year.[42] The last naval trial for sodomy which resulted in execution was in 1829.

The scale, however, of active prosecution of such an offence was not high and the navy seems to have attempted to avoid the death penalty where possible – after all it meant one less sailor when trained sailors were a valuable commodity. During the course of the Seven Years' War, for example, there were some eleven trials for sodomy, four of which resulted in acquittals. The remaining seven were convicted on such lesser, non-capital offences as indecency or 'uncleanliness'[43] – a very vague term which could range from sodomy to relieving oneself on board, very tempting when the alternative was to make one's way to the head in a heaving sea.[44]

No doubt, in many case such matters were dealt with less formally, leaving no trial record behind. In Cook's journal as master of the *Pembroke*, while at Halifax, Canada on 2 June 1758, he records matter-of-factly that he punished a member of his crew for attempting sodomy (and then immediately continues on to give the number of bread bags received).[45] In other cases, even when guilt was formally established, the punishment inflicted fell well short of death. On his first naval vessel, the *Eagle*, Cook had in 1756 been witness to the punishment of a midshipman who had been convicted of sodomy by a court martial. The punishment was twenty lashes alongside every ship (much less than the penalty for desertion).[46] While in Halifax on 25 November 1758 Cook recorded that another such court martial was held to try a marine 'for Attempting to commit Sodomy' (but does not note the outcome).[47]

One would expect that on the long Pacific voyages the incidence of homosexuality would have increased and there is some evidence for this. On the voyage of the *Dolphin* under John Byron, from 1764 to 1766, there were two recorded examples of men being punished for attempted sodomy by running the gauntlet so that the punishment was inflicted by their fellow crew members wielding ropes acting as whips[48] – which, given the depth of homophobia among the common sailors, would have been a severe penance.

British sexual practice, like all other aspects of society, was coloured by its hierarchical character. Religious sanctions could be very real to at least some members of the elite, but their lives were not subject to the same community pressure to conform, nor was the issue of who would be 'left holding the baby' such a problem to those with the means to pay for the upbringing of their illegitimate offspring. The behaviour of the elite (and, in many cases, that of members of the royal family) therefore diverged significantly from the injunctions by which the rest of society was meant to conduct their lives.

Cook's contact with Joseph Banks would have given him an insight into the sexual licence that at least some of the elite allowed themselves. On the first voyage there were Banks' celebrated amours in Tahiti, which prompted much satire on his return.[49] Such behaviour was in many ways a continuation of Banks' practice at home, for Banks was later to boast 'that he had tasted Women's flesh in almost every part of the known habitable World'.[50] A year before the *Endeavour* set sail Banks greeted the return from France of one of his old Etonian school-friends with the remark that 'every man who goes to see a people chuses to make Experiments upon the women' – a guide to his own practice abroad.[51] Banks could also tell stories against himself claiming that after a night with Queen Oberea of Tahiti 'she dismissed him with evident Contempt, informing him that he was not to be compared with her own Men and requesting that for the future he would devote his attentions to the Girls of his suite'.[52] Though Banks withdrew in high dudgeon from the second voyage, Cook was much amused to find that when they reached Madeira in August 1772 the botanist who was meant to join Banks was indeed a woman.[53] No doubt Cook was much relieved that Banks' mistress did not join the ship, since, as the young sailor John Elliott wrote, 'she might have been the cause of much mischief'.[54] Such activities of Banks resulted in a least one illegitimate child who is only fleetingly mentioned but, as was often the way with the eighteenth-century elite, acknowledged without any great fuss.[55] Cook's patron, Sir Hugh Palliser, who never married, left much of his property to his illegitimate son who later took the Palliser name.[56]

These libertine ways were one of the bonds between Banks' and Cook's patron, Lord Sandwich. In 1776 David Hume reported, for example, that Banks and his school-friend, Lord Mulgrave (Constantine Phipps), together with Sandwich, were on a fishing trip near Newbury with 'two or three Ladies of pleasure' and later that year the *Morning Post* recorded that Banks had been seen in the company of Sandwich 'who is almost the only surviving member of that club (formerly called the Hell-Fire Club)' at Medmenham.[57] This brief note conveyed much significance: though the link with the original Hell-Fire Club which attracted an elite free-thinking and free-living elite in London in the 1720s was rather tenuous, the name came to be applied to a shadowy body, the Monks of Medmenham, founded by Sir Francis Dashwood. The Tory politician Dashwood embodied the elite anticlerical Enlightenment impulses which can also be seen in Banks. The garden at his seat at High Wycombe was laid out to resemble a naked woman, complete with a Temple of Venus – a play on the frequent linkage between maps of the world and pornographic explorations of the female body.[58]

Joseph Banks. Engraving by John Smith after Benjamin West (Australian National
Library, Rex Nan Kivell Collection, Nk265)

His resort at Medmenham was on the site of a former Cistercian monastery – hence the parody of the monks with much dressing up and the importing of 'nuns' (prostitutes) from London 'convents' (brothels).[59]

Sandwich did not get involved with this body until after 1763, when it had been disrupted by internal political debates stirred up by that great stormy petrel of the age, John Wilkes. By then Medmenham seems to have become a much quieter place and by 1776 it was probably a spent force. Sandwich himself made little secret of his licentious ways, entertaining the visiting Ra'iatean Mai at his seat at Hinchinbrooke along with his mistress, Martha Ray (who appears to have been a little wary of Mai's close observation of her connection with another admirer). Sexual scandal seems to have had little impact on a politician's standing and Sandwich could write in 1781 that 'I have never pretended to be free from indiscretion, and those who know me have been … long accustomed to forgive my weaknesses, when they do not interfere with my conduct as a public man'.[60]

Cook himself showed no inclination to emulate such goings on by his social superiors. To the best of our knowledge, Cook led a chaste life and was faithful to his wife – 'a decent, plump Englishwoman', as Boswell described her[61] – even though over the course of their seventeen years of married life they only spent some four years together.[62] The sailor Heinrich Zimmerman remarked in his journal of the third voyage that 'Never, however, was there a breath of suspicion in regard to his dealings with women', and in his account of the second voyage John Elliott noted that he 'never had any connection with any our fair friends; I have often seen them *jeer* and *laugh* at him, calling him Old, and *good for nothing*'.[63] Such virtue may have proceeded from some osmosis of Quaker values or perhaps it simply reflected Cook's inveterate dislike of lack of discipline. On the Pacific voyages he was watched closely and any indulgence could have considerably weakened his authority (though this certainly did not constrain his officers).

Cook, however, also had a principled objection to the behaviour of his men in relation to native women, even though he could do little to stop it. When at Queen Charlotte Sound, at the top of the South Island of New Zealand on the second voyage, Cook reflected on how the women had become more ready to sell sexual favours to his men than on his first visit. Such, he sadly concluded, 'are the concequences of a commerce with Europeans and what is still more to our Shame civilized Christians, we debauch their Morals already too prone to Vice'.[64] When he returned on the third voyage he again turned sadly to the same theme. While acknowledging that 'A connection with Women I allow because I cannot prevent it, but never encourage', he dismissed the view that such contact between Europeans and natives could bring advantage. Such a view might have some truth 'when you intend to settle amongst them; but with travelers and strangers, it is generally otherwise'. How could such transient couplings by his sailors be of benefit, he continued, when 'all their View are selfish without the least mixture of regard or attatchment whatever; at least my observations which have been pretty general, have not pointed out to me one instance to the contrary'.[65]

Though ready to judge his own men, Cook was more indulgent when considering the behaviour of the peoples of the Pacific and inclined to voice sentiments that would not have been well received at a Quaker meeting. The sexual mores of the Tahitians he reflected on the second voyage were scarcely to be condemned, since 'Incontency in the unmarried people can hardly be called a Vice sence neither the state or Individuals are the least injured by it. Maried Women are perhaps as faithfull to their husband[s] as any others'.[66] When it came to publishing his journal, however, he was a little uneasy about making public some of what he had seen, bidding his editor, the Reverend John Douglas, to avoid mention of the 'Amours of my People at Otaheite & other places ... unless it be by way of throwing a light on the Characters, or Customs of the People we are then among'. In any case, there should be nothing that 'might be unexceptionable to the nicest readers'.[67]

Cook must often have been very much on his own during the ships' sojourns on Pacific shores. He hints as much in his journal of his first visit to Tahiti, when he remarked that his attempt to limit sexual fraternization to reduce the risk of spreading venereal disease were 'not assisted by any one person in ye Ship'.[68] It would seem that he had some support from the young Quaker draughtsman, Sydney Parkinson, who denounced his fellow crewmen's errant ways. At Tahiti, Parkinson wrote, 'Most of our ship's company procured temporary wives ... an indulgence which even many reputed virtuous Europeans allow themselves, in uncivilized parts of the world, with impunity; as if a change of place altered the moral turpitude of fornication'.[69] Perhaps, however, there was an element of autobiography here, for that 'philosophical gossip', the Swedish botanist Daniel Solander, reported that once when Banks returned with a Tahitian woman 'the first thing he saw was Shyboots Parkinson in bed with the girl's sister'.[70] Less probable is the public insinuation by the astronomer, William Wales, that the two Forsters also succumbed on the second voyage, Wales coyly referring in his pamphlet war with the Forsters to 'the affair of the *old man and his son* at Uliatea, where a girl and a *knife* was concerned'.[71]

However imperfect a guide to his own practice, Parkinson's comments underline the extent to which the often thin veneer of sexual restraint largely dissolved once Europeans left home. Pacific sailors had a saying that 'There was no God on this side of Cape Horn'.[72] Even within Britain such restraint was only very effective in small communities where the weight of public scrutiny and opinion could be readily felt; the behaviour of sailors in port towns would not have been all that different to that adopted in the Pacific. The official sexual morality might be taught from the pulpits but it was only spasmodically observed and probably least of all by the aristocratic elite. Well might John Wesley, the founder of Methodism, lament: 'Where is male chastity to be found? Among the nobility, among the gentry, among the tradesmen, or among the common people of England? How few can lay any claim to it at all?'[73]

When the European strangers entered the Pacific one of their first questions when they attempted to make sense of other societies was to enquire about the institution of marriage. Families were the building blocks of their own societies and, they assumed, of others as well. They were surprised to learn, however, that marriage was a much more fluid affair in the strange new world of the Pacific. The young Joseph Banks, who was to put off his own (seemingly successful) marriage as long as possible, noted with some interest that in Tahiti marriage was a much more flexible arrangement than in Europe: 'Marriage is [in] these Islands no more than an agreement between man and woman totaly independent of the preist, it is in general I believe pretty well kept unless they agree to seperate, which is done with as little trouble as they come together'.[74] Such an arrangement may well have suited the young traveller who, the previous year, had confided to a school friend that 'Matrimony never would have come under my dispraise but from its uncertain consequences'.[75] On the second voyage, James Burney (whose own marriage was later to be disturbed by a long affair with his half-sister) also remarked on the readiness with which Tahitian marriages could be undone: 'If a women [sic] after 6 or 7 months cohabitation with her Husband does not prove with Child, their Union, if they please, may be dissolved & each party at liberty to choose another mate'. In some ways it was not unlike the English folk practice of permitting sexual relations between courting couples until the girl 'proved' pregnant. Burney, however, noted an important difference in Tahiti: for 'if a girl becomes pregnant the man cannot be forced to marry her'.

Burney's account indicated that, though there was a ritual element to Tahitian marriage, it was much less pronounced than in Britain: having obtained the 'relations consent' the male suitor 'sleeps 3 nights at their house – if the bride is a Virgin he is allowed to take no liberties till the 3d. Night, though he lyes with her each Night'. The suitor then 'makes the Relations a present & the 4th takes the Bride home'. Burney noted with particular interest that there did not appear to be a system of dowries, a practice which so dominated the marriage considerations of the English elite: 'They give no portions with the girls unless the Bride's father has no Male children or other Male Relations to bestow his property on'.[76] When Bligh visited Tahiti in 1788–89, on the *Bounty* expedition, he came to a similar conclusion to Burney, noting that 'any ceremony attending Marriage is not general'.[77] Practice varied, however, according to one's station, with the Tahitian elite having more elaborate rituals and, as in Britain, there was a great deal of emphasis on marrying within one's own class.[78]

A Māori Warrior (armed with a Patu) and his Wife. Engraving by W. Darling after Parkinson (From Sydney Parkinson, *A Journal of a Voyage to the South Seas* (London, 1773), plate 17, facing p. 98)

Tahiti also harboured a unique social institution, the *Arioi*, who, to the mixed indignation and fascination of the voyagers, defied any norms of married life. This select society of trained dancers and actors provided entertainment for major occasions such as a birth or the inauguration of a noble – their ceremonies, like those dedicated to Dionysius in ancient Greece, were intended to highlight the forces of fertility.[79] Possibly, too, they acted as a reservoir of warriors unencumbered by domestic ties.[80] They travelled widely and their freedom of movement extended to exemption from marriage, though they were certainly not celibate. If a child was conceived it was killed at birth: keeping the child and thus settling down to normal domestic life meant leaving the *Arioi*. As Thomas Edgar wrote of them in his account of the third voyage, among them there was 'an agreement between the Man & Woman to live together as long as they can do it with mutual happiness & the offspring of their enjoyments is as soon as brought into the World destroyed'. Sometimes, however, they decided to keep the child 'that done there is an end' to their life as a member of the *Arioi* and 'they are married for life'.[81]

Though there was no equivalent to the *Arioi* elsewhere in Polynesia, generally marriage was marked with less ceremony and was less of a lifelong commitment than in Europe. The Marion du Fresne expedition to New Zealand of 1772 remarked how little ritual seemed to accompany marriage;[82] in Tonga, as in Tahiti, there was a high incidence of divorce (only obtainable in England through a private act of parliament until 1857). William Mariner, who lived in Tonga from 1805 to 1810, thought that about a third of married women were divorced.[83] In Tonga it was not so important, thought Surgeon Anderson, 'that the marriages should be rigidly binding where the free intercourse between the sexes amongst the younger sort is not at all reckoned criminal but rather encouraged'.[84]

For Cook and his men Hawai'i stood out both for its degree of sexual freedom and its relaxed understanding of marriage, even among the chiefs. As Captain Clerke observed: 'Marriage, if at all known among them, is very little encouraged, we saw no traces of it'.[85] Ledyard thought that in Hawai'i 'the custom [of marriage] does not seem to be respectable, at least among the chiefs, and we were told that a man could discard his wife at pleasure'.[86] At least one of Cook's crew was intrigued how the society could function without a stable system of marriage, writing that 'indeed we never could discover that any man ever acknowledged any particular woman as his wife, but yet such an Institution must have been as I don't see how we can Raise our Society without it'.[87] Indeed, ancient Hawai'i did not have a strongly developed system of ritual marking for marriage, at least for the lower classes, nor definite words for husband and wife, so that domestic relations were characterized by much mobility.[88] For the upper classes marriage had a political dimension which would have been very familiar to the European aristocracy. As the missionary William Ellis wrote in 1826: 'Among the higher ranks, marriage seems to be conducted on principles of political expediency, with a view to strengthen alliances and family influence'. What would have been less familiar to Europeans was the practice of brothers and sisters marrying to maintain rank and family influence,[89] a practice, wrote Ellis, with a passion that reflected the strength of the incest taboo in European and most other societies, which was 'revolting to every idea of moral propriety'.[90]

In Pacific societies such as New Zealand birth was marked with much more ritual attention than marriage.[91] For Polynesians, birth exposed society to some of the most powerful and potentially dangerous creative forces. Therefore care had to be taken to shield oneself from its effects. In Tahiti, the Marquesas and New Zealand, expectant mothers (or at least those of high degree) were often secluded in a special dwelling.[92] One early nineteenth-century English traveller to New Zealand noted that after a birth both father and mother were particularly *tapu* and could not touch food, having to be fed by hand.[93] A similar ritual marking of the time after birth appears to have taken place in Tonga, where, noted

Tahitian Mother and Child. Engraving by T. Chambers after Parkinson (From Sydney Parkinson, *A Journal of a Voyage to the South Seas* (London, 1773), plate 5, facing p. 23)

Surgeon Samwell, 'After lying in the women stain their bodies & faces of a yellow Colour & this they continue to do for a certain time'.[94]

There was a certain analogy with the English ritual of 'churching' a woman after child birth, a practice that went back to purification rituals laid down in the Old Testament. Officially, church teaching moved to emphasise the element of thanksgiving rather than purification, but the older beliefs continued until relatively recent times. One Staithes woman remarked that 'you *had* to be churched before you could go into other houses'.[95] The Christian practice of christening with water also had some parallels with the Māori practice of dipping a new-born child in a stream, after which the parents were freed from the constraints of the birth *tapus*.[96]

For Polynesians the umbilical cord had particular importance, being integral to the spiritually charged and fraught process of birth. In Tahiti a priest ritually cut it to ward off potential dangers and in New Zealand it was often buried.[97] In Hawai'i Cook was intrigued to find that Hawaiian women brought the cords 'tyed up in little slips of Cloth and hide them in any little holes they can find about the Ship'.[98] Since for Hawaiians the great symbol of their connection with others was the umbilical cord the practice may well have been prompted by the desire to maintain their ties with the Europeans and their hope that the children might one day be reunited with them (and especially with those sailors who had fathered them). It may also have simply represented a desire for the children to become seafarers.[99]

In Polynesian (or European) society ritual practices soon brought one back to the all-pervading issue of social hierarchy. The scale and opulence of marriages and birthing rituals in both worlds naturally reflected one's place in the social order. In both societies, too, there was a greater expectation that aristocratic males should have both greater sexual freedom and a virgin bride (though this was by no means uniform). Cook's men made much of the sexual freedom of Polynesia but generally agreed that aristocratic women were unavailable. Surgeon Samwell, an authority in such matters, wrote, for example, of the 'Agee Girls' of Tonga that 'nor were their favours to be purchased for Hatchets or any thing else that we had, they are kept inviolate for the Chiefs who marry them'.[100]

Social hierarchy was more marked in Tonga than on Tahiti, but at Tahiti, too, Cook's men generally found the aristocratic women off limits, though seemingly not to quite the same extent as on Tonga. The astronomer Bayly found that the sisters of 'king' Tu 'would almost do anything with us except cohabiting with us & that was not to be done on any consideration whatever – Either with them or any other Aree woman'. Plainly, however, Bayly came to know these princesses well, since they told him of the social bars to their 'cohabit[ing] with any of us except we were invested with a rank among them equal to their own', and the fact that a woman of their class would be barred from being 'ever married if it is once

known she has once lost her virginity'. He also learnt in detail of the ingenious
ways such aristocratic women could maintain technical virginity while indulging
in a considerable degree of sexual freedom. Things, of course, were very different
when one moved down to the ranks of the commoners. 'Every Aree', wrote Bayly,
'has a number of young girls Daughters of his towtows & servants these he uses
as he pleases & during our residence among them the Chiefs let them out to sleep
with our people for what they can get'.[101]

Others, however, were less certain that the Tahitian aristocratic women were
so out of reach. Another third voyage journalist, the unpopular Lieutenant
Williamson, boasted that 'these women are as fond of attention & flattery, &
being danced after as any woman in Europe, & I can take upon me positively to
assert that C. Cook was mistaken, & that they are comeatable'.[102] Though Johann
Reinhold Forster had, no doubt, done less fieldwork than Williamson, he was
inclined to agree, writing in his account of the second voyage about the lack of
sexual restraint in Tahiti that 'Women of all ranks follow these practices from the
earliest times, and ... are married to the first people of the isle'.[103] Nonetheless,
Bayly, who seems to have researched the matter thoroughly, was probably right in
his insistence that Tahitian aristocratic brides needed to be virgins, even though
lesser favours might be granted before marriage.

The hierarchical character of Polynesian society was reflected in the way, too,
that women commoners sought sexual connections with the higher born which,
on Hawai'i at least, seems to have included the European voyagers. When Cook's
expedition first arrived in Hawai'i at Kaua'i, Lieutenant King remarked on the
way in which the local women readily made themselves available: 'They were very
desirous of coming on board, & their action were too unequivocal to leave us
in any doubt of their intentions of gratifying us in all the pleasures the Sex can
give'.[104] To the amazement of the men, the women did not even seem to expect
payment in return. Surgeon Ellis wrote with some surprise that the Hawaiian
'ladies are very lavish of their favours, but are far from being so mercenary as
those of the Friendly or Society Isles, and some of their attachments seemed
purely the effect of affection'.[105]

A more likely explanation, however, than infatuation with British sailors was
the desire to attach themselves to these seemingly powerful strangers through the
most basic of all social ties, that of common parenthood. By doing so they were
following the well-established local practice of offering a virgin to a chief with
the hope that any pregnancy that might result would be a claim on his political
and religious power.[106] In legend, at least, such a connection even extended to
Cook himself, whose high status demanded no less than a royal princess. Hence
the Hawaiian myth that one of the Kauaian chieftesses gave her own daughter
to Cook.[107] In a manner similar to the European practice of royal marriages to
cement alliances, other Polynesian societies also sought to draw the new arrivals

into their social system through marriage. On one of the Cook Islands, for example, there was a tradition that the local chief had sought to make Cook his son-in-law.[108]

There is no denying, however, that in much of the Pacific sex was a trading commodity (as it was, of course, in Europe). To Lieutenant Williamson the sexual trade available at Queen Charlotte Sound, New Zealand, seemed very much like that available back in London, with young women offering themselves 'with as much ease & assurance as the oldest Strand walker in London would do'.[109] The astronomer William Wales was also struck by the parallel when he visited Tahiti on the second voyage: 'That there are Prostitutes here as well as in London is true', but emphasized that this did not apply to the whole female population any more than it did in Britain even in the port cities. 'On the whole', he continued, 'I am firmly of opinion that a stranger who visits England might with equal justice draw the Characters of the Ladies there, from those which he might meet with on board the Ships in Plymouth Sound, at Spithead, or in the Thames; on the point at Plymouth, or in the Purlieus of Wapping'.[110] George Forster wondered what sort of tales Mai might bring back from London 'because he did not find the ladies cruel in the Strand'. He also was of the opinion that 'the women who made a practice of this intercourse were all of the common or lowest class'[111] – an indication of the extent to which those at the bottom of the hierarchy were used to buy the goods the society as a whole and particularly the chiefs wanted. Cook pointed out, however, that in Tahiti prostitution was not as shameful as in Britain and that a woman indulging in it was not considered 'to have committed a crime of so deep a die as to exclude her from the Esteem and Society of the Community in general'.[112]

When the demand for precious goods increased, access to Tahitian women, including those of higher social rank, also seemed to increase. On the third voyage, wrote Bayly, 'the women are thought to be more friendly than on former voyages which we Attribute to the great desire for red Feathers'. The result, he continued, was that 'numbers of fine women have come on board the ship though, having 'obtained a small Quantity by cohabiting once', they promptly disappeared.[113] On the previous voyage when red feathers were even rarer, Anders Sparrman reported that 'the paramount chief Potataw, in his overwhelming desire for red feathers, actually gave his wife over to the rites of Eros', adding caustically that in Europe men were willing to wear the horns of a cuckold 'provided that they were gilded. Why, then, marvel if the Otaheitian viceroy adorned his with red plumes'.[114] The use of Tahitian married women for sexual trade seems, however, to have been unusual. On the second voyage Elliott remarked that 'a Married woman was never known to be got at; though many trials were made with very high offers'.[115] Cook thought that 'the favours of Maried women and also the unmarried of the better sort, are as difficult to obtain here as in any other

Country whatever', and another of the second voyage journalists affirmed his belief in the importance of marriage by writing that 'the ladies of Otaheite are never known to break that solemn union which holds society together'.[116] Wales' endorsement of this point was slightly more qualified, writing that 'the favours of Maried Women are not to be purchased, except of their Husbands, to whose commands they seem to pay implicit obedience'.[117]

Wales was here pointing to a general principle, that the Europeans' access to local women depended very much on the attitude of their menfolk. Cook made the same point when commenting on the way in which his men were denied sexual contact with the Tasmanian Aborigines at Adventure Bay: 'I believe it has generally been found amongst uncivilized people that where the Women are easy of access, the Men are the first who offer them to strangers, and where this is not the case they are not easily come at'.[118] It might be surmised that societies that had little use for European goods (such as the hunter and gatherer Tasmanians) were less open to such sexual trade.

There were also examples of societies, however, which were quite familiar with such goods, where the sailors made little sexual headway. One such was the island of Savu in the East Indies (Indonesia) encountered on the *Endeavour* voyage, where, wrote Cook, approvingly though perhaps a little sweepingly, 'Fornication and Adultery is hardly known among them'.[119] The Nootka were very keen indeed to obtain European goods, but, wrote Bayly, 'They are willing to part with any thing they have except their Women'.[120] Predictably, the boastful Lieutenant Williamson claimed that 'the Women have no objection to barter their Favours'[121] – but this may well refer to the way in which the Nootka used slave women to obtain goods. Ellis described the pathetic scene when such women who, he speculated, had been 'overcome in battle', were paraded before his fellow crewmen, being 'mute', 'dejected' and 'totally under the command of those who brought them'.[122] By contrast, on Hawai'i, where, as we have seen, marriage ties were particularly weak, Surgeon Samwell affirmed that there was little bar to contact with the married women. This was even more marked on the island of Unalaska in the Bering Strait where, wrote Samwell, the men did not have 'the least Objections to our lying with their Wives' – perhaps because of traditional notions of sexual hospitality.[123]

These European strangers, then, received very varying sexual receptions, ranging from brisk sexual trade in Tahiti and enthusiastic embrace in Unalaska and Hawai'i to outright rejection in Tasmania and Savu. On occasions, too, their sexual eagerness prompted taunting from some of the local people, who obviously were not all in awe of these strange beings. When the *Endeavour* was in New Zealand one crew member bought, as he thought, the services of a young woman. He found, however, that his companion was a boy. When he complained he was sent another boy, after which, wrote Banks, 'he could get no redress but was laught at by the Indians'.[124] On New Caledonia on the second voyage the voyagers also met with more mockery. 'The Ladies here', wrote Cook, 'would frequently devert themselves by going a little aside with our gentlemen as if they meant to grant them the last favour and then run away laughing at them'.[125]

Ironically, in other contexts, Europeans declining sex could also be met with derision. When he would not avail himself of the services of a pretty Tongan girl, Cook was abused by her elderly female relative interested in securing a trade with a stinging comment to the effect that 'what sort of a man are you thus to refuse the embraces of so fine a young Woman'.[126] The Spanish were also looked down on for their sexual restraint – a part of their eighteenth-century determination to live down the 'Black Legend' of their Conquistador past. The Tahitian women, wrote Surgeon Samwell, 'frequently complained to us of this unmanly Behaviour of the flesh-subduing Dons', adding slyly that 'We gave them every consolation in our power'.[127] The energies of Samwell, the parson's son turned sexual athlete, were undiminished by the fact that he had left behind in London a mistress and child, both of whom died by the time he returned.[128]

There were also misunderstandings across the cultural divide about gender identity, especially as some of the sailors were only boys with no facial hair and performed tasks such as carrying burdens which, in some parts of the Pacific, were reserved for women. At Dusky Sound, New Zealand on the second voyage a Māori girl became very friendly with one of the sailors 'untill she discovered his sex and then', wrote Cook, 'she would not suffer him to come near her'.[129] Later in the voyage at Tanna (Vanuatu) there was speculation that some of the population were homosexually inclined because they followed some of the young sailors into the bushes. Wales questioned this, noting that a man being followed had 'either a softness in his features' or was carrying 'bundles of one kind or other which is the Office of their own Women'. Thus he set a sort of trap and confirmed that when the Tannan men found out that their European companion was male they returned 'very much abashed'.[130] A similar situation arose on the third voyage at Adventure Bay, Tasmania – though things did not go quite so far. There, Bayly recorded, the local people 'took some of our young Gentlemen to be women & wanted to be friendly with them – which was by no means agreeable'.[131]

Sexual encounters brought with them not only a crop of (generally) unwanted pregnancies but also the terrible scourge of venereal disease. Cook tried to prevent men with overt symptoms having sexual relations, but such restraints had only limited effect and, in any case, those without symptoms could still be carriers. Indeed, it has been calculated that about half the *Endeavour*'s crew contracted some form of venereal disease.[132] The knowledge that the voyages brought with them such a black legacy gnawed at Cook's conscience and that of many of his officers. When at Tonga on the third voyage, Lieutenant King found that a consequence of his countrymen's previous visit was 'that the Venereal disorder had been left among them; so it is, that wherever we go, we spread an incurable distemper which nothing we can do can ever recompence'. Britain would have to live with the knowledge, realized King, that 'we have left them an incurable disorder which will for ever embitter, their quiet & happy lives, & make them curse the hour they ever saw us'.[133] Surgeon Anderson thought similarly, writing of the Tongans: 'The injury these people have received from us by communicating this certain destroyer of mankind is not to be repaired by any method whatever'. It was, he continued, a particularly heavy cross for a people for whom 'intercourse between the sexes' was 'a principal ingredient of happiness in a country where custom has laid but little restraint upon it, and religion has not branded it with the name of a crime'.[134] When reflecting on the damage done to the New Zealanders, Johann Reinhold Forster was particularly animated on the subject, arguing that it would have been better if the first Māori woman infected by the Europeans had been killed to save the country from the scourge of venereal disease and 'that nothing is capable to compensate in the slightest manner the great injury done to their Society'.[135]

There was some attempt to mitigate the guilt by passing the blame for infection in Tahiti onto the French who had visited there the year before Cook's *Endeavour*. Or, perhaps, it was argued, there was some form of the disease which was already endemic in the Pacific – a view that seems to have had some substance, since modern research has established the similarity between yaws, which was common in places such as Tahiti, and some forms of venereal disease.[136] Both Joseph Banks and the astronomer Wales, for example, remarked on the way that the Tahitians seemed to have a cure for venereal disease, which suggested that they were long familiar with it.[137] Though in Hawai'i, too, Samwell reported that there was a traditional cure for such diseases, suggesting that it preceded European contact,[138] it was difficult to escape the knowledge that the local people considered that the British had brought the disease with them. Cook was grieved that his attempts at preventing its spread there had broken down – predictable though that was.[139] Thereafter in the Hawaiian mind venereal disease was 'the curse of Cook'.[140]

Male–female relations were very familiar territory for the voyagers, including, sadly, the spread of venereal disease. Some Pacific sexual practices might differ from what the voyagers were used to, but these rarely provoked moral indignation. Pre-marital and even post-marital sexual freedom or more 'open' marriages prompted philosophical reflections on human variety or, in many cases, scarcely disguised envy. The voyagers were, however, shocked to find that on Hawai'i homosexuality was openly practised in the highest circles. In awed tones Ledyard reported that the Hawaiian upper aristocracy practised 'a custom among them contrary to nature, and odious to a delicate mind … the custom alluded to is that of sodomy, which is very prevalent if not universal among the chiefs'. Though he thought that 'we had no right to attack or even to disapprove of customs in general that differed from our own yet this one so apparently infringed and insulted the first and strongest dictate of nature'.[141] Even Samwell breathlessly wrote of the Hawaiian chiefs 'that Unnatural Crime which ought never to be mentioned is not unknown among them'.[142] He was shocked, too, that the Hawaiians 'have frequently asked us on seeing a handsome young fellow if he was not an Ikany [aikane, homosexual lover] to some of us'.[143]

As we have seen, over the course of the eighteenth century in Britain the image of homosexual practice had changed from something indulged in by libertines seeking every possible form of sexual pleasure with male or female to a particular type of individual who generally sought single sex relations. In the journalists' responses to the practice of Hawaiian homosexuality there were, however, traces of both the more traditional view as well as that of the more recent stereotype of the homosexuality. The well-educated Lieutenant King was more inclined to the latter: hence he took the view that 'the foulest pollutions [which] disgrace the Men' meant that women would be neglected and 'deprived of the natural affections of their Husbands'. Indeed, he thought that the Hawaiian female consorts were paid 'little attention or regard'. Ledyard agreed, contending that such chiefs 'bestow all those affections upon them [their aikane] that were intended for the other sex'.[144] By contrast, Clerke's description of what he termed 'this infernal practice' was more in the same vein as seventeenth-century English critiques of court debauchery, with courtiers indulging in every possible form of sexual licence: 'every Aree according to his rank keeps so many women and so many young men ... for the amusement of his leisure hours'.[145] Similarly, Samwell wrote that the great chiefs 'have as many Concubines and Wives as they please, and a number of young fellows'.[146] The strongest reaction against such practices, Ledyard tells us, came not from the more philosophically inclined officers but from the men – reflecting the depth of plebeian homophobia.[147] Though the journalists had a good deal to say about Hawaiian homosexuality, they made no mention of its practice in Tahiti or elsewhere in the Pacific. Bligh, however, discovered when he visited Tahiti on the Bounty expedition that there was a class of males on Tahiti (the mahu) who were 'Selected when Boys and kept with the Women solely for the caresses of men'.[148]

The observations of Cook and his men of homosexuality in Hawai'i and probably, too, those of Bligh in Tahiti made the British ponder whether the practice was as contrary to nature as orthodoxy had it. Strangely enough, however, when the philosopher and legal reformer Jeremy Bentham came to consider the matter, in his Theory of Legislation (1802), he thought that the travel accounts had been too circumspect on the matter and that it was the missionaries who had made plain the extent of the 'improlific appetite' on the 'newly discovered islands of the Pacific Ocean'. Moreover, in contrast to the increasingly accepted view that homosexuals were preoccupied with same sex relations, he thought the accounts from the Pacific showed that they did not change male–female behaviour – all of which he saw as providing grounds for mitigating laws against homosexuality.[149] This was one instance of the way in which one of the effects of Pacific travel was to prompt a reassessment of homosexual as well as heterosexual mores.[150]

The voyagers' discussion of homosexuality was linked with the issue of the role of women in Hawaiian and, indeed, Pacific society. In their view homosexuality represented one extreme of the way in which Hawaiian women were excluded from many aspects of the male world. Lieutenant King qualified his often positive description of Hawai'i with the remark that 'they fall very short of the other islanders in that best test of civilization, the respect paid to women', arguing that 'In their domestic life, they appear to live almost by themselves'.[151] Like many of his colleagues, he made much of the way in which some parts of Polynesia (with major exceptions such as New Zealand and Tonga) women were not permitted to eat with men or to eat particular foods. In Polynesian thinking, the basic cosmic dualism between male and female had its parallel in the distinction between raw and cooked food, the former being the domain of the male and the latter of the females. In Hawai'i this was carried to the point of having separate cook houses for men's and women's food.[152] From such a binary opposite arose the deeply-engrained insistence that men and women should eat separately, and this was further strengthened by male fears of being polluted by women, especially in relation to menstruation (particularly, again, in Hawai'i).[153] Many of the journalists make much of the way in which on board the European ships women would eat with men and indulge with delight in foods which were normally tapu. Samwell described with relish the way in which Hawaiian women on board ate 'very heartily' the forbidden pork and plantain.[154] Sometimes, however, they were caught out: King noted that 'A Girl got a terrible beating on board our Ship for eating the wrong sort of Plantain'.[155]

Similar dietary restrictions applied on Tahiti, much to the astonishment of Joseph Banks, who thought it very odd that 'Fond as the sexes are of each others company the Customs of the Country will not allow them to Eat together'. Some of the younger Tahitian women would permit the British males to eat with them, but one of the older women responded to such an infringement of tapu by destroying the vessels that European males had inadvertently touched. When Banks told the Tahitian that men and women commonly ate together in England, they 'expressed much disgust'.[156] Nonetheless, on board ship there was surreptitious mixed dining with women eating tapued food, though, added Thomas Edgar, 'they did [so] with great caution fearing to be seen by the Men'.[157] Edgar very much took the side of the Tahitian women, viewing them as 'Angels' and the time he lived with one 'the happiest 3 Months I ever spent'. He was therefore rather more sympathetic to Tonga where, he thought, women were much less in a state of 'vassalage' and where the men allowed 'them I believe nearly equal privileges with themselves'.[158] In making such a judgement, he was no doubt greatly influenced by the fact that, as Cook put it, 'It is not the custom here as at Otaheite for the men and women to have seperated Messes, here they eat at the same Table'.[159] Surgeon Anderson thought, however, that there the women were treated by the men 'as a set of beings every way inferior to them'. This prompted a more general disquisition on the way that, 'as civilization has advanced', women were 'treated with that respect to which they are often more justly entitled than their lordly masters'.[160]

It was a theme taken up by a number of the journalists reflecting the Enlightenment preoccupation with measuring the upward progress of civilization, with what they considered the progressive improvement of the lot of women being one of its markers. Anderson's fellow Scot, the influential social theorist, Lord Kames, for example, spoke of 'the gradual progress of women, from their low state in savage tribes, to their elevated state in civilized nations'.[161] By modern standards the 'elevated state' of British women of the period was far from clear, though women did play a more active role in society than hitherto. It has been suggested, for example, that women's purchasing power was one of the drivers of the early Industrial Revolution, with the mass production of textiles and household goods.[162] The emphasis on the family as the building block of society with the male as its head meant, however, that women had no direct role in politics or in many other areas, and that they rarely had independent rights to property. 'In marriage', intoned the great eighteenth-century legal authority Sir William Blackstone, 'husband and wife are one person and that person is the husband'.[163] So deeply engrained was the notion that the authority of a husband over a wife was fundamental to the stability of the society that there were still occasional eighteenth-century instances of women receiving savage punishment for murdering their husbands, since the crime was regarded as a form of treason – one such case leading to the execution by burning of Ann Sowerby at York in 1767.[164]

Nonetheless, the belief that the treatment of Western women illustrated a clear and upward advance in civilization was well entrenched in educated circles. The philosophically-inclined Forsters, though open-minded about many other aspects of the way of life of the peoples of the Pacific, adopted a more critical tone when discussing the lot of women (though one wonders what Johann Reinhold Forster's long-suffering wife would have said while at home coping with a large family and larger debts). 'It is the practice of all uncivilized nations', wrote George Forster in his account of Tanna, 'to deny their women the common privileges of human beings and to treat them as creatures inferior to themselves'.[165] Lieutenant King made even more overt the view that the treatment of women offered a gauge of social progress and a means 'to judge how near Barbarous people approach in manners to civilized Nations'. Using this yardstick he thought that the people of Tahiti 'are far removed from a savage state'.[166] Another of his shipmates, however, flattered himself by using the same contrast between the treatment of women in 'polished' and 'barbarous' nations to explain why the Hawaiian women were attracted to the British sailors – even though, as he conceded with some understatement, 'we were not the most polished of our nation'.[167]

Sailing the Pacific made Cook and his men well aware of the way that sex, that most basic of human impulses, could manifest itself in many different social forms. Exposure to a wider world made them reflect on their own society's way of ordering matters. This could prompt both praise and criticism of the practices of the peoples of the Pacific. Assumptions about what was inscribed in the law of nature were challenged, though the voyagers remained judgemental about some of the more radical departures from their own accustomed ways in matters such as infanticide or homosexuality. While generally loud in their praises of the women of the Pacific they regarded what they considered as their generally downtrodden condition as an index of the distance that Pacific societies had to climb up the ladder that led to civilization.

When the voyagers returned home, and published their accounts of the new world of the Pacific, distance often meant magnifying difference still further – particularly when it came to that great staple of the best seller, the extent of sexual freedom in sunnier climes. The judicious Cook sought to dampen down some of the more lurid excesses of the travel accounts that sprang from his own voyages. When dining with James Boswell, Dr Johnson's biographer and a well-seasoned authority on matters sexual, Cook attempted to put right some of what he considered the exaggerations of John Hawkesworth who had gained the lucrative rights to publish the official account of Cook's first voyage. 'He said', wrote Boswell, 'that a disregard of chastity in unmarried women was by no means general at Otaheite, and he said that Hawkesworth's story of an *initiation* he had no reason to beleive' [168] – referring to the account of a public sexual initiation of a young girl. Highly coloured though it may have been, however, Hawkesworth's work drew on plentiful material in the journals of Cook and, still more, of Banks.[169] Whether he liked it or not, the sober Cook and his voyages (together with ample help from the accounts of those of Bougainville and others) had implanted in the European imagination an image of a sexually blissful South Pacific which neither further scrutiny nor the passage of time would altogether erase.

8

Death

Eighteenth-century Britain may have been more reticent than many Pacific societies in publicly acknowledging sex, but it gave death – that other great central biological fact of human existence – at least as much prominence as did the peoples of the Pacific. 'In the midst of life we are in death' intoned the prayerbook, and the inevitability of death and the need to prepare for it and the life to come was the abiding theme of the preachers. Cook's devout employer, John Walker, though vigilant in the affairs of this world, reflected the preoccupation with death's dark shadow in the preamble to his will: 'Whereas it is the duty of every man to consider of his latter end to let his house in order whilst opportunity permits knowing the certainty of death and uncertainty of this life'.[1]

Everywhere there were reminders of death: few families escaped its clutches for long and in village society death, in the form of the churchyard, was given a central place. The ravages that death could exact were spelt out in full public view in the gravestone erected by Cook's father and carved with his own hand outside All Saints, Great Ayton, to mark the final resting place of Cook's mother, Grace, and her offspring. It serves as a monument to the quite common toll that the grim reaper had exacted from one by no means out of the ordinary family. Grace herself (who died in 1765) came close to the biblical three score and ten, dying at the age of sixty-three, but the lives of most of her progeny were cut short, with only three living to something approaching a full span: James and his sisters, Margaret (Mrs Fleck) and Christiana (Mrs Cocker) – and, of course, James' life was brutally cut short at fifty. Thus the gravestone records the roll-call of early death in the Cook family:

> To ye memory of Mary, and Mary, Jane, and William, daughters and sons of James and Grace Cook. Mary died June 30th 1737 in ye fifth year of her age; Mary, died June 17th, 1741, aged 10 months and 6 days; Jane, died May ye 12th, 1742, in the 5th year of her age; William, died January ye 29th, 1747/8, aged 2 yrs, 12months, 16 days and 7 hours; and also John their son, dyed Sept. 20, 1750, aged 23 years.[2]

The repetition of Mary is a reminder that it was common practice for a child to be given the same name as a deceased sibling: so common was infant death that not even the name was regarded as the exclusive property of a particular child. After all, in an age when something like one in five children died before their

Photograph of the Old Cemetery, Great Ayton (Mitchell Library, Frame Order Number: GPO 1-31941)[4]

first birthday, it was not worth investing too much emotional capital in such a precarious little life.[3] In death Cook's parents were separated, for poor transport and the family's straitened means resulted in his father being buried in the churchyard at Marske near his daughter's house at Redcar where he died. Though widely dispersed, Cook and his two adult sisters seem to have good relations: both were accorded a legacy of ten pounds in his will and he and later his widowed wife paid close attention to the tangled affairs of the Flecks.[4]

James Cook's own family re-enacted a similarly grim saga of early deaths. His first-born son, James, was born in 1763 and lived to man's estate but, like his father before him, died in the service of the Royal Navy, drowning in Poole Harbour in 1794. A similar fate had earlier befallen his second son, Nathaniel, who was born in 1764 but drowned in the West Indies in 1780. By contrast, Elizabeth, the only daughter, lived for only five years from 1766 to 1771, while the next two offspring had an even more fragile purchase on life: the third son, Joseph, died after a few weeks of fitful existence in 1768, and the next son, George, survived for only a little longer, dying after a few months in 1775. The last son, Hugh, whom Cook never saw since he was born on 23 May 1776 after the third voyage had set sail, was, understandably, not exposed by his mother to the hazards of the navy but nonetheless died of scarlet fever in 1793. He was buried in the church of Great St Andrew's Cambridge, just across the road from Christ's College, Cambridge, where he was studying to become an Anglican minister. This became the vault for the remainder of the sadly depleted family. While the children who died before Hugh were buried at St Dunstan's church in Stepney, London, James, the eldest, followed his brother to the graveyard at Cambridge and it was there that Elizabeth herself was eventually laid to rest in 1835. True to the provisions of her will, the Cook family monument is still maintained.

Confronted thus by death's every-present demands, rituals formed an essential means of reaffirming the permanence of society in the face of the manifest impermanence of the individual. Attendance at funerals became a way of defining the community to which the deceased belonged. The smaller the community, the more inclusive funerals were likely to be. In the North Riding villages of Cook's Yorkshire, funerals were one of the most important of all social gatherings and many of the customs were of ancient lineage. The custom of women dressed in mourning clothes going around the village 'bidding' relatives and neighbours to attend a funeral went back to Scandinavian times.[5] Custom also dictated different forms of funeral observance to mark the passing of the different sorts and conditions of the dead. The death of a young maiden was publicly proclaimed by the female bearers wearing white and carrying a garland, while a woman who died in childbirth had a white sheet thrown over her coffin. In the North Yorkshire fishing town of Flamborough the coffins of men drowned at sea were carried shoulder high, while those who died on land were carried lower.[6]

But even within such villages the funeral ceremonies were becoming less all-embracing of the community as a whole – a trend which was to intensify as time went by. The old custom of inviting all to the funeral 'arvel' and the feast that followed had shrunk somewhat, and specially baked biscuits (which might be stamped with a skull and crossbones) appear to have taken the place of a general distribution of bread.[7] At eighteenth-century funerals a select few were often marked out by the bestowal of marks of remembrance. Black kid gloves were one sign of special connection to the dead, while among wealthier families the deceased was often commemorated by funeral rings bestowed on those closest to him or her. When the wealthy Ralph Jackson of Great Ayton buried his wife at Guisborough in 1777 (along with his late child, who was disinterred from his grave at Great Ayton to be with his mother in death), funeral rings were afterwards distributed to relatives and close friends. This reflected the character of the funeral party more generally, which was restricted in size and consisted largely of relatives and tenants.[8] As always the concerns of the dead were intertwined with those of the living: when Mr William Osbaldeston, the

MP for Scarborough, died in 1765, forty-two memorial rings were given to the forty-two members of the town corporation. His brother, Fontayne, was duly and promptly elected as MP in his place.[9] Though Cook (or what remained of him after the Hawaiians returned his depleted corpse) was buried in distant Hawai'i, Mrs Cook had a funeral ring made for herself which she wore in the portrait painted when she was over eighty and which still survives.[10]

In Europe more generally there were some signs that by the late eighteenth century death was being pushed towards the outer edges of the community. From 1776, in France burials inside churches were forbidden on the grounds of hygiene. In England the relatively new profession of the funeral director was establishing itself, especially among the wealthier middling order, as a way of freeing the family from the necessity of having to deal directly with the stark realities of death and corruption.[11] In the Yorkshire that Cook knew death was still accorded very considerable attention and respect, and such practices as funeral wakes acted as an affirmation of the community's continued existence. In the small closely-knit fishing village of Staithes there remained, for example, something of the old practice of reaffirming the community in the face of death through a meal – somewhat depleted though this meal might be. There, after the coffin lid was fixed in position, sweet funeral biscuits were consumed along with glasses of port or spirits.[12]

Within English society the increasing extent of religious division made funerals less inclusive than of yore. This was most notably true among the Quakers, with whom Cook had much to do. Symbolically, in death the Quakers withdrew from the larger society by being buried in their own graveyards. Consistent with their religion more generally, Quakers believed that death should be marked with as much simplicity as possible and that ritual should be minimal. Quakers were discouraged from holding or attending wakes, being urged to 'abstain from all Superfluities in meat and drink and at the Burials of their dead'.[13] They also regarded all but the most rudimentary form of gravestones as a form of vanity. The Whitby Quakers were advised in 1717 to forego 'the vain custome of erecting monuments over the dead bodies of Friends' and to ensure 'that all such monuments should be removed, as much as may be with discretion and conveniency'.[14] True to such precepts, the eighteenth-century headstones in the Great Ayton Quaker cemetery remain devoid of any decoration, bearing only the basic facts of name, age and date of death.[15] They offer mute testimony to Quaker aversion to vanity and ritual and to the retreat of death to a private sector outside the reach of the wider community – a trend that was eventually to become more pronounced in English society more generally.

In the closely-knit communities of the Pacific death was likely to be a much more public event, with few of the buffers between the larger society and the deceased, and his or her immediate family, which the European world was gradually erecting. As in Europe and elsewhere the fact of death was given meaning and social recognition by a set of rituals intended both to mourn the dead and to reaffirm society's ongoing existence. What struck both Cook and his fellow travellers most was the extent to which ritualized grief demanded considerable sacrifices of the living to an extent unknown in Europe. As Surgeon Anderson put it: 'Their mourning is ... not in words but deeds' – which he saw as a great 'proof of their humanity'.[16] Mourning in Europe had become more and more controlled and private, and outward displays of grief in northern Europe were seen as signs of a lack of that emotional control which society more and more expected of individuals.[17] In the Pacific, by contrast, the sense of loss required outward and visible expression in forms quite alien to the Europeans.

Above all, the voyagers remarked on the frequent practice of mutilation of the living as a means of mourning the dead – something they encountered throughout Polynesia. The loss of blood relatives meant that the living lost blood.[18] At Tahiti, noted Banks, the mourners would stand in the presence of the dead and lacerate themselves, stemming the flow of blood (and tears) with rags which they would throw near the corpse as a tribute to the dead.[19] Sydney Parkinson, however, thought that the practice could become ritualized, commenting that after one of the wives of a Tahitian deceased chief had duly struck herself with a shark's tooth 'and covered the blood with some pieces of cloth; and, having bled about a pint, she gathered up as much of it as she could, threw it into the sea, and then assumed a cheerful countenance, as if nothing had happened'.[20]

Elsewhere, as at Tonga, grief could, as Lieutenant Burney put it in his *Discovery* journal, take the form of 'cutting off a little finger, burning their Arms in circular Rings, beating the Skin off their Arms in circular Rings, beating the Skin off their cheek bones, or cutting the Hair Short and rubbing the Head with a mixture of Lime and Oil'.[21] In the view of William Ellis, Burney's fellow *Discovery* shipmate, the more the Tongans 'torture themselves in this manner the greater esteem they are supposed to have entertained for the deceased'.[22] Clerke perceived a graduated scale whereby the death of a brother or a sister would result in the loss of 'a joint of one of their little fingers, but when a Father dies they cut the whole of the little finger off the right hand and for a Mother the same off the left hand'.[23] The philosophical George Forster saw the practice of cutting off fingers as a tribute to the dead as having parallels elsewhere in the world among such peoples as the African Hottentots, the Guaranos in Paraguay and among the residents of California.[24] On Hawai'i respect for the dead often took the form of knocking out teeth, a practice which, as Surgeon Samwell remarked, 'bears some resemblance to that of cutting the little fingers off by the Inhabitants of the friendly Isles'.[25]

The New Zealanders followed Tahitian practice in marking the passing of the dead with laceration of the living – 'they proportion the depth of their cuts', speculated Banks, 'to the regard they have for the deceased'.[26] On occasions the dye for making tattoos was applied to such cuts and it has even been suggested that the stains thus made could act as a form of design to commemorate the departed.[27] Cook indeed wondered if the scars made by 'cuting and scarifying their bodies' had 'some signification such as to shew how near related the deceased was to them'.[28] In any case, it was certainly true that throughout the Pacific bodies were deliberately marked by the process of grieving, just as they were permanently marked by tattooing. As an early nineteenth-century missionary, William Smith, remarked of the Māoris' lack of gravestones: 'the living themselves are the monuments; for scarcely a single person is to be seen of either sex, whose body is not marked'.[29] There was no parallel to this in European society, though memory of the dead was marked in the outward and visible form of mourning dress and the codes that dictated how long it should be worn according to the closeness of the kin that had died. In Staithes the colours of the women's bonnets, a distinctive feature of village dress, served to act as a marker of the mourning process, with black worn for the first year then lilac for the second, before reverting to the more usual colours.[30]

Though European men wore mourning and Pacific men would wound themselves to honour their dead, women in both societies played a particularly conspicuous part in the ceremonies of mourning. Banks regarded the readiness with which Tahitian women would lacerate themselves as an instance of 'The superior strength of affection which the Soft Sex are capable of in preference to men'.[31] On Hawai'i, Samwell thought that it was women particularly who sacrificed their front teeth to mark the death of their husband or chief.[32] Māori women acted as chief mourners and this also appears to have been true of the Tahitians – Banks remarking that 'the men seem to think lamentations below their dignity'.[33] At North Riding Yorkshire funerals, too, women were particularly prominent in the rituals of mourning. It was women who acted as 'bidders', summoning the mourners, and as 'servers', dispensing the food and drink at the funeral – a meal being the most expressive statement of community solidarity. The 'bidders' and 'servers' would also frequently walk at the head of the funeral procession.[34] Quite why women figured so prominently in marking the passage of the dead is open to speculation: one possibility is that as the bearers of children they were the most potent symbol of society's capacity to renew itself.

Funerals brought together men and women and, to some extent, that other great social divide: those of different rank. In traditional English society the social standing of a lord was marked by the number of those attending his funeral, and the poor would often be attracted by the funeral doles handed out after the burial.[35] Attendance at the funeral was not only a way of paying one's respect for the dead but also of acknowledging the power of the aristocratic family, as the heir took his (or, rarely, her) place to maintain the dynasty's continuity:

'the lord is dead, long live the lord'. By Cook's time the gentry and aristocracy were demanding more privacy when it came to funerals, just as they withdrew from the masses in other ways, whether through private galleries at church (as at Great Ayton) or greater seclusion of their houses and their dining practices therein. This may help to account for the popularity of the 'night funeral' in the seventeenth and eighteenth centuries as a way of cutting down both the numbers and the pomp. By the nineteenth century these nocturnal burials had faded out but, by that time, the quasi-feudal expectations of 'good lordship', which required much largesse and a very large funeral, had greatly diminished.[36]

In Polynesian society, too, death, like all other aspects of society, was marked by hierarchy. Cook noted that on Tonga the length of time that the women who prepared a chief's body for burial had to remain *tapued* and be fed by others varied according to the status of the chief.[37] In Tahiti the death of a major chief might require general restrictions on everyday activities, such as lighting of fires and fishing, while in New Caledonia the death of a chief could result in the destruction of precious possessions along with bodily laceration as a mark of respect.[38] A chief's passing required greater time for society to readjust than the death of a commoner, so the mourning ceremonies were often more prolonged. Hence deceased notables were sometimes embalmed (as, traditionally, were members of the European aristocracy, for similar reasons). Because such ceremonies linked with the upper echelons of Pacific society were so much more visible than those of commoners, the accounts of funeral customs by the voyagers were much more likely to reflect aristocratic practice. What they did see of commoners' funerals indicated that they could be pretty perfunctory. William Ellis saw one such in the highly stratified society of Hawai'i, which consisted of a gathering of friends and relatives who 'deplored his loss, with loud lamentations and expressions of grief, which continued till the following day, when they threw his body into the sea' (a practice that also seems to have been commonly employed in disposing of Māori commoners).[39] By contrast, Hawaiian chiefs were buried with ceremony in large stone structures (*heiaus*) for which Cook and his men used the Tahitian term '*morais*'. The size of the piles of stone laid on the grave, suggested King, correlated with 'the rank of the person'.[40] Their passing could, he also remarked, be marked by human sacrifices, 'a Barbarous & horrid Custom' he regarded as 'more prevalent here, than in any Island we have visited' (though there were cases in New Zealand).[41]

While mortuary sacrifice tested the limits of the voyagers' detachment, the concept of a chiefly burying place was readily understandable to these visitors from the hierarchical world of Europe. When the naturalist Andrew Bloxam visited what he called the great *morai* at Kealakekua Bay in 1825, he likened it to Westminster Abbey as the place 'where the bones of the kings had for generations been deposited'.[42] On Tonga both commoner and aristocrat were, according to

A Burying Place, Tonga. Engraving by Byrne from a lost original by Hodges (From J. Cook, *A Voyage towards the South Pole and Round the World* … (2 vols, London, 1777), ii, plate 27, facing p. 183)

Surgeon Anderson, buried 'after being wrapped up in matts and cloths, much after our manner'. While the commoners were 'interred in no particular spot', however, the chiefs were buried in state.[43] The astronomer Bayly described these Tongan burying places much in the manner of a European family vault: 'Every great Family has a … burying place belonging to it … formed into a small eminence either by Nature or Art'.[44] Cook found something similar on the sacred Tahitian island of Ra'iatea: 'It is the Custome here as well as in most other Nations for all the great families to have burial places of their own'.[45]

The role of gender and hierarchy in shaping funeral customs was relatively familiar ground to Cook and his men; what was much less familiar was the way in which Pacific mortuary customs dealt with the lingering presence of the dead. Protestant England drew a sharp line between the living and the dead. The dead had left their human community to meet their eternal reward, whether that be bliss or woe, and no longer had a role to play in the society of which they had once been a part. In the Pacific the dead might have lost the use of their body but their spirit could still be present in some form of which society had to take account. The result was that many of the mortuary customs that the voyagers encountered in the Pacific and found most foreign were those intended to placate the dead.

Pre-Reformation England had given rather more attention to the dead and had accorded them some role in society's concerns. It was possible to pray to the dead and to seek their intercession. Reciprocally, the living could help out the dead by lessening their time in Purgatory (assuming that, like much of humanity, their sins were not so black as to condemn them to hell or their lives so exemplary as to send them straight to heaven). Particularly in out-of-the-way places, such as the North Riding villages, the residue of such beliefs, along with pre-Christian folk practice, meant that funeral ceremonies gave some scope to recognizing the continuing presence of the spirit of the departed – despite the lack of any Protestant theological basis for such practices. Herbs were sometimes thrown into the grave to help make the spirit rest. An unquiet spirit could be a nuisance: hence the practice of switching around the furniture in the room in which someone had died to deceive the ghost and discourage it from lingering.[46] It was important, too, that the dead be given a proper farewell: hence the belief that unless one touched the corpse it would haunt one's dreams for six months.[47] Not only did the deceased need to make his or her peace with the human community but also with other living things. It was thought particularly important that bees be involved in the funeral ceremonies: hence the death was announced to the hive, which was then draped in black, and the bees were given a small share of all that was offered to the bidden guests. The departing spirit also had to be helped to deal with other malign spirits on its upward flight: hence the belief that the passing bell helped to drive away evil spirits.[48]

But such folk residues were very much at the margin of English practice and had no secure foundation in the system of beliefs by which the larger society at least professed to understand their lives and eternal destiny. In the Pacific, by contrast, the notion of a disembodied spirit was part and parcel of a world view which did not distinguish clearly between matter and spirit or the natural and the supernatural. In Tahitian society it was held that the spirit could leave the body temporarily while a person was sleeping or in a trance – a foretaste of the more permanent quitting of the body by the spirit at death.[49] So long as some residue of the dead body remained, the spirit with which it had been united might also remain and be capable of doing mischief.[50] Many of the Polynesian mortuary rituals were, then, intended to placate the spirit of the departed and to protect the living against the powers that could still be connected with the remains of the dead.

Banks wrote at length of the Tahitian mortuary customs, as he considered them to be 'so remarkable that they deserve particular description'. Since it still retained some of its spirit the dead body had to be disposed of in a manner which would show suitable respect and placate the deceased. Following prayers and sprinkling with sea water by the priests, the body was placed in a small temporary structure at the centre of which were posts on which a bier with the body was placed. Here, in what Banks called these 'houses of corruption', the body was allowed to decay. While this occurred it was important that the body be protected from other spirits and, to this end, food was placed near the corpse. This was not

A Tahitian Toupapow (Funeral Platform) with the Chief Mourner: Engraved by
W. Woollett after Hodges (from J. Cook, *A Voyage towards the South Pole and Round
the World* ... (2 vols, London, 1777), i, plate 44, facing p. 184)

meant for the corpse itself but, rather, because they 'think that if any of their gods
should descend upon that place and being hungry find that these preparations
had been neglected he would infallibly satisfy his appetite with the flesh of the
dead corps'. The installing of the dead body in its temporary house ushered in the
formal mourning and, with it, the bodily mutilation which was a very potent way
of demonstrating one's regard for the dead – thus ensuring that the dead would
rest in peace. As Banks wrote, the blood was regarded as 'an acceptable present to
the deceased, whose soule they believe to exist and hover about the place where
the body lays observing the actions of the survivors'.

After a few days of such largely female mourning, wrote Banks, 'the men, who
till now seemed to be intirely insensible of their loss, begin their part'.[51] This took
the form of one of the practices which most fascinated the voyagers: the use of
the striking costume of the chief mourner and the rituals associated with it. So
valuable were these costumes that the Tahitians would not trade them until the
second and third voyages, when red feathers were offered in payment – quite
apart from their value the feathers with their sacred associations may have been
considered an appropriate form of exchange.[52] This remarkable garb was made
chiefly of bark cloth but with a breast ornament of tiny slips of mother-of-pearl
shell and an apron of coconut shell disks, the whole surmounted by a face mask
of pearl shell-edged with feathers of the tropical bird and a turban of bark
cloth. Once clothed in it, the chief mourner appears to have taken on a new

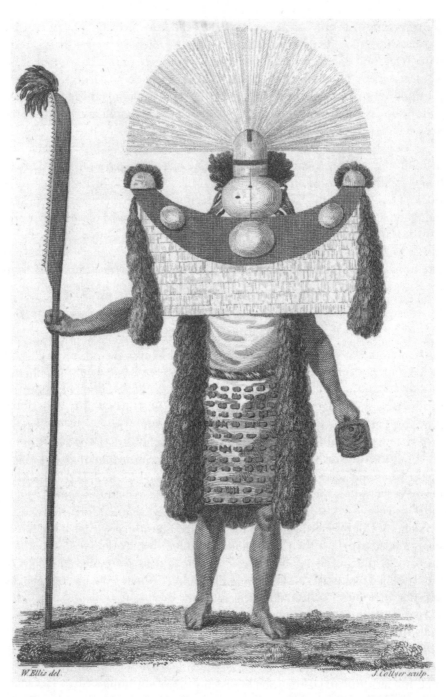

Tahitian Chief Mourner's Costume. Engraving by S. Collyer after W. Ellis (from W. Ellis, *An Authentic Narrative of a Voyage* ... (2 vols, London, 1782), i, p. 131)

and anonymous *persona* as the spirit of the dead. Anyone caught by him or his assistants could be cut 'with his stick the edge of which is set with sharks teeth', though few remained anywhere near them, having generally been warned of his whereabouts by the clapping together of shells. The chief mourner's role could continue for up to five months, after which the body had practically disintegrated and the bones could be scrapped clean 'and buried according to the rank of the person either within or without some one of their *Marais*'.[53]

Among the Māoris the belief in the force of the spirit or *mana* still remaining in bodily remains was so strong that it was considered dangerous to leave human bones about in places where they could be used by enemies. Such secretive ways led both Cook and Banks to remark on the seeming absence of funeral rites. Cook thought that if burial occurred 'it must be in some secrete or by place for we never saw the least signs of a burying place in the whole Country' – a sentiment echoed by Banks, who wrote that 'The Burial of the Dead instead of being a Pompous ceremony as in the [Society] Islands is here kept secret'.[54] These comments from the first voyage underline Māori caution about the disposal of bones with their potential store of *mana*, though Māoris did, indeed, hold elaborate mourning as opposed to funeral ceremonies.[55]

Bones were to be important in the aftermath of Cook's own death in distant Kealakekua Bay on the big island of Hawai'i, an event that brought together in forceful and dramatic form the Yorkshire-born Cook and the world of the Pacific to which he had devoted so much of his adult life. Through his death Cook became a part of Hawaiian society and the *mana* that resided in his bones was used to give spiritual force to the Hawaiian chiefs who had played a part in his death. At the time of his death, his bones were 'distributed amongst the chiefs … the head and several other parts were in the possession of Kerriebo [King Kalaniopu'u] and his hair was given to Maya Maya [Kamehameha] who is a great Chief and is to succeed Kerriebo'[56] – a remarkably accurate prediction. Such remnants of Cook continued to be valued: by 1801 it was reported that his 'Bones were divided amongst the Cheifs' and continued to be 'preserved as Relics'.[57] Reportedly, the great King Kamehameha, who forged the united kingdom of Hawai'i, incorporated a casket containing Cook's bones into the ceremonies linked to the central Makahiki festival.[58]

His death in Hawai'i was of a piece with the last stage of his life there. Unintended though it was on Cook's part, he was integrated into the Hawaiian world view from the moment he first arrived in Hawai'i. In a society where, in contrast to Britain, there was no clear frontier between the natural and the supernatural, the arrival of such an extraordinary personage with two such fantastic ships, containing vast treasures in the form of iron goods, was, in Hawaiian terms, naturally explained by the merging of the divine and the human.

A View of Kealakekua Bay. Engraving by W. Byrne after Webber (from J. Cook and J. King, *Voyage to the Pacific Ocean* ... (3 vols, London, 1784), iii, plate 68)

Cook was plainly a chief but more than that he was a manifestation (though one of many) of the god Lono. It was this 'Title and Dignity ... a Character that is looked upon them as partaking something of divinity', wrote Samwell, that was formally conferred on him by the priests on 19 January 1779, soon after he first landed at Kealakekua Bay, but oral tradition indicates that it was used when Cook encountered Hawai'i at Kaua'i a year before.[59]

Whether he was killed because he returned with a broken mast when it was time for Lono, the god of fertility and festival, to give way to the more spartan regime of Ku, the god of war, has been vigorously debated.[60] Though everything that Cook did in Hawai'i was probably linked to the Lono identity that the Hawaiians had ascribed to him, one has also to leave room for the contingent and the unplanned in the events that brought about his death. Testimony from those who discussed the matter with the Hawaiians places a good deal of emphasis on how Cook's death was a spur of the moment event, much regretted afterwards. After interviewing a number of Hawaiians present at Cook's death, the missionary William Ellis concluded that the killing 'was unpremeditated'.[61] At the time Lieutenant King had taken the same view, writing in his published account that 'the late melancholy accident did not appear to have arisen from any premeditated design'.[62] Given the supreme status accorded to chiefs in Hawaiian society it is not difficult to see how Cook's attempt to carry off King Kalaniopu'u as a hostage for the return of the stolen cutter might have inflamed Hawaiian feeling. One of Cook's crew, in a letter of 1781, wrote forcefully of the anger of the Hawaiians 'for they thought he meant to decoy the King on board and then kill him', while Surgeon Samwell wrote that 'The Indians say that they thought Kariopoo would have been killed if he had gone on board with Captain

Cook'.[63] A later source from 1801 also records that one of those who killed Cook responded to the cry 'that the White men were going to kill the King'.[64] Fears about the fate of their king may well have been exacerbated by apprehensions that the British return to Keakaelulea Bay might be connected, as Midshipman Gilbert wrote, with an 'attempt to settle there, and deprive them of part if not the whole of their country'.[65]

Cook's own men also placed a good deal of emphasis on the random nature of events that led to his death, and to the strong possibility that it could have been avoided if he had acted differently or if events had taken another path. Though an event as momentous as Cook's death later called for a number of scapegoats,[66] many of the officers most immediately involved thought that Cook mismanaged the whole thing – perhaps because of overweening confidence born of his handling of many similar events in the past. 'And had Captain [Cook] come down to the Boats Directly', wrote Surgeon Law in fractured prose, 'as he was advised its most probably would have hindered some bloodshed – But too warmly thought as he said that the flash of a musquet would disperse the whole Island'. Even after he was knocked down, continued Law, 'he immediately got up & rashly went alone into the Middle of the Crowd'. [67] Midshipman William Harvey thought his commander guilty of 'an infatuation that is altogether unaccountable' and, in more sober terms, even Captain Clerke, his second-in-command, wrote that 'matters would not have been carried to the extremities they were had not Captain Cook attempted to chastise a man in the midst of this multitude'.[68] Clerke was alluding here to Cook's lack of judgement in firing at a man who was threatening him – especially as Cook's musket, loaded with small shot, had little effect and only served to spark a general attack on himself and his men.

Whatever Cook's culpability in his own death, there was more than enough blame to spread around afterwards, and the guilt was compounded by the fact that the Hawaiians had been allowed to take his body away along with that of the four marines who were killed with him.[69] Very different, noted some of Cook's men, was the value that the Hawaiians placed on the value of the corpses of their fallen comrades. In the view of Alexander Home, the Hawaiians despised the British for 'Not Attempting to Carry off the Dead Bodies when they First Fell. For we see that Amongst them there is Nothing so Honorable as carrying off the Dead and the Risque that they will run is most astonishing'.[70] When some Hawaiians were decapitated in retaliation for Cook's death, and their heads were exposed, it inspired such horror in their countrymen that Midshipman Trevenen was moved to write that this, along with the 'exposing themselves to carry off the dead bodies of their friends, served to convince us that they have some superstitious notions with regard to their treatment after death, depending on their internment with proper ceremonies'.[71] For the British a dead body had no longer any real connection with the community to which it had once belonged, even though a decent burial was seen as an appropriate mark of respect to acknowledge the previous existence of the deceased. To the Hawaiians, by contrast, death did not sunder all ties and the spiritual force that had animated a person's life could still be attached to the physical remains – remains which needed to be disposed of with due ceremony lest they be used malignly or result in a troubled and possibly vengeful ghost.

Cook's death may have owed something to the fact that the initial attack revealed how human and mortal he was, subject to pain and wounding like all humans. Reportedly one of the chiefs who attacked him said words to the effect that, if Cook were hit, 'if he be a God he will not make a noise, if a man he will cry like ourselves'. When he duly cried out, 'the multitude immediately shouted he his [sic] no god let us kill him, he his only a man'.[72] Nonetheless, the belief that he was an incarnation of Lono did not die with him. Captain Clerke refers to the way in which Hawaiians took Cook's body and burnt off much of the flesh 'at different places with some peculiar kind of ceremony'.[73] Perhaps such ceremonies were linked to those traditionally used to deify a chief after his death, which also involved removing the flesh and keeping the bones in a casket.[74]

Whether because of his status before his death or that conferred on him posthumously, many of the Hawaiians continued to regard Cook as having the divine status of a manifestation of Lono. In his published account, Lieutenant King reported that after Cook's death the British were asked 'When the Oran [Orono or Lono] would come again? and what he would do to them on his return?' – a question which he considered 'agrees with the general tenor of their conduct towards him, which shewed that they considered him as a being of a superior nature'.[75] Other crewmen recorded similar beliefs: one was asked, for example, if 'Capt. Cook would come to the Ship and resume his former station and if he would not appear in three days', while Samwell in the same vein wrote that 'the Indians have a Notion that Captain Cook as being Orono will come amongst them again in a short time'.[76]

The belief persisted long after Cook's ships had departed. Joshua Dimsdell, who lived on Hawai'i from 1792 to 1801, spoke to the man who claimed to be responsible for the fatal blow that felled Cook, who 'hoped the Oroner [Lono] (so they term Captain Cook) would forgive him as he had built several Morais to his Memory & sacrificed a Number of Hogs Annually at each of them'. More generally, reported Dimsdell, the Hawaiians held to the 'Belief that he will come again'.[77] Such beliefs explain why the dead Cook was almost as important as the live one. Though his flesh (or a good deal of it) might be given back to the British as something of little value which would soon decompose, his bones with their store of spiritual power were important trophies well worth retaining.

In death as in life Cook was integrated by the Hawaiians into their world and became a part of their spiritual armoury. Some of his remains might have been

The Apotheosis of Captain Cook, 1794. Engraving after Philippe de Loutherbourg and
John Webber (Australian National Library, pic-an7678295-1)

given a Christian naval burial, but, when his men sailed away, Cook's bones remained. Indeed, according to officers of Vancouver's expedition who visited Hawai'i in 1793, his remains were kept in the great temple on the shore of Kealakekua Bay along with those of King Kalaniopu'u[78] – the man whom Cook had attempted to take hostage, triggering the skirmish that led to his death. On the second voyage Cook had been asked on the Tahitian island of Ra'iatea, the religious and ceremonial centre of the Society Islands, where his *marae*, his last resting place, would be for, to the Tahitians, that was where he truly belonged. His answer was the London parish church of Stepney, where three of his children were buried.[79] By the third voyage Cook had become much more a part of the Pacific and it was to be a Hawaiian *heiau* that was to be his *marae*.

Notes

Notes to Preface

1 ML, R198.
2 D. Howse, *Captain Cook's Pendulum Clocks* (London, 1969), p. 12.
3 B. Smith, 'Cook's Posthumous Reputation', in R. Fisher and H. Johnston (eds), *Captain James Cook and his Times* (Vancouver, 1979), p. 185.
4 R. Brooke, *Remarks and Conjectures on the Voyage of the Ships* Resolution *and* Discovery ... *after the Death of Captain James Cook* ... (London, 1780), p. 45.
5 R. Barker, *The Book of Whitby* (Buckingham, 1990), and 'Cook's Nursery: Whitby's Eighteenth-Century Merchant Fleet', in G. Williams (ed.), *Captain Cook: Explorations and Reassessments* (Woodbridge: Suffolk, 2004), pp. 7–21; B. Farnill, *A History of Robin Hood's Bay* (North York Moors National Park, 1990); J. Howard, *Staithes: Chapters from the History of a Seafaring Town* (Scarborough, 2000); D. O'Sullivan, *Great Ayton: A History of the Village* (Great Ayton, 1996); J. Rae [née Hunt], *Captain James Cook Endeavours* (London, 1997), J. Hunt [Rae], *From Whitby to Wapping: The Story of the Early Years of Captain James Cook* (London, 1991); T. and C. Stamp, *James Cook: Maritime Scientist* (Whitby, 1995); and C. Thornton, *Captain Cook in Cleveland: A Study of his Early Years* (Middlesbrough, 1978).
6 J.C. Beaglehole (ed.), *The Journals of Captain James Cook on his Voyage of Discovery* (3 vols, in 4, Cambridge, 1955–69).
7 J.C. Beaglehole, *The Life of Captain James Cook* (Stanford, 1974); A. Salmond, *The Trial of the Cannibal Dog: Captain Cook in the South Seas* (London, 2003); N. Thomas, *Discoveries: The Voyages of Captain Cook* (London, 2003).
8 R. Joppien, and B. Smith, *The Art of Captain Cook's Voyages* (3 vols in 4, London, 1985–88); B. Smith, *European Vision and the South Pacific* (2nd edn, New Haven, 1985) and *Imagining the Pacific: In the Wake of the Cook Voyages* (New Haven, 1992).
9 A. David, *The Charts and Coastal Views of Captain Cook's Voyages* (3 vols, London, 1988–97).
10 A. Kaeppler, *'Artificial Curiosities': Being An Exposition of Native Manufactures Collected on the Three Pacific Voyages of Captain James Cook, RN* (Honolulu, 1978).
11 M.K. Beddie, *Bibliography of Captain James Cook, RN, FRS, Circumnavigator* (The Library of New South Wales: Sydney, 1970); J. Robson, *Captain Cook's World* (Sydney, 2000) and *The Captain Cook Encyclopaedia* (London, 2004); http://southseas.nla.gov.au

Notes to Chapter 1: Worlds

1 John Walker Ord, *The History and Antiquities of Cleveland: Comprising the Wapentake of East and West Langbaurgh, North Riding, County York* (London, 1846), pp. 70–71; E. Baines, *Yorkshire, Past and Present* (2 vols in 4 parts, London, [?1870]), i, pt 2, pp. 392–93.

2 Cook to W. Hammond, 3 January 1772, J.C. Beaglehole, *The Journals of Captain James Cook on his Voyage of Discovery* (3 vols in 4, Cambridge, 1955–69), ii, p. 909.

3 Robert Brown, *Staithes in Olden Times* (published in three parts in the *Whitby Gazette*, March 1924).

4 W. Page (ed.), *The Victoria History of the County of York: North Riding* (2 vols, London, 1923), ii, p. 506.

5 J. Howard, *Staithes: Chapters from the History of a Seafaring Town* (Scarborough, 2000), p. 92.

6 J. Tuke, *General View of the Agriculture of the North Riding of Yorkshire: With Observations on the Means of its Improvement* (London, 1794), p. 35.

7 Tuke, *General View*, p. 35.

8 D. Spratt (ed.), *The Archaeology of Cleveland* (Middlesbrough, 1979), p. 49.

9 E. Evans, *The Forging of the Modern State: Early Industrial Britain, 1783–1870* (Harlow, 1983), p. 139.

10 D. Gerrard, *North Riding of One Hundred Years Ago* (Stroud, 1993), p. 93.

11 J. Wardell, *The Economic History of Tess-Side* (Stockton, 1960), p. 9.

12 Page, *The Victoria History: North Riding*, ii, p. 269.

13 Ibid., ii, p. 225; R.P. Hastings, *Essays in North Riding History, 1780–1850* (Northallerton, 1981), p. 29.

14 E. Proctor, Great Ayton Estates, NYCRO, ZLT (guide).

15 C. Thornton, *Captain Cook in Cleveland: A Study of his Early Years* (Middlesbrough, 1978), p. 18.

16 Thornton, *Captain Cook in Cleveland*, p. 13.

17 J. Graves, *The History of Cleveland* (Carlisle, 1808), p. 455.

18 Spratt, *The Archaeology of Cleveland*, pp. 36–37.

19 J. Blakeborough, *A Guide to … Great Ayton* (Middlesbrough, 1900).

20 P. Skottowe, *The Leaf and the Tree: The Story of an English Family* (London, 1963), p. 20.

21 R. Kettlewell, *Cleveland Village* (Redcar, 1938), p. 25; P. Rowe, *The Archaeology of East Marton, Captain Cook's Birthplace* (n.p., 1998).

22 E. Wrigley and R. Schofield, *The Population History of England, 1547–1871: A Reconstruction* (London, 1981), pp. 577, 595.

23 G. Young, *The Life and Voyages of Captain James Cook* (London, 1836), p. 10.

24 J. Cook (snr), Documents regarding the Great Ayton Cottage, Victoria State Library, Melbourne, store map case, drawer 2/4, H6405, H6407.

25 Cook to Admiralty Secretary, 14 December 1771, *Cook's Journals*, ii, p. 906.

26 J. Dixon, *History under the Hammer* (North York Moors National Park, 1996).

27 C. Healy, *From the Ruins of Colonialism: History as Social Meaning* (Cambridge, 1997), pp. 11, 33.

28 Young, *Life and Voyages*, p. 283.

29   D. O'Sullivan, *Great Ayton: A History of the Village* (Great Ayton, 1996), p. 144. Cook's schoolroom was demolished in 1785 but the school continued.

30   B. Rudd to Banks, 23 August 1801, Auckland Public Library, GMSS 67/GMSS D8.

31   R. Malcolmson, *Life and Labour in England, 1700–1780* (London, 1981), p. 62.

32   Thornton, *Captain Cook in Cleveland*, p. 12.

33   On the extent and importance of the belief in the possibilities of agricultural improvement, see J. Gascoigne, *Joseph Banks and the English Enlightenment: Useful Knowledge and Polite Culture* (Cambridge, 1994), Chapter 5, 'The Principles and Practice of Improvement'; J. Gascoigne, *The Enlightenment and the Origins of European Australia* (Cambridge, 2002), pt 2, 'The Possibilities of Improvement'.

34   N. Thomas, *Discoveries: The Voyages of Captain Cook* (London, 2003), p. 333.

35   *Cook's Journals*, iii, pt 1, p. 23.

36   Ibid., ii, p. 297.

37   J. King, 'An Account of the late Captain Cook, and Some Memoirs of His Life', *Universal Magazine*, July 1784, p. 38.

38   Cook to Sandwich, 26 November 1776, *Cook's Journals*, iii, pt 2, p. 1520.

39   H. Roberts, *Resolution* journal, 8 March 1779, DL, Q 151–52; J. Burney, *Discovery* journal, 4 February 1779, ML, safe 1/79.

40   *Cook's Journals*, iii, pt 1, p. 194.

41   J. Bigge to Earl Bathurst, 27 February 1823, ML, Bonwick Transcripts, series 1, Box 28.

42   *Cook's Journals*, ii, p. 322.

43   Thornton, *Captain Cook in Cleveland*, p. 23.

44   R. Barker, 'Cook's Nursery: Whitby's Eighteenth-Century Merchant Fleet', in G. Williams (ed.), *Captain Cook: Explorations and Reassessments* (Woodbridge, Suffolk: 2004), p. 12.

45   A. Sparrman, *A Voyage Round the World with Captain James Cook in HMS* Resolution, translated from Swedish by H. Beamish and A. Mackenzie-Grieve (London, 1953), p. 3.

46   J.C. Beaglehole, 'On the Character of Captain James Cook', *Geographical Journal*, 122 (1956), p. 427.

47   *Cook's Journals*, iii, pt 1, p. 480n.

48   Howard, *Staithes*, p. 73.

49   W. East, 'The Historical Geography of the Town, Port and Roads of Whitby', *Geographical Journal*, 80 (1932), p. 484.

50   T. Hinderwell, *The History and Antiquities of Scarborough and the Vicinity* (York, 1811), p. 291.

51   Barker, 'Cook's Nursery', p. 9.

52   Hinderwell, *The History and Antiquities of Scarborough*, p. 293.

53   C. Preston, *Captain James Cook, RN, FRS and Whitby* (Whitby, 1965), p. 6.

54   Tuke, *A General View*, p. 92.

55   Page, *The Victoria History: North Riding*, ii, p. 512.

56   P. Jeffrey, *Whitby Lore and Legend* (Whitby, 1952), p. 3.

57   R. Gaskin, *The Old Seaport of Whitby: Being Chapters from the Life of its Bygone People* (Whitby, 1909), p. 63.

58   With considerable local support, I have the temerity to depart here from the view of J.C. Beaglehole, the doyen of Cook scholars, that Cook did not serve his apprenticeship at the

Grape Lane house but rather at a house at Haggersgate. J.C. Beaglehole, *The Life of Captain James Cook* (Stanford, 1974), p. 6n. Beaglehole appears to have been confused by another John Walker, also a mariner, who was a cousin of Cook's employer and lived at Haggersgate. T. and C. Stamp, *James Cook: Maritime Scientist* (Whitby, 1995), pp. 11–12. Furthermore, the Haggersgate house would not have accommodated Walker's full complement of apprentices.

59   J. Trevenen, 'Notes on Passages from December 1777 to October 1779 published in 1784 Quarto Edition of Captain Cook's Third Voyage', ATL, q MS-2041, p. 8.

60   J. Hunt, *From Whitby to Wapping: The Story of the Early Years of Captain James Cook* (London, 1991), p. 4.

61   Barker, 'Cook's Nursery', p. 14; G. Graham, *Incidents in the Life of Captain James Cook: Illustrated by Authentic Material in Whitby Museum* (Whitby, 1980), p. 7.

62   For an imaginative, empathetic but necessarily largely fictional account of Mrs Cook's meagrely documented life, see M. Day, *Mrs Cook: The Real and Imagined Life of the Captain's Wife* (Sydney, 2002).

63   J.G. Graham, *Muster Rolls of Whitby Ships in which James Cook Sailed, 1747–1755* (Whitby, 1983).

64   Beaglehole, *The Life of Captain James Cook*, p. 15.

65   Graves, *The History of Cleveland*, p. 457.

66   G. Ritchie, 'Captain's Cook's Influence on Hydrographic Surveying', *Pacific Studies*, 1 (1978), pp. 80–83; V. Suthren, *To Go Upon Discovery: James Cook and Canada, 1758–1767* (Toronto, 1999), p. 62.

67   J. Cook and J. King, *Voyage to the Pacific Ocean … in the Years 1776, 1777, 1778, 1779 and 1780: In Three Volumes: vol. 1 and 2 written by Captain J. Cook, vol. 3 by Captain J. King* (London, 1784), iii, p. 47.

68   Suthren, *To Go Upon Discovery*, p. 108.

69   R. Skelton, 'Captain James Cook as a Hydrographer', *Mariner's Mirror*, 40 (1954), p. 102.

70   R. Skelton, 'Explorer's Maps: James Cook and the Mapping of the Pacific', *Geographical Magazine*, 28 (1955), p. 101.

71   Cook and King, *Voyage to the Pacific Ocean*, iii, p. 47.

72   F. Bladen, (ed.), *Historical Records of New South Wales* (8 vols, Sydney, 1892–1901), i, pt 1, p. 305.

73   R. Skelton, *Captain James Cook after Two Hundred Years* (London, 1969), p. 16.

74   W. Whiteley, 'James Cook and British Policy in the Newfoundland Fisheries, 1763–7', *Canadian Historical Review*, 54 (1973), pp. 253, 272.

75   A. David, *The Charts and Coastal Views of Captain Cook's Voyages* (3 vols, London, 1988–97), iii, p. xxviii.

76   P. O'Brian, *Joseph Banks: A Life* (London, 1987), p. 64.

77   *Cook's Journals*, i, pp. cciv–ccxiv.

78   Cook to Banks, 18 November 1772, *Cook's Journals*, ii, p. 688.

79   *Philosophical Transactions of the Royal Society*, 66 (1776), pp. 402–6.

80   B. Rudd to Banks, 11 August 1801, 10 September 1801, 29 January 1802, Auckland Public Library, Grey MSS 66/GMSS D8.

81 C. Newbury, *Tahiti Nui: Change and Survival in French Polynesia, 1767–1945* (Honolulu, 1980), Chapter 1, 'The Market at Matavai Bay'.

82 D. Oliver, *Ancient Tahitian Society* (3 vols, Canberra, 1974), iii, p. 1250.

83 Bayly, *Discovery* journal, TNA, Adm. 55/20, fol. 83v. Its importance is also referred to in Henry Adams, *Memoirs of Arii Taimai* (Paris, 1901), 'Indigenous Histories', p. 109, http://southseas.nla.gov.au

84 A. D'Alleva, *Shaping the Body Politic: Gender, Status and Power in the Art of Eighteenth-Century Tahiti and the Society Islands* (PhD, University of Columbia, 1997), pp. 45, 181.

85 *Cook's Journals*, iii, pt. 2, p. 980.

86 Cook and his contemporaries used the name 'Omai' but the initial 'O' was not a part of the name but rather was an honorific term of address though it was much valued by Mai himself who aspired to a higher status than he actually enjoyed at home. Indeed he may have assumed the name for that reason. Lieutenant Williamson wrote in his third journey journal: 'we found that Mai was an assum'd name, his real name being Parridero' though, as he had reportedly told Cook, he had taken the name Mai since 'ye names of all the great chiefs began with an O. & that he thought to pass for a great Man, by assuming ye name of a chief who was dead'. *Cook's Journals*, iii, pt 2, p. 1343.

87 Beaglehole, *The Life of Captain James Cook*, p. 194.

88 J. Robson, *The Captain Cook Encyclopaedia* (London, 2004), p. 207.

89 For Parkinson's illustration of this together with two by Herman Spöring, one by Charles Praval and another by John Barralet, see R. Joppien and B. Smith, *The Art of Captain Cook's Voyages* (3 vols in 4, London, 1985–88), i, pp. 172–73.

90 For an exploration of the Māori response to Cook's voyages, see A. Salmond, *Two Worlds: First Meetings* (Auckland, 1991), pp. 87–298, and A. Salmond, *Between Worlds: Early Exchanges between Maori and Europeans, 1773–1815* (Auckland, 1997), pp. 36–170.

91 Though Banks mentions taking possession of some forty to fifty spears, only four appear to have survived and these are now housed (in a cut-down form) in the University of Cambridge Museum of Archaeology and Anthropology (UCMAA) (D 1914.1–4). Banks gave these objects to Lord Sandwich, who in turn passed them on to his old college, Trinity, Cambridge, whence they came to the university museum. P. Gathercole, 'Lord Sandwich's Collection of Polynesian Artefacts', in M. Lincoln, *Science and Exploration in the Pacific: European Voyages to the Southern Oceans in the Eighteenth Century* (Woodbridge, Suffolk, 1998), pp. 103–15. One is a hunting spear with a single, fire-hardened point and the other three are fishing spears with three or four prongs made sharp by slivers of fish or mammal bone. J. Megaw, 'Captain Cook and Bone Barbs at Botany Bay', *Antiquity*, 48 (1969), pp. 213–16.

92 J. Megaw, Captain Cook and Bone Barbs', p. 214.

93 E. Kolig, 'Captain Cook in the Western Kimberleys', in R.M. and C.H. Brendt (eds), *Aborigines of the West: Their Past and Present* (Perth, 1980), pp. 274–82; D. Rose, 'The Saga of Captain Cook: Morality in Aboriginal and European Law', *Australian Aboriginal Studies*, 2 (1984), pp. 24–39; C. Mackinolty and P. Wainburranga, 'Too Many Captain Cooks', R. Rose and T. Swain (eds), *Aboriginal Australian Christian Missions* (Canberra, 1988), pp. 355–60.

94 *Cook's Journals*, i, p. 399.

95   Robson, *The Captain Cook Encyclopaedia*, p. 149.

96   A relic of Johann Reinhold Forster's presence on board is his sea trunk (in which he would
      have kept his journals and possibly some of the artefacts he collected), now in the Bishop
      Museum, Honolulu (1977.070.001).

97   For photographs and a description of the site see Mark Adams and Nicholas Thomas,
      Cook's Sites: Revisiting History (Dunedin, 1999), pp. 15–96.

98   A. Salmond, *The Trial of the Cannibal Dog: Captain Cook in the South Seas* (London, 2003),
      p. 305.

99   Beaglehole, *The Life of Captain James Cook*, p. 289.

100   Cook to John Walker, 19 August 1775, *Cook's Journals*, ii, pt 2, p. 960.

101   Beaglehole, 'On the Character of Captain James Cook', p. 423.

102   J. Watt, 'Medical Aspects and Consequences of Cook's Voyages', in R. Fisher and H. Johnston
      (eds), *Captain James Cook and his Times* (Vancouver, 1979), pp. 129–57; A. Salmond, 'Tute:
      the Impact of Polynesia on Captain Cook', in Williams, *Captain Cook*, p. 86.

103   Thomas, *Discoveries*, p. 332.

104   H. Zimmerman, *Account of the Third Voyage of Captain Cook, 1776–1780*, translated from
      the German by U. Tewsley (Wellington, 1926), p. 42.

105   J. Williamson, *Resolution* journal, TNA, Adm. 55/117, fol. 74v.

106   *Cook's Journals*, i, p. 101.

107   Ibid., iii, pt 1, p. 228.

108   G. Gilbert, 'Journal 1776–1780', BL, Add. MS 38530, fol. 35v.

109   Cook and King, *Voyage to the Pacific*, iii, p. 49.

110   Zimmerman, *Account*, pp. 48–49.

111   T. Horwitz, *Into the Blue: Boldly Going Where Captain Cook Has Gone Before* (Sydney, 2002),
      p. 418.

Notes to Chapter 2: The Sea

1   A lecture based on some parts of this chapter was delivered at the 2003 Australian
      Association for Maritime History Conference on Norfolk Island and subsequently
      published in the association's journal under the title, 'Cook, The Sea and Culture Contact in
      the Pacific', *The Great Circle*, 26 (2004), pp. 3–18. I am grateful to the editor of this journal
      for permission to reproduce this material.

2   J. Cook, *A Voyage towards the South Pole* (2 vols, London, 1777), i, p. xxxvi.

3   G. Forster, 'Cook the Discoverer', preface to his 1787 translation of Cook's third voyage.
      Translated from the German by P.E. Klarwill. ATL, MS Papers 1485, p. 45.

4   St Cuthbert's Church, Marton, Middlesbrough, *James Cook, FRS, RN* (Middlesbrough,
      n.d.), p. 5.

5   D. O'Sullivan, *Great Ayton: A History of the Village* (Great Ayton, 1996), p. 145.

6   A. Godfrey, *Yorkshire Fishing Fleets: The Story of Yorkshire's Oldest and Most Dangerous
      Industry* (Clapham, North Yorkshire, 1974), p. 11.

7   B. Farnill, *A History of Robin Hood's Bay* (North York Moors National Park, 1990), p. 63;
      R. Hastings, *Essays in North Riding History, 1780–1850* (Northallerton, 1981), p. 50.

8   R. Robinson, 'The Fish Trade in the Pre-Railway Era: The Yorkshire Coast, 1780–1840', *Northern History*, 25 (1989), p. 234.

9   Farnill, *A History of Robin Hood's Bay*, pp. 63, 66.

10   J. Howard, *Staithes: Chapters from the History of a Seafaring Town* (Scarborough, 2000), p. 182.

11   Ibid., p. 57.

12   W. Mitchell, *Life on the Yorkshire Coast* (Clapham, North Yorkshire, 1982), p. 69.

13   Farnill, *A History of Robin Hood's Bay*, p. 66.

14   R. Barker, *The Book of Whitby* (Buckingham, 1990), p. 54.

15   Farnill, *A History of Robin Hood's Bay*, p. 69.

16   A. White, *A History of Whitby* (Chichester, 1993), p. 86.

17   R. Gaskin, *The Old Seaport of Whitby* (Whitby, 1909), p. 251.

18   J. Dykes, *Yorkshire Whaling Days* (Clapham, North Yorkshire, 1980), p. 7.

19   F. Payne, *Whaling and Whitby* (Whitby, n.d.), pp. 2, 5, 9, 14.

20   J. Beaglehole (ed.), *The* Endeavour *Journal of Joseph Banks, 1768–1771* (Sydney, 1962), 2 vols, ii, p. 13.

21   W. Page (ed.), *The Victoria History of the County of York: North Riding* (2 vols, London, 1923), ii, p. 512.

22   C. Preston, *Captain William Scoresby, 1760–1829: Whitby's Most Successful Whaler* (Whitby, 1964), pp. 16–17.

23   J. Banks to Scoresby, 8 September 1810, Whitby Museum.

24   G. Young, *A Picture of Whitby and its Environs* (Whitby, 1840), pp. 194–95.

25   L. Charlton, *The History of Whitby* (York, 1779), p. 358.

26   J. and C. Stamp, *Captain Cook and his Ships* (Whitby, 1981), pp. 7, 11.

27   S. Jones, *A Maritime History of the Port of Whitby, 1700–1914* (University of London, Ph.D, 1982), p. 27.

28   Charlton, *The History of Whitby*, p. 358.

29   R.S. Porter, *English Society in the Eighteenth Century* (Harmondsworth, 1982), p. 203.

30   J. Rae, *Captain James Cook Endeavours* (London, 1997), p. 14.

31   J. King, 'An Account of the late Captain Cook, and Some Memoirs of His Life', *Universal Magazine*, July 1784, p. 38.

32   C. Thornton, *Captain Cook in Cleveland: A Study of his Early Years* (Middlesbrough, 1978), p. 39.

33   R. Finch, *Coals from Newcastle: Coal Trade in the Days of Sail* (Lavenham, Suffolk, 1973), p. 27.

34   J.C. Beaglehole, 'Cook, the Navigator', *Explorer's Journal*, 48 (1970), p. 265.

35   Rae, *Captain James Cook Endeavours*, p. 15.

36   Gaskin, *The Old Seaport of Whitby*, p. 267.

37   'Log', 'South Sea Companion', http://southseas.nla.gov.au/biogs/P000053b

38   G. Graham, *Captain James Cook: Servant and Friend of Captain John Walker* (Whitby, 1986), n.p.

39   R. Smith, *Sea-Coal for London: History of the Coal Factors in the London Market* (London, 1961), p. 7.

40   M. Flinn, *The History of the British Coal Industry*, ii, *1700–1830: The Industrial Revolution* (Oxford, 1984), p. 275.

41 Rae, *Captain James Cook*, pp. 18–19; J. Hunt [Rae], *From Whitby to Wapping: The Story of the Early Years of Captain James Cook* (London, 1991), pp. 11–12.

42 Thornton, *Cook in Cleveland*, p. 40.

43 N.A.M. Rodger, *The Wooden World: An Anatomy of the Georgian Navy* (New York, 1996), p. 29.

44 D. Baugh, 'The Eighteenth Century Navy as a National Institution, 1690–1815', in J.R. Hill (ed.), *The Oxford Illustrated History of the Royal Navy* (Oxford, 1995), p. 157; J. Brewer, *The Sinews of War: War, Money and the English State 1688–1783* (London, 1989), p. 40.

45 Ibid., p. 31.

46 Rodger, *The Wooden World*, p. 113.

47 M. Lewis, *A Social History of the Navy, 1783–1815* (London, 1960), p. 136.

48 R. Holt, *Whitby Past and Present* (Whitby, [1897?]), p. 13.

49 J. Cook, *Eagle* log, 23 February 1756, ATL, q MS-0537-0539. Transcription by J. Robson, http://pages.quicksilver.net.nz/jcr/eagle1756

50 W. Falconer, *An Universal Dictionary of Marine* (London, 1780), p. 301, 'Reference Works', http://southseas.nla.gov.au/refs/falc/0301.

51 *General Evening Post*, 27 July, 1771; F. Bladen, (ed.), *Historical Records of New South Wales* (8 vols, Sydney, 1892–1901), i, pt 1, p. 487.

52 *Banks' Endeavour Journal*, ii, p. 349.

53 Rodger, *The Wooden World*, p. 86.

54 R. Parkin, *H.M. Bark* Endeavour: *Her Place in Australian History* (Melbourne, 1997), p. 47.

55 Forster. 'Cook the Discover', p. 46.

56 Ibid., p. 69.

57 *Cook's Journals*, ii, p. 187.

58 J. Trevenen, 'Notes on Passages from December 1777 to October 1779 published in 1784 Quarto Edition of Captain Cook's Third Voyage', ATL, qMS-2041, p. 7.

59 P. O'Brian, *Men-of-War: Life in Nelson's Navy* (New York, 1995), p. 56.

60 E. Morris, 'Captain's Cook's First Log in the Royal Navy [from June 27, 1755 – December 31, 1756]', *Cornhill Magazine*, 7 (1899), p. 524.

61 J.C. Beaglehole, *The Life of Captain James Cook* (Stanford, 1974), p. 54.

62 A. Salmond, *The Trial of the Cannibal Dog: Captain Cook in the South Seas* (London, 2003), 'Calender of Punishments during Captain Cook's Three Pacific Voyages', pp. 433–37.

63 G. Dening, *Mr Bligh's Bad Language: Passion, Power and Theatre on the* Bounty (Cambridge, 1992), p. 114.

64 J. Robson, *The Captain Cook Encyclopaedia* (London, 2004), p. 86.

65 Dening, *Mr Bligh's Bad Language*, p. 384.

66 J. Elliott, 'Memoirs of the Early Life of John Elliott', BL, Add. MS 42714, fol. 42v.

67 M. Hoare (ed.), *The* Resolution *Journal of Johann Reinhold Forster, 1772–1775* (4 vols, London, 1982), ii, p. 369.

68 Parkin, *H.M. Bark* Endeavour, p. 100.

69 J. Trevenen, 'Notes', pp. 3–4.

70 G. Forster, *A Voyage Round the World*, edited by N. Thomas and O. Berghof (2 vols, Honolulu, 2000), i, p. 290.

71 *Banks' Endeavour Journal*, i, p. 242.

72 *Cook's Journals*, i, p. 323.

73 Ibid., p. 324.

74 R. Hough, *Captain James Cook: A Biography* (London, 1994), p. 371.

75 *Cook's Journals*, i, p. 131.

76 N. Rigby and P. Van der Merwe, *Captain Cook in the Pacific* (London, 2001), p. 66.

77 Forster, 'Cook the Discover', p. 40.

78 Parkin, *H.M. Bark* 'Endeavour', pp. 71, 338.

79 J. Cook, *A Voyage towards the South Pole* (2 vols, London, 1777), i, p. xxviii.

80 *Cook's Journals*, iii, pt 1, p. 246.

81 G. Badger, *The Explorers of the Pacific* (Sydney, 1996), p. 18.

82 [J. Marra], *Journal of the* Resolution's *Voyage* (London, 1775), p. 217.

83 G. Irwin, *The Prehistoric Exploration and Colonisation of the Pacific* (Cambridge, 1992), pp. 7, 217–18, 220.

84 W. Bayly, *Adventure* journal, ATL, fms-015, fol. 63.

85 Salmond, *The Trial*, p. 243.

86 Irwin, *The Prehistoric Exploration*, p. 47.

87 A. Salmond, 'Their Body is Different, Our Body is Different: European and Tahitian Navigators in the Eighteenth Century', *History and Anthropology*, 16 (2005), pp. 167–87.

88 Banks' Endeavour *Journal*, i, p. 312.

89 *Cook's Journals*, i, p. 600.

90 D. Oliver, *Ancient Tahitian Society* (3 vols, Canberra, 1974), i, p. 195; 'Canoes in the Society Islands', 'South Seas Companion', http://southseas.nla.gov.au, cs-ss-biogs-P000422

91 *Cook's Journals*, i, p. 131.

92 Ibid., i, pp. 153–54.

93 Ibid., ii, p. 848.

94 *Banks' Endeavour Journal*, ii, p. 23.

95 S.Cherry, *The Te Ao Maori: The Maori World* (Dublin, 1990), p. 13.

96 J. Roberts, *Endeavour* Journal, ML, safe 1/65, fol. 42.

97 G. Gilbert, Journal, 1776–80, BL, Add. MS 38530, fol. 131.

98 *Cook's Journals*, iii, pt 1, p. 626.

99 Gilbert, Journal, 1776–80, fos 131v–132.

100 *Banks' Endeavour Journal*, i, p. 283.

101 Ibid., ii, p. 93.

102 *Cook's Journals*, i, pp. 396–97.

103 Ibid., ii, p. 865.

104 Ibid., iii, pt 2, p. 1102; iii, pt 1, p. 316.

105 Ibid., i, p. 283.

106 Ibid., iii, pt 2, p. 1112.

107 Gilbert, Journal, 1776–80, fol. 73.

108 D. Livingstone, *The Geographical Tradition* (Oxford, 1993), p. 98.

109 M. Edney, 'Reconsidering Enlightenment Geography and Mapping', in D. Livingstone and C. Withers (eds), *Geography and Enlightenment* (Chicago, 1999), p. 165.

110 Now collected and authoritatively edited, along with reproductions of Cook's maps, in three massive volumes, A. David, *The Charts and Coastal Views of Captain Cook's Voyages* (3 vols, London, 1988–97).

111 D. Cosgrove, *Mappings* (London, 1999), pp. 129–30.

112 'Think of the moon', writes Howse, 'as the hand of a clock and the sun and stars as time markers on the clock dial'. D. Howse, 'Navigation and Astronomy in the Voyages', in D. Howse (ed.), *Background to Discovery: Pacific Exploration from Dampier to Cook* (Berkeley, 1990), p. 165.

113 Forster, A *Voyage Round the World*, i, p. 299.

114 Howse, 'Navigation and Astronomy', p. 171.

115 David, *The Charts and Coastal Views*, iii, p. xxviii.

116 Badger, *Explorers*, p. 218; L. Withey, *Voyages of Discovery: Captain Cook and the Exploration of the Pacific* (Berkeley, 1989), p. 246.

117 Tupaia's original chart was lost but a copy made by Cook survives. Johann Reinhold Forster later had it engraved 'as a monument of the ingenuity and geographical knowledge of the people of the Society Islands, and of Tupaya in particular'. David, *The Charts and Coastal Views*, i, p. 130.

118 D. Turnbull, 'Cook and Tupaia: A Tale of Cartographic *Méconnaissance*', in M. Lincoln (ed.), *Science and Exploration in the Pacific: European Voyages in the Southern Oceans in the Eighteenth Century* (Woodbridge, Suffolk, 1998), pp. 117–32.

119 Ibid., p. 120.

120 *Cook's Journals*, iii, pt 1, p. 279.

121 Ibid., i, p. 154.

122 Ibid., iii, pt 1, p. 87.

123 Irwin, *The Prehistoric Exploration*, p. 7.

124 N. Thomas, *Discoveries: The Voyages of Captain Cook* (London, 2003), p. 342.

125 For examples of Māori paddles UCMAA, Z 17170 and 1922.933; bailer D1914.66, photos J. Tanner, *From Pacific Shores: Eighteenth-Century Ethnographic Collections at Cambridge: The Voyages of Cook, Vancouver and the First Fleet* (Cambridge, 1999), cover, pp. 21, 32. For Marquesan paddles Australian Museum H304 and H310.

126 *Banks' Endeavour Journal*, i, p. 361.

127 Trevenen, 'Notes', p. 16. The collection of the Cook-derived Pacific artefacts at the Museo Nazionale di Anthropologico e Ethnologia, Florence, for example, includes an Hawaiian two-piece fishhook with a turtle shell shank and a bone point. On the Forster provenance of this material see A. Kaeppler (ed.), *Cook Voyage Artefacts in Leningrad, Berne, and Florence Museums* (Honolulu, 1978), pp. 71–74. There is a similar Cook-derived Hawaiian two-piece fishhook with a sharpened bone point in the Museo Nazionale Preistorico Ethnografico ('Luigi Pigorini'), Rome 1193 – a collection that derives from the collection of Cardinal Borgia which probably also has a Forster provenance.

128 There is a Tongan example in the Institut für Ethnologie, Göttingen (Inv. Oz 219). This derives from the large and well-catalogued collection of five hundred objects from the Cook voyages that George III presented to the university of Göttingen, Hanover (then still a part of the lands of the Hanoverian dynasty, which had ruled Britain since 1714). See B. Hauser-Schäublin and G.Krüger (ed.), *James Cook: Gifts and Treasures from the South Seas* (Munich, 1998), p. 323. There are further Tongan examples in the National Museum of Ireland, nos 3892–96. The University of Cambridge Museum of Archaeology and Anthropology (UCMAA) has a Tahitian example, D1922.930, photo, Tanner, *From Pacific Shores*, p. 10.

129 Pitt Rivers Museum, Oxford, Foster Coll. No. 62. The Forster collection is particularly valuable because of the surviving documentation that establishes clearly its links with Cook's voyages. See J. Coote, P. Gathercole, and N. Meister, '"Curiosities Sent to Oxford": The Original Documentation of the Forster Collection at the Pitt Rivers Museum', *Journal of the History of Collections*, 12 (2000), pp. 177–92; and J. Coote, C. Knowles, N. Meister, and A. Petch, 'Computerising the Forster ("Cook"), Arawe, and Founding Collections at the Pitt Rivers Museum', *Pacific Arts*, 19/20 (1999), pp. 48–80.

130 Hauser-Schäublin and Krüger, *James Cook*, p. 331; J. Belich, *Making Peoples: A History of New Zealanders: From Polynesian Settlement to the End of the Nineteenth Century* (Auckland, 1996), p. 74.

131 A fine Tongan example in the Florence Museo Anthropologico (203) has floats made of wooden sticks and stone sinkers. There is a similarly large Tahitian net (1100 cm x 100 cm) at Göttingen (Inv. Oz 403).

132 E. Best, *Fishing Methods and Devices of the Maori* (Wellington, 1977), p. 10.

133 *Banks' Endeavour Journal*, ii, p. 25.

134 Best, *Fishing Methods*, p. 4.

135 For example, the polished multi-coloured abalone shell attached to a Māori fish hook in the Australian Museum (H386).

136 Cherry, *Te Ao Maori*. This work is based on the extensive collections in the National Museum of Ireland (which unfortunately are not on public display). These originated in the collections given to Trinity College, Dublin by the surgeon James Patten after the second voyage and by Lieutenant James King after the third. J. Freeman, 'The Polynesian Collection of Trinity College, Dublin and the National Museum of Ireland', *Journal of the Polynesian Society*, 58 (1949), pp. 1–18. Purportedly, a few items from the Dublin Cook voyage collection were donated to the Otago Museum, Dunedin (D09.1–8) including some Pacific paddles (though the fact that these include one from New Ireland which the Cook expeditions did not visit indicates that the provenance is not secure).

137 Pitt Rivers, 1887.1.378. As Jeremy Coote has recently shown Banks' collection of Tahitian and New Zealand artefacts was passed on by Christ Church to the Pitt Rivers Museum where it now forms a discrete collection. See his 'An Interim Report on a Previously Unknown Collection from Cook's First Voyage: The Christ Church Collection at the Pitt Rivers Museum, University of Oxford', *Journal of Museum Ethnology*, 16 (2004), pp. 111–21. I am grateful to Jeremy Coote for showing me this collection.

138 *Cook's Journals*, ii, p. 503.

139 Ibid., i, p. 396.

140 K. Kohen and R. Lambert, 'Hunters and Fishers in the Sydney Region', in D. Mulvaney and J. P. White (eds), *Australians to 1788* (Sydney, 1988), p. 352.

141 E. Ferdon, *Early Tonga: As the Explorers Saw It 1616–1810* (Tucson, Arizona, 1987), p. 204; J. Burkinshaw, *Klaya-Ho-Alth: Collections from the Northwest Coast of North America in the Royal Albert Memorial Museum, Exeter* (Exeter, 1999), p. 6.

142 Hauser-Schäublin and Krüger, *James Cook*, pp. 339–41.

143 *Cook's Journals*, iii, pt 2, p. 1325.

144 Hauser-Schäublin and Krüger, *James Cook*, pp. 274, 269.

145 *Cook's Journals*, iii, pt 1, p. 320.

146 For examples of a Tahitian sting ray point (UCMAA, D1914.23A) and of a Tongan rasp (1922.937), photos Tanner, *From Pacific Shores*, pp. 13, 42; Tongan sting ray examples (Inv. Oz 217–18) in Hauser-Schäublin and Krüger, *James Cook*, p. 323.

147 The National Museum of Ireland has one such Hawaiian shark-tooth knife (3664). There is another example of comparable size at the Royal Albert Memorial Museum, Exeter (E1226) with twenty-one teeth (though three are missing). It is from the Vaughan collection that goes back to the large collection of Sir Ashton Lever, who purchased many specimens from Cook's third voyage for his private museum. Burkinshaw, *Klaya-Ho-Alth*, p. 22. Among those from whom Lever purchased his specimens was Mrs Cook, A. Kaeppler, 'Tracing the History of Hawaiian Cook Voyage Artefacts in the Museum of Mankind', in T. Mitchell (ed.), *Captain Cook and the South Pacific* (London, 1979), p. 175. The Australian Museum, Sydney has an example of another type of shark knife with a single large tooth at the end of a curved wooden handle (H111). At the Berne Historisches Museum (which holds the collection deriving from John Webber, artist on the third voyage) there are two Hawaiian shark-tooth rings with holders made of a thin plate of turtle shell formed into a ring holding a sharp shark's tooth (HAW 3a and b).

148 For examples of Nootkan clubs with the characteristic bird's head, see Royal Albert Memorial Museum, Exeter E1222 (along with a Māori whalebone cloak pin E1231) and UCMAA, 1949.190, 1921.567.1 and 1922.954. Christchurch Museum's E149.139 probably also derives from Cook's third voyage. For examples of whalebone Māori clubs (*patu paraoa*) see UCMAA, D1914.57 (photos, Tanner, *From Pacific Shores*, pp. 33, 67, 69) or Göttingen, Inv. Oz 276 (photo, Hauser-Schäublin and Krüger, *James Cook*, p. 298). The Australian Museum has an example of a highly decorated whalebone club that may have been used as a handle (possibly for an axe). H 364.

149 Göttigen, Inv. Am 14. Photo, Hauser-Schäublin and Krüger, *James Cook*, p. 339.

150 Seal skin coat, Pitt Rivers, Forster Coll. No. 165. Seal skin quiver (UCMAA, 1925.380). Photo, Tanner, *From Pacific Shores*, p. 8 (derives originally from the collection of Thomas Pennant, a Welsh naturalist closely linked with Joseph Banks).

151 Tanner, *From Pacific Shores*, p. 84; Pitt Rivers Museum, Oxford, Forster Collection, no. 131/2.

152 It eventually made its way to the Otago Museum, Dunedin (D62.998FF) via Mrs Cook's sister's granddaughter.

153 UCMAA, D1925.374, Colour photo, Tanner, *From Pacific Shores*, pp. 31. On which see P. Gathercole, 'A Maori Shell Trumpet at Cambridge' in G. Sieveking, I. Longworth and K. Wilson (eds), *Problems in Economic and Social Anthropology* (London, 1976), pp. 187–99.

154 For Tahitian, Marquesan and Tongan examples see respectively: UCMAA, D1914.37, Colour photo, Tanner, *From Pacific Shores*, p. 8; Institut für Ethnologie, Göttingen, Inv. Oz. 326, photo, Hauser-Schäublin and Krüger, *James Cook*, p. 324 and Berne Historisches Museum, FR 24.

Notes to Chapter 3: Trade

1 R.S. Porter, *English Society in the Eighteenth Century* (Harmondsworth, 1982), p. 202.

2   N.A.M. Rodger, *The Command of the Ocean: A Naval History of Britain, 1649–1815* (London, 2004), p. 310.

3   I. R. Christie, *Wars and Revolutions: Britain, 1760–1815* (London, 1982), p. 8.

4   J. Black, *An Illustrated History of Eighteenth-Century Britain* (Manchester, 1996), p. 41.

5   F. B. Singleton and S. Rawnsley, *A History of Yorkshire* (Chichester, 1986), p. 90.

6   W.A. Speck, *Stability and Strife: England, 1714–1760* (London, 1977), p. 136.

7   D. Sullivan, *Great Ayton: A History of the Village* (Great Ayton, 1996), p. 61.

8   Porter, *English Society*, p. 25.

9   A. Smith, *An Inquiry into the Nature and Causes of the Wealth of Nations* (Chicago, 1952), i, Chapter 3, pp. 8–9.

10 R. Floud, D. Mc Closkey (ed.), *The Economic History of Britain since 1700*, i, *1700–1860* (Cambridge, 1981), p. 234.

11 F.M.L. Thompson (ed.), *The Cambridge Social History of Britain, 1750–1950*, i, *Regions and Communities* (Cambridge, 1990), p. 424.

12 H. Perkin, *The Origins of Modern English Society, 1780–1880* (London, 1972), pp. 17, 24.

13 N. McKendrick, J. Brewer and J. H. Plumb, *The Birth of a Consumer Society: The Commercialization of Eighteenth-Century Britain* (Bloomington, Indiana, 1985), p. 20.

14 Ibid.; Floud and McCloskey, *The Economic History*, i, p. 102.

15 G. Newman (ed.), *Britain in the Hanoverian Age, 1714–1837* (New York, 1997), p. 154.

16 R. Price, *British Society, 1680–1880* (Cambridge, 1999), p. 62.

17 Robert Campbell, cited in J. Rule, *Albion's People: English Society, 1714–1815* (London, 1992), p. 73.

18 T.S. Ashton, *An Economic History of England: The Eighteenth Century* (London, 1955), p. 165.

19 Cook to John Harrison Esq., attorney at law of Guisborough, 24 February 1776, NLA, MS 7.

20 Newman, *Britain in the Hanoverian Age*, p. 153.

21 J. Black, *Eighteenth-Century Europe, 1700–1789* (Houndmills, 1990), p. 75.

22 C. Thornton, *Captain Cook in Cleveland: A Study of his Early Years* (Middlesbrough, 1978), p. 19; J. Wardell, *The Economic History of Tees-side* (Stockton, 1960), p. 6.

23 Ashton, *An Economic History*, p. 63.

24 R. Holt, *Whitby Past and Present* (Whitby, [1897?]), p. 11.

25 J. Graves, *The History of Cleveland* (Carlisle, 1808), p. 197.

26 Ashton, *An Economic History*, pp. 68–69.

27 Rule, *Albion's People*, p. 78.

28 Smith, *Wealth of Nations*, iv, Chapter 7, p. 266.

29 J. Gascoigne, *Science in the Service of Empire* (Cambridge, 1998), p. 122.

30 G. Young, *A Picture of Whitby* (Whitby, 1840), p. 218; P. Mathias, 'The People's Mint in the Eighteenth Century: The Royal Mint, Trade Tokens and the Economy', in his *The Transformation of England* (London, 1979), p. 197.

31 J.C. Beaglehole, *The Life of Captain James Cook* (Stanford, 1974), p. 5.

32 Ashton, *An Economic History*, p. 185.

33 A. Briggs, *The Age of Improvement, 1783–1867* (London, 1964), p. 31.

34 M. Phillips, *A History of Banks, Bankers and Banking in Northumberland, Durham and North Yorkshire* (London, 1894), p. 59.

35   Floud and McCloskey, *The Economic History*, p. 58.

36   Black, *Eighteenth-Century Europe*, p. 326.

37   J. Baker, *History of Scarborough, from the Earliest Date* (London, 1882), pp. 315–17; A. Rowntree (ed.), *The History of Scarborough* (London, 1931), p. 107.

38   I. McCalman (ed.), *An Oxford Companion to the Romantic Age: British Culture, 1776–1832* (Oxford, 1999), p. 504.

39   Thornton, *Captain Cook*, p. 13.

40   Ibid., p. 19.

41   H. Cunningham, *Leisure in the Industrial Revolution* (London, 1980), pp. 30–31.

42   A. Salmond, *The Trial of the Cannibal Dog: Captain Cook in the South Seas* (London, 2003), p. 257.

43   McCalman, *An Oxford Companion*, p. 504.

44   A. Mendel, *The Essential Works of Marxism* (New York, 1965), p. 15.

45   M. Quanchi and R. Adams, *Culture Contact in the Pacific* (Cambridge, 1993), p. 58.

46   J.C. Beaglehole (ed.), *The Journals of Captain James Cook on his Voyage of Discovery* (3 vols, Cambridge, 1955–69), i, p. 116.

47   Bayly, *Discovery* journal, ATL, fms 016, fol. 157.

48   W. Shawcross, 'The Cambridge University Collection of Maori Artefacts, Made on Captain Cook's First Voyage', *Journal of the Polynesian Society*, 17 (1970), p. 312.

49   I. Goldman, *Ancient Polynesian Society* (Chicago, 1970), pp. 478, 509.

50   *Cook's Journals*, iii, pt 2, p. 1371.

51   Salmond, *The Trial*, p. 78.

52   C. Holmes (ed.), *Captain Cook's Final Voyage: The Journal of Midshipman George Gilbert* (London, 1982), p. 62.

53   A. Salmond, *Two Worlds: First Meetings between Maori and Europeans, 1642–1772* (Harmondsworth, 1993), p. 216; Salmond, *Trial*, p. 129.

54   *Cook's Journals*, i, p. 195.

55   J. C. Beaglehole (ed.), *The* Endeavour *Journal of Joseph Banks, 1768–1771* (2 vols, Sydney, 1962), i, p. 429.

56   [Recollections of Captain Cook's Visit in 1769, by Taniwha, a Māori Chief. Statement made by him on 15th November 1852], in Great Britain–New Zealand, *Further Papers Relative to the Affairs of New Zealand* (London, 1854), p. 180.

57   While on the *Endeavour* voyage Tupaia learnt to use European drawing implements. This picture depicts Banks trading a nail for a lobster with Banks, wary of his Māori trading partner, keeping, as he later wrote, 'a firm fist on the Lobster detemined not to Quit the nail till I had Livery and Seizin of the article purchasd'. H.B. Carter, 'Note on the Drawings by an Unknown Artist from the Voyage of HMS *Endeavour*', in M. Lincoln (ed.), *Science and Exploration in the Pacific: European Voyages to the Southern Oceans in the Eighteenth Century* (Woodbridge, Suffolk, 1998), pp. 133–34.

58   Salmond, *Two Worlds*, pp. 176, 395; Thomas, *Discoveries*, p. 213.

59   I. Barber, 'Early Contact Ethnography and Understanding: An Evaluation of the Cook Expeditionary Accounts of the Grass Cove Conflict', in A. Calder, J. Lamb and B. Orr (eds), *Voyages and Beaches: Pacific Encounters, 1769–1840* (Honolulu, 1999), pp. 170–72.

60   [J. Marra], *Journal of the* Resolution*'s Voyage* (London, 1775), p. 45.

61 *Banks'* Endeavour *Journal*, ii, p. 96.

62 D. Connor and L. Miller, *Master Mariner: Captain James Cook and the Peoples of the Pacific* (Edinburgh, 1978), p. 93; W. Bayly, *Discovery* Log, ATL, fms 016, fol. 107.

63 *Cook's Journals*, iii, pt 2, p. 1401.

64 Ibid, p. 1396. Among the artefacts collected by John Webber at Nootka Sound was a scraper made from an iron blade set in wood (Berne Historisches Museum, AL10). Three of the nine arrows from the American Northwest coast in the collection of Cook-derived artefacts in the South African Museum, Cape Town have metal tips (SAM 2192).

65 Ibid, p. 1407.

66 *Cook's Journals*, iii, pt 2, p. 1091.

67 R. Fisher, 'Cook and the Nootka', in R. Fisher and H. Johnston (ed.), *Captain James Cook and his Times* (Seattle, 1979), p. 88.

68 *Cook's Journals*, iii, pt 1, pp. 298–99.

69 B. Gough, 'Nootka Sound in James Cook's Pacific World', *Sound Heritage*, 7 (1978), p. 15.

70 Bayly, *Discovery* journal, ATL, Ms fms 016, fol. 93.

71 R. Inglis and J. Haggarty, 'Cook to Jewitt: Three Decades of Change in Nootka Sound', in B. Trigger, T. Morantz, L. Dechêne (eds), *Le Castor Fait Tout: Selected Papers of the Fifth North American Fur Trade Conference, 1985* (Montreal, 1987), pp. 196–97.

72 M. Hoare (ed.), *The* Resolution *Journal of Johann Reinhold Forster* (4 vols, London, 1982), iii, p. 427.

73 I owe this observation to Dr Peter Gathercole.

74 R. Borkfsky and A. Howard, 'The Early Contact Period', in A. Howard and R. Borkfsky (eds), *Developments in Polynesian Ethnology* (Honolulu, 1989), p. 259; A. Henare, *Museums, Anthropology and Imperial Exchange* (Cambridge, 2005), p. 33.

75 Salmond, *The Trial*, pp. 67, 79.

76 *Banks'* Endeavour *Journal*, ii, p. 12.

77 *Cook's Journals*, ii, p. 294.

78 Ibid., iii, pt 2, p. 1161.

79 Ibid., pp. 1207, 1193.

80 *J.R. Forster's* Resolution *Journal*, iii, p. 401.

81 Borkfsky and Howard, 'The Early Contact Period', p. 257.

82 R. Darnton, *The Great Cat Massacre and Other Episodes in French Cultural History* (Harmondsworth, 1984), pp. 61–67.

83 Salmond, *Trial*, p. 64.

84 J. Rickman, *Journal of Cook's Last Voyage to the Pacific Ocean* (London, 1781), p. 98.

85 *J.R. Forster's* Resolution *Journal*, iii, p. 401.

86 *Banks'* Endeavour *Journal*, i, p. 437.

87 Borkfsky and Howard, 'The Early Contact Period', p. 253.

88 *Cook's Journals*, iii, pt 2, p. 1164.

89 Ibid., ii, p. 236.

90 Ibid., ii, p. 366; Borosky and Howard, 'The Early Contact Period', p. 254.

91 *Cook's Journals*, iii, pt 2, p. 1149.

92 J. Martin, *Discovery* journal, TNA, Adm. 51/4531/47, 6 April 1777. Though Pacific Islanders had often heard of Europeans and their goods well before first-hand contact through

encounters with other islanders who had had dealings with them. H. Driessen, 'Outrigger Canoes and Glorious Beings', *Journal of Pacific History*, 17 (1982), p. 3.

93   *Cook's Journals*, iii, pt 1, p. 171.

94   Ibid., p. 160.

95   E. Ferdon, *Early Tonga: As the Explorers Saw It, 1616–1810* (Tucson, Arizona, 1987), p. 234. In the late nineteenth century the Tongans even traded back some of the goods that Cook had sold to them – goods now greatly enhanced in value because of the Cook connection. Bristol City Museum holds a knife and scissors (E1172, E1173) which allegedly derive from Cook's voyages, having been brought back by the Reverend Charles Tucker in 1876.

96   *Banks' Endeavour Journal*, ii, p. 98.

97   H.B. Carter, *Sir Joseph Banks, 1743–1820* (London, 1988), p. 97.

98   *Cook's Journals*, i, p. 186.

99   George Forster, *A Voyage Round the World*, N. Thomas and O. Berghof (eds) (2 vols, Honolulu, 2000), i, p. 363; ii, p. 525.

100   T. Edgar, *Discovery* Journal, BL, Add. MS 37528, fol. 22v.

101   Forster, *Voyage*, i, p. 353.

102   Thomas, *Discoveries*, p. 226.

103   D. Oliver, *Ancient Tahitian Society* (3 vols, Canberra, 1974), i, pp. 75–76. At the Museo Anthropologico, Florence (196, 235, 243, 302) there are the remains of four such girdles (though from Tonga) made from red feathers and sennit.

104   C. Holmes, *Captain Cook's Second Voyage: The Journals of Lieutenants Elliott and Pickersgill* (London, 1984), p. 30.

105   *Cook's Journals*, iii, pt 1, p. 164.

106   Salmond, *The Trial*, p. 217.

107   *Cook's Journals*, ii, p. 369.

108   Ibid., ii, p. 411.

109   Edgar's *Discovery* Journal, fol. 44.

110   *Cook's Journals*, iii, pt. 2, 1014.

111   Ibid., iii, pt. 1, p. 187.

112   Ibid., ii, p. 369.

113   Ibid., iii, pt 2, p. 1164.

114   *Banks' Endeavour Journal*, i, p. 286.

115   *J.R. Forster's Resolution Journal*, iv, p. 679.

116   *Cook's Journals*, iii, pt 2, p. 1527.

117   Ibid.

118   Ibid., iii, pt. 2, p. 1150.

119   Ibid., ii, p. 411.

120   Edgar, *Discovery* Journal, fol. 22v.

121   J. Burney, *Discovery* journal, ML, safe 1/64, fol. 25.

122   *Cook's Journals*, iii, pt 1, p. 483.

123   Ibid., iii, pt 2, p. 1186.

124   Ibid., iii, pt 1, p. 474.

125   Ibid., iii, pt 2, p. 1171.

126 A. Kaeppler, 'Eighteenth-Century Tonga: New Interpretations of Tongan Society and Material Culture at the Time of Captain Cook', *Man*, 6 (1971), p. 206.

Notes to Chapter 4: War

1 J. Cookson, 'War', in I. McCalman (ed.), *An Oxford Companion to the Romantic Age: British Culture, 1776–1832* (Oxford, 1999), p. 27; P. Mackesy, 'Strategic Problems of the British War Effort', in H.T. Dickinson (ed.), *Britain and the French Revolution, 1789–1815* (London, 1989), p. 148.

2 P. Langford, *A Polite and Commercial People: England, 1727–1783* (Oxford, 1989), p. 640.

3 R. Price, *British Society, 1680–1880* (Cambridge, 1999), p. 62.

4 C. Tilly, 'Reflections on the History of European State-Making', in his *The Formation of the Nation States in Western Europe* (Princeton, 1975), p. 42.

5 J. Brewer, *The Sinews of War: War, Money and the English State, 1688–1783* (London, 1989), pp. 31, 40.

6 Brewer, *Sinews*, p. 12.

7 J. Black, 'Introduction', in J. Black and P. Woodfine (eds), *The British Navy and the Use of Naval Power in the Eighteenth Century* (Leicester, 1998), p. 3.

8 G. Young, *A Picture of Whitby and its Environs* (Whitby, 1840), p. 43; R. Barker, *The Book of Whitby* (Buckingham, 1990), p. 65.

9 Quoted from *Calendar of Close Rolls, 1327–30, Edward III*, p. 280 in Friends of Whitby Abbey, *Whitby in the Middle Ages* (CD, n.d.), item 4.220.

10 J. Charles, 'The Yorkshire Haunts of Captain Cook', in J. Hurd and M. Kodama (eds), *Captain Cook and the Pacific Islands: The Proceedings of the Third Annual Pacific Islands Studies Conference* (Honolulu, 1978), p. 37.

11 *Cook's Journals*, iii, pt 2, p. 1456.

12 S. Ashley, 'How Navigators Think: The Death of Captain Cook Revisited', *Past and Present* (2007, forthcoming). This study calculates that, as a percentage of those whose origins are known, 43 per cent of the men and 50 per cent of the offices on Cook's third voyage 'came from outside the metropolitan centres of lowland Britain'. (I am grateful to Dr Ashley for providing me with a preprint of this article.)

13 R. Barker, *The Book of Whitby* (Buckingham, 1990), p. 51.

14 J. Rae, *Captain James Cook Endeavours* (London, 1997), pp. 54, 57.

15 J. Cook, *Pembroke* log, TNA, Adm. 52/978.

16 R. Kettlewell, *Cleveland Village ...* (Redcar, 1938), p. 28.

17 R. Parkin, *H.M.Bark* Endeavour: *Her Place in Australian History* (Melbourne, 1997), p. 73.

18 J. Robson, *The Captain Cook Encyclopaedia* (London, 2004), p. 143.

19 'Marines' in 'South Sea Companion', http://southseas.nla.gov.au/biogs/P000033b

20 'Carriage Gun' and 'Sea Service Musket', Ibid., /biogs/P000073b and P000043b

21 C. Hotimsky, *The Death of Captain James Cook: A Letter from Russia* (Sydney, 1962), pp. 12–13.

22 W. Griffin, *Resolution* journal, DL, MS Q155A, p. 22.

23   G. Newman (ed.), *Britain in the Hanoverian Age, 1714–1837* (New York, 1997), p. 740.

24   E. Robson, 'The Armed Forces and the Art of War', in J.O. Lindsey (ed.), *The Old Regime*, vii, *The New Cambridge Modern History* (Cambridge, 1963), pp. 169, 176.

25   G. Parker, *The Military Revolution: Military Innovation and the Rise of the West, 1500–1800* (Cambridge, 1988), p. 153.

26   G. Parker, 'Warfare', in P. Burke (ed.), *Companion Volume*, xiii, *The New Cambridge Modern History* (Cambridge, 1979), p. 205.

27   Ibid., p. 70.

28   J. Childs, *Armies and Warfare in Europe, 1648–1789* (Manchester, 1982), p. 104.

29   P. O'Brien, *Men-of-War: Life in Nelson's Navy* (New York, 1974), p. 32.

30   Childs, *Armies and Warfare*, p. 22.

31   M. Howard, *War in European History* (Oxford, 1976), p. 54.

32   J. Houlding, *Fit for Service: The Training of the British Army, 1715–95* (Oxford, 1981), p. 77.

33   Brewer, *Sinews*, p. 32.

34   D. and V. Neave, *Georgian Yorkshire* (Clapham, 1972), p. 20.

35   V. Suthren, *To Go Upon Discovery: James Cook and Canada, 1758–1767* (Toronto: 1999), p. 66; J.C. Beaglehole, *The Life of Captain James Cook* (Stanford, 1974), p. 34.

36   F.E. Maning, *Old New Zealand and Other Writings*, A. Calder (ed.) (Leicester, 2001), pp. 19, 34.

37   Anon to Mrs Strachan, 23 January 1781, ML, safe 1/67.

38   R.T. Gould, 'Bligh's Notes on Cook's Last Voyage', *Mariner's Mirror*, 14 (1928), p. 383.

39   The Australian Museum has examples from Cook's voyages of a wooden and a well-sharpened basalt *patu* (H363 and H85) which, characteristically, have a hole bored near the top to attach a cord to hold on to the weapon in battle. There is an example of the rare and very valuable greenstone *patu* in the Forster collection in the Pitt-Rivers Museum (no. 115).

40   E. Riou, *Discovery* journal, TNA, Adm. 51/4529/41-4, fol. 79v. Two such Nootka bone clubs are in the Museo Anthropologica, Florence, 242, 242b.

41   S. Cherry, *Te Ao Maori: The Maori World* (Dublin, 1990), p. 13.

42   D. Oliver, *Ancient Tahitian Society* (3 vols, Canberra, 1974), i, p. 379.

43   W. Bayly, *Discovery* journal, ATL, fms 016, fol. 163.

44   E. Ferdon, *Early Tahiti: As the Explorers Saw It, 1767–1797* (Tucson, 1981), p. 261.

45   J.C. Beaglehole (ed.), *The Journals of Captain James Cook on his Voyage of Discovery* (3 vols, Cambridge, 1955–69), iii, pt.2, p. 1312.

46   A. Kaeppler, 'Artificial Curiosities', being An Exposition of Native Manufactures Collected on the Three Pacific Voyages of Captain James Cook, R.N. (Honolulu, 1978), p. 279.

47   G. Forster, *A Voyage Round the World*, ed. N. Thomas and O. Berghof (2 vols, Honolulu, 2000). ii, p. 813.

48   G. Gilbert, Journal 1776–1780, BL, Add. MS 38530, fol. 67.

49   *Cook's Journals*, iii, pt. 2, p. 1133.

50   There is a Forster-derived example of a New Caledonian sling in the Museo Anthropologico, Florence (154) and another (complete with four sling stones and a bag for such missiles) at the Göttingen Institut für Ethnologie (Inv. Oz 693–94, 696–98, 705). Slings were also

used in Hawai'i, Tahiti and Tierra del Fuego (for examples of the latter two with Cook provenances see Göttingen, Inv. Oz 702 and Inv. Am. 15).

51 *Cook's Journals*, iii, pt 2, p. 1112.

52 Bayly, *Discovery* journal, fol. 140.

53 For an example Göttingen, Inv. Am. 655, 685.

54 *Cook's Journals*, iii, pt 2, p. 1112. There is a fine example (perhaps the one that Thomas Edgar mentions purchasing, ibid., iii, i, p. 351n) in the UCMAA, 1922.950B. Colour photo, J. Tanner, *From Pacific Shores: Eighteenth-Century Ethnographic Collections at Cambridge. The Voyages of Cook, Vancouver and the First Fleet* (Cambridge, 1999), p. 75.

55 Oliver, *Ancient Tahitian Society*, i, p. 380.

56 E. Best, *Notes on the Art of War*, ed. J. Evans (Wellington, 2001), p. 62.

57 Ferdon, *Early Tahiti*, p. 264.

58 Oliver, *Ancient Tahitian Society*, i, p. 402.

59 *Cook's Journals*, i, p. 130.

60 S. Parkinson, *A Journal of a Voyage to the South Seas, in His Majesty's Ship, the* Endeavour … (London, 1773), p. 24.

61 A. Home, 'Journal of the Account of Otaheite and our Transactions there', ANL, MS 690 (typescript), pp. 1–2.

62 V. Valieri, *Kingship and Sacrifice: Ritual and Society in Ancient Hawaii* (Chicago, 1985), p. 348.

63 P. Kirch, *The Evolution of the Polynesian Chiefdoms* (Cambridge, 1984), pp. 196–67.

64 I. Goldman, *Ancient Polynesian Society* (Chicago, 1970), p. 193.

65 Jane Austen, *Pride and Prejudice, Northanger Abbey, Persuasion, Emma* (London, 1982), pp. 363, 372.

66 *Cook's Journals*, iii, pt 1, p. 505.

67 A. Home, 'A Journal', p. 12.

68 *Cook's Journals*, i, p. 396.

69 Bayly, *Discovery* log, fol. 45.

70 J. Forster, *Observations Made during a Voyage round the World*, edited by Nicholas Thomas, Harriet Guest and Michael Dettelbach (Honolulu, 1996), p. 355.

71 *Cook's Journals*, iii, pt 1, p. 174.

72 E. Bott, *Tongan Society at the Time of Captain Cook's Visits* (Wellington, 1982), p. 47; Bayly, *Discovery* journal, fol. 107.

73 Thus a Tongan club with a mushroom-shaped head which derives from Cook's voyages resembles a Fijian design though the pierced lug for hanging the weapon is distinctively Tongan. Royal Albert Museum, Exeter, E1211; Gilbert, Journal 1776–1780, fol. 26 v.

74 E. Ferdon, *Early Tonga: As the Explorers Saw It, 1616–1810* (Tucson, Arizona, 1987), pp. 261–72.

75 J.C. Beaglehole (ed.), *The* Endeavour *Journal of Joseph Banks 1768–1771* (2 vols., Sydney, 1962), ii, p. 59.

76 *Cook's Journals*, ii, p. 740.

77 Ibid., i, p. 203.

78 C. Holmes, *Captain Cook's Second Voyage: The Journals of Lieutenants Elliott and Pickersgill* (London, 1984), p. 75.

79   A.P. Vayda, *Maori Warfare* (Wellington, 1960), pp. 2, 61.

80   A. Sparrman, *A Voyage Round the World with Captain James Cook in HMS* Resolution, translated from the Swedish by H. Beamish and A. Mackenzie-Grieve (London, 1953), pp. 32–33.

81   Childs, *Armies and Warfare*, p. 133.

82   E. Best, *The Pa Maori* (Wellington, 1975), p. 12.

83   *Banks'* Endeavour *Journal*, ii, p. 31.

84   J. Matra, *A Journal of a Voyage Round the World in His Majesty's Ship* Endeavour (London, 1771), p. 98. Matra was known as Magra until 1775.

85   Vayda, *Maori Warfare*, p. 79.

86   Sparrman, *A Voyage*, p. 38.

87   A. Salmond, *Between Worlds: Early Exchanges between Maori and Europeans, 1773–1815* (Auckland, 1997), p. 177.

88   A.P. Vayda, *War in Ecological Perspective* (New York, 1976), p. 81.

89   H. Robley, *Moko: or Maori Tattooing* (London, 1896), p. 160.

90   Best, *Notes on the Art of War*, p. 109; A. Salmond, *The Trial of the Cannibal Dog: Captain Cook in the South Seas* (London, 2003), p. 225.

91   Salmond, *The Trial*, p. 312.

92   T. Edgar, *Discovery* journal, BL, Add. MS 37528, fol. 22v.

93   E. Handy, *Polynesian Religion* (Honolulu, 1927), p. 265.

94   Sparrman, *A Voyage*, p. 71.

95   [J. Rickman], *Journal of Captain Cook's Last Voyage to the Pacific Ocean* (London, 1781), p. 111.

96   M. Duffy, *Man of Honour: John Macarthur* (Sydney, 2003), pp. 38, 197.

97   [J. Matra], *A Journal*, p. 57.

98   W. Griffin, 'Short Narrative', p. 4.

99   Ashley, 'How Navigators Think'.

100 M. Hoare (ed.), *The* Resolution *Journal of Johann Reinhold Forster* (4 vols, London, 1982), iii, p. 502.

101 Anon. to Mrs Strachan, 23 January 1781.

102 W. Shawcross, 'The Cambridge University Collection of Maori Artefacts, Made on Captain Cook's First Voyage', *Journal of the Polynesian Society*, 17 (1970), p. 318.

103 *Cook's Journals*, i, p. 281.

104 W. Bayly, *Adventure* journal, ATL, fms-015, fol. 63.

105 For example, Francis Wilkinson describing the weapons of the Māoris of Poverty Bay, *Endeavour* Journal, TNA, Adm. 51/4547, 149–50, 9 October 1769.

106 Vayda, *Maori Warfare*, p. 41.

107 J. Cook and J. King, *Voyage to the Pacific Ocean* (London, 1784), iii, p. 26.

108 *Cook's Journals*, iii, pt 2, p. 1193.

109 Ibid., ii, p. 493.

110 Bayly, *Discovery* journal, fol. 55.

111 *Cook's Journals*, iii, pt 1, p. 501.

112 H. Zimmerman, *Account of the Third Voyage of Captain Cook, 1776–1780*, translated by U. Tewsley (Wellington, 1926), p. 39.

113   C. Clerke, *Resolution* journal (second voyage), TNA, Adm. 55/103, fol. 168.

114   G. Forster, *A Voyage*, i, p. 100.

115   *Banks'* Endeavour *Journal*, ii, p. 12; *Cook's Journals*, i, p. 282.

116   *Banks'* Endeavour *Journal*, ii, p. 55. This is very likely the same shield now on display in the British Museum (Ethno Q78.Oc.839), which has a hole probably made by a bullet in the incident which Banks describes.

117   *Cook's Journals*, iii, pt 2, p. 1202.

118   Sparrman, *A Voyage*, pp. 71–72.

119   *Cook's Journals*, ii, p. 398.

120   Riou, *Discovery* journal, fol. 80v.

121   J. Elliott, 'Memoirs of the Early Life of John Elliott', BL, Add. MS 42714, fol. 22.

122   *Cook's Journals*, ii, p. 752.

123   Ibid., iii, pt 2, p. 1197.

124   A. Home, *Memoirs of an Aristocrat* (London, 1838), p. 303.

125   Gould, 'Bligh's Notes', p. 380.

126   Bayly, *Discovery* journal, fol. 7.

127   *Cook's Journals*, iii, pt 2, p. 985.

128   Bayly, *Discovery* journal, fol. 107.

129   Childs, *Armies and Warfare*, p. 118.

130   Parker, *The Military Revolution*, p. 154; J. Black, *A Military Revolution? Military Change and European Society, 1550–1800* (Atlantic Highlands, New Jersey, 1991), pp. 52, 93.

Notes to Chapter 5:   Politics

1   Rudd Family Letters and Papers 1792–1863, NYCRO, ZLT (MIC 3995/0423).

2   G. Newman (ed.), *Britain in the Hanoverian Age, 1714–1837* (New York, 1997), p. 27.

3   L. Withey, *Voyages of Discovery: Captain Cook and the Exploration of the Pacific* (London, 1987), p. 384.

4   G. Forster, *A Voyage Round the World*, ed. N. Thomas and O. Berghof (2 vols, Honolulu, 2000). i, pp. 199, 340.

5   P. Kirch, *The Evolution of the Polynesian Chiefdoms* (Cambridge, 1984). p. 261.

6   M. Hoare (ed.), *The* Resolution *Journal of Johann Reinhold Forster, 1772–1775* (4 vols, London, 1982), iv, p. 635.

7   G. Gilbert, Journal 1776–80, BL, Add. MS 38530, fol. 68.

8   L. Stone, *The Family, Sex and Marriage in England, 1500–1800* (London, 1979), pp. 94–97.

9   W.A. Speck, *Stability and Strife: England, 1714–1760* (London, 1977), p. 169.

10   J.C. Beaglehole (ed.), *The Journals of Captain James Cook on his Voyage of Discovery* (3 vols, Cambridge, 1955–69), ii, p. 798.

11   Ibid., iii, pt 2, p. 1022.

12   Ibid, iii, pt 2, p. 1323.

13   [J. Marra], *Journal of the* Resolution's *Voyage* (London, 1775), p. 224.

14 This is not vastly different, however, to the way in which in the United States and Australian constitution each state has the same number of representatives in the Senate whatever the size of the state.

15 D. and V. Neave, *Georgian Yorkshire* (Clapham, North Yorkshire, 1972), p. 16.

16 Hull Election of 1796: Sir Charles Turner Candidate, NYCRO, ZK 13095, items 13099–13278, 13292–98, 13450–60.

17 L. Namier and J. Brooke (eds), *History of Parliament: The House of Commons, 1754–1790* (3 vols, London, 1964), i, p. 329.

18 Ibid, pp. 439, 434, 432–33, 335, 10.

19 H. Dickinson, 'Democracy', in I. McCalman (ed.), *An Oxford Companion to the Romantic Age: British Culture, 1776–1832* (Oxford, 1999), p. 35.

20 Newman, *Britain in the Hanoverian Age*, p. 26.

21 Namier and Brook, *History of Parliament*, iii, pp. 234–5, i, pp. 439–40.

22 J. Graves, *The History of Cleveland* (Carlisle, 1808), p. 457; J.C. Beaglehole, *The Life of Captain James Cook* (Stanford, 1974), p. 25.

23 'Sir Hugh Palliser', in F. Bladen (ed.), *Historical Records of New South Wales* (8 vols, Sydney, 1892–1901), i, pt 1, p. 481.

24 V. Suthren, *To Go Upon Discovery: James Cook and Canada, 1758–1767* (Toronto, 1999), p. 134.

25 Namier and Brooke, *History of Parliament*, i, p. 439.

26 Ibid ii, p. 247.

27 Ibid ii, p. 246.

28 J. Baker, *The History of Scarborough, from the Earliest Date* (London, 1882), p. 233.

29 Ibid., p. 240; F.B. Singleton and S. Rawnsley, *A History of Yorkshire* (Chichester, 1986), p. 113.

30 Benjamin Stephenson to Joseph Banks, 21 March, 1768, Yale University, Manuscripts and Archives, Banks Correspondence.

31 Banks to Sandwich, 1 September 1775, NMM, Sandwich Papers, 41/80.

32 J.C. Beaglehole, *The Life of Captain James Cook* (Stanford, 1974), p. 450.

33 H.B. Carter, *Sir Joseph Banks, 1743–1820* (London, 1988), p. 132.

34 A. Kippis, *A Narrative of the Voyages Round the World Performed by Captain James Cook* (London, 1883), p. ix.

35 Sandwich's draft reply to Banks, submitted to the king, 20 June 1772, J.C. Beaglehole (ed.), *The Endeavour Journal of Joseph Banks 1768–1771* (2 vols., Sydney, 1962), ii, p. 354.

36 Sandwich to Lord North, 8 June 1772, ibid., ii, p. 348.

37 M. Hoare, *The Tactless Philosopher: Johann Reinhold Forster (1729–98)* (Melbourne, 1976), pp. 159–162.

38 N. Thomas, *Discoveries: The Voyages of Captain Cook* (London, 2003), p. 263.

39 Cook to Sandwich, 11 July 1776, *Cook's Journals*, iii, pt 2, p. 1512.

40 Cook to Sandwich, 23 October 1776, ibid., p. 1515.

41 Sandwich to Banks, 10 January 1780, ibid., pp. 1552–3; Banks to Sandwich, 14 September, 16 September, 20 September, 2 October, 9 October, 21 October 1782, ANL, MS 7218/14–15, 17–20.

42 Elizabeth Cook to Sandwich, 17 December 1783, ANL, MS 7218/25.

43 B. Rudd to Banks, 11 August, 1801, 29 January 1802, Auckland Public Library, Grey MSS 66, 73, GMSS D8.

44 D. Baugh, *British Naval Adminstration in the Age of Walpole* (Princeton, 1965), p. 139.

45 Molesworth Phillips to 'My Dear Doctor [?Burney]', n.d., NLA, MS 333.

46 Scottish and Irish peers not included. H.J. Habbakuk, 'England', in A. Goodwin (ed.), *The European Nobility in the Eighteenth Century* (London, 1953), p. 17.

47 A. Frost, *The Voyage of the* Endeavour: *Captain Cook and the Discovery of the Pacific* (Sydney, 1998), p. 110.

48 Banks' Endeavour *Journal*, i, p. 384.

49 *Cook's Journals*, ii, p. 410.

50 G. Forster, *A Voyage Round the World*, N. Thomas and O. Berghof (eds) (2 vols, Honolulu, 2000), i, p. 199.

51 *Cook's Journals*, i, p. 134.

52 A. Home, 'Journal of the Account of Otaheite and our Transactions there' (typescript), ANL, MS 690, p. 6.

53 *Cook's Journals*, iii, pt 1, p. 174 and pt 2, p. 950.

54 Banks' Endeavour *Journal*, i, p. 384n.

55 Gilbert, Journal, 1776–1780, fol. 52v.

56 B. Hooper (ed.), *With Captain James Cook in the Antarctic and Pacific: The Journal of James Burney, Second Lieutenant of the* Adventure *on Cook's Second Voyage, 1772–1773* (Canberra, 1975), p. 69.

57 *Cook's Journals*, ii, p. 836.

58 E. Bott, *Tongan Society at the Time of Captain Cook's Visits* (Wellington, 1982), p. 15.

59 J. Burney, *Discovery* journal, ML, safe 1/64, fol. 66.

60 A. Salmond, *The Trial of the Cannibal Dog: Captain Cook in the South Seas* (London, 2003), p. 327; H. Cummins, 'Tongan Society at the Time of European Contact', in N. Rutherford (ed.), *Friendly Islands: A History of Tonga* (Melbourne, 1977), p. 64.

61 C. Clerke, *Discovery* journal, ML, MS A559, fol. 158.

62 A. Kaeppler, 'Eighteenth-century Tonga: New Interpretations of Tongan Society and Material Culture at the Time of Captain Cook', *Man*, 6 (1971), p. 208.

63 *Cook's Journals*, iii, pt 1, p. 178.

64 Kirch, *Evolution of the Polynesian Chiefdoms*, p. 219.

65 *Cook's Journals*, i, p. 281; ii, p. 294.

66 Anon, *A Second Voyage Round the World ... by James Cook* (London, 1776), p. 43.

67 *Cook's Journals*, iii, pt 2, p. 1304.

68 Bayly, *Discovery* journal, fol. 59.

69 Home, Journal, p. 7.

70 Bayly, *Adventure* journal, fol. 85

71 Kaeppler, 'Eighteenth-century Tonga', p. 211.

72 Burney, *Discovery* journal, fol. 66.

73 A. Kaeppler, *'Artificial Curiosities': Being An Exposition of Native Manufactures Collected on the Three Pacific Voyages of Captain James Cook, R.N.* (Honolulu, 1978), p. 223. The National Maritime Museum, Greenwich has, for example, a Tongan fly-whisk the handle of which is made from a spear. L15/94/C. The one in the Berne Historisches Museum (TAH33) more

conventionally has a handle made of whalebone while the whisk itself consists of coconut fibre and that at the Museo Anthropologico, Florence (195) has a wooden handle.

74   A. Kaeppler, 'Rank in Tonga', *Ethnology*, 10 (1971), p. 174, and G. Forster, *Journey*, i, p. 453.

75   *Cook's Journals*, iii, pt 2, p. 1179.

76   V. Valieri, *Kingship and Sacrifice: Ritual and Society in Ancient Hawaii* (Chicago, 1985), p. 153.

77   *Cook's Journals*, iii, pt 2, p. 1392.

78   King's journal in *Cook's Journals*, iii, pt 1, p. 512. Clerke's cloak probably made its way to the British Museum (Ethno HAW 134). It is made from black cocks' feathers but is edged with the valuable red and yellow feathers. Clerke (who left his artefacts to Banks, much of whose collection then passed to the British Museum) was probably also the source of the British Museum's feathered helmet (HAW 108), decorated principally with yellow and red feathers (though it also includes some black). The splendid red and yellow feathered cloak in Te Papa, Wellington (FE327) derives from Cook and was a gift from Kalani'op'u (Kaeppler, *Artificial Curiosities*, p. 62). The feathered cape (H104) in the Australian Museum (where the Cook material goes back to Mrs Cook) probably also derives from Cook. Presumably the red and yellow feathered cloak and helmet in the Webber collection at the Berne Historisches Museum (HAW1) were purchased by Webber. It would be interesting to know what European goods he could provide which the Hawaiians considered of comparable value to these rare and culturally highly-prized objects.

79   A. Kaeppler, 'Hawaiian Art and Society', in A. Hooper and J. Huntsman (eds), *Transformations of Polynesian Culture*, Polynesian Society Memoir 45 (Auckland, 1985), p. 118.

80   'Extracts from the Journal of A. Bloxam ... General Naturalist on HMS *Blonde* at the Sandwich Islands in the Year 1825', ATL, MS-0247, fol. 11.

81   Thomas, *Discoveries*, p. 387.

82   G. Forster, *Voyage*, i, p. 254.

83   Burney, *Discovery* journal, fol. 60.

84   Gilbert, Journal, 1776–1780, fos 129v–130.

85   Clerke, *Discovery* journal, fos 127–28.

86   J. King, *Resolution* journal, TNA, Adm. 55/116, fol. 124.

87   *Cook's Journals*, iii, pt 1, p. 596.

88   *Cook's Journals*, iii, pt 1, p. 175.

89   J. Munford (ed.), *John Ledyard's Journal of Captain Cook's Last Voyage* (Corvallis, Oregan, 1963), pp. 130–31.

90   *Cook's Journals*, iii, pt 2, p. 1022.

91   Ibid., iii, pt 1, p. 174.

92   King, *Resolution* journal, fol. 90v.

93   G. Forster, *A Voyage*, i, pp. 256, 132.

94   I. Goldman, *Ancient Polynesian Society* (Chicago, 1970), p. 96.

95   G. Forster, *A Voyage*, i, p. 322.

96   *Cook's Journals*, ii, p. 354.

97   A. Home, 'Journal', p. 7.

98   G. Forster, *A Voyage*, i, p. 199.

99   Goldman, *Ancient Polynesian Society*, p. 7.

100 Bayly, *Discovery* journal, fol. 9.

101 Home, Journal, p. 10.

102 Burney, *Discovery* journal, fol. 66.

103 J. Rae, *Captain James Cook Endeavours* (London, 1997), p. 92.

104 In his wide-ranging recent book, *Longitude and Empire: How Captain Cook's Voyages Changed the World* (Vancouver, 2005), Brian Richardson argues that Cook's mapping, and especially his use of longitude, was a major stimulus for the division of the world into separate states. For a critique see my review in *Journal of Pacific Studies*, 40 (2005), pp. 359–60.

Notes to Chapter 6: Religion

1 E. Davies, *Episcopacy and the Royal Supremacy in the Church of England in the Sixteenth Century* (Oxford, 1950), p. 60.

2 C. Thornton, *Captain Cook in Cleveland: A Study of his Early Years* (Middlesbrough, 1978), p. 20.

3 R. Butlin, *Historical Atlas of North Yorkshire* (Otley, 2003), p. 109.

4 H. Davies, *Worship and Theology in England* (5 vols, Grand Rapids, 1996), iii, *From Watts and Wesley to Martineau, 1690–1900*, p. 114.

5 R. Kettlewell, *Cleveland Village* (Redcar, [1938]), p. 50.

6 Davies, *Worship and Theology*, iii, p. 43.

7 D. O'Sullivan, *Great Ayton: A History of the Village* (Great Ayton, 1996), p. 134.

8 Society of Friends, NYCRO, Ayton Women's Preparatory Meeting; Minute of Quarterly Meeting Held at York 28 June 1781; Women's Quarterly Meeting Queries nos. 4, 5, 'From the Yearly Meeting of Women Friends held in London … 21 May 1785', RGG 1/52 (MIC 1301, frames 919–21, 2609). Disownments 1751–93, Guisborough, R/Q/G3/1 (MIC 1301, frame 1323). Women's Quarterly Meeting Queries no. 6, RGG 1/52 (MIC 1301, frames 921).

9 T. Woodwark, *The Quakers of Whitby* (n.p, n.d.), p. 3.

10 L. Charlton, *The History of Whitby* (York, 1779), p. 349.

11 Ibid.

12 Cook to John Walker, 13 September 1771, J.C. Beaglehole (ed.), *The Journals of Captain James Cook on his Voyage of Discovery* (3 vols in 4, Cambridge, 1955–69), i, pp. 507–8.

13 Cook to John Walker, 20 November 1772, *Cook's Journals*, ii, p. 689.

14 Ibid., iii, pt. 1, p. 389.

15 H. Zimmerman, *Account of the Third Voyage of Captain Cook, 1776–1780*, translated by U.Tewsley (Wellington, 1926), p. 41.

16 C[harles] H[atchett], 'Banksiana Written at the Request of my Friend Dawson Turner Esq. of Great Yarmouth', Banks Archive Project, Natural History Museum, London.

17 K. Popp, (ed.), *Georg Forster, Georg Chr. Lichtenberg. Cook der Entdecker* (Leipzig, 1980), p. 170.

18 R. Allen, 'Cook and the North Yorkshire Quakers', in G. Williams (ed.), *Captain Cook: Explorations and Reassessments* (Woodbridge, Suffolk, 2004), p. 36.

19 Woodwark, *The Quakers of Whitby*, pp. 9–10.

20 A. Smith, 'Captain James Cook: Londoner', *East London Papers*, 11 (1968), p. 94.

21 J. Robson, *The Captain Cook Encyclopaedia* (London, 2004), p. 65.

22 J. Rae, *Captain James Cook Endeavours* (London, 1997), p. 98.

23 E. Willams, *The Eighteenth-Century Constitution: Documents and Commentary* (Cambridge, 1960), p. 325.

24 G. Young, *A Picture of Whitby and its Environs* (Whitby, 1840), p. 228.

25 D. Neave, *Port, Resort and Market Town: A History of Bridlington* (Hull, 2000), p. 131.

26 R. Barker, *The Book of Whitby* (Buckingham, 1990), p. 107.

27 O'Sullivan, *Great Ayton*, p. 140.

28 J. Baker, *The History of Scarborough, from the Earliest Date* (London, 1882), p. 497.

29 Barker, *The Book of Whitby*, p. 107.

30 C.J. Sommerville, *The Secularization of Early Modern England: From Religious Culture to Religious Faith* (New York, 1992), pp. 124–27.

31 Ibid., p. 3.

32 N.A.M. Rodger, *Articles of War: The Statutes which Governed our Fighting Navies, 1661, 1749, and 1886* (Homewell, Hampshire, 1982), p. 22.

33 *Cook's Journals*, i, p. 95.

34 Ibid., i, p. 515.

35 'Articles of War, 1749', 'South Sea Companion', http://southseas.nla.gov.au/biogs/P000354b

36 Sommerville, *The Secularization*, p. 75.

37 K. Thomas, *Religion and the Decline of Magic* (New York, 1971), p. 71.

38 Kettlewell, *Cleveland Village*, pp. 114–16.

39 Captain Cook Tourism Association, *Captain Cook Country Tour* (Yarm, 1994), p. 5.

40 A. Marchant, *Great Ayton: Church History* (n.p., 1989), p. 9.

41 I owe this point to Rosalin Barker.

42 W.E. Tate and F.B. Singleton, *A History of Yorkshire* (Beaconsfield, 1965), p. 29; K. McCutcheon, *Yorkshire Fairs and Markets to the End of the Eighteenth Century* (Leeds, 1940), p. 7.

43 Sommerville, *The Secularization*, p. 62.

44 Thomas, *Religion and the Decline of Magic*, p. 75.

45 Kettlewell, *Cleveland Village*, p. 31.

46 At the Ryedale Folk Museum there are two examples of such witchposts, one dating from 1704.

47 G. Home, *Memoirs of an Aristocrat* (London, 1838), p. 26.

48 Thomas, *Religion and the Decline of Magic*, pp. 201–2.

49 R. Blakeborough, *Wit, Character, Folklore and Customs of the North Riding of Yorkshire* (London, 1898), p. 161.

50 Kettlewell, *Cleveland Village*, p. 113.

51 J. Brown and I. Croden, *Staithes: A Collection of Fact and Fantasy about a North Yorkshire Fishing Community* (Staithes, 1977), p. 20.

52 *Cook's Journals*, ii, p. 424.

53 On Māori witchcraft, for example, see M. Pomare and J. Cowan, *Legends of the Maori*

(2 vols, Wellington, 1930–34), i, p. xxiii; E. Best, *Maori Religion and Mythology* (2 vols, Wellington, 1976), i, p. 374, ii, pp. 104, 139.

54 Ibid., i, pp. 39, 51, 259, 265.

55 *Cook's Journals*, i, p. 286; ii, p. 294.

56 J.C. Beaglehole (ed.), *The* Endeavour *Journal of Joseph Banks, 1768–1771* (2 vols., Sydney, 1962), ii, p. 34.

57 Ibid, i, p. 277.

58 *Cook's Journals*, i, p. 113.

59 [J. Matra], *A Journal of a Voyage Round the World in His Majesty's Ship* Endeavour, ... (London, 1771), p. 48.

60 *Cook's Journals*, iii, pt 1, p. 620.

61 E. Ferdon, *Early Tonga: As the Explorers Saw It, 1616–1810* (Tucson, Arizona, 1987), p. 73; E. Best, *Tuhoe: The Children of the Mist* (2 vols, Wellington, 1996), i, p. 1019.

62 A. Home, 'Journal of the Account of Otaheite and our Transactions there' (typescript), ANL, MS 690, p. 12.

63 [J. Matra], *A Journal*, pp. 48–49.

64 *Cook's Journals*, ii, p. 797.

65 W. Bayly, *Discovery* journal, TNA, Adm. 55/2, fol. 73.

66 *Cook's Journals*, iii, pt 2, p. 1185.

67 M. Hoare (ed.), *The* Resolution *Journal of Johann Reinhold Forster, 1772–1775* (4 vols, London, 1982), iii, p. 393.

68 *Cook's Journals*, ii, p. 797.

69 *Banks'* Endeavour *Journal*, i, p. 383.

70 M. Sahlins, *Historical Metaphors and Mythical Realities: Structure in the Early History of the Sandwich Islands Kingdom* (Ann Arbor, Michigan, 1981), p. 31.

71 As was probably true of the Hawaiian feathered god acquired during Cook's third voyage and now in the British Museum (Ethno Van 231).

72 H. Cobbe, *Cook's Voyages and the Peoples of the Pacific* (London, 1979), p. 52.

73 There is an example in the British Museum from the eighteenth century (and possibly Cook's third voyage), BM, Ethno. Q79 Am 1.

74 B. Shore, 'Manu and Tapu', in Alan Howard and R. Boroksky (eds), *Developments in Polynesian Ethnology* (Honolulu, 1989), p. 143.

75 E. Best, *Tuhoe*, i, p. 1020.

76 E. Handy, *Polynesian Religion* (Honolulu, 1927), p. 28.

77 G. Dening, *Beach Crossings: Voyaging across Times, Cultures and Self* (Melbourne, 2004), p. 163.

78 R. Oppenheim, *Maori Death Customs* (Wellington, 1973), p. 120.

79 Shore, 'Manu and Tapu', p. 165.

80 Sahlins, *Historical Metaphors*, p. 54.

81 A. Salmond, *The Trial of the Cannibal Dog: Captain Cook in the South Seas* (London, 2003), p. 100.

82 T. Edgar, *Discovery* journal, TNA, Adm. 55/21, f. 114v.

83 J. King, *Resolution* journal, TNA, Adm. 55/116, fol. 90.

84 *Cook's Journals*, iii, pt 2, p. 1161.

85 S. Allott, *Friends in York: The Quaker Story in the Life of a Meeting* (York, 1978), p. 52.

86 Friends of Whitby Abbey, *Whitby in the Middle Ages* (CD, n.d.), 6.

87 *Banks' Endeavour Journal* i, p. 383.

88 J. Morrison, *Account of Tahiti*, Indigenous Histories, http://southseas.nla.gov.au/journals/morrison, p. 50.

89 *J.R. Forster's Resolution Journal*, iii, p. 530.

90 J. Burney, *Discovery* log, ML safe 1/79, fol. 8.

91 E. Handy, *Polynesian Religion* (Honolulu, 1927), pp. 158, 118.

92 H. Zimmerman, *Account of the Third Voyage of Captain Cook, 1776–1780*, translated by U. Tewsley (Wellington, 1926), p. 20.

93 H. Cummins, 'Tongan Society at the Time of European Contact', in N. Rutherford (ed.), *Friendly Islands: A History of Tonga* (Melbourne, 1977), p. 76.

94 John Williamson, *Resolution* journal, TNA, Adm. 55/117, fol. 64v.

95 E. Bott, *Tongan Society at the Time of Captain Cook's Visits* (Wellington, 1982), pp. 39, 46.

96 *Cook's Journals*, iii, pt 1, p. 205.

97 N. Thomas, *Discoveries: The Voyages of Captain Cook* (London, 2003), p. 388.

98 Home, 'Journal', p. 12.

99 G. Forster, *A Voyage Round the World*, ed. N. Thomas and O. Berghof (2 vols, Honolulu, 2000), i, p. 401.

100 J. Munford, (ed.), *John Ledyard's Journal of Captain Cook's Last Voyage* (Corvallis, Oregan, 1963), p. 58.

101 R. Williamson, *Social and Political Systems of Central Polynesia* (3 vols, Cambridge, 1924), i, p. 418.

102 M. Sahlins, *Islands of History* (Chicago, 1985), p. 125.

103 W. Harvey, *Resolution* journal, TNA, Adm. 55/121, fol. 118v.

104 J. Forster, *Observations Made during a Voyage round the World*, edited by Nicholas Thomas, Harriet Guest and Michael Dettelbach (Honolulu, 1996), p. 339.

105 *G. Forster's Voyage*, i, pp. 400, 171.

106 Ibid., i, p. 249.

107 [J. Marra], *Journal of the Resolution's Voyage* (London, 1775), p. 227.

108 *Cook's Journals*, i, p. 84.

109 Ibid, i, p. 135.

110 *Banks' Endeavour Journal*, i, pp. 379, 382.

111 Home, 'Journal', p. 12.

112 G. Gilbert. 'Journal, 1776–1780', BL, Add. MS 38530, fol. 33v.

113 C. Holmes (ed.), *Captain Cook's Final Voyage: The Journal of Midshipman George Gilbert* (London, 1982), p. 59.

114 *Cook's Journals*, ii, p. 274; iii, pt 2, p. 1169.

115 A. Sparrman, *A Voyage Round the World with Captain James Cook in HMS* Resolution, translated from the Swedish by H. Beamish and A. Mackenzie (London, 1953), p. 126.

116 Munford, *John Ledyard's Journal*, p. 95

117 J. Morrison, *Account of Tahiti*, 'Indigenous Histories', http://southseas.nla.gov.au/journals/morrison, p. 50.

118 Sparrman, *A Voyage*, p. 136.

119 [Marra], *Journal of the* Resolution's *Voyage*, p. 227.

120 M. Sahlins, *How 'Natives' Think about Captain Cook, For Example* (Chicago, 1996), p. 134.

121 Based on a oral tradition recorded by a European trader. A. Salmond, *Two Worlds: First Meetings between Maori and Europeans, 1642–1772* (Harmondsworth, 1993), p. 124.

122 Best, *Tuhoe*, ii, p. 554.

123 Ibid., p. 553; Salmond, *Two Worlds*, pp. 198, 206, 221.

124 B. Gough, 'Nootka Sound in James Cook's Pacific World', in B. Efrat and W. Langlois (eds), *Nu.tka. Captain Cook and the Spanish Explorers on the Coast, Sound Heritage*, 7 (1978), p. 13.

125 Cobbe, *Cook's Voyages*, p. 107.

126 D. Clayton, *Islands of Truth: The Imperial Fashioning of Vancouver Island* (Vancouver, 2006), pp. 23–25.

127 Sahlins, *How 'Natives' Think*, p. 164; I.C. Campbell, 'The Culture of Culture Contact: Refractions from Polynesia', *Journal of World History*, 14 (2003), pp. 63–86.

128 W. Gill, *Historical Sketches of Savage Life in Polynesia* (Wellington, 1880), p. 187.

129 J. King, *Resolution* journal, DL, MS 98, fol. 39.

130 *J.R. Forster's* Resolution *Journal*, iii, p. 528.

131 Prince Frederick Augustus to Bishop William Markham, 18 July 1774, ATL, 78–058.

132 *J.R. Forster's* Resolution *Journal*, iii, p. 395.

Notes to Chapter 7: Sex

1 T. S. Eliot, 'Sweeney Agonistes' (1932).

2 J.C. Beaglehole (ed.), *The Journals of Captain James Cook on his Voyage of Discovery* (3 vols in 4 parts, Cambridge, 1955–69), i, p. 359.

3 G. Forster, *A Voyage Round the World*, ed. N. Thomas and O. Berghof (2 vols, Honolulu, 2000), i, p. 250.

4 Friends of Whitby Abbey, *Whitby in the Middle Ages* (CD), Church Historians, i, pt 2, p. 44.

5 M. Hoare (ed.), *The* Resolution *Journal of Johann Reinhold Forster, 1772–1775* (4 vols, London, 1982), iv, p. 759.

6 J.C. Beaglehole (ed.), *The* Endeavour *Journal of Joseph Banks, 1768–1771* (2 vols, Sydney, 1962), i, p. 382.

7 John Watts, *Resolution* journal (third voyage), TNA, Adm. 55/117, fol. 41.

8 V. Valieri, *Kingship and Sacrifice: Ritual and Society in Ancient Hawaii* (Chicago, 1985), p. 302.

9 E. Handy, *Polynesian Religion* (Honolulu, 1927), p. 145.

10 G. Newman (ed.), *Britain in the Hanoverian Age, 1714–1837* (New York, 1997), p. 439.

11 T. Laqueur, 'Sex and Desire in the Industrial Revolution', in P. O'Brien and R. Quinault (eds), *The Industrial Revolution and British Society* (Cambridge, 1993), p. 101.

12 L. Stone, *The Family, Sex and Marriage in England, 1500–1800* (London, 1979), pp. 324, 399–400.

13 J. Jago, *Aspects of the Georgian Church: Visitation Studies of the Diocese of York, 1761–1776* (London and Cranbury, New Jersey, 1997), p. 214.

14 Ibid., p. 215.

15 D. Clark, *Between Pulpit and Pew: Folk Religion in a North Riding Yorkshire Fishing Village* (Cambridge, 1982), p. 49.

16 Stone, *The Family, Sex and Marriage*, p. 399.

17 Ibid., p. 400.

18 Society of Friends, Guisborough Monthly Meeting, Disownments, NYCRO, R/Q/G 3/1, frame 1359.

19 S. Allott, *Friends in York: The Quaker Story in the Life of a Meeting* (York, 1978), p. 60.

20 J. Brown and I. Croden, *Staithes: A Collection of Fact and Fantasy about a North Yorkshire Fishing Community* (Staithes, 1977), p. 16.

21 R. Holt, *Whitby Past and Present* (Whitby, [?1897]), p. 31; G. Walker, *The Costume of Yorkshire* (London, 1814), p. 70.

22 Laqueur, 'Sex and Desire', p. 101.

23 A. Burnicle, *A Genealogical Study of the Families of Captain James Cook* (Middlesbrough, [1985]).

24 J. Fairfax-Blakeborough, *Yorkshire Days and Yorkshire Ways* (London, 1935), p. 144.

25 J. Gillis, 'Married but not Churched: Plebeian Sexual Relations and Marital Nonconformity in Eighteenth-Century Britain', in R. Maccubbin (ed.), *'Tis Nature's Fault: Unauthorized Sexuality during the Enlightenment* (Cambridge, 1987), p. 33.

26 Stone, *Family, Sex and Marriage*, p. 32.

27 James Cook and Elizabeth Batts, Marriage Bond, Lambeth Palace, VM 11/165 (copy ANL, MS 7).

28 Will of James Cook, TNA, no. D. 3394 (copy ML, MSS 826X).

29 Gillis, 'Married but not Churched', pp. 36–37.

30 R.S. Porter, 'Mixed Feelings: the Enlightenment and Sexuality in Eighteenth-Century Britain', in P. Boucé (ed.), *Sexuality in Eighteenth-Century Britain* (Manchester, 1982), p. 9.

31 N. Thomas, *Discoveries: The Voyages of Captain Cook* (London, 2003), p. 156.

32 J. Black, *An Illustrated History of Eighteenth-Century Britain, 1688–1793* (Manchester, 1996), p. 68.

33 T. Hitchcock, *English Sexualities, 1700–1800* (New York, 1997), p. 67.

34 K. Wilson, 'Gender Misrecognition and Polynesian Subversions aboard the Cook Voyages', in K. Wilson (ed.), *A New Imperial History: Culture, Identity and Modernity in Britain and the Empire, 1660–1840* (Cambridge, 2004), p. 355.

35 Porter, 'Mixed Feelings', p. 17.

36 I. McCalman (ed.), *An Oxford Companion to the Romantic Age: British Culture, 1776–1832* (Oxford, 1999), p. 547; Hitchcock, *English Sexualities*, p. 66.

37 Hitchcock, *English Sexualities*, p. 63.

38 N.A.M. Rodger, *The Command of the Ocean: A Naval History of Britain, 1649–1815* (London, 2004), p. 407.

39 B. Shuster and S. Shuster, 'Buggery in the British Merchant Navy in the mid Nineteenth Century', in J. Covacevich, *et al.*, *History, Heritage and Health: Proceedings of the Fourth*

Biennial Conference of the Australian Society of the History of Medicine (Brisbane, 1996), pp. 277–83.

40 N.A.M. Rodger, *Articles of War: The Statutes which Governed our Fighting Navies, 1661, 1749 and 1886* (Homewell, Hampshire, 1982), p. 27.

41 A. N. Gilbert, 'Buggery and the British Navy, 1700–1861', *Journal of Social History*, 10 (1976–77), p. 86.

42 G. Dening, *Mr Bligh's Bad Language: Passion, Power and Theatre on the* Bounty (Cambridge, 1992), p. 117.

43 N.A.M. Rodger, *The Wooden World: An Anatomy of the Georgian Navy* (New York, 1996), p. 80. In her discussion of naval homosexuality K. Wilson mentions two occasions on which Cook's men were flogged for 'uncleanliness'. K. Wilson, *The Island Race: Englishness, Empire and Gender in the Eighteenth Century* (London, 2003), p. 177. The one case that I could trace was for the offender 'easing himself betwixt decks'. *Cook's Journals*, ii, pt 2, p. 361n.

44 Rodger, *Wooden World*, p. 228.

45 J. Cook, *Pembroke* log, TNA, Adm.52/978.

46 J. Cook, *Eagle* log (27 June 1755–31 December 1756), 23 February 1756. ATL, q MS-0537-0539 (transcript by John Robson, http://pages.quicksilver,net.nz/jcr/eagle 1756).

47 J. Cook, *Pembroke* log, TNA, Adm.52/978.

48 N. Hegarty, 'Unruly Subjects: Sexuality, Science and Discipline in Eighteenth-Century Pacific Exploration', in M. Lincoln (ed.), *Science and Exploration in the Pacific: European Voyages to the Southern Oceans in the Eighteenth Century* (Woodbridge, Suffolk, 1998), p. 189.

49 C. Roderick, 'Sir Joseph Banks, Queen Oberea and the Satirists', in W. Veit (ed.), *Captain James Cook: Image and Impact* (2 vols, Melbourne, 1970–72), ii, pp. 67–89.

50 C[harles] H[atchett], 'Banksiana written at the Request of my Friend Dawson Turner Esq. of Great Yarmouth', Banks Archive Project, Natural History Museum, London, p. 24.

51 Banks to William Perrin, 21 March 1767, Derbyshire Record Office, Fitzherbert MSS D239M.

52 Hatchett, 'Banksiana', p. 24.

53 Cook to ?, 1 August 1772, *Cook's Journals*, ii, p. 685.

54 J. Elliott, 'Memoirs of the Early Life of John Elliott', BL, Add. MS 42714, fol. 13v.

55 H.B. Carter, *Sir Joseph Banks, 1743–1820* (London, 1988), pp. 150, 234–45.

56 E. Craig, 'Notes on Sir Hugh Palissier', ATL, MS-7888-031, fol. 49.

57 Carter, *Sir Joseph Banks, 1743–1820*, p. 152.

58 K. Harvey, 'Spaces of Erotic Delight', in M. Ogden and C. Withers (eds), *Georgian Geographies: Essays on Space, Place and Landscape in the Eighteenth Century* (Manchester, 2004), p. 145.

59 N.A.M. Rodger, *The Insatiable Earl: A Life of John Montagu, Fourth Earl of Sandwich, 1718–1792* (London, 1993), p. 81.

60 Rodger, *The Insatiable Earl*, p. 80.

61 J.C. Beaglehole, *The Life of Captain James Cook* (Stanford, 1974), p. 475.

62 S. Sinclair, *Elizabeth Cook, the Captain's Wife, 1741–1835* (Sydney, 1995), p. 10.

63 H. Zimmerman, *Account of the Third Voyage of Captain Cook, 1776–1780*, translated by U. Tewsley (Wellington, 1926), p. 41; Elliott, 'Memoirs', fol. 30.

64 *Cook's Journals*, ii, p. 175.

65 Ibid., iii, pt 1, pp. 61–62.

66 Ibid., ii, p. 236.

67 Cook to J. Douglas, 7 January 1776, BL, Egerton MS 2180, fol. 3.

68 *Cook's Journals*, i, p. 99; B. Orr, '"Southern Passions Mix with Northern Art": Miscegenation and the *Endeavour* Voyage', *Eighteenth-Century Life*, 18 (1994), p. 225.

69 S. Parkinson, *A Journal of a Voyage to the South Seas, in His Majesty's Ship, the* Endeavour (London, 1773), pp. 25–26.

70 E. Duyker, *Nature's Argonaut: Daniel Solander, 1733–1782* (Melbourne, 1998), p. 140.

71 W. Wales, *Remarks on Mr Forster's Account* in G. Forster, *Voyage*, ii, p. 726.

72 M. Sahlins, *Historical Metaphors and Mythical Realities: Structure in the Early History of the Sandwich Islands Kingdom* (Ann Arbor, Michigan, 1981), p. 40.

73 Porter, 'Mixed Feelings', p. 10.

74 *Banks' Endeavour Journal*, i, pp. 381–82.

75 Banks to William Perrin, 28 February 1768, Derbyshire Record Office, Fitzherbert MSS D239M.

76 B. Hooper (ed.), *With Captain James Cook in the Antarctic and Pacific: The Journal of James Burney, Second Lieutenant of the* Adventure *on Cook's Second Voyage, 1772–1773* (Canberra, 1975), p. 68.

77 D. Oliver, *Ancient Tahitian Society* (3 vols, Canberra, 1974), i, p. 450.

78 Ibid., pp. 452, 454; E. Handy, *Polynesian Religion* (Honolulu, 1927), pp. 230–31.

79 Beaglehole, *James Cook*, p. 176.

80 J. Saquet, *The Tahiti Handbook* ([Papeete], 1998), p, 55.

81 T. Edgar, *Discovery* journal, TNA, Adm. 55/21, fol. 114.

82 A. Salmond, *Two Worlds: First Meetings between Maori and Europeans, 1642–1772* (Harmondsworth, 1993), p. 423.

83 H. Cummins, 'Tongan Society at the Time of European Contact', in N. Rutherford (ed.), *Friendly Islands: A History of Tonga* (Melbourne, 1977), p. 86.

84 *Cook's Journals*, iii, pt. 2, p. 945.

85 Ibid., pt. 1, p. 596.

86 J. Munford (ed.), *John Ledyard's Journal of Captain Cook's Last Voyage* (Corvallis, Oregan, 1963), p. 132.

87 Anon to Mrs Strachan, 23 January 1781, ML, safe 1/67, fol. 11.

88 M. Sahlins, *Islands of History* (Chicago, 1985), p. 23.

89 P. Kirch, *The Evolution of the Polynesian Chiefdoms* (Cambridge, 1984), p. 254.

90 W. Ellis, *Narrative of a Tour Through Hawaii* (London, 1826), p. 414.

91 E. Best, *Maori Religion and Mythology* (2 vols, Wellington, 1924), i, p. 366.

92 Handy, *Polynesian Religion*, p. 212.

93 A. Salmond, *Between Worlds: Early Exchanges between Maori and Europeans, 1773–1815* (Auckland, 1997), p, 358.

94 *Cook's Journals*, iii, pt 2, p. 1042.

95 Clark, *Between Pulpit and Pew*, p. 119.

96 Salmond, *Between Worlds*, p. 358

97 Handy, *Polynesian Religion*, p. 213; Best, *Maori Religion*, i, p. 359.

98   *Cook's Journals*, iii, pt 2, p. 1225.

99   Sahlins, *Islands of History*, p. 5n.; D. Chappell, 'Shipboard Relations between Pacific Island Women and Euroamerican Men, 1767–1887', *Journal of Pacific History*, 27 (1992), p. 134.

100 *Cook's Journals*, iii, pt 2, p. 1042.

101 W. Bayly, *Discovery* Log, ATL, fms 016, fol. 15.

102 *Cook's Journals*, iii, pt 2, p. 1344.

103 J. Forster, *Observations Made during a Voyage round the World* edited by Nicholas Thomas, Harriet Guest and Michael Dettelbach (Honolulu, 1996), p. 298.

104 J. King, *Resolution* Journal, DL, MS 98, fol. 40.

105 W. Ellis, *An Authentic Narrative*, ii, p. 153.

106 Sahlins, *Historical Metaphors*, p. 40; C. Ralston, 'Ordinary Women in Early Post-Contact Hawaii', in M. Jolly and M. Macintyre (eds), *Family and Gender in the Pacific: Domestic Contradictions and the Colonial Impact* (Cambridge, 1989), pp. 55–57.

107 A. Taylor, *Sesquicentennial Celebration of Captain Cook's Discovery of Hawaii (1778–1928)* (Honolulu, 1929), p. 66.

108 W. Gill, *Historical Sketches of Savage Life in Polynesia* (Wellington, 1880), p. 176.

109 J. Williamson, *Resolution* journal, TNA, Adm. 55/117, fos. 64v, 45.

110 *Cook's Journals*, ii, p. 797.

111 G. Forster, *Voyage*, i, p. 351.

112 *Cook's Journals*, ii, p. 239.

113 Bayly, *Discovery* journal, ATL, Ms fms 016, fol. 5.

114 A. Sparrman, *A Voyage Round the World with Captain James Cook in* HMS Resolution, translated [from the Swedish] by H. Beamish and A. Mackenzie-Grieve (London, 1953), p. 126.

115 J. Elliott, 'Memoirs of the Early Life of John Elliott', BL, Add. MS 42714, fol. 30.

116 *Cook's Journals*, ii, p. 238; Anon, *A Second Voyage Round the World* (London, 1776), p. 69.

117 *Cook's Journals*, ii, p. 796.

118 Ibid., iii, pt. 1, p. 56.

119 Ibid., i, p. 424.

120 Bayly, *Discovery* journal, 3 April 1778.

121 Williamson, *Resolution* journal, TNA, Adm. 55/117, fol. 100.

122 Ellis, *An Authentic Narrative*, i, p. 216.

123 *Cook's Journals*, iii, pt 2, pp. 1182, 1142; pt 1, p. 468n.

124 *Banks' Endeavour Journal*, i, p. 461.

125 *Cook's Journals*, ii, p. 546.

126 Ibid., ii, p. 444.

127 Ibid., iii, pt 2, p. 1149.

128 Ibid., iii, pt 1, lxxxvi.

129 Ibid., ii, p. 119.

130 Ibid., ii, pp. 859–60.

131 Bayly, *Discovery* log, fol. 44.

132 F. Cuppage, *James Cook and the Conquest of Scurvy* (Westport, Connecticut, 1994), p. 46.

133 King, *Resolution* log, TNA, Adm. 55/116, fos. 72v, 91.

134 *Cook's Journals*, iii, pt 2, p. 927.

135 *J.R. Forster's* Resolution *Journal*, ii, p. 308.

136 I. Van Der Sluis, *The Treponematois of Tahiti: Its Origin and Evolution. A Study of the Sources* (PhD thesis, University of Amsterdam, 1969), pp. 76, 13–4.

137 *Banks' Endeavour Journal*, i, p. 375; *Cook's Journals*, ii, p. 797.

138 *Cook's Journals*, iii, pt 2, p. 1186.

139 Ibid., iii, pt 1, p. 265.

140 M. Jolly, 'Desire, Difference and Disease: Sexual and Venereal Exchanges on Cook's Voyages to the Pacific', in R. Gibson (ed.), *Exchanges: Cross-Cultural Encounters in Australia and the Pacific* (Sydney, 1977), p. 203.

141 Munford, *John Ledyard's Journal*, p. 132.

142 *Cook's Journals*, iii, pt 2, p. 1184.

143 Ibid., iii, pt 2, pp. 1171–12.

144 Ibid., iii, pt 1, p. 624; Munford, *John Ledyard's Journal*, p. 132.

145 *Cook's Journals*, iii, pt 1, p. 596.

146 Ibid., iii, pt 2, p. 1184.

147 Munford, *John Ledyard's Journal*, p. 133.

148 D. Oliver, *Ancient Tahitian Society* (3 vols, Canberra, 1974), i, p. 369. Wilson, *The Island Race*, p. 195, quotes Wales's remark about Tahitian men who 'are forbid the use of Women' in relation to the issue of homosexuality. However, Wales here seems to be making a muddled reference to the *arioi*. In any case he goes on to add that such men 'hold not short Dalliance with them [women] in private'. *Cook's Journals*, ii, p. 839.

149 R. Morris, 'Aikane: Accounts of Hawaiian Same-Sex Relationships in the Journals of Captain Cook's Third Voyage', *Journal of Homosexuality*, 19 (1990), p. 25.

150 L. Wallace, *Sexual Encounters: Pacific Texts, Modern Sexualities* (Ithaca, New York, 2003).

151 J. Cook, and J. King, *Voyage to the Pacific Ocean* (London, 1784), iii, p. 130.

152 I. Goldman, *Ancient Polynesian Society* (Chicago, 1970), pp. 215, 538–9.

153 V. Valieri, *Kingship and Sacrifice: Ritual and Society in Ancient Hawaii* (Chicago, 1985), p. 85

154 *Cook's Journals*, iii, pt 2, p. 1181.

155 Ibid., iii, pt 1, p. 624.

156 *Banks' Endeavour Journal*, i, 348.

157 Edgar, *Discovery* journal, TNA, Adm. 55/21, fol. 114v.

158 T. Edgar, *Discovery* journal, BL, Add. MS 37528, fol. 77.

159 *Cook's Journals*, ii, p. 268.

160 Ibid., iii, pt. 2, p. 933.

161 E. Evans-Prichard, *A History of Anthropological Thought* (London, 1981), p. 16.

162 N. McKendrick, J. Brewer and J.H. Plumb, *The Birth of a Consumer Society: The Commercialization of Eighteenth-Century Britain* (Bloomington, Indiana, 1985), p. 9.

163 R.S. Porter, *English Society in the Eighteenth Century* (Harmondsworth, 1982), p. 38.

164 J. Mayhall, *The Annals of Yorkshire, from the Earliest Period to the Present Time* (3 vols, London, [1876]), i, p. 147.

165 G. Forster, *A Voyage*, ii, p. 537.

166 *Cook's Journals*, iii, pt. 2, p. 1366.

167 Anon to Mrs Strachan, 23 January 1781, ML, safe1/67, fol. 11.

168 Beaglehole, *Cook*, p. 458.

169 Even the much-remarked initiation scene had a real foundation in Cook's journal (i, p. 93), though Hawkesworth exercised considerable poetical licence. N. Rennie, 'The Point Venus "Scene"', in M. Lincoln (ed.), *Science and Exploration in the Pacific: European Voyages in the Southern Oceans in the Eighteenth Century* (Woodbridge, Suffolk, 1998), pp. 134–46.

Notes to Chapter 8: Death

1 Will of John Walker, 22 February 1742, NYCRO, PB 2872 (copy in Captain Cook Memorial Museum).

2 J. Ord, *The History and Antiquities of Cleveland* (London, 1846), p. 410.

3 R. Malcolmson, *Life and Labour in England, 1700–1780* (London, 1981). p. 60.

4 Will of James Cook, TNA, no. D3394 (copy ML, MSS 826X).

5 R. Blakeborough, *Wit, Character, Folklore and Customs of the North Riding of Yorkshire* (1898), p. 118; J. Fletcher, *Recollections of a Yorkshire Village* (London, 1910), p. 129.

6 D. Clark, *Between Pulpit and Pew: Folk Religion in a North Riding Yorkshire Fishing Village* (Cambridge, 1982), p. 130.

7 R. Kettlewell, *Cleveland Village* (Redcar, 1938), p. 118; A. White, *A History of Whitby* (Chichester, 1993), p. 138.

8 D. O'Sullivan, *Great Ayton: A History of the Village* (Great Ayton, 1996), p. 60.

9 J. Baker, *The History of Scarborough from the Earliest Date* (London, 1882), p. 233.

10 Now in the Mitchell Library, Sydney (R363).

11 J. Whaley (ed.), *Mirrors of Mortality: Studies in the Social History of Death* (London, 1981), p. 6; M. Vovelle, 'Death', in A Kors, *Encyclopedia of the Enlightenment* (4 vols, New York, 2003), i, pp. 324–27.

12 Clark, *Between Pulpit and Pew*, p. 129.

13 Society of Friends, Ayton Women's Preparatory Meeting, 'From the Yearly Meeting of Women Friends held in London … 21 May 1785', NYCRO, RGG 1/52, MIC 1301, frame 2611.

14 T. Woodwark, *The Quakers of Whitby* (n.p, n.d.), p. 14.

15 O'Sullivan, *Great Ayton*, p. 9.

16 J.C. Beaglehole (ed.), *The Journals of Captain James Cook on his Voyage of Discovery* (3 vols in 4, Cambridge, 1955–69), iii, pt 2, p. 946.

17 J. Amelang, 'Mourning Becomes Eclectic: Ritual Lament and the Problems of Continuity', *Past and Present*, no. 187 (2005), pp. 20, 28.

18 E. Handy, *Polynesian Religion* (Honolulu, 1927). p. 191.

19 J.C. Beaglehole (ed.), *The Endeavour Journal of Joseph Banks, 1768–1771* (2 vols., Sydney, 1962), i, p. 286.

20 S. Parkinson, *A Journal of a Voyage to the South Seas, in His Majesty's Ship, the Endeavour* (London, 1773), p. 21.

21 J. Burney, *Discovery* journal, ML safe, 1/64, fol. 71.

22 W. Ellis, *An Authentic Narrative of a Voyage* (2 vols, London, 1782), i, p. 112.

23 C. Clerke's *Discovery* Journal, ML, MS A 559, fol. 159.

24 G. Forster, *A Voyage Round the World*, N. Thomas and O. Berghof (eds) (2 vols, Honolulu, 2000), i, p. 236.

25 *Cook's Journals*, iii, pt 2, p. 1178.

26 *Banks' Endeavour Journal*, i, p. 430.

27 H. Robley, *Moko: or Maori Tattooing* (London, 1896), p. 45.

28 *Cook's Journals*, i, p. 286.

29 A. Salmond, *Between Worlds: Early Exchanges Between Maori and Europeans, 1773–1815* (Auckland, 1997), p. 278.

30 Staithes Bonnets, Teeside Archives, Cook Material, CC/PR(3)/3–4.

31 *Banks' Endeavour Journal*, ii, p. 333.

32 *Cook's Journals*, iii, pt 2, p. 1181.

33 Robley, *Moko*, p. 45; *Banks' Endeavour Journal*, i, p. 377.

34 R. Holt, *Whitby Past and Present* (Whitby, [1897?]), p. 32.

35 C. Gittings, *Death, Burial and the Individual in Early Modern England* (London, 1998), p. 161.

36 White, *Whitby*, p. 137.

37 *Cook's Journals*, iii, pt 1, p. 135.

38 D. Oliver, *Ancient Tahitian Society* (3 vols, Canberra, 1974), i, p. 492; B. Douglas, 'A Contact History of the Balad People of New Caledonia, 1774–1845', *Journal of the Polynesian Society*, 79 (1970), p. 189.

39 Ellis, *An Authentic Narrative*, ii, p. 179; A. Salmond, *Two Worlds: First Meetings between Maori and Europeans, 1642–1772* (Harmondsworth, 1993), p. 423.

40 *Cook's Journals*, iii, pt 1, p. 621.

41 King, 'Resolution Journal', TNA Adm. 55/116, fol. 124v; R. Oppenheim, *Maori Death Customs* (Wellington, 1973), p. 52.

42 A. Bloxam, Extracts from the Journal of the visit of HMS *Blonde* at the Sandwich Islands in the year 1825, ATL, MS-0247.

43 *Cook's Journals*, iii, pt. 2, p. 947.

44 W. Bayly, *Discovery* Log, ATL, fms 016, fol. 73.

45 *Cook's Journals*, ii, p. 426.

46 A. Crowther, *Yorkshire Customs: Traditions and Folk Lore of Old Yorkshire* (Clapham, North Yorkshire, 1974), p. 55.

47 J. Fairfax-Blakesborough, *Yorkshire Days and Yorkshire Ways* (London, 1935), p. 170.

48 Blakeborough, *Wit, Character, Folklore*, pp. 119, 121.

49 'Death in Maohi Society', South Sea Companion, http://southseas.nla.gov.au/biogs/P000417b.

50 Oliver, *Ancient Tahiti*, i, p. 64.

51 *Banks' Endeavour Journal*, i, p. 378.

52 A. Kaeppler, 'Pacific Culture and European Voyages', in W. Esler and B. Smith (eds), *Terra Australia: The Furthest Shore* (Sydney, 1988), p. 143. There are complete Tahitian mourning dresses in the Pitt Rivers Museum, Oxford (Forster coll. 1–4); the Museo Anthropoligico (202), Florence; the British Museum (TAH 78); Bishop Museum, Honolulu (1971.198) and the Institut für Ethnologie, Göttingen (Oz 1522) together with various pieces scattered around the world, for example the apron with the thin slivers of mother-of-pearl

ingeniously stitched together in the Australian Museum (H149) or the feathered mask, chest apron and pair of pearl-shell clappers at the Berne Historisches Museum (TAH 3). Along with the substantial Webber collection this museum also holds had a few items which were passed down through the Forster family (the Rheiberger collection) including a shell from a mourning dress (Rh.82.450.18c).

53 *Banks' Endeavour Journal*, i, pp. 378.

54 *Cook's Journals*, i, p. 285; *Banks'* Endeavour *Journal*, ii, p. 34.

55 E. Best, *Maori Religion and Mythology* (2 vols, Wellington, 1924), i, pp. 375–77; Oppenheim, *Maori Death Customs*, p. 15 and passim.

56 Anon, 'Eye-Witness Account of the Death of Captain James Cook', ANL, MS 8.

57 J. Dimsdell, 'Account of the Death and Remains of Capt. Cook – at Owyhee received from Joshua Lee Dimsdell Quarter Master of the *Gunjara* Capt. James Barber' 1801, DL, MS Q154.

58 P. King, 'Some Thoughts on Native Hawaiian Attitudes towards Captain Cook', in G. Williams (ed.), *Captain Cook: Explorations and Reassessments* (Woodbridge, Suffolk, 2004), p. 102.

59 *Cook's Journals*, iii, pt 2, pp. 1161–62; A. Taylor (ed.), *Sesquicentennial Celebration of Captain Cook's Discovery of Hawaii (1778–1928)* (Honolulu, 1929), pp. 66–67.

60 See the celebrated dispute between Obeyesekere and Sahlins: the latter argues strongly that Cook was assimilated into the Hawaiians' conceptions of a deity (and, in particular, that of Lono) to the extent that Cook's death was largely occasioned by the annual cycle of Lono giving way to Ku; by contrast, the former questions such an approach as being shaped by Western imperialism which gives too much importance to iconic white explorers such as Cook and which downplay the extent of a generalized human 'practical rationality'. The main works in the debate are G. Obeyesekere, *The Apotheosis of Captain Cook: European Mythmaking in the Pacific* (Princeton, 1992) and M. Sahlins, *How 'Natives' Think about Captain Cook, For Example* (Chicago, 1996). For a overview and critique of the controversy see R. Brodsky *et al.*, 'Cook, Lono, Obeyesekere, and Sahlins', *Current Anthropology* 38 (1997), pp. 255–282.

61 K. Howe, 'The Death of Cook: Exercises in Explanation', *Eighteenth-Century Life*, 18 (1994), p. 206.

62 J. Cook and J. King, *Voyage to the Pacific Ocean* (London, 1784), p. 60.

63 Anon to Mrs Strachan, 23 January 1781, ML, safe 1/67; *Cook's Journals*, iii, pt 2, p. 1218.

64 J. Dimsdell, 'Account'.

65 G. Gilbert, Journal 1776–1780, BL, Add. MS 38530, fol. 99v.

66 G. Kennedy, *The Death of Cook* (London, 1978), p. 55.

67 J. Law, *Discovery/Resolution* Journal, BL, Add. 37327, fos. 24–25.

68 W. Harvey, *Resolution* journal, TNA, Adm. 55/121, fol. 116; *Cook's Journals*, iii, pt 1, p. 538.

69 On the dynamics of the apportionment of the post-mortem blame, see S. Ashley, 'How Navigators Think: The Death of Captain Cook Revisited', *Past and Present*, 2007 (forthcoming).

70 A. Home, 'Journal of the Account of the Death of Captain James Cook', ANL, MS 7, fol. 4.

71 C. Lloyd and R.C. Anderson (eds), *A Memoir of James Trevenen* (London, 1959), p. 24.

72　William Dalton's Journal (1823–29), including visit to Kealakekua Bay, 5 May 1827, ANL, MS 7230, fol. 74.

73　*Cook's Journals*, iii, pt 1, p. 542.

74　Obeysekere, *The Apotheosis*, p. 90.

75　J. Cook and J. King, *Voyage to the Pacific Ocean*, iii, p. 69.

76　Anon, 'Eye-Witness Account', fol. 13; *Cook's Journals*, iii, pt 2, p. 1217.

77　Dimsdell, 'Account'.

78　Sahlins, *How 'Natives' Think*, p. 96.

79　*Cook's Journals*, ii, p. 425.

Bibliography

MANUSCRIPT SOURCES

Anon, 'Eye-Witness Account of the Death of Captain James Cook', ANL, MS 8.

Anon to Mrs Strachan, 23 January 1781, ML, safe 1/67.

Banks, J., to William Perrin, 21 March 1767, 28 February 1768, Derbyshire Record Office, Fitzherbert MSS D239M.

Banks, J., to Sandwich, 14 September, 16 September, 20 September, 2 October, 9 October, 21 October, 1782, ANL, MS 7218/14–15, 17–20.

Banks, J., to William Scoresby, 8 September 1810, Whitby Museum.

Bayly, W., *Adventure* journal, ATL, fms-015.

—, *Discovery* journal, ATL, fms 016 and TNA, Adm. 55/20.

Bigge, J., to Earl Bathurst, 27 February 1823, ML, Bonwick Transcripts, series 1, Box 28.

Bloxam, A., 'Journal … on HMS *Blonde* at the Sandwich Islands in the Year 1825', ATL, MS-024.

Burney, J., *Discovery* journal, ML, safe 1/64 and 79.

Clerke, C., *Discovery* journal, ML, MS A559 and TNA, Adm. 55/22 (AJCP, PRO, reels 1575–76).

—, *Resolution* journal (second voyage), TNA, Adm. 55/103 (AJCP, PRO, reel 1590).

Cook, E., to Lord Sandwich, 17 December 1783, ANL, MS 7218/25.

Cook, J. (snr), Documents regarding the Great Ayton Cottage, Victoria State Library, Melbourne, store, map case, drawer 2/4, H6405, H6407.

Cook, J., *Eagle* log (27 June 1755–31 December 1756), ATL, q MS-0537-0539.

—, *Pembroke* log, TNA, Adm. 52/978.

—, Will, TNA, no. D. 3394 (copy ML, MSS 826X).

Cook, J., to John Douglas, 7 January 1776, BL, Egerton MS 2180.

Cook, J., to John Harrison, 24 February 1776, NLA, MS 7.

Cook, J., and Batts, E., marriage bond, Lambeth Palace, VM 11/165 (copy ANL, MS 7).

Craig, E., 'Notes on Sir Hugh Palissier', ATL, MS-7888-031.

Dalton, W. Journal (1823–29, ANL, MS 7230.

Dimsdell, J., 'Account of the Death and Remains of Capt. Cook – at Owyhee received from Joshua Lee Dimsdell Quarter Master of the *Gunjara* Capt. James Barber. 1801, DL, MS Q154.

Edgar, T., *Discovery* journal, BL, Add. MS 37528 and TNA, Adm. 55/21 (AJCP, PRO, Reel 1575).

Elliott, J., 'Memoirs of the Early Life of John Elliott', BL, Add. MS 42714.

Forster, G., 'Cook the Discover', preface to his 1787 translation of Cook's third voyage. Translated from the German by P.E. Klarwill. ATL, Ms Papers 1485.

Gilbert, G., Journal 1776–80, BL, Add. MS 38530.

Griffin, W., *Resolution* journal (third voyage), DL, MS Q 155 (typescript).

Harvey, W., *Resolution* journal (third voyage), TNA, Adm. 55/121 (AJCP, PRO, reel 1594).

H[atchett], C[harles], 'Banksiana written at the Request of my Friend Dawson Turner Esq of Great Yarmouth', Banks Archive Project, Natural History Museum, London.

Home, A., 'Journal of the Account of the Death of Captain James Cook', ANL, MS 7.

—, 'Journal of the Account of Otaheite and our Transactions there' (typescript), ANL, MS 690.

Hull Election of 1796: Sir Charles Turner Candidate, NYCRO, ZK 13095, items 13099–13278, 13292–98, 13450–60.

King, J., *Resolution* journal (third voyage), TNA, Adm. 55/116; another copy DL, MS 98.

Law, J., *Discovery/Resolution* Journal, BL, Add. MS 37327.

Martin, J., *Discovery* journal, TNA, Adm. 51/4531/47 (AJCP, PRO, reel 1555).

Phillips, M., to 'My Dear Doctor [?Burney]', n.d., NLA, MS 333.

Prince Frederick Augustus to Bishop William Markham, 18 July 1774, ATL, 78–058.

Proctor, E., Great Ayton Estates, NYCRO, ZLT (guide).

Riou, E. *Discovery* journal, TNA, Adm. 51/4529/41-4 (AJCP, PRO, reel 1554).

Roberts, H., *Resolution* journal (third voyage), DL, Q 151–52.

Roberts, J., *Endeavour* journal, ML, safe 1/65.

Rudd, B., to Banks, 11 August, 23 August, 10 September, 1801, 29 January 1802, Auckland Public Library, Grey MSS 66–68, 73/GMSS D8.

Rudd Family Letters and Papers, 1792–1863, NYCRO, ZLT (MIC 3995/0423).

Society of Friends, NYCRO, Ayton Women's Preparatory Meeting; Minute of Quarterly Meeting Held at York 28 June 1781; Women's Quarterly Meeting Queries nos 4, 5, 'From the Yearly Meeting of Women Friends held in London … 21 May 1785', RGG 1/52 (MIC 1301, frames 919–21, 2609, 2611); Guisborough, Monthly Meeting, Women's Quarterly Meeting Queries no. 6,

RGG 1/52 (MIC 1301, frames 921); Disownments 1751–93, R/Q/G3/1 (MIC 1301, frames, 921, 1323, 1359).

Staithes Bonnets, Teeside Archives, Cook Material, CC/PR(3)/3–4.

Stephenson, B., to Joseph Banks 21 March, 1768, Yale University, Manuscripts and Archives, Banks Correspondence.

Trevenen, J., 'Notes on Passages from December 1777 to October 1779 published in 1784 Quarto Edition of Captain Cook's Third Voyage', ATL, q MS-2041.

Walker, J., Will, 22 February 1742, NYCRO, PB 2872 (copy in Captain Cook Memorial Museum).

Watts, J., *Resolution* journal (third voyage), TNA, Adm. 55/117 (AJCP, PRO, reel 1593).

Wilkinson, F., *Endeavour* Journal, TNA, Adm. 51/4547.

Williamson, J., *Resolution* journal (third voyage), TNA Adm. 55/117 (AJCP, PRO, Reel 1593).

PRINTED SOURCES

Adams, M. and Thomas, N., *Cook's Sites: Revisiting History* (Dunedin, 1999).

Allen, R., 'Cook and the North Yorkshire Quakers', in G. Williams (ed.), *Captain Cook. Explorations and Reassessments* (Woodbridge, Suffolk, 2004), pp. 21–36.

Allott, S., *Friends in York: The Quaker Story in the Life of a Meeting* (York, 1978).

Amelang, J., 'Mourning becomes Eclectic: Ritual Lament and the Problems of Continuity', *Past and Present*, no. 187 (2005), pp. 3–31.

Anon, *A Second Voyage Round the World … by James Cook, Esq. Commander of His Majesty's Bark the* Resolution (London, 1776).

Ashley, S., 'How Navigators Think: The Death of Captain Cook Revisited', *Past and Present*, 2007 (forthcoming).

Ashton, T.S., *An Economic History of England: The Eighteenth Century* (London, 1955).

Austen, J., *Pride and Prejudice, Northanger Abbey, Persuasion, Emma* (London, 1982).

Badger, G., *The Explorers of the Pacific* (Sydney, 1996).

Baines, E., *Yorkshire, Past and Present* (2 vols in 4 parts, London, [?1870]).

Baker, J., *The History of Scarborough, from the Earliest Date* (London, 1882).

Barber, I., 'Early Contact Ethnography and Understanding: An Evaluation of the Cook Expeditionary Accounts of the Grass Cove Conflict', in A. Calder, J. Lamb and B. Orr (eds), *Voyages and Beaches: Pacific Encounters, 1769–1840* (Honolulu, 1999), pp. 156–79.

Barker, R., *The Book of Whitby* (Buckingham, 1990).

—, 'Cook's Nursery: Whitby's Eighteenth-Century Merchant Fleet',
in G. Williams (ed.), *Captain Cook: Explorations and Reassessments*
(Woodbridge: Suffolk, 2004), pp. 7–20.

Baugh, D. *British Naval Adminstration in the Age of Walpole* (Princeton, 1965).

—, 'The Eighteenth Century Navy as a National Institution, 1690–1815', in
J.R. Hill (ed.), *The Oxford Illustrated History of the Royal Navy* (Oxford,
1995), pp. 120–60.

Beaglehole, J.C. (ed.), *The Journals of Captain James Cook on his Voyage of
Discovery* (3 vols, in 4, Cambridge, 1955–69).

—, 'On the Character of Captain James Cook', *Geographical Journal*, 122
(1956), pp. 417–29.

—, (ed.), *The* Endeavour *Journal of Joseph Banks, 1768–1771* (2 vols., Sydney,
1962).

—, 'Cook, the Navigator', *Explorer's Journal*, 48 (1970), pp. 264–73.

—, *The Life of Captain James Cook* (Stanford, 1974).

Beddie, M.K., *Bibliography of Captain James Cook, RN, FRS, Circumnavigator*
(The Library of New South Wales: Syndey, 1970).

Belich, J., *Making Peoples: A History of New Zealanders, i, From Polynesian
Settlement to the End of the Nineteenth Century* (Auckland, 1996).

Best, E., *Maori Religion and Mythology* (2 vols, Wellington, 1924).

—, *The Pa Maori* (Wellington, 1975).

—, *Fishing Methods and Devices of the Maori* (Wellington, 1977).

—, *Tuhoe: The Children of the Mist* (2 vols, Wellington, 1996).

—, *Notes on the Art of War: As Conducted by the Maoris of New Zealand*
ed. J. Evans (Wellington, 2001).

Black, J., *Eighteenth-Century Europe, 1700–1789* (Houndmills, 1990).

—, *A Military Revolution? Military Change and European Society, 1550–1800*
(Atlantic Highlands, New Jersey, 1991).

—, *An Illustrated History of Eighteenth-Century Britain* (Manchester, 1996).

Black, J. and Woodfine, P. (eds), *The British Navy and the Use of Naval Power in
the Eighteenth Century* (Leicester, 1998).

Bladen, F. (ed.), *Historical Records of New South Wales* (8 vols, Sydney,
1892–1901).

Blakeborough, J., *A Guide to … Great Ayton* (Middlesbrough, 1900).

Blakeborough, R., *Wit, Character, Folklore and Customs of the North Riding of
Yorkshire* (London, 1898).

Borkfsky, R. and Howard, A., 'The Early Contact Period', in A. Howard and
R. Borkfsky (eds), *Developments in Polynesian Ethnology* (Honolulu, 1989),
pp. 241–75.

Bott, E., *Tongan Society at the Time of Captain Cook's Visits* (Wellington, 1982).

Brewer, J., *The Sinews of War: War, Money and the English State, 1688–1783* (London, 1989).

Briggs, A., *The Age of Improvement, 1783–1867* (London, 1964).

Brodsky, R. *et al.*, 'Cook, Lono, Obeyesekere, and Sahlins', *Current Anthropology*, 38 (1997), pp. 255–82.

Brooke, R., *Remarks and Conjectures on the Voyage of the Ships* Resolution *and* Discovery ... *after the Death of Captain James Cook* (London, 1780).

Brown, J. and Croden, I., *Staithes: A Collection of Fact and Fantasy about a North Yorkshire Fishing Community* (Staithes, 1977).

Brown, R., *Staithes in Olden Times* (published in three parts in the *Whitby Gazette*, March 1924).

Burkinshaw, J., *Klaya-Ho-Alth: Collections from the North-West Coast of North America in the Royal Albert Memorial Museum, Exeter* (Exeter, 1999).

Burnicle, A., *A Genealogical Study of the Families of Captain James Cook* (Middlesbrough, [1985]).

Butlin, R., *Historical Atlas of North Yorkshire* (Otley, 2003).

Campbell, I.C., 'The Culture of Culture Contact: Refractions from Polynesia', *Journal of World History*, 14 (2003), pp. 63–86.

Captain Cook Country Tourism Association, *Captain Cook Country Tour* (Yarm, 1994).

Carter, H.B., *Sir Joseph Banks, 1743–1820* (London, 1988).

—, 'Note on the Drawings by an Unknown Artist from the Voyage of HMS *Endeavour*', in M. Lincoln (ed.), *Science and Exploration in the Pacific: European Voyages to the Southern Oceans in the Eighteenth Century* (Woodbridge, Suffolk, 1998), pp. 133–34.

Chappell, D., 'Shipboard Relations between Pacific Island Women and Euroamerican Men, 1767–1887', *Journal of Pacific History*, 27 (1992), pp. 131–49.

Charles, J., 'The Yorkshire Haunts of Captain Cook', in J. Hurd and M.Kodama (eds), *Captain Cook and the Pacific Islands: The Proceedings of the Third Annual Pacific Islands Studies Conference* (Honolulu, 1978), pp. 35–47.

Charlton, L., *The History of Whitby* (York, 1779).

Cherry, S., *The Te Ao Maori: The Maori World* (Dublin, 1990).

Childs, J., *Armies and Warfare in Europe, 1648–1789* (Manchester, 1982).

Christie, I.R., *Wars and Revolutions: Britain, 1760–1815* (London, 1982).

Clark, D., *Between Pulpit and Pew: Folk Religion in a North Riding Yorkshire Fishing Village* (Cambridge, 1982).

Clayton, D., *Islands of Truth: The Imperial Fashioning of Vancouver Island* (Vancouver, 2006).

Cobbe, H., *Cook's Voyages and the Peoples of the Pacific* (London, 1979).

Connor, D. and Miller, L., *Master Mariner: Captain James Cook and the Peoples of the Pacific* (Edinburgh, 1978).

Cook, J., *A Voyage towards the South Pole* (2 vols, London, 1777).

Cook, J, and King, J., *Voyage to the Pacific Ocean … in the Years 1776, 1777, 1778, 1779 and 1780. In Three Volumes:* vol. 1 and 2 written by Captain J. Cook, vol. 3 by Captain J. King (London, 1784).

Cookson, J., 'War', in I. McCalman (ed.), *An Oxford Companion to the Romantic Age: British Culture, 1776–1832* (Oxford, 1999), pp. 26–34.

Cosgrove, D., *Mappings* (London, 1999).

Coote, J., 'An Interim Report on a Previously Unknown Collection from Cook's First Voyage: The Christ Church Collection at the Pitt Rivers Museum, University of Oxford', *Journal of Museum Ethnology*, 16 (2004), pp. 111–21.

Coote, J., Gathercole, P. and Meister, N., '"Curiosities Sent to Oxford": The Original Documentation of the Forster Collection at the Pitt Rivers Museum', *Journal of the History of Collections*, 12 (2000), pp. 177–92.

Coote, J., Knowles, C., Meister, N. and Petch, A., 'Computerising the Forster ("Cook"), Arawe, and Founding Collections at the Pitt Rivers Museum', *Pacific Arts*, 19/20 (1999), 48–80.

Crowther, A., *Yorkshire Customs: Traditions and Folk Lore of Old Yorkshire* (Clapham, North Yorkshire, 1974).

Cummins, H., 'Tongan Society at the Time of European Contact', in N. Rutherford (ed.), *Friendly Islands: A History of Tonga* (Melbourne, 1977), pp. 63–89.

Cunningham, H. *Leisure in the Industrial Revolution* (London, 1980).

Cuppage, F., *James Cook and the Conquest of Scurvy* (Westport, Connecticut, 1994).

D'Alleva, A., *Shaping the Body Politic: Gender, Status and Power in the Art of Eighteenth-Century Tahiti and the Society Islands* (PhD, University of Columbia, 1997).

Darnton, R., *The Great Cat Massacre and Other Episodes in French Cultural History* (Harmondsworth, 1984).

David, A., *The Charts and Coastal Views of Captain Cook's Voyages* (3 vols, London, 1988–97).

Davies, E., *Episcopacy and the Royal Supremacy in the Church of England in the Sixteenth Century* (Oxford, 1950).

Davies, H., *Worship and Theology in England* (5 vols, Grand Rapids, Michigan, 1996).

Day, M., *Mrs Cook: The Real and Imagined Life of the Captain's Wife* (Sydney, 2002).

Dening, G., *Mr Bligh's Bad Language: Passion, Power and Theatre on the* Bounty (Cambridge, 1992).

—, *Beach Crossings: Voyaging across Times, Cultures and Self* (Melbourne, 2004).

Dickinson, H., 'Democracy', in I. McCalman (ed.), *An Oxford Companion to the Romantic Age: British Culture, 1776–1832* (Oxford, 1999), pp. 35–42.

Dixon, J., *History under the Hammer* (North York Moors National Park, 1996).

Douglas, B., 'A Contact History of the Balad People of New Caledonia, 1774–1845', *Journal of the Polynesian Society*, 79 (1970), pp. 180–200.

Driessen, H., 'Outrigger Canoes and Glorious Beings', *Journal of Pacific History*, 17 (1982), pp. 3–28.

Duffy, M., *Man of Honour: John Macarthur* (Sydney, 2003).

Duyker, E., *Nature's Argonaut: Daniel Solander, 1733–1782* (Melbourne, 1998).

Dykes, J., *Yorkshire Whaling Days* (Clapham, North Yorkshire, 1980).

East, W., 'The Historical Geography of the Town, Port and Roads of Whitby', *Geographical Journal*, 80 (1932), pp. 484–97.

Edney, M., 'Reconsidering Enlightenment Geography and Mapping', in D. Livingstone and C. Withers (eds), *Geography and Enlightenment* (Chicago, 1999), pp. 165–98.

Ellis, W., *An Authentic Narrative of a Voyage Performed by Captain Cook and Captain Clerke, in His Majesty's Ships* Resolution *and* Discovery *during the Years 1776–80* (2 vols, London, 1782).

Ellis, W., *Narrative of a Tour Through Hawaii* (London, 1826).

Evans, E., *The Forging of the Modern State: Early Industrial Britain, 1783–1870* (Harlow, 1983).

Evans-Prichard, E., *A History of Anthropological Thought* (London, 1981).

Fairfax-Blakeborough, J., *Yorkshire Days and Yorkshire Ways* (London, 1935).

Farnill, B., *A History of Robin Hood's Bay* (North York Moors National Park, 1990).

Ferdon, E., *Early Tahiti: As the Explorers Saw It, 1767–1797* (Tucson, Arizona, 1981).

—, *Early Tonga: As the Explorers Saw It, 1616–1810* (Tucson, Arizona, 1987).

Finch, R., *Coals from Newcastle: Coal Trade in the Days of Sail* (Lavenham, Suffolk, 1973).

Fisher, R., 'Cook and the Nootka', in R. Fisher and H. Johnston (eds), *Captain James Cook and his Times* (Vancouver, 1979), pp. 81–98.

Fletcher, J., *Recollections of a Yorkshire Village* (London, 1910).

Flinn, M., *The History of the British Coal Industry*, ii, *1700–1830: The Industrial Revolution* (Oxford, 1984).

Floud, R. and Mc Closkey, D. (eds), *The Economic History of Britain since 1700*, i, *1700–1860* (Cambridge, 1981).

Forster, G., *A Voyage Round the World*, N. Thomas and O. Berghof (eds) (2 vols, Honolulu, 2000).

Forster, J., *Observations Made during a Voyage round the World*, Nicholas Thomas, Harriet Guest and Michael Dettelbach (eds) (Honolulu, 1996).

Freeman, J., 'The Polynesian Collection of Trinity College, Dublin and the National Museum of Ireland', *Journal of the Polynesian Society*, 58 (1949), pp. 1–18.

Friends of Whitby Abbey, *Whitby in the Middle Ages* (CD, n.d.).

Frost, A., *The Voyage of the* Endeavour: *Captain Cook and the Discovery of the Pacific* (Sydney, 1998).

Gascoigne, J., *Joseph Banks and the English Enlightenment: Useful Knowledge and Polite Culture* (Cambridge, 1994).

—, *Science in the Service of Empire: Joseph Banks, the British State and the Uses of Science in the Age of Revolution* (Cambridge, 1998).

—, *The Enlightenment and the Origins of European Australia* (Cambridge, 2002).

Gaskin, R., *The Old Seaport of Whitby: Being Chapters from the Life of its Bygone People* (Whitby, 1909).

Gathercole, P., 'Lord Sandwich's Collection of Polynesian Artefacts', in M. Lincoln, *Science and Exploration in the Pacific: European Voyages to the Southern Oceans in the Eighteenth Century* (Woodbridge, Suffolk, 1998), pp. 103–15.

—, 'A Maori Shell Trumpet at Cambridge', in G. Sieveking, I. Longworth and K. Wilson (eds), *Problems in Economic and Social Anthropology* (London, 1976), pp. 187–99.

Gerrard, D., *North Riding of One Hundred Years Ago* (Stroud, 1993).

Gilbert, A., 'Buggery and the British Navy, 1700–1861', *Journal of Social History*, 10 (1976–77), pp. 72–98.

Gill, W., *Historical Sketches of Savage Life in Polynesia* (Wellington, 1880).

Gillis, J., 'Married but not Churched: Plebeian Sexual Relations and Marital Nonconformity in Eighteenth-Century Britain', in R. Maccubbin (ed.), *'Tis Nature's Fault: Unauthorized Sexuality during the Enlightenment* (Cambridge, 1987), pp. 31–42.

Gittings, C., *Death, Burial and the Individual in Early Modern England* (London, 1998).

Godfrey, A., *Yorkshire Fishing Fleets: The Story of Yorkshire's Oldest and Most Dangerous Industry* (Clapham, North Yorkshire, 1974).

Goldman, I., *Ancient Polynesian Society* (Chicago, 1970).

Gough, B., 'Nootka Sound in James Cook's Pacific World', in B. Efrat and W. Langlois (eds), *Nu.tka: Captain Cook and the Spanish Explorers on the Coast, Sound Heritage*, 7 (1978), pp. 1–31.

Gould, R.T., 'Bligh's Notes on Cook's Last Voyage', *Mariner's Mirror*, 14 (1928), pp. 371–85.

Graham, G., *Incidents in the Life of Captain James Cook: Illustrated by Authentic Material in Whitby Museum* (Whitby, 1980).

—, *Muster Rolls of Whitby Ships in which James Cook Sailed, 1747–1755* (Whitby, 1983).

—, *Captain James Cook: Servant and Friend of Captain John Walker* (Whitby, 1986).

Graves, J., *The History of Cleveland* (Carlisle, 1808).

Great Britain–New Zealand, *Further Papers Relative to the Affairs of New Zealand* (London, 1854).

Habbakuk, H.J., 'England', in A. Goodwin (ed.), *The European Nobility in the Eighteenth Century* (London, 1953), pp. 1–21.

Handy, E., *Polynesian Religion* (Honolulu, 1927).

Harvey, K., 'Spaces of Erotic Delight', in M. Ogden and C. Withers (eds), *Georgian Geographies: Essays on Space, Place and Landscape in the Eighteenth Century* (Manchester, 2004), pp. 131–50.

Hastings, R.P., *Essays in North Riding History, 1780–1850* (Northallerton, 1981).

Hauser-Schäublin, B. and Krüger, G. (ed.), *James Cook: Gifts and Treasures from the South Seas* (Munich, 1998).

Healy, C., *From the Ruins of Colonialism: History as Social Meaning* (Cambridge, 1997).

Hegarty, N., 'Unruly Subjects: Sexuality, Science and Discipline in Eighteenth-Century Pacific Exploration', in M. Lincoln (ed.), *Science and Exploration in the Pacific: European Voyages to the Southern Oceans in the Eighteenth Century* (Woodbridge, Suffolk, 1998), pp. 183–98.

Henare, A., *Museums, Anthropology and Imperial Exchange* (Cambridge, 2005).

Hinderwell, T., *The History and Antiquities of Scarborough and the Vicinity* (York, 1811).

Hitchcock, T., *English Sexualities, 1700–1800* (New York, 1997).

Hoare, M., *The Tactless Philosopher: Johann Reinhold Forster (1729–98)* (Melbourne, 1976).

— (ed.), *The* Resolution *Journal of Johann Reinhold Forster, 1772–1775* (4 vols, London, 1982).

Holmes, C. (ed.), *Captain Cook's Final Voyage: The Journal of Midshipman George Gilbert* (London, 1982).

— (ed.), *Captain Cook's Second Voyage: The Journals of Lieutenants Elliott and Pickersgill* (London, 1984).

Holt, R., *Whitby Past and Present* (Whitby, [1897?]).

Home, G., *Memoirs of an Aristocrat* (London, 1838).

Hooper, B. (ed.), *With Captain James Cook in the Antarctic and Pacific: The Journal of James Burney, Second Lieutenant of the* Adventure *on Cook's Second Voyage, 1772–1773* (Canberra, 1975).

Horwitz, T., *Into the Blue: Boldly Going Where Captain Cook Has Gone Before* (Sydney, 2002).

Hotimsky, C.M., *The Death of Captain James Cook: A Letter from Russia* (Sydney, 1962).

Hough, R., *Captain James Cook: A Biography* (London, 1994).

Houlding, J.A., *Fit for Service: The Training of the British Army, 1715–95* (Oxford, 1981).

Howard, J., *Staithes: Chapters from the History of a Seafaring Town* (Scarborough, 2000).

Howard, M., *War in European History* (Oxford, 1976).

Howe, K., 'The Death of Cook: Exercises in Explanation', *Eighteenth-Century Life*, 18 (1994), pp. 198–211.

Howse, D., *Captain Cook's Pendulum Clocks* (London, 1969).

—, 'Navigation and Astronomy in the Voyages', in D. Howse (ed.), *Background to Discovery: Pacific Exploration from Dampier to Cook* (Berkeley, 1990), pp. 160–84.

Hunt [Rae], J., *From Whitby to Wapping: The Story of the Early Years of Captain James Cook* (London, 1991).

Inglis, R. and Haggarty, J., 'Cook to Jewitt: Three Decades of Change in Nootka Sound', in B. Trigger, T. Morantz, L. Dechêne (eds), *Le Castor Fait Tout: Selected Papers of the Fifth North American Fur Trade Conference, 1985* (Montreal, 1987), pp. 193–235.

Irwin, G., *The Prehistoric Exploration and Colonization of the Pacific* (Cambridge, 1992).

Jago, J., *Aspects of the Georgian Church: Visitation Studies of the Diocese of York, 1761–1776* (London and Cranbury, New Jersey, 1997).

Jeffrey, P., *Whitby Lore and Legend* (Whitby, 1952).

Jolly, M., 'Desire, Difference and Disease: Sexual and Venereal Exchanges on Cook's Voyages to the Pacific', in R. Gibson (ed.), *Exchanges: Cross-Cultural Encounters in Australia and the Pacific* (Sydney, 1977), pp. 187–217.

Jones, S., *A Maritime History of the Port of Whitby, 1700–1914* (University of London Ph.D, 1982).

Joppien, R. and Smith, B., *The Art of Captain Cook's Voyages* (3 vols in 4, London, 1985–88).

Kaeppler, A., 'Eighteenth-Century Tonga: New Interpretations of Tongan Society and Material Culture at the Time of Captain Cook', *Man*, 6 (1971), pp. 206–20.

—, 'Rank in Tonga', *Ethnology*, 10 (1971), pp. 174–93.

—, *'Artificial Curiosities': Being An Exposition of Native Manufactures Collected on the Three Pacific Voyages of Captain James Cook, RN* (Honolulu, 1978).

—, *Cook Voyage Artefacts in Leningrad, Berne, and Florence Museums* (Honolulu, 1978).

—, 'Tracing the History of Hawaiian Cook Voyage Artefacts in the Museum of Mankind', in T. Mitchell (ed.), *Captain Cook and the South Pacific* (London, 1979), pp. 167–97.

—, 'Hawaiian Art and Society', in A. Hooper and J. Huntsman (eds), *Transformations of Polynesian Culture*, Polynesian Society Memoir, no. 45 (Auckland, 1985).

—, 'Pacific Culture and European Voyages', in W. Esler and B. Smith (eds), *Terra Australis: The Furthest Shore* (Sydney, 1988), pp. 141–46.

Kennedy, G., *The Death of Cook* (London, 1978).

Kettlewell, R., *Cleveland Village: Being Notes … on Some of the Records of the Parish of Great Ayton, Mainly the Churchwarden's Book, 1734–1844;* to which is added a Chapter by J.Fairfax-Blakeborough on Village Lore (Redcar, 1938).

King, J., 'An Account of the late Captain Cook, and Some Memoirs of His Life', *Universal Magazine*, July 1784, pp. 33–40.

King, P., 'Some Thoughts on Native Hawaiian Attitudes towards Captain Cook', in G. Williams (ed.), *Captain Cook: Explorations and Reassessments* (Woodbridge, Suffolk, 2004), pp. 94–109.

Kippis, A., *A Narrative of the Voyages Round the World Performed by Captain James Cook* (London, 1883).

Kirch, P., *The Evolution of the Polynesian Chiefdoms* (Cambridge, 1984).

Kolig, E., 'Captain Cook in the Western Kimberleys', in R.M. and C.H. Brendt (eds), *Aborigines of the West: Their Past and Present* (Perth, 1980), pp. 274–82.

Kohen, K, and Lambert, R. 'Hunters and Fishers in the Sydney Region', in D. Mulvaney and J. P. White (eds), *Australians to 1788* (Sydney, 1988), pp. 342–65.

Langford, P., *A Polite and Commercial People: England, 1727–1783* (Oxford, 1989).

Laqueur, T., 'Sex and Desire in the Industrial Revolution', in P. O'Brien and R. Quinault (eds), *The Industrial Revolution and British Society* (Cambridge, 1993), pp. 100–23.

Lewis, M., *A Social History of the Navy, 1783–1815* (London, 1960).

Livingstone, D., *The Geographical Tradition* (Oxford, 1993).

Lloyd, C. and Anderson, R.C. (eds), *A Memoir of James Trevenen* (London, 1959).

McCalman, I. (ed.), *An Oxford Campanion to the Romantic Age: British Culture, 1776–1832* (Oxford, 1999).

McCutcheon, K., *Yorkshire Fairs and Markets to the End of the Eighteenth Century* (Leeds, 1940).

McKendrick, N., Brewer, J. and Plumb, J.H., *The Birth of a Consumer Society: The Commercialization of Eighteenth-Century Britain* (Bloomington, Indiana, 1985).

Mackesy, P., 'Strategic Problems of the British War Effort', in H.T.Dickinson (ed.), *Britain and the French Revolution, 1789–1815* (London, 1989), pp. 147–64.

Mackinolty, C. and Wainburranga, P., 'Too Many Captain Cooks', in R. Rose and T. Swain (eds), *Aboriginal Australian Christian Missions* (Canberra, 1988), pp. 355–60.

Malcolmson, R., *Life and Labour in England, 1700–1780* (London, 1981).

Maning, F.E., *Old New Zealand and Other Writings*, A. Calder (ed.) (Leicester, 2001).

Marchant, A., *Great Ayton: Church History* (n.p., 1989).

[Marra, J.], *Journal of the* Resolution*'s Voyage* (London, 1775).

Mathias, P., 'The People's Mint in the Eighteenth Century: The Royal Mint, Trade Tokens and the Economy', in his *The Transformation of England* (London, 1979), pp. 190–208.

[Matra, J.], *A Journal of a Voyage Round the World in His Majesty's Ship Endeavour, in the Years 1768, 1769, 1770 and 1771* (London, 1771).

Mayhall, J., *The Annals of Yorkshire, from the Earliest Period to the Present Time* (3 vols, London, [1876]).

Megaw, J., 'Captain Cook and Bone Barbs at Botany Bay', *Antiquity*, 48 (1969), pp. 213–16.

Mendel, A., *The Essential Works of Marxism* (New York, 1965).

Mitchell, W., *Life on the Yorkshire Coast* (Clapham, North Yorkshire, 1982).

Morris, E., 'Captain's Cook's First Log in the Royal Navy', *Cornhill Magazine*, 7 (1899), pp. 519–32.

Morris, R., 'Aikane: Accounts of Hawaiian Same-Sex Relationships in the Journals of Captain Cook's Third Voyage', *Journal of Homosexuality*, 19 (1990), pp. 21–54.

Munford, J. (ed.), *John Ledyard's Journal of Captain Cook's Last Voyage* (Corvallis, Oregan, 1963).

Namier, L. and Brooke, J. (eds), *History of Parliament: The House of Commons, 1754–1790* (3 vols, London, 1964).

Neave, D. and V., *Georgian Yorkshire* (Clapham, North Yorkshire, 1972).

Newbury, C., *Tahiti Nui: Change and Survival in French Polynesia, 1767–1945* (Honolulu, 1980).

Newman, G. (ed.), *Britain in the Hanoverian Age, 1714–1837* (New York, 1997).

Obeyesekere, G., *The Apotheosis of Captain Cook: European Mythmaking in the Pacific* (Princeton, 1992).

O'Brian, P., *Joseph Banks: A Life* (London, 1987), p. 64.

—, *Men-of-War: Life in Nelson's Navy* (New York, 1995).

Oliver, D., *Ancient Tahitian Society* (3 vols, Canberra, 1974).

Oppenheim, R., *Maori Death Customs* (Wellington, 1973).

Ord, J., *The History and Antiquities of Cleveland: Comprising the Wapentake of East and West Langbaurgh, North Riding, County York* (London, 1846).

Orr, B., '"Southern Passions Mix with Northern Art": Miscegenation and the *Endeavour* Voyage', *Eighteenth-Century Life*, 18 (1994), pp. 212–31.

O'Sullivan, D., *Great Ayton: A History of the Village* (Great Ayton, 1996).

Page, W. (ed.), *The Victoria History of the County of York: North Riding* (2 vols, London, 1923).

Parker, G., 'Warfare', in P. Burke (ed.), *Companion Volume*, xiii, *The New Cambridge Modern History* (Cambridge, 1979), pp. 201–19.

—, *The Military Revolution: Military Innovation and the Rise of the West 1500–1800* (Cambridge, 1988).

Parkin, R., *H.M. Bark* Endeavour: *Her Place in Australian History* (Melbourne, 1997).

Parkinson, S., *A Journal of a Voyage to the South Seas, in His Majesty's Ship, the* Endeavour (London, 1773).

Payne, F., *Whaling and Whitby* (Whitby, n.d).

Perkin, H., *The Origins of Modern English Society, 1780–1880* (London, 1972).

Phillips, M., *A History of Banks, Bankers and Banking in Northumberland, Durham and North Yorkshire* (London, 1894).

Pomare, M. and Cowan, J., *Legends of the Maori* (Wellington, 1930–34).

Popp, K. (ed.), *Georg Forster, Georg Chr. Lichtenberg. Cook der Entdecker* (Leipzig, 1980).

Porter, R.S., *English Society in the Eighteenth Century* (Harmondsworth, 1982).

—, 'Mixed Feelings: The Enlightenment and Sexuality in Eighteenth-Century Britain', in P. Boucé (ed.), *Sexuality in Eighteenth-Century Britain* (Manchester, 1982).

Preston, C., *Captain William Scoresby, 1760–1829: Whitby's Most Successful Whaler* (Whitby, 1964).

—, *Captain James Cook, RN, FRS and Whitby* (Whitby, 1965).

Price, R., *British Society, 1680–1880* (Cambridge, 1999).

Quanchi, M. and Adams, R., *Culture Contact in the Pacific* (Cambridge, 1993).

Rae [née Hunt], J., *Captain James Cook Endeavours* (London, 1997).

Ralston, C., 'Ordinary Women in Early Post-Contact Hawaii', in M. Jolly and M. Macintyre (eds), *Family and Gender in the Pacific: Domestic Contradictions and the Colonial Impact* (Cambridge, 1989), pp. 45–64.

Rennie, N., 'The Point Venus "Scene"', in M. Lincoln (ed.), *Science and Exploration in the Pacific: European Voyages in the Southern Oceans in the Eighteenth Century* (Woodbridge, Suffolk, 1998), pp. 134–46.

Richardson, B., *Longitude and Empire: How Captain Cook's Voyages Changed the World* (Vancouver, 2005).

[Rickman, R.], *Journal of Captain Cook's Last Voyage to the Pacific Ocean* (London, 1781).

Rigby, N. and Van der Merwe, P., *Captain Cook in the Pacific* (London, 2001).

Ritchie, G., 'Captain's Cook's Influence on Hydrographic Surveying', *Pacific Studies*, 1 (1978), pp. 78–95.

Robinson, R., 'The Fish Trade in the Pre-Railway Era: The Yorkshire Coast 1780–1840', *Northern History*, 25 (1989), pp. 223–34.

Robley, H., *Moko: or Maori Tattooing* (London, 1896).

Robson, E., 'The Armed Forces and the Art of War', in J.O.Lindsey (ed.), *The Old Regime*, vii, *The New Cambridge Modern History* (Cambridge, 1963), pp. 163–90.

Robson, J., *Captain Cook's World* (Sydney, 2000).

—, *The Captain Cook Encyclopaedia* (London, 2004).

Roderick, C., 'Sir Joseph Banks, Queen Oberea and the Satirists', in W. Veit (ed.), *Captain James Cook: Image and Impact* (2 vols, Melbourne, 1970–72), ii, pp. 67–89.

Rodger, N.A.M., *Articles of War: The Statutes which Governed our Fighting Navies, 1661, 1749 and 1886* (Homewell, Hampshire., 1982).

—, *The Insatiable Earl: A Life of John Montagu, Fourth Earl of Sandwich, 1718–1792* (London, 1993).

—, *The Wooden World: An Anatomy of the Georgian Navy* (New York, 1996).

—, *The Command of the Ocean: A Naval History of Britain, 1649–1815* (London, 2004).

Rose, D., 'The Saga of Captain Cook: Morality in Aboriginal and European Law', *Australian Aboriginal Studies*, 2 (1984), pp. 24–39.

Rowe, P., *The Archaeology of East Marton, Captain Cook's Birthplace* (n.p., 1998).

Rowntree, A. (ed.), *The History of Scarborough* (London, 1931).

Rule, J., *Albion's People: English Society, 1714–1815* (London, 1992).

Sahlins, M., *Historical Metaphors and Mythical Realities: Structure in the Early History of the Sandwich Islands Kingdom* (Ann Arbor, Michigan, 1981).

—, *Islands of History* (Chicago, 1985).

—, *How 'Natives' Think about Captain Cook, For Example* (Chicago, 1996).

St Cuthbert's Church, Marton, Middlesbrough, *James Cook, FRS, RN* (Middlesbrough, n.d.).

Salmond, A., *Two Worlds: First Meetings between Maori and Europeans, 1642–1772* (Harmondsworth, 1993).

—, *Between Worlds: Early Exchanges Between Maori and Europeans, 1773–1815* (Auckland, 1997).

—, *The Trial of the Cannibal Dog: Captain Cook in the South Seas* (London, 2003).

—, 'Tute: The Impact of Polynesia on Captain Cook', in G. Williams (ed.), *Captain Cook: Explorations and Reassessments* (Woodbridge, Suffolk, 2004), pp. 77–93.

—, 'Their Body is Different, Our Body is Different: European and Tahitian Navigators in the Eighteenth Century', *History and Anthropology*, 16 (2005), pp. 167–87.

Saquet, J., *The Tahiti Handbook* ([Papeete], 1998).

Shawcross, W., 'The Cambridge University Collection of Maori Artefacts, Made on Captain Cook's First Voyage', *Journal of the Polynesian Society*, 17 (1970), pp. 305–48.

Shore, B., 'Manu and Tapu', in A. Howard and R. Boroksky (eds), *Developments in Polynesian Ethnology* (Honolulu, 1989), pp. 137–73.

Shuster, B. and Shuster, S., 'Buggery in the British Merchant Navy in the mid Nineteenth Century', in J. Covacevich *et al.*, *History, Heritage and Health: Proceedings of the Fourth Biennial Conference of the Australian Society of the History of Medicine* (Brisbane, 1996), pp. 277–83.

Sinclair, S., *Elizabeth Cook, the Captain's Wife, 1741–1835* (Sydney, 1995).

Singleton, F.B. and Rawnsley, S., *A History of Yorkshire* (Chichester, 1986).

Skelton, R., 'Captain James Cook as a Hydrographer', *Mariner's Mirror*, 40 (1954), pp. 92–119.

—, 'Explorer's Maps: James Cook and the Mapping of the Pacific', *Geographical Magazine*, 28 (1955), pp. 95–106.

—, *Captain James Cook after Two Hundred Years* (London, 1969).

Skottowe, P., *The Leaf and the Tree: The Story of an English Family* (London, 1963).

Smith, A., *An Inquiry into the Nature and Causes of the Wealth of Nations* (Chicago, 1952).

Smith, A., 'Captain James Cook: Londoner', *East London Papers*, 11 (1968), pp. 94–97.

Smith, B., 'Cook's Posthumous Reputation', in R. Fisher and H. Johnston (eds), *Captain James Cook and his Times* (Vancouver, 1979), pp. 159–85.

—, *European Vision and the South Pacific* (2nd edn, New Haven, 1985).

—, *Imagining the Pacific: In the Wake of the Cook Voyages* (New Haven, 1992).

Smith, R., *Sea-Coal for London: History of the Coal Factors in the London Market* (London, 1961).

Sommerville, C.J., *The Secularization of Early Modern England: From Religious Culture to Religious Faith* (New York, 1992).

Sparrman, A., *A Voyage Round the World with Captain James Cook in HMS Resolution*, translated from Swedish by H. Beamish and A. Mackenzie-Grieve. Introduction and Notes by O. Rutter (London, 1953).

Speck W., *Stability and Strife: England, 1714–1760* (London, 1977).

Spratt, D. (ed.), *The Archaeology of Cleveland* (Middlesbrough, 1979).

Stamp, J. and C., *James Cook: Maritime Scientist* (Whitby, 1995).

—, *Captain Cook and his Ships* (Whitby, 1981).

Stone, L., *The Family, Sex and Marriage in England, 1500–1800* (London, 1979).

Sullivan, D., *Great Ayton: A History of the Village* (Great Ayton, 1996).

Suthren, V., *To Go Upon Discovery: James Cook and Canada 1758–1767* (Toronto: 1999).

Tanner, J., *From Pacific Shores: Eighteenth-Century Ethnographic Collections at Cambridge. The Voyages of Cook, Vancouver and the First Fleet* (Cambridge, 1999).

Tate, W.E. and Singleton, F.B., *A History of Yorkshire* (Beaconsfield, 1965).

Taylor, A., *Sesquicentennial Celebration of Captain Cook's Discovery of Hawaii (1778–1928)* (Honolulu, 1929).

Thomas, K., *Religion and the Decline of Magic* (New York, 1971).

Thomas, N., *Discoveries: The Voyages of Captain Cook* (London, 2003).

Thompson, F.M.L. (ed.), *The Cambridge Social History of Britain, 1750–1950*, i, *Regions and Communities* (Cambridge, 1990).

Thornton, C., *Captain Cook in Cleveland: A Study of his Early Years* (Middlesbrough, 1978).

Tilly, C., 'Reflections on the History of European State-Making', in his *The Formation of the Nation States in Western Europe* (Princeton, 1975), pp. 3–83.

Tuke, J., *General View of the Agriculture of the North Riding of Yorkshire: With Observations on the Means of its Improvement* (London, 1794), p. 35.

Turnbull, D., 'Cook and Tupaia, a Tale of Cartographic *Méconnaissance*', in M. Lincoln (ed.), *Science and Exploration in the Pacific: European Voyages in the Southern Oceans in the Eighteenth Century* (Woodbridge, Suffolk, 1998), pp. 117–32.

Valieri, V., *Kingship and Sacrifice: Ritual and Society in Ancient Hawaii* (Chicago, 1985).

Van Der Sluis, I., *The Treponematois of Tahiti: Its Origin and Evolution. A Study of the Sources* (Ph.D thesis, University of Amsterdam, 1969).

Vayda, A.P., *Maori Warfare* (Wellington, 1960).

—, *War in Ecological Perspective* (New York, 1976).

Vovelle, M., 'Death', in A. Kors, *Encyclopedia of the Enlightenment* (4 vols, New York, 2003), i, pp. 324–27.

Wallace, L., *Sexual Encounters: Pacific Texts, Modern Sexualities* (Ithaca, New York, 2003).

Wardell, J., *The Economic History of Tees-Side* (Stockton, 1960), p. 9.

Watt, J., 'Medical Aspects and Consequences of Cook's Voyages', in R. Fisher
    and H. Johnston (eds), *Captain James Cook and his Times* (Vancouver, 1979),
    pp. 129–57.
Whaley, J., *Mirrors of Mortality: Studies in the Social History of Death* (London,
    1981).
White, A., *A History of Whitby* (Chichester, 1993).
Whiteley, W., 'James Cook and British Policy in the Newfoundland Fisheries,
    1763–7', *Canadian Historical Review*, 54 (1973), pp. 245–72.
Willams, E., *The Eighteenth-Century Constitution: Documents and Commentary*
    (Cambridge, 1960).
Williamson, R., *Social and Political Systems of Central Polynesia* (3 vols,
    Cambridge, 1924).
Wilson, K., *The Island Race: Englishness, Empire and Gender in the Eighteenth
    Century* (London, 2003).
—, 'Gender Misrecognition and Polynesian Subversions aboard the Cook
    Voyages', in K. Wilson (ed.), *A New Imperial History: Culture, Identity
    and Modernity in Britain and the Empire, 1660–1840* (Cambridge, 2004),
    pp. 345–62.
Withey, L., *Voyages of Discovery: Captain Cook and the Exploration of the Pacific*
    (London, 1987).
Woodwark, T., *The Quakers of Whitby* (n.p, n.d.).
Wrigley, E. and Schofield, R., *The Population History of England, 1547–1871:
    A Reconstruction* (London, 1981).
Young, G., *The Life and Voyages of Captain James Cook* (London, 1836).
—, *A Picture of Whitby and its Environs* (Whitby, 1840).
Zimmerman, H., *Account of the Third Voyage of Captain Cook, 1776–1780*,
    translated from the German by U. Tewsley (Wellington, 1926).

WEB SOURCES

http://pages.quicksilver.net.nz/jcr/~cooky.html. Many useful links to Cook
    material compiled by John Robson including bibliography and notes and
    transcripts of Cook's *Eagle* log and logs from his years in Newfoundland.
http://southseas.nla.gov.au. Gives much valuable material including the text
    of Cook's journals and related works together with much cartographical
    information, bibliography and articles on key topics ('the South Sea
    Companion').

Index

Page numbers in italics (e.g. *109*) refer to illustrations.
Page numbers in bold type (e.g. **24–26**) refer to detailed discussion of the topic.